Windows 3.11 For Dummies, 3rd Edition

Helpful Hints

When you're doing a lot of cutting and pasting, keep the Windows Clipboard as an icon at the bottom of your screen. By double-clicking on the Clipboard's icon, you can see the Clipboard's current contents.

If you're baffled, try pressing F1, that *function key* in the top left corner of your keyboard. A help window appears, bringing hints on your current program.

To quickly organize your desktop, double-click anywhere on your wallpaper. The Windows Task List appears, listing all your currently open windows. Click on the Tile button, and all your open windows are neatly tiled across your screen.

Double-click here to close the window

Point here, hold down the mouse button, and move the mouse to move the window

Click here to shrink the window

Click here to enlarge the window

Click here to move up the page

Click here to move down the page

Point here, hold down the mouse button, and move the mouse to change the window's size

Notepad - HELPFUL.TXT

File   Edit   Search   Help

```
Push the mouse across your desk,
and the mouse's arrow will move
across your screen.

Push the mouse's left button with
your finger to "click" the mouse.
Push the button twice in rapid
succession to "double-click."

By pointing to different parts of
the window and either "clicking"
or "double-clicking," you can
perform different chores.
```

W9-ALU-438

File Manager Stuff

To Do This . . .	Do This . . .
Copy a file to another location on the *same* disk drive	Hold down Ctrl and drag it there.
Copy a file to a *different* disk drive	Drag it there.
Move a file to another location on the *same* disk drive	Drag it there.
Move a file to a *different* drive	Hold down Alt and drag it there.
Select several files	Hold down Ctrl and click on their names.
Tile windows	Press Shift+F4.
Cascade windows	Press Shift+F5.
Look at a different directory	Click on that directory's icon at the window's top.
Put a different directory in its own separate window	Double-click on that directory's icon at the window's top.

Cut and Paste Stuff

To Do This . . .	Do This . . .
Highlight stuff with a mouse	Hold down the mouse button while sliding the pointer over the information.
Highlight with the keyboard	Hold down Shift and press an arrow key.
Highlight a word quickly	Double-click on the word.
Copy highlighted stuff to the Clipboard	Press Ctrl+C or Ctrl+Insert.
Cut highlighted stuff to the Clipboard	Press Ctrl+X or Shift+Delete.
Paste stuff from the Clipboard to the current window	Press Ctrl+V or Shift+Insert.
Copy the entire screen to the Clipboard	Press Print Screen (Shift+Print Screen on some keyboards).
Copy the current window to the Clipboard	Press Alt+Print Screen.

COMPUTER BOOK SERIES FROM IDG

Windows 3.11 For Dummies, 3rd Edition

Cheat Sheet

General Stuff

To Do This . . .	Do This . . .
Start Windows	Type **WIN**.
Call up the Help menu	Press F1.
Undo the mistake you just made	Press Ctrl+Z or Alt+Backspace.
Close a window	Press Alt+F4.
See a list of all open windows	Press Ctrl+Esc.
Exit Windows	Press Alt+F4 in the Program Manager.

Organizing a Pile of Windows

To Do This . . .	Do This . . .
See a list of all open windows	Press Ctrl+Esc.
Move from one window to another window	Press Alt+Tab+Tab.
Tile the windows across the screen	Press Ctrl+Esc, Alt+T.
Cascade the windows across the screen	Press Ctrl+Esc, Alt+C.
Shrink a window into an icon	Press Alt+spacebar, N.
Make a window fill the screen	Press Alt+spacebar, X.

Handling Files within a Program

To Do This . . .	Do This . . .
Start a new file	Press Alt, F, N.
Open an existing file	Press Alt, F, O.
Save a file	Press Alt, F, S.
Save a file under a new name	Press Alt, F, A.
Print a file	Press Alt, F, P.

DOS Window Stuff

To Do This . . .	Do This . . .
Toggle a DOS program from a screen display to a window-sized display	Press Alt+Enter.
Toggle a DOS program from an icon to a full-screen display	Press Alt+Esc.
Close a DOS window	Use that program's normal exit command.

How To Format a Floppy Disk

Most new floppy disks won't work straight out of the box. Unless the box specifically says the word *formatted,* you'll have to format them yourself.

Place the unformatted disk into drive A or drive B and close the latch. From inside the File Manager, click on the word <u>D</u>isk and then <u>F</u>ormat Disk. A Format Disk box appears. If you're formatting your disk in drive A, merely click on the OK button. If you're formatting a disk in drive B, click on the little arrow next to the <u>D</u>isk In box and click on the words Drive B from the little menu that shoots out. Then click on the OK button. Your drives will whir as Windows formats your disk.

. . . For Dummies: #1 Computer Book Series for Beginners

References for the Rest of Us

COMPUTER BOOK SERIES FROM IDG

Are you intimidated and confused by computers? Do you find that traditional manuals are overloaded with technical details you'll never use? Do your friends and family always call you to fix simple problems on their PCs? Then the *...For Dummies™* computer book series from IDG is for you.

...For Dummies books are written for those frustrated computer users who know they aren't really dumb but find that PC hardware, software, and indeed the unique vocabulary of computing make them feel helpless. *...For Dummies* books use a lighthearted approach, a down-to-earth style, and even cartoons and humorous icons to diffuse computer novices' fears and build their confidence. Lighthearted but not lightweight, these books are a perfect survival guide for anyone forced to use a computer.

Already, hundreds of thousands of satisfied readers agree. They have made *...For Dummies* books the #1 introductory level computer book series and have written asking for more. So, if you're looking for the most fun and easy way to learn about computers, look to *...For Dummies* books to give you a helping hand.

IDG BOOKS

WINDOWS™ 3.11 FOR DUMMIES®

3RD EDITION

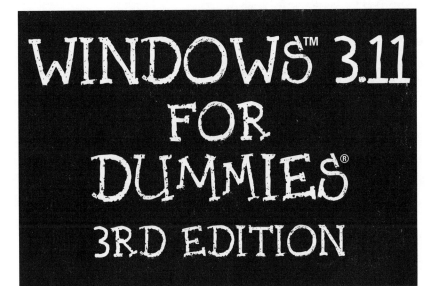

WINDOWS™ 3.11 FOR DUMMIES®
3RD EDITION

by **Andy Rathbone,**
coauthor of best-selling *PCs For Dummies*

IDG BOOKS

IDG Books Worldwide, Inc.
An International Data Group Company

Foster City, CA ♦ Chicago, IL ♦ Indianapolis, IN ♦ Braintree, MA ♦ Dallas, TX

Windows™ 3.11 For Dummies,® 3rd Edition

Published by
IDG Books Worldwide, Inc.
An International Data Group Company
919 E. Hillsdale Blvd.
Suite 400
Foster City, CA 94404

Library of Congress Catalog Card No.: 94-76643

ISBN: 1-56884-370-4

Printed in the United States of America

10 9 8 7 6 5 4 3

3E/RX/QU/ZV

Distributed in the United States by IDG Books Worldwide, Inc.

Distributed by Macmillan Canada for Canada; by Computer and Technical Books for the Caribbean Basin; by Contemporanea de Ediciones for Venezuela; by Distribuidora Cuspide for Argentina; by CITEC for Brazil; by Ediciones ZETA S.C.R. Ltda. for Peru; by Editorial Limusa SA for Mexico; by Transworld Publishers Limited in the United Kingdom and Europe; by Al-Maiman Publishers & Distributors for Saudi Arabia; by Simron Pty. Ltd. for South Africa; by IDG Communications (HK) Ltd. for Hong Kong; by Toppan Company Ltd. for Japan; by Addison Wesley Publishing Company for Korea; by Longman Singapore Publishers Ltd. for Singapore, Malaysia, Thailand, and Indonesia; by Unalis Corporation for Taiwan; by WS Computer Publishing Company, Inc. for the Philippines; by WoodsLane Pty. Ltd. for Australia; by WoodsLane Enterprises Ltd. for New Zealand.

For general information on IDG Books in the U.S., including information on discounts and premiums, contact IDG Books at 800-434-3422 or 415-655-3000.

For information on where to purchase IDG Books outside the U.S., contact IDG Books International at 415-655-3021 or fax 415-655-3295.

For information on translations, contact Marc Jeffrey Mikulich, Director, Foreign & Subsidiary Rights, at IDG Books Worldwide, 415-655-3018 or fax 415-655-3295.

For sales inquiries and special prices for bulk quantities, write to the address above or call IDG Books Worldwide at 415-655-3000.

For information on using IDG Books in the classroom, or ordering examination copies, contact Jim Kelly at 800-434-2086.

For authorization to photocopy items for corporate, personal, or educational use, please contact Copyright Clearance Center, 222 Rosewood Drive, Danvers, MA 01923, or fax 508-750-4470.

 is a registered trademark under exclusive license to IDG Books Worldwide, Inc., from International Data Group, Inc.

About Microsoft Windows 95

The programming information in this book is based on information for developing applications for Windows 95 made public by Microsoft as of 03/16/95. Since this information was made public before the final release of the product, there may have been changes to some of the programming interfaces by the time the product is finally released. We encourage you to check the updated development information that should be part of your development system for resolving issues that might arise.

The end-user information in this book is based on information on Windows 95 made public by Microsoft as of 03/16/95. Since this information was made public before the release of the product, we encourage you to visit your local bookstore at that time for updated books on Windows 95.

If you have a modem or access to the Internet, you can always get up-to-the-minute information on Windows 95 direct from Microsoft on WinNews:

On CompuServe: GO WINNEWS

On the Internet: ftp://ftp.microsoft.com/PerOpSys/Win_NewsChicago
        hup://www.microsoft.com

On AOL: keyword WINNEWS

On Prodigy: jumpword WINNEWS

On GEnie: WINNEWS file area on Windows RTC

You can also subscribe to Microsoft's WinNews electronic newsletter by sending Internet e-mail to news@microsoft.nwnet.com and putting the words SUBSCRIBE WINNEWS in the text of the e-mail.

About the Author

Andy Rathbone started geeking around with computers in 1985 when he bought a boxy CP/M Kaypro 2X with lime-green letters. Like other budding nerds, he soon began playing with null-modem adapters, dialing up computer bulletin boards, and working part-time at Radio Shack.

In between playing computer games, he served as editor of the *Daily Aztec* newspaper at San Diego State University. After graduating with a comparative literature degree, he went to work for a bizarre underground coffee-table magazine that sort of disappeared.

Andy began combining his two interests, words and computers, by selling articles to a local computer magazine. During the next few years, Andy started ghostwriting computer books for more-famous computer authors, as well as writing several hundred articles about computers for technoid publications like *Supercomputing Review*, *CompuServe Magazine*, *ID Systems*, *DataPro*, and *Shareware*.

In 1992, Andy and *DOS For Dummies* author/legend Dan Gookin teamed up to write *PCs For Dummies*, which was a runner-up in the Computer Press Association's 1993 awards. Andy subsequently wrote the first edition of *Windows For Dummies*, *OS/2 For Dummies*, *Upgrading & Fixing PCs For Dummies*, *Multimedia & CD-ROMs For Dummies*, and *MORE Windows For Dummies*.

Andy is currently contributing regularly to *CompuServe Magazine*, a magazine mailed monthly to CompuServe members. (Feel free to drop him a line at 75300,1565.) Andy lives with his most-excellent wife, Tina, and their cat in San Diego, California. When not writing, he fiddles with his MIDI synthesizer and tries to keep the cat off both keyboards.

Dedication

To my wife, parents, sister, and cat.

Acknowledgments

Thanks to Dan Gookin and his wife Sandy, Matt Wagner, Wally Wang, Sandy Blackthorn, Kristin Cocks, Leigh Davis, Pat Seiler, Alice Martina Smith, Bob Garza, Terrie and David Solomon, the Kleskes, the Tragesers, and the Dooleys.

(The publisher would like to give special thanks to Patrick J. McGovern, without whom this book would not have been possible.)

Credits

Contents at a Glance

Cartoons at a Glance
By Rich Tennant

Table of Contents

Part II: Making Windows Do Something *73*

Chapter 5: Starting Windows **75**

Chapter 6: Examining All Those Buttons, Bars, and Boxes **87**

Foreword

• •

Remember *Highlights* magazine, one of the only things you could read while waiting at the dreaded doctor's office when you were a kid? I find that *Highlights* contains many parallels for the modern computer user. For example, *Highlights* magazine tries to make an extremely unpleasant experience (like going to the doctor) into a more enjoyable one. And books such as this one try to make the unpleasant computer experience more palatable.

As a kid, my favorite part of *Highlights* magazine was the Hidden Picture, where you can find all sorts of hidden goodies in what looks like a normal picture (provided that some jerk doesn't let his or her child mark all the hidden goodies beforehand with a pencil). Anyone who has ever used a computer knows that there are lots of hidden treasures secretly stored inside the box. No matter how hard you stare at the keyboard, you'll never see the command you need — the hidden hammer that will let you smash your work into shape. You know it's there, but how can you find it?

One of the treasures of the . . .*For Dummies* series from IDG Books Worldwide is that these books contain lots of hidden information, presented in an uncluttered and entertaining manner. And unlike with the Hidden Picture in *Highlights,* with these books you can look up *hammer* in the index, find exactly on which page the hammer is explained, and then read how to use it. No other knowledge is assumed; there's no learning involved. After all, you know what you need the hammer for, so these books aren't going to waste time explaining that to you.

Specific to this book is the subject of Microsoft Windows, an operating "environment" that makes the PC easier to use. Windows is definitely easier than DOS, the Disk Operating System, which displays crude prompts, uses ugly and confusing commands, and has been known to induce hysteria the most sedate of humans.

Going back to *Highlights* magazine, DOS and Windows are like Goofus and Gallant, the twins who know the proper and improper ways of doing things. (Little old ladies love Gallant. When I was growing up, it was my dream to become Goofus incarnate.)

DOS is Goofus. Goofus walks up to the confused user and says, "I have something for you that will help you get your work done. It's beautiful!" And then he hands her a short, dirty stick. "Ha, ha! Joke's on you, Granny."

Windows, posing as Gallant and looking a lot like Goofus with his hair combed, walks up to the user and says, "I have something for you to help you get your work done, ma'am. And it is truly beautiful." Then he hands her a lovely bouquet of flowers. The user is impressed and sweet on Gallant. It brings tears to Granny's eyes.

Goofus and Gallant represent the attitude the computer has toward you. Goofus is DOS — rude and hideous to look at. It laughs when you make a mistake. Gallant is Windows, which tries very hard to please. Windows is a graphical environment, where everything is laid out on the table for you to see. There may be more to learn, but the graphical environment is consistent. Essentially, if you learn one Windows program, you've learned them all. That's the promise of Windows, but sometimes the promise gets broken.

One thing you need to remember is that Gallant Windows is still related to Goofus DOS. Therein lies the rub and the reason that a book like *Windows For Dummies* is necessary.

Dan Gookin
Coeur d'Alene, Idaho

The 5th Wave   By Rich Tennant

"GATHER AROUND, KIDS. YOUR MOTHER'S WINDOWING!"

Introduction

● ●

Welcome to *Windows 3.11 For Dummies,* 3rd Edition! This edition is almost identical to the first, but everything's been given an overhaul to make sure that the information is as up-to-date as possible.

The basic premise of this edition remains the same as for earlier versions, and it boils down to this: Some people want to be Windows wizards. They love interacting with dialog boxes. In their free moments, they randomly press keys on their keyboards, hoping to stumble onto a hidden, undocumented feature. They memorize long strings of computer commands while they're organizing their socks-and-underwear drawer.

And you? Well, you're no dummy, that's for sure. In fact, you're light-years ahead of most computer nerds. You can make conversation with a neighbor without mumbling about "stacked RAM drives," for example. But, when it comes to Windows and computers, the fascination just isn't there. You just want to get your work done, fill the cat's water dish, and relax for a while. You have no intention of changing, and there's nothing wrong with that.

That's why this book will come in handy. It won't try to turn you into a Windows wizard, but you'll pick up a few chunks of useful computing information while reading it. You won't become a Windows wizard, but you'll know enough to get by quickly, cleanly, and with a minimum of pain so you can move on to the more pleasant things in life.

About This Book

Don't try to read this book at one sitting; there's no need to. Instead, treat this book like a dictionary or an encyclopedia. Turn to the page with the information you need and say, "Ah, so that's what they're talking about." Then put down the book and move on.

Don't bother trying to remember all the Windows buzz words, like "Select the menu item from the drop-down list box." Leave that stuff for the computer geeks. In fact, if anything technical comes up in a chapter, a road sign warns you well in advance. That way you can either slow down to read it or speed on around it.

You won't find any fancy computer jargon in this book. Instead, you'll find subjects like these, discussed in plain old English:

- Finding a lost window in the pile
- Running favorite DOS programs under Windows
- Dumping information from one window into another
- Finding the file you saved yesterday
- Starting programs by clicking on an icon

There's nothing to memorize and nothing to learn. Just turn to the right page, read the brief explanation, and get back to work. Unlike other books, this one enables you to bypass any technical hoopla and yet still get your work done.

How to Use This Book

Something in Windows will eventually leave you scratching your head. No other program brings so many buttons, bars, or babble to the screen. When something in Windows has you stumped, use this book as a reference. Look for the troublesome topic in this book's table of contents or index. The table of contents lists chapter and section titles and page numbers. The index lists topics and page numbers. Page through the table of contents or index to the spot that deals with that particular bit of computer obscurity, read only what you have to, close the book, and apply what you've read.

There's no learning involved. There's no remembering, either, unless you want to remember something so you don't have to grab the book the next time the same situation comes up.

If you're feeling spunky and want to learn something, read a little further. You'll find a few completely voluntary extra details or some cross-references to check out. There's no pressure, though. You won't be forced to learn anything that you don't want to or that you simply don't have time for.

If you have to type something into the computer, you'll see easy-to-follow text like this:

```
C:\> TYPE THESE LETTERS
```

In the preceding example, you type **TYPE THESE LETTERS** after the C:\> and then press the keyboard's Enter key. Typing words into a computer can be confusing, so a description of what you're supposed to type usually follows. That way, you can type the words exactly as they're supposed to be typed.

You won't, for example, accidentally type **"TYPE THESE LETTERS"** — complete with quotation marks — like many users do after seeing text like *At the DOS prompt, type "TYPE THESE LETTERS"* in computer manuals.

Whenever I describe a message or information that you'll see on the screen, I present it as follows:

```
This is a message on-screen.
```

This book doesn't wimp out by saying, "For further information, consult your manual." No need to pull on your wading boots. This book covers everything you need to know to use Windows. The only thing you won't find is general information about using DOS or other software packages. The best crowbar for DOS is this book's grandfather, *DOS For Dummies,* published by IDG Books Worldwide. Other . . .*For Dummies* books mercifully explain other popular software packages, as well.

Note that if you do need to know something about DOS to use Windows, that part of DOS is covered here in enough detail for you to get the job done. You'll also find help for some of the more popular Windows programs.

Please Don't Read This!

Computers thrive on technical stuff. Luckily, you're warned in advance when you're heading for something even vaguely obtuse. Chances are it's just more minute detail concerning something you've already read about. Feel free to skip any section labeled Technical Stuff. Those niblets of information aren't what this book's about. But, if you're feeling particularly ornery, keep reading and you may learn something. (Just don't let anybody see you do it.)

And What about You?

Well, chances are that you have a computer. You have Windows. And you do something with both of them. You know what *you* want to do. The problem is with making the computer do what you want to do. You've gotten by one way or another, hopefully with the help of a computer guru — either a friend at the office or somebody down the street. Unfortunately, though, that computer guru isn't always around. This book can be a substitute for the computer guru during your times of need. Keep a fresh bag of Chee-tos in your desk drawer, however, just in case you need a quick bribe.

How This Book Is Organized

The information in this book has been well sifted. This book contains seven parts, and each part is divided into chapters related to the part's theme. Each chapter is divided into short sections to help you navigate Windows' stormy seas. Sometimes you may find what you're looking for in a small, boxed tip. Other times you may need to cruise through an entire section or chapter. It's up to you and your particular task at hand.

Here are the categories (the envelope, please):

Part I: Introducing Windows (Bare-Bones Stuff)

This book starts out with the basics. You learn how to turn on your computer, and you examine all your computer's parts and what Windows does to them. This part walks you through the steps for installing Windows and explains all the Windows stuff that everybody thinks you already know. And you end this part (with great relief) by turning off your computer.

Part II: Making Windows Do Something

The biggest problem with using Windows isn't opening programs or moving windows around on-screen. It's making Windows do something *useful*. Here, you find ways to overcome Windows' frustratingly playful tendencies and force it to shovel the walkway or blow leaves off the driveway.

Part III: Using Windows Applications (Those Free Programs)

Good news. Windows comes with a whole bunch of free programs that aren't even listed on the box. In this part, you find practical information about your new word processor, calendar, electronic Rolodex, and a few other goodies.

Part IV: Looking at That Darn DOS Stuff

Bad news. Windows is fancy clothing over an ugly DOS belly — curly hairs and all. This part offers tips to keep you from falling into its navel — especially if you still cling to a few DOS programs under Windows.

Part V: Getting Help

Are your windows stuck? Broken? Do you need new screens? Although glass doesn't shatter when Windows crashes, it can still hurt. In this part, you find some soothing salves for the most painful and irritating maladies.

Part VI: Windows for Workgroups

A computer can be pretty confusing. But imagine strings of computers linked together with cables — a *network* of computers, often found in an office. Networked computers often use a special version of Windows called Windows for Workgroups, and you'll find instructions and snapshots in this section.

Part VII: The Part of Tens

Everybody loves lists (unless they're published by the IRS). This part contains lists of Windows-related trivia — ten aggravating things about Windows (and how to fix them), ten DOS commands you shouldn't run under Windows, ten programs that make Windows easier, ten expensive things that make Windows easier, and ten mystifying acronyms.

Icons Used in This Book

Already seen Windows? Then you've probably noticed its *icons,* which are little pictures for starting various programs. The icons in this book fit right in. They're even a little easier to figure out:

Watch out! This signpost warns you that pointless technical information is coming around the bend. Swerve away from this icon, and you'll be safe from the nerdy technical drivel.

This icon alerts you to juicy information that makes computing easier. For example, keep a damp sponge on hand in case your Saint Bernard decides to sniff your keyboard.

Don't forget to remember these important points. (Or at least dog-ear the pages so you can look them up again a few days later.)

The computer itself won't explode while you're performing the delicate operations associated with this icon. Still, wearing gloves and proceeding with caution is a good idea when this icon is near.

Where to Go from Here

Now you're ready for action. Give the pages a quick flip and maybe scan through a few sections that you know you'll need later. Oh, and this is *your* book — your weapon against the computer criminals who've inflicted this whole complicated computer concept on you. So personalize your sword: Circle the paragraphs you find useful, highlight key concepts, cover up the technical drivel with sticky notes, and draw smiley faces in the margins.

Part I

Introducing Windows (Bare-Bones Stuff)

The 5th Wave   **By Rich Tennant**

While upgrading to Windows 3.1, Tonto the scout embarrasses himself by taking the wrong path reference back to the directory.

In this part...

Windows is an exciting, modern way to use the computer. That means it's as confusing as a new car's dashboard. Even the most wizened old computer buffs will stumble in this strange new land of boxes, bars, and bizarre oddities like *PIF options*.

Never used a computer before but bought Windows because it's "easy to use"? Well, Windows can be intuitive, but that doesn't mean it's as easy to figure out as a bowling ball.

In fact, most people are dragged into Windows without a choice. Your new computer probably came with Windows already installed. Or maybe they installed Windows at the office, where everyone has to learn it except for Scott, who plays racquetball with the boss. Or perhaps your favorite program, like PageMaker, requires Windows, so you've had to learn to live with the darn thing.

And you can adjust to Windows, just like you eventually learned to live comfortably with that funky college roommate who kept leaving hair clogs in the shower.

Whatever your situation, this part keeps things safe and sane, with the water flowing smoothly. If you're new to computers, the first chapter answers the question you've been afraid to ask around the lunch room: "Just what is this Windows thing, anyway?"

Chapter 1
What Is Windows?

*O*ne way or another, you've probably already heard about Windows. Windows posters line the walls of computer stores. All the flashy computer magazines are shouting "Windows" loudly enough to disturb sleeping animals. And you've probably heard at least one person tell you that Windows is a computer paradise, filled with beautiful graphics and relaxing menus.

But be prepared: Windows is no panacea, no matter how you want to pronounce that word. Windows may be a paradise compared with DOS, but even Hawaii has cockroaches. And they're huge! (At least the one I saw in a fancy Kona restaurant last year was. It was so huge that my wife thought it was fake — part of the jungle decor and all. Then it started to clean its antennae. The waitress picked it up and let it go outside. Didn't like to kill animals, she said.)

You probably won't find a cockroach in your Windows box, but be prepared for a few other surprises. . . .

This chapter fills you in on the basics of Windows. It explains what Windows is and what it does. You also examine how Windows and DOS work together.

What Is Windows?

Windows is just another computer program, like the zillions of others lining the store shelves. But it's not a program in the normal sense — something that enables you to write letters or play Spatula Invaders. Rather, Windows changes the way you work with your computer.

For years, computer programs have made computers cling to the typewriter look. Just as on a typewriter, people type letters and numbers into the computer. The computer listens and then places letters and numbers onto the screen. This time-tested system works well. But it takes a long time to learn, and it's as boring as an oral hygiene pamphlet.

It's boring because computer geeks designed computers for other computer geeks many moons ago. They thought that computers would be forever isolated in narrow hallways where somber young people with clipboards and white lab coats jotted down notes while the big reels whirled. Nobody expected normal people to use computers — especially not in their offices, their dens, or, heaven help us, their kitchens.

- ✓ Windows dumps the typewriter analogy and updates the *look* of computers. It replaces the words and numbers with pictures and buttons. It's splashy and modern, like an expensive new coffee maker.

- ✓ Because Windows looks and acts differently from traditional computer programs, learning it can take a few days. After all, you probably couldn't make perfect coffee the first day, either.

What Does Windows Do?

Like the mother with the whistle in the lunch court, Windows controls all the parts of your computer. You turn on your computer, start Windows, and start running Windows programs. Each program runs in its own little *window* on-screen. Yet Windows keeps things safe, even if the programs start throwing food at each other.

While it's keeping order, Windows makes computing a little easier. Windows purges an ugly computing custom called the *DOS command line.* The command line lives next to a confusing little symbol, *the DOS prompt,* which looks something like this:

```
C:\>
```

With DOS, people boss around their computers by typing a command at the prompt. To start the WhipIt program, for example, they type the program's name and then press Enter, like this:

```
C:\> WHIPIT
```

That is, they type **WHIPIT** at the prompt and then press Enter. The computer dutifully loads the WhipIt program and brings it to the screen. DOS is tense, shoulder-tightening stuff. You must memorize the names of all your programs because DOS doesn't offer any clues — not even a quick spelling tip. (For more information on DOS, see the section "What Is DOS, and Why Do I Still Need It?")

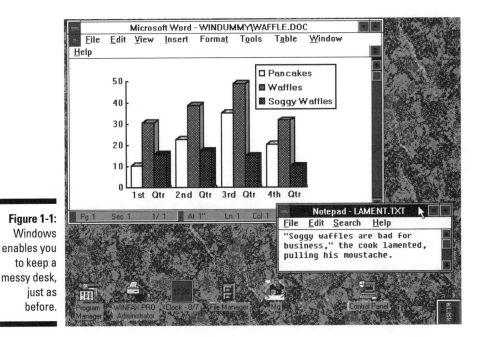

Figure 1-1:
Windows
enables you
to keep a
messy desk,
just as
before.

Windows, in contrast, replaces that dreary DOS prompt with little pictures. To start your WhipIt program in Windows, for example, you look for the picture representing your WhipIt program. It may look something like this:

By selecting the picture of the whip, Windows users can start the WhipIt program even if they can't spell. Figures 1-1 and 1-2 compare the way Windows and DOS look.

Windows fills the screen with lots of fun little boxes and pictures; DOS is for no-nonsense minimalists who never put bumper stickers on their cars.

   ✔ Some people say that colorful pictures make Windows easier to use; others say that Windows is a little too arty. To write a letter in Windows, for example, do you select the picture of the notepad, the quill, or the clipboard? And what do you do with the icon of the little man juggling?

   ✔ A computer environment that uses little pictures and symbols is called a *graphical user interface,* or *GUI.* (It's pronounced *gooey,* believe it or not.) Pictures require more computing horsepower than letters and numbers, so Windows requires a relatively powerful computer. (You'll find a list of its requirements in Chapter 2.)

```
C:\>
```

Figure 1-2:
The DOS
screen
shows only
the prompt.

- Windows gets its name from all the cute little windows on the screen. Each window shows some information: a picture, perhaps, or a program you're running. You can put several windows on the screen at the same time and jump from window to window, visiting different programs. (Actually, the windows look like little squares, but who would buy a program called Squares?)

- When the word *Windows* starts with a capital letter, it refers to the Windows program. When the word *windows* starts with a lowercase letter, it refers to windows you see on-screen.

Because Windows uses graphics, it's much easier to use than to describe. To tell someone how to move through a document in a DOS-based program, you simply say, "Press the PgDn key." In Windows, you say, "Click in the vertical scroll bar beneath the scroll box." Those directions sound awfully weird, but after you've done it, you'll say, "Oh, is that all? Golly!" (Plus, you can still press the PgDn key in Windows. You don't have to "click in the vertical scroll bar beneath the scroll box" if you don't want to.)

What Is DOS, and Why Do I Still Need It?

MS-DOS is as boring as the words it stands for: Microsoft Disk Operating System. DOS handles the chores required to make the computer do its traditional computer stuff: shuffle information to and from various parts of your computer and put it on your screen for you to labor over.

When you turn on your computer, DOS wakes up, takes control, and starts making things happen. It handles all the dreadful, background computing mechanics so you can concentrate on what's happening on the screen.

DOS protects you from that internal computer stuff, but DOS is kind of technical itself. So Windows rides on top of DOS, insulating you from your computer's technical side even more. When you tell Windows to do something, it turns around and tells DOS to do something. Windows is just a translator, converting languages and collecting cash for its services.

And you still need DOS to run Windows. Because Microsoft wrote both programs, it can collect twice as much money!

 ✔ Windows and DOS are two separate programs. DOS controls your computer's sticky internal mechanics, and Windows controls DOS. You then control Windows. Windows and DOS act as two layers of insulation that protect you from your computer's guts.

 ✔ Windows doesn't have to be running on your computer all the time. In fact, after installing Windows, you don't even have to use it. You can still use your favorite DOS programs, just as before. When you get up the nerve, you can start Windows, run some Windows programs, and see what all the fuss is about.

 ✔ Although Windows programs can insulate you from DOS, DOS still lurks in the background. In fact, you see DOS when you start Windows and when you exit Windows. You can't get away from it. (You can even run a DOS session in an on-screen Windows window if you miss seeing that `C:\>` stuff.)

 ✔ DOS is too disgusting to be discussed in detail this early. If you're into it, turn to Chapter 16.

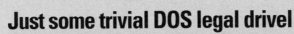

Just some trivial DOS legal drivel

Microsoft's version of DOS is called MS-DOS. Microsoft sells licenses to other companies so that those companies can sell DOS with their own line of computers. The other companies change the name slightly so customers think that they're getting something special. You'll find PC DOS, COMPAQ DOS, Tandy DOS, DIP DOS, and a plethora of others. They're all pretty much the same thing. A DOS is a DOS.

Oh, and no matter who's selling it, DOS rhymes with boss. Don't pronounce it as *dose* unless you're pretending you're a novice at the software store to see whether the salesperson will try to rip you off.

Even worse technical glop

Computer nerds spend their idle hours arguing whether Windows is an operating system or a shell.

An *operating system* controls a computer's innards at a bare-bones, blood-pumping level. DOS is an operating system because it handles all the raw, messy mechanics of computing. When you tell DOS to copy something to a floppy disk, DOS wakes up the floppy drives and tells the computer to find the appropriate information and move it, one morsel at a time, to the floppy disk. All you do is type the COPY command; DOS jumps in there and does the rest.

A *shell,* on the other hand, rides on top of DOS, making DOS easier to use. (Sure, the DOS COPY command is easy enough, but try remembering other commands, like MODE LPT1:=COM2:.) Shells always have DOS in the background, just as Windows does.

But, because Windows takes over the computer completely, handling all the pesky maintenance chores (using DOS as a background helper), some people say that Windows itself is an operating system. Besides, right on the front of the box Microsoft calls Windows an operating system.

The debate rages. Luckily, computer nerds tend to mumble, so you don't have to listen.

Why Should I Bother Using Windows?

DOS is time tested and traditional, but, like IRS forms, it's a bunch of cryptic words and numbers. It's a mean, spiteful computer program. You have to know what strange words to type at the DOS prompt before your computer will even listen to you.

Windows, in contrast, puts all its cards on the table. You don't have to memorize any program names; you just look for the right pictures. Just as the international symbols over rest rooms help when you drink too much espresso in Paris, pictures can make computing easier.

Windows outdoes DOS in another way. All DOS programs work differently from each other. For example, your word processor and your database require different commands for printing. If you work with four different programs, you have to memorize four different print commands.

Microsoft bossed around all the companies that write software for Windows, so all Windows programs work pretty much the same way. No matter who wrote the program, you use the same three keystrokes in any Windows program to print your work. Imagine relying on just one yellow sticky note rather than having dozens of sticky notes circling your monitor!

In DOS, only one program can be on the screen at a time. Because Windows programs run in little windows, you can run as many programs as you can fit on your screen. This feature makes it easier to, say, grab an address from one window and stick it into a letter you're writing in another window. (Finding that other window is another problem. Chapter 8 can help you locate lost windows.)

Finally, you'll probably have to start using Windows sooner or later. Windows has become so fashionable that most software companies are abandoning their DOS programs and writing Windows versions instead. It was bound to happen. Make room in the garage to dump those DOS programs next to the 8-tracks.

- ✔ The box doesn't say so, but Windows comes with a free word processor, an address book, a calendar, a drawing program, and a few other goodies. These freebies, which can handle the computing needs of many people, are described in Part III of this book.

- ✔ Windows can run your DOS programs as well as Windows programs. Depending on your computer, Windows either places the DOS program in its own little window or steps back and lets it fill the entire screen, just as it normally does.

- ✔ The store shelves are packed with programs that say "For Windows" on the box. Those programs don't include Microsoft Windows, however. They're designed to run from within Microsoft Windows. You have to buy Windows separately and install it on your computer first.

What Are the Best Versions of Windows and DOS?

Computer programs are never finished. If a company sold a perfect program, its programmers would be out of a job. So programmers keep fiddling with the programs — adding new features or removing the older ones that didn't go over very well. Eventually, when they've tweaked with the program enough, the marketing department dubs the program a new *version,* puts it on the store shelves, and tries to convince everybody to buy it and upgrade to the latest, greatest version.

Windows and DOS have been around for a long time, so they've gone through a plethora of versions. Currently, Windows 3.11 is the latest version of Windows, and DOS 6.21 is the latest version of DOS. They work very well together, as if they were made for each other. (In fact, they were made for each other because Microsoft made both of them.)

Skip this stuff about versions and vegetables

When programmers make a bunch of changes to a program, they release a new version: Carrot Version 1.0, for example, becomes Carrot Version 2.0. People start buying the new version, leaving the old one outside for the raccoons.

But, if the programmers make just a few changes to fix their old mistakes, they release a minor

upgrade by adding a decimal: Carrot Version 1.0 becomes Carrot Version 1.1. The latest version of Windows fixed a great deal of problems found in Windows 3.0, but it still can't park cars or do anything worthy enough to merit a Version 4.0.

It's just a little computer oddity. You were supposed to skip this part anyway.

To find out what name and version of DOS is driving your computer, use the VER command:

```
C:\> VER
```

That is, type **VER** at the DOS prompt and press Enter. Your computer then coughs up the information.

✔ To find out what version of Windows you're using, click on <u>H</u>elp from the menu along the top of Program Manager. When a new menu drops down, click on <u>A</u>bout Program Manager. A box pops up, listing bunches of gibberish. The third line of gibberish gives you the version number. Click on the OK button to get rid of this box.

✔ Windows 3.1 and DOS 6.2 work together better than any other combination of versions, although DOS 5.0 comes close. Don't rush right out and buy DOS 6.21, however; that version is merely a legalese, "lost-the-lawsuit" version. (Nerdy note: DOS 6.21 removes a utility called *DoubleSpace* that was supposed to give people more space on their hard disks. It also gave Microsoft more time in court.)

✔ Some early Windows programs don't run under Windows 3.1. The only way to tell whether they work is to try to run them. (Give it a shot; they won't damage your computer if they don't work.)

✔ If you're not using DOS 3.1 or a later version, Windows won't even come out of the box. Buy DOS 6.2 at the same time you buy Windows 3.1.

✔ To create Version 3.11, Microsoft just updated a few of its older files. If Windows already works fine on your computer, don't bother with the new version. There's nothing noticeably different in it, like a new game of Solitaire. (In fact, the opening screen for Windows 3.11 still says *Windows 3.1.*) This version is designed mainly for people with computer networks.

Can I Still Use My DOS Programs?

Sure, you can still use your DOS programs. You can either run them while using Windows or run them the same as before — as if Windows isn't even there.

See, even though Windows has been installed on your hard drive, you don't have to use it. Just pretend that Windows isn't taking up space on your hard drive and don't run it. Run your favorite DOS programs from the DOS prompt, the same as in the old days.

However, Windows is good-natured enough to let you run your DOS programs from within Windows (if you want to). With a powerful enough computer, Windows treats a DOS program just like a Windows program: It puts it into a little window and lets it do its stuff.

But, because DOS programs weren't designed to run with Windows, the two program flavors don't mix well. DOS programs run more slowly in a Windows window, for example, than if they had the computer all to themselves.

To make matters worse, you have to fool some particularly mulish DOS programs into thinking that they're running normally by performing bizarre technical tweaks to something called a *PIF*. (You can find more information about PIFs in Chapter 16.)

But it can be done.

- ✔ Just because something can be done doesn't mean it should be done. Sure, you can use Windows to run your DOS programs. Nobody will run up and hit you with a pig bladder. But it's not a very efficient way to run your computer. Your DOS programs run better without Windows.

- ✔ If you're using Windows just to run DOS programs, you're probably better off not even installing Windows. Head back to the computer store and ask for a program called DESQview.

- ✔ DOS programs are hoggy, and they eat a great deal of your computer's resources. If your computer doesn't have a lot of memory, Windows may not be capable of heaving any of your DOS programs onto the screen at all.

- ✔ DOS programs are so hoggy, in fact, that they eat up all of Chapter 16 in this book.

Bracing Yourself for Windows

DOS, for all its faults, at least looks simple because the programs run one at a time. They take their time on the center stage and then exit politely, letting another program hit the spotlight.

With Windows, however, everything happens at the same time. Its many different parts run around like hamsters with an open cage door. Programs cover each other up on the screen. They overlap corners, hiding each other's important parts. Occasionally, they simply disappear.

Be prepared for a bit of frustration when things don't behave properly. You'll be tempted to stand up, bellow, and toss a nearby stapler across the room. After that, calmly pick up this book, find the trouble spot listed in the index, and turn to the page with the answer.

(And don't forget to pick up the stapler. Jerry Schuster from Anaheim reports that his stapler jammed in the janitor's vacuum cleaner, and the guy stopped emptying the trash cans in the whole department.)

✔ Windows may be accommodating, but that can cause problems, too. For example, Windows often offers more than three different ways for you to perform the same computing task. Don't bother memorizing each command. Just choose one method that works for you and stick with it. For example, Andrew and Deirdre Kleske use scissors to cut their freshly delivered pizza into slices. It stupefies the house guests, but it gets the job done.

✔ Windows runs best on a powerful computer with the key word *386, 486, Pentium,* or *testosterone* somewhere in the description. Look for lots of RAM (random-access memory) too, as well as a huge hard disk. You'll find the finicky computer requirements for Windows in Chapter 2.

Chapter 2
Your PC's Parts

In This Chapter

▶ Learning the names for the gizmos and gadgets on the computer

▶ Understanding what all those things do

▶ Finding out what stuff you need in order to use Windows

▶ Making a list of what computer equipment you have

---

*T*his chapter introduces computer gizmos and gadgets. Go ahead and ignore it. Who cares what all your PC gadgetry is called? Unless your PC's beeping at you like a car alarm, don't bother messing with it. Just dog-ear the top of this page, say, "So, that's where all that stuff is explained," and keep going.

In Windows, you just press the buttons. Windows scoots over to the right part of your computer and kick-starts the action. If Windows stubs a toe, this chapter holds the Band-Aids. And, as always, the foul-smelling technical chunks are clearly marked; just hold your nose while stepping over them gingerly.

The Computer

The computer is that beige box with all the cables. It probably answers to one of three names: IBM (called *True Blue* when people try to dump their old one in the classifieds), an *IBM compatible* or *clone,* or a plain old PC.

Most people just call their computers *PCs* because that's what IBM called its first *personal computer* back in 1981. In fact, IBM's first PC started this whole personal computing craze, although some people lay the blame on video games.

The concept of a small computer that could be pecked on in an office or den caught on well with the average Joe, and IBM made gobs of money. So much money, in fact, that other companies immediately ripped off IBM's design. They *cloned,* or copied, IBM's handiwork to make a computer that worked just like it. These clone computers are *compatible* with IBM's own PC; they can use the same software as IBM's PC without spitting up.

Clones generally have an obscure brand name and a lower price on their invoice, but they work just as well (or better) than IBM's own line of computers. In fact, more people own clones than personal computers from IBM's own line. (Just look at IBM's latest quarterly earnings statements for proof.)

✔ People used to say that *IBM-compatible* computers were made by big corporations, like COMPAQ and Toshiba. A *clone*, on the other hand, was thrown together by a kid in a back room. The distinction has waned through the years. If it's not IBM's computer, it's a clone.

✔ Windows runs equally well on IBM-compatible computers and on IBM's own computers; the key word is *IBM*. Computers from other planets, like the Macintosh, can't run Windows, but their owners don't care. They just stifle their giggles when you try to figure out how to create a Windows *program group*.

✔ Some muscular people heft their desktop PCs onto one side and put them in a special stand. Other computers are designed to work sideways. These upright PCs are called *tower PCs*. The tilt doesn't affect their performance, but it makes them look really cool — especially when they use Windows' Black Leather Jacket color scheme. (The hairy-armed crowd can check out Chapter 10 for leather jacket tips.)

✔ If your PC has a CD-ROM drive, *don't* turn your PC onto one side; CD-ROM drives don't like to be run sideways, and doing so can damage your discs. If your CD-ROM drive's manual says it's okay, however, then go for it.

✔ As other companies built *compatible* computers, they strayed a bit from IBM's design. Tandy, for example, added sound. A few years ago, IBM itself strayed from its classic design by launching a new *PS series* of computers. Some of these design quirks can befuddle Windows — especially when you first install it. After you tell Windows what brand of computer it's dealing with, however, any hard feelings are soothed. All this stuff is covered in Chapter 3.

✔ Laptop and notebook computers can run Windows with no problems. Airplane-bound laptoppers should check out this chapter's mouse section for a mouse substitute.

When laptopping on an airplane, drop a few smoked almonds on your neighboring passenger's thigh. If he doesn't wake up, you can use his kneecap as a makeshift mousepad for a few double-clicks.

The Computer's Microprocessor

The computer's *brain* is a small black chip of silicon, buried deep inside the computer's case. Resembling a Girl Scout's Thin Mint with square corners, this flat little wafer is the *microprocessor*, but nerds tend to call it a *central processing unit*, or *CPU*. (You may have seen flashy microprocessor TV commercials that say, "Intel Inside." Intel is a leading CPU developer.)

The computer's microprocessor determines how fast and powerful the computer can toss information around. Refer to Table 2-1 for a look at the power of your particular computer.

Table 2-1		Microprocessor Power Ratings		
Computer Name	*Fancy Name*	*Micro-processor*	*Vintage*	*Power*
PC	Personal Computer	8088	1981	A mere babe. This one was not strong enough to run Windows.
XT	eXtended Technology	8088	1983	A toddler. The XT used the same microprocessor as the PC, but it came with a 10MB hard drive (Windows won't baby-sit).
AT	Advanced Technology	80286	1984	A hyper teenager. This one was the start of the newer, more powerful class of chips that ends with the number *86*. Windows barely tolerates this chip.
386, 486, Pentium	386-class	80386 80386SX 80486 80486SX 80486DX 80486DX2 80486DX4 Pentium	1986-today	The powerhouse pictured on "bulging muscle" magazines. Windows prefers this chip series.

✔ A microprocessor is the current evolution of the gadget that powered those little 1970s pocket calculators. It performs all the computer's background calculations, from juggling spreadsheets to putting a picture of "Calvin and Hobbes" on the screen.

✔ Microprocessors are described by two numbers: the chip's class (8088, 286, 386, and so on) and the chip's processing speed, measured in *megahertz,* or *MHz.* The bigger the numbers, the faster Windows performs. For example, a 50 MHz 486 microprocessor is faster than a 33 MHz 486 microprocessor.

✔ I apologize for all the numbers in the preceding paragraph.

General obfuscation about 386DX and 386SX code words

Today, the 386-class microprocessors are the most fashionable CPUs. They're the most powerful, and they can take advantage of the special memory features of Windows. The first 386 chip really scared people, and so did its price tag. Corporations snapped them up; everyone else saved their allowance.

Intel, the chip's creator, wanted to capture the thin-wallet crowd, so Intel's engineers hunkered down in the coffee room and released a less powerful (and less expensive) 386 chip called the *386SX*.

To avoid confusion between the 386 and its new little brother, Intel renamed its first 386 chip as a *386DX*. Technically speaking (and that's why this information is fenced into a little box), 386DX and 386SX chips can handle the same computing tasks: They can divvy up the computer's memory among greedy programs and enable them all to run wild at the same time.

But the programs run a little more slowly with a 386SX chip. Both the SX and DX versions of the 386 can take advantage of Windows' special 386 Enhanced mode.

Windows is even faster with a 486 chip, and the *SX* and *DX* stuff applies to 486 chips, as well. But those chips are another story with their own technical gobbledygook. (And, strangely enough, 486 chips and Pentiums are still referred to as "386-class" chips.)

Windows works best with the 386 and higher classes of microprocessors, which include 486 chips and the lofty Pentium. It's slow on a 286, and it doesn't let you run your favorite DOS programs in little windows on-screen. Don't bother trying to run Windows on an XT or an age-old original IBM PC. It chokes.

Disks and Disk Drives

The computer's disk drive, that thin slot in its front side, is like the drawer at the bank's drive-up teller window. That disk drive enables you to send and retrieve information from the computer.

You can push anything that's flat into a disk drive, but the computer recognizes only one thing: *floppy disks*. Things get a little weird here, so hang on tight. See, by some bizarre bit of mechanical wizardry, computers store information as a stream of magnetic impulses.

TECHNICAL STUFF

Math coprocessors and 486 stuff that only scientists care about

Microprocessors perform mathematical calculations all day. They absorb numbers, scratch their heads, and spit out the right answer. Everything a computer does requires calculations, from figuring out California's latest sales tax to moving a dot across the screen three inches.

Strangely enough, computer graphics require the largest number of calculations. The microprocessor can get bogged down by all those calculations — especially when scientists do important science stuff, like simulating a drop of milk splashing into a bowl.

To speed things up, scientists and other hardcore computer folk place a second computer chip called a *math coprocessor* inside their computers. Although the regular microprocessor handles the calculations required for everyday computing, the math coprocessor jumps in to handle the extra hard-core, number-crunching stuff. Windows works slightly faster with a math

coprocessor — especially if you're working with gargantuan spreadsheets (or milk drops).

The 486DX is the first chip to include a built-in math coprocessor. None of the other chips, including the 486DX's little brother, the 486SX, has one. (With those other chips, you need to buy a separate math coprocessor and have Dave at the computer store stick it on your computer's motherboard.) Finally, the latest 486DX2 varieties use new technology to make them a little faster.

Oh, and because of some legal oddities, buying a single 486DX chip is cheaper than buying a 486SX chip and adding a separate math coprocessor.

And here's one last little technical oddity: Math coprocessor chips end with the number 7. A math coprocessor for an 8088 is an 8087. A math coprocessor for a 286 is a 287. A math coprocessor for a — well, you get the idea.

A disk drive spits those little magnetic impulses onto the floppy disk for safe storage. The drive can slurp them back up, too. You just push the disk into the disk drive and tell Windows whether to slurp or spit. That's known as *copy to* or *copy from* in computer parlance.

Disks come in two main sizes: a sturdy 3½-inch disk and a rather flimsy 5¼-inch disk. Both are called floppy disks, but only one of them flops around when you dangle it by one corner.

✔ The 3 ½-inch disk drives automatically grab the disk when you push it in far enough. You hear it *clunk,* and the disk sinks down into the drive. If it doesn't, you're putting it in the wrong way. (The disk's silver edge goes in first, with the little round silver thing in the middle facing down.) To retrieve the disk, push the button protruding from around the drive's slot and then grab the disk when the drive kicks it out.

✔ The 5 ¼-inch disks require an extra step. Push the disk into the drive until it doesn't go in any farther and then flip down the drive's little lever. (The disk's oval-shaped hole edge goes in first; the disk's smooth side faces up, with the rough-edged side facing down.) To retrieve the disk, flip the little lever back up and grab the disk as the drive kicks it out.

✔ A disk you can carry around the house is a *floppy disk.* A hidden disk that lurks deep in the bowels of the computer is a *hard disk,* or *hard drive.*

✔ Hard disks are thick little Frisbees inside the computer that can hold hundreds of times more information than floppy disks. They're also much quicker at reading and writing information. (They're a great deal quieter, too, thank goodness.) Windows insists on a hard drive because it's such a huge program. The programs that run under Windows can be pretty huge, too.

✔ Because floppy disks are portable, using them is the easiest way to move information from one computer to another. You install Windows or any other program onto the computer by using floppy disks. You take the floppy disks out of the box and place them into the disk drive, one at a time, when a message on the computer screen tells you to. The computer copies the information from the floppy disk onto its hard drive.

✔ Computer stores sell blank disks so that you can copy your work onto them and put them in a safe place. Unless your new box of blank disks has the word *preformatted,* you can't use them straight out of the box. They must be *formatted* first. This merry little chore is covered in Chapter 12.

✔ Computers love to *copy* things. When you're copying a file from one disk to another, you aren't *moving* the file. You're just placing a copy of that file onto that other disk.

✔ Floppy disks come in many flavors, each holding different amounts of information. Different disks are designed for different sizes and types of disk drives. The disk's box describes what sort of disks are inside, but the bare disks rarely offer a clue as to their capacity. Table 2-2 provides a handy identification chart for that disk you found behind the bookcase.

Table 2-2		True-to-Life Disk Facts		
Size	*Name*	*Storage Capacity*	*Label Jargon*	*Looks Like This*
5¼-inch	Low-density	360K, or about 240 pages of double-spaced text	DS/DD 40 tpi	Square, bendable, and usually black; has a large hole in the center that's lined with a little plastic reinforcing ring.
5¼-inch	High-density	1.2MB, or about 800 pages of text	HD DS/HD 96 tpi	Most common. Square, bendable, and usually black; has a large hole in the center *without* a little plastic reinforcing ring, but that's not always a good indicator.
3½-inch	Low-density	760K, or about 500 pages of text	DS/DD DD 135 tpi	Square and rigid; has a little arrow in one corner. The arrow points away from a single, small square hole in another corner.
3½-inch	High-density	1.4MB, or about 900 pages of text	DS/HD HD	Most common. Square and rigid; has a little arrow in one corner and two small square holes in corners opposite from the arrow. The letters *HD* are often stamped on the disk.
3½-inch	Extended density	2.8MB, or about 1,800 pages of text	DS/ED ED	Square and rigid; very new and still quite shy. Chances are that you'll never have to recognize it by looking for little *ED* letters stamped on the disk.

Fun CD-ROM Drive Stuff

Most people think compact discs contain music. Nope. Compact discs contain numbers. That's all the information they can handle. The CD factory translates music into numbers, and the CD player translates those numbers back into music.

Computer nerds snapped up compact discs pretty quickly when they realized that they could store numbers, and many companies now sell their programs and information on compact discs. A single compact disc can hold more information than hundreds of floppy disks.

Disk do's and doughnuts

Do label your disks so you know what's on them.

Do at least make a valiant effort to peel off a disk's old label before sticking on a new one. (After a while, those stacks of old labels make the disk too fat to fit into the drive.)

Do feel free to write on the label after it has been placed on the disk. But use a felt-tipped pen if you're writing on a 5¼-inch disk; ballpoint pens can damage the fragile disk inside.

Do not touch the exposed part of the 5¼-inch disks.

Do not write on the disk's sleeve rather than the label. Disks always end up in each other's sleeves, leading to mistaken identities and a *faux pas*.

Do not fold a floppy disk in half.

Do copy important files from your hard disk to floppy disks on a regular basis. (This routine is called *backing up* in computer lingo. You can buy

special backup packages to make this chore a little easier. Not much, but a little.)

Do not try to use high-density disks in a low-capacity drive. They don't work.

Do use low-density disks in a high-capacity drive but only if you have to. They weren't designed for high-capacity drives, and they can cause problems.

Do not listen to silver-tongued people who say you can *notch* a low-density disk to turn it into a high-density disk. It just doesn't work consistently and reliably.

Do not leave disks lying in the sun.

Do not place disks next to magnets. Don't place them next to magnets disguised as paper clip holders, either, or next to other common magnetized desktop items like older telephones.

To use them, however, you have to buy a CD-ROM drive for the computer. The CD player with your stereo won't cut it. If you spend enough money, though, you can buy a CD-ROM drive that hooks up to your computer *and* plays music. Then you can sell the one attached to your stereo. It's getting old anyway.

✔ Compact discs can store a great deal of information, but they're notoriously slow in bringing it back up. They're even slower than floppy disks. Buy a comfortable chair.

✔ You can't write information to a compact disc. Only the people at the CD factory can write to it, and that's because they have an expensive machine. Compact discs can't ever be erased, either.

✔ Compact discs are spelled with a *c* to confuse people accustomed to seeing disks spelled with a *k*.

> ✔ Do you plan to use that new Kodak PhotoCD stuff or watch any fancy multimedia videos of Venus Flytraps eating frogs? If so, you'll want Windows to display at least 256 colors on-screen. Chapter 10 shows you how to make Windows' video modes more palatable.
>
> ✔ Multimedia computers need a sound card and a CD-ROM drive; the drive alone isn't enough. It's the computer industry's special way of making people spend more money.

What disk drives does Windows like?

On the box, Windows recommends that you have a hard drive with at least 6MB of free space, but it's keeping its fingers crossed behind its back. Windows can easily eat up 15MB of space. Windows programs can eat up even more space. Nobody will laugh if you use a 200MB hard disk and reserve at least half of that for Windows and your Windows programs.

Also, Windows requires a 5¼-inch, high-capacity floppy disk drive or a 3½-inch disk drive.

Finally, be aware that the terms *capacity* and *density* are often used interchangeably. The important part is the first part — *high* or *low*.

Be forewarned, however that Windows comes with *high-density* disks. If your 3½-inch disk drive isn't *high-capacity,* you won't be able to use the Windows disks straight out of the box. Instead, you'll have to mail a coupon to Microsoft asking for the low-density, 720K disks that are designed for your antiquated drives. Getting the disks can take from two weeks to a month, which can stifle the excitement of bringing home a new piece of software.

What does write-protected mean?

Write protection is supposed to be a helpful safety feature, but most people discover it through an abrupt bit of computer rudeness: File Manager stops them short with the threatening message shown in Figure 2-1 while they are trying to copy a file to a floppy disk.

A *write-protected disk* has simply been tweaked so nobody can copy or delete the files it contains. Write protection is a simple procedure, surprisingly enough, requiring no government registration. You can write-protect and unwrite-protect disks in the privacy of your own home.

Figure 2-1:
File
Manager's
error
message
that a disk
is write-
protected.

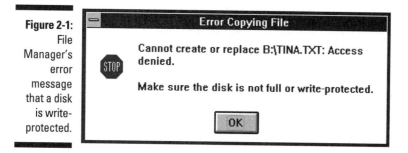

✔ To write-protect a 5 ¼-inch disk, fold a little black write-protect sticker over that big square notch on the disk's side. That cheap little sticker protects your disk's priceless contents from any changes or accidental deletions. You can *copy* information from the disk, but you can't *write* any information to it. You can't delete any information from it, either. (Those cheap little write-protect stickers come inside your expensive box of disks. If you can't find yours, a little piece of masking tape does the trick.)

✔ To remove the write protection on a 5 ¼-inch disk, simply peel off that little tab. Rub any leftover stickum off the disk and wipe your fingers on your pants.

✔ To write-protect a 3 ½-inch disk, look for a tiny black sliding tab in a square hole in its corner. Slide the tab with a pencil or your thumbnail so that the hole is uncovered. The disk is now write-protected.

✔ To remove the write protection on a 3 ½-inch disk, slide the little black plastic thingy so that the hole is covered up.

✔ Yes, it's confusing. The notch must be *covered* for you to write-protect a 5 ¼-inch disk. The square hole must be *uncovered* for you to write-protect a 3 ½-inch disk.

✔ If you encounter the write-protect error shown in Figure 2-1, then wait until the drive stops making noise. Remove the disk, unwrite-protect the disk, and put it back in the drive. Then repeat what you were doing before you were so rudely interrupted.

The Mouse and That Double-Click Stuff

The *mouse* is that rounded plastic thing that looks like a bar of electronic soap. Marketing people thought that the word *mouse* sounded like fun, so the name stuck. Actually, think of your mouse as your electronic finger because you'll be using it in Windows to point at stuff on the screen.

TECHNICAL STUFF

The breeds of mice

A serial mouse and a bus mouse look the same; both are plastic things with tails stretching toward the computer's back side. At the back side, serial and bus mice differ. A serial mouse plugs into an oblong doodad called a *serial port*. Almost all computers come with a preinstalled serial port that nerds call *COM1*.

The tail from a bus mouse doesn't head for the serial port. Instead, it creeps into a special *card* that's plugged into a slot in the computer's *expansion bus*. How did the card get there? Well, the person who sold you the computer took off the computer's case and plugged it in.

Also, some computers, like IBM's PS/2 series, come with a mouse already built in.

You can install a serial mouse yourself by just plugging it into the serial port. If you buy a bus mouse, however, you'd better buy a bag of Doritos, too, so you can bribe a computer guru to pull off your computer's case and slide that card in there.

A mouse has a little roller, or mouse ball, embedded in its belly. (Where were the animal-rights people?) When you move the mouse across your desk, the ball rubs against electronic sensor gizmos. The gizmos record the mouse's movements and send the information down the mouse's tail, which connects to the back of the computer.

As you move the mouse, you see an *arrow,* or *pointer,* move simultaneously across the computer screen. Here's where your electronic finger comes in: When the arrow points at a picture of a button on the screen, you press, or *click,* the left button on the mouse. The Windows button is selected, just as if you'd pressed it with your finger. It's a cool bit of 3-D computer graphics that makes you want to click buttons again and again.

- ✔ You control just about everything in Windows by pointing at it with the mouse and pressing and releasing the mouse button, or *clicking*. (The mouse pitches in with a helpful clicking noise when you press its button.)

- ✔ The plural of mouse is *mice,* just like the ones cats chew on. It's not *mouses.*

- ✔ Fold-down airline trays don't have enough room for a laptop, a mouse, *and* a beverage, so laptoppers often substitute trackballs for mice. A *trackball* is a small *upside-down mouse* that clips to the keyboard. You roll the mouse's ball with your thumb to move the on-screen arrow. You use your other fingers to inadvertently spill your beverage.

✔ Trackballs must be *purchased*. You can't just turn your normal mouse upside down and use masking tape. (I already tried.)

✔ Most mice run in two modes: Microsoft compatible or some funky third-party way. Microsoft created Windows, so you'll have fewer problems if you run the mouse in the Microsoft-compatible mode.

✔ Mice come in two breeds: bus and serial. Windows doesn't care which you have, so neither should you. And ignore the technical trivia listed in the sidebar "The breeds of mice."

✔ A mouse won't work by itself; it needs software called a *driver*. A driver listens to the mouse location information coming down the tail and puts the mouse's location in a special spot in the computer's memory. All your other programs can glance at that spot to see where you've pushed the mouse this time. For still more information on drivers, scurry to the section on installing drivers in Chapter 17.

✔ If your mouse doesn't work with Windows (it gets the shivers, it scurries around at random, or the arrow doesn't move), the driver (the software — not your hand) is probably to blame. Visit Chapter 17 for help.

The mouse arrow changes shape, depending on what it's pointing at in Windows. When it changes shape, you know it's ready to perform a new task. Table 2-3 is a handy reference for the different uniforms the mouse pointer wears for different jobs.

Don't worry about memorizing all the various shapes that the pointer takes on. The pointer changes shape automatically at the appropriate times. The shapes are described here so you won't think that your pointer's goofing off when it changes shape.

Table 2-3	The Various Shapes of the Mouse Pointer	
Shape	*What It Points At*	*What to Do When You See It*
▷	Just about anything on-screen	Use this pointer for moving from place to place on-screen.
⬦	A single window	Uh-oh. You've somehow selected the annoying size or move option from the Control menu. Moving the mouse or pressing the cursor-control keys now makes the current window bigger or smaller. Press Enter when you're done or press Esc if you want to get away from this uncomfortable bit of weirdness.

Shape	What It Points At	What to Do When You See It
⬍	The top or bottom edge of a window	Hold down the mouse button and move the mouse back and forth to make the window grow taller or shorter. Let go when you like the window's new size.
⬌	The left or right side of a window	Hold down the mouse button and move the mouse back and forth to make the window fatter or skinnier. Let go when you like the window's new size.
⬂	The corner of a window	Hold down the mouse button and move the mouse anywhere to make the window fat, skinny, tall, or short. Let go when you're through playing.
I	A program or box that accepts text (this pointer is called an *I-beam*)	Put the pointer where you want words to appear, click the button, and start typing the letters or numbers.
🖑	A word with a hidden meaning in the Windows help system	Click the mouse, and Windows will trot out some more helpful information about that particular subject.
⧗	Nothing (Windows is busy ignoring you)	Move the mouse in wild circles and watch the hourglass spin around until Windows catches up with you. This shape usually appears when you are loading files or copying stuff to a floppy disk.

Cards and Monitors

The monitor is the thing you stare at all day until you go home to watch TV. The front of the monitor, called its *screen* or *display,* is where all the Windows action takes place. The screen is where you can watch the windows as they bump around, occasionally cover each other up, and generally behave like nine people eyeing a recently delivered eight-slice pizza.

Monitors have *two* cords so they won't be mistaken for a mouse. One cord plugs into the electrical outlet; the other heads for the *video card,* a special piece of electronics poking out from the computer's back. The computer tells the video card what it's doing; the card translates the events into graphics information and shoots it up the cable into the monitor, where it appears on the screen.

> ✔ Like herbivores and cellulose-digesting gut microorganisms, monitors and video cards come in symbiotic pairs. Neither can function without the other, and you buy them in matched sets so that they'll get along.

> ✔ Unlike other parts of the computer, the video card and monitor don't require any special care and feeding. Just wipe the dust off the screen every once in a while.

Ignore these awful graphics terms

Some people describe their monitors as *boxy* or *covered with cat hair;* others use the following strange scientific terms:

Pixel: A pixel is a fancy name for an individual dot on the screen. Everything on the screen is made up of bunches of graphic dots, or pixels. Each pixel is a different shade or color, which creates the image. (Squint up close and you may be able to make out an individual pixel.) Monochrome monitors are often called *gray-scale monitors* because their pixels can only show shades of gray.

Resolution: The resolution is the number of pixels on a screen — specifically, the number of pixels across (horizontal) and down (vertical). More pixels mean greater resolution: smaller letters and more information packed onto the same-sized screen. People with small monitors usually use 640 × 480 resolution. People with larger monitors often switch to 1024 × 768 resolution so that they can fit more windows on-screen.

Color: This term describes the number of colors the card and monitor display on-screen. The number of colors can change, however, depending on the current resolution. When the card runs

at a low resolution, for example, it can use its leftover memory to display more colors. At super-duper-high 1024 × 768 resolution, you may see only 16 colors on-screen. With a lower resolution of 640 × 480 — and an expensive video card — you may be able to see 16.7 million. Windows runs fastest with 16 colors. (Windows looks the flashiest — especially if you're using Kodak PhotoCD — with 256 colors or more.)

Mode: A predetermined combination of pixels, resolution, and colors is described as a *graphics mode.* Right out of the box, Windows can handle the mode needs of most people. If the video card hails from a weird mode planet, you need a *driver* from the folks who made the card (see Chapter 17 for help).

16-bit, 24-bit: These are fancy ways of describing the number of on-screen colors. The 16-bit mode stands for 65,000 possible colors, whereas 24-bit mode allows 16.7 million colors.

You don't need to know any of this stuff. If you're feeling particularly modular, however, you can change the Windows graphics modes after reading Chapter 10.

  ✔ Spray plain old glass cleaner on a rag and then wipe off the dust with the newly dampened rag. If you spray glass cleaner directly on the screen, it drips down into the monitor's casing, annoying the trolls who sleep under the bridge.

  ✔ When you first install Windows, it interrogates the video card and monitor until they reveal their brand name and orientation. Windows almost always gets the right answer from them and sets itself up automatically so that everything works fine the first time.

✔ If everything *doesn't* work fine, however, and Windows looks weird on the screen (or doesn't even show up at all), then try this: First, exit Windows. (If you can't even see Program Manager, press Ctrl+Alt+Del to get to DOS.) Next, move to your Windows directory and type the command **SETUP**. When the DOS version of the Windows Setup program arises, choose VGA from the various Display options. Save the new setting and exit the Setup program; Windows should look much better when you reload it.

✔ Windows may be dominating, but it's accommodating, too. It can handle a wide variety of monitors and cards. In fact, most monitors and cards can switch to different *modes,* putting more or fewer colors on the screen and shrinking the text so that you can cram more information onto the screen. Windows enables you to play around with all sorts of different video settings if you're in that sort of mood. (If you are, check out Chapter 10.)

✔ For such simple gadgets, monitors and cards command a dazzling array of nerdy terms. Ignore them all. Windows picks the appropriate video settings automatically and moves on to the hard stuff, like mouse drivers.

Keyboards

Computer keyboards looks pretty much like typewriter keyboards with a few dark growths around the perimeter. In the center lie the familiar white typewriter keys. The grayish keys with obtuse code words live along the outside edges. They're described next.

Groups of keys

Obtuse code-word sorters divvy those outside-edge keys into key groups:

Function keys: These keys either sit along the top of the keyboard in one long row or clump together in two short rows along the keyboard's left side. Function keys boss around programs. For example, you can press F1 to demand help anytime you're stumped in Windows.

Numeric keypad: Zippy-fingered bankers like this thingy: a square, calculator-like pad of numbers along the right edge of most keyboards. (You have to press a key called Num Lock above those numbers, though, before they'll work. Otherwise, they're *cursor-control keys,* described next.)

Cursor-control keys: If you *haven't* pressed the magical Num Lock key, the keys on that square, calculator-like pad of numbers are the cursor-control keys. These keys have little arrows that show which direction the cursor will be moved on-screen. (The arrowless 5 key doesn't do anything except try to overcome its low self-esteem.) Some keyboards have a second set of cursor-control keys next to the numeric keypad. Both sets do the same thing. Additional cursor-control keys are Home, End, PgUp, and PgDn. To move down a page in a word processor, for example, you press the PgDn key.

More key principles

Other keyboard keys you need to be familiar with follow:

Shift: Just as on a typewriter, this key creates uppercase letters or the symbols %#@$, which make great G-rated swear words.

Alt: Watch out for this one! When you press Alt (which stands for *Alternate*), Windows moves the cursor to the little menus at the top of the current window. If you're trapped up there and can't get out, you probably pressed Alt by mistake. Press Alt again to free yourself.

Ctrl: This key (which stands for *Control*) works like the Shift key, but it's for weird computer combinations. For example, holding down the Ctrl key while pressing Esc (described next) brings up a special Windows Task List box that tracks down missing windows. (Check out "The Way-Cool Task List" section in Chapter 7.)

Esc: This key, which stands for *Escape,* was a pipe dream of the computer's creators. They added Esc as an escape hatch from malfunctioning computers. By pressing Esc, the user was supposed to be able to escape from whatever inner turmoil the computer was currently going through. Esc doesn't always work that way, but give it a try. It sometimes enables you to escape when you're trapped in a menu or a dastardly dialog box. (Those traps are described in Chapter 6.)

Scroll Lock: This one's too weird to bother with. Ignore it. (It's no relation to a *scroll bar,* either.) If a little keyboard light glows next to your Scroll Lock key, press the Scroll Lock key to turn it off. (The key's often labeled Scrl Lk or something equally obnoxious.)

Delete: Press the Delete key (sometimes labeled Del), and the unlucky character sitting to the *right* of the cursor disappears. Any highlighted information disappears as well. Poof.

Backspace: Press the Backspace key, and the unlucky character to the *left* of the cursor disappears. The Backspace key is on the top row, near the right side of the keyboard; it has a left-pointing arrow on it. Oh, and the Backspace key deletes any highlighted information, too.

If you've goofed, hold down Alt and press the Backspace key. This action undoes your last mistake in most Windows programs.

Insert: Pressing Insert (sometimes labeled Ins) puts you in Insert mode. As you type, any existing words are scooted to the right, letting you add stuff. The opposite of Insert mode is Overwrite mode, where everything you type replaces any text that's in its way. Press Insert to toggle between these two modes.

Ugly disclaimer: Some Windows programs — Notepad, Cardfile, Write, and Calendar — are always in Insert mode. There's simply no way to move to Overwrite mode, no matter how hard you pound the Insert key.

Enter: This key works pretty much like a typewriter's Return key but with a big exception. Don't press Enter at the end of each line. A word processor can sense when you're about to type off the edge of the screen. It herds your words down to the next line automatically. So just press Enter at the end of each paragraph.

You'll also want to press Enter when Windows asks you to type something — the name of a file, for example, or the number of pages you want to print — into a special box.

Caps Lock: If you've mastered the Caps Lock key on a typewriter, you'll be pleased to find no surprises here. (OK, there's one surprise. Caps Lock affects only your letters. It has no effect on punctuation symbols or the numbers along the top row.)

Tab: There are no surprises here, either, except that Tab is equal to five spaces in some word processors and eight spaces in others. Still other word processors enable you to set Tab to whatever number you want. Plus, a startling Tab Tip follows.

Press Tab to move from one box to the next when filling out a form in Windows. (Sometimes these forms are called *dialog boxes.*)

✔ A mouse works best for most Windows tasks, like starting programs or choosing among various options. Sometimes the keyboard comes in handy, however. Windows comes with *shortcut keys* to replace just about anything you can do with a mouse. Sometimes pressing a few keys can be quicker than wading through heaps of menus with a mouse. (The shortcut keys are described in Chapter 5 in the section on when to use the keyboard.)

> ✔ If you don't own a mouse or a trackball, you can control Windows exclusively with a keyboard. But it's awkward, like when Freddy from *Nightmare on Elm Street* tries to floss his back molars.

Print Screen: the one, fun, weird code key

Windows fixed something dreadfully confusing about an IBM computer's keyboard: the Print Screen key (sometimes called PrtScr, Print Scrn, or something similar). In the old days of computing, pressing the Print Screen key sent a snapshot of the screen directly to the printer. Imagine the convenience!

Unfortunately, nobody bothered to update the Print Screen key to handle graphics. If a screen shows anything other than straight text, pressing the Print Screen key sends a wild jumble of garbled symbols to the printer. And, if the printer isn't connected, turned on, and waiting, the computer stops cold.

Windows fixes the Print Screen woes. Pressing the Print Screen key now sends a picture of the screen to a special place in Windows that is known as the *Clipboard.* When the image is on the Clipboard, you can *paste* it into your programs or save it to disk. You can even print the screen's picture if you paste the image from the Clipboard into Paintbrush, the Windows drawing program.

> ✔ With some computers, you have to hold down Shift while you press Print Screen, or you get just an asterisk on the screen. Not nearly as much fun.
>
> ✔ The Clipboard is described in Chapter 9.

Modems

Modems are the things those youngsters down the street use to break into the computer of a defense contractor and order tanks, billing them to your credit card number.

Although modems are surrounded by intrigue, they're really just little mechanical gadgets that translate a computer's information into squealing sounds that can be sent and received over plain, ordinary, phone lines.

> ✔ The computers on both ends of the phone lines need modems in order to talk to each other.
>
> ✔ Modems need special *communications software* to make them work. Windows comes with a communications program called Terminal. The program is just waiting for you to buy a modem.

✔ Modems come in two breeds: *internal* and *external.* Internal modems come on special *cards* that must be buried inside the computer — a process best left to professional buriers.

✔ An external modem comes in its own little case. A cable runs from the modem's case to a *serial port,* or *COM port,* which is a special receptacle in the back of the computer. (Plugging an external modem into the port is easy, unless you have only one serial port and you've already plugged the mouse into it. Then it's time to drive back to the computer store, with your computer in the back seat, and tell the teenager to put another serial port in the computer when he's through setting a new high score.)

✔ Most people use modems to call the Internet and Prodigy, CompuServe, and other *on-line services.* On-line services are huge computers stuffed with information like stock prices, weather updates, news, and *message areas,* where people can swap talk about flatware, UFOs, and how much the on-line service is costing them. (On-line services cost anywhere from $8.95 a month to more than $20 an hour, all billed through a credit card.)

✔ For more information about CompuServe, call (800) 848-8199. For more information about Prodigy, call (800) PRODIGY. And, for more information about your credit rating, call those youngsters down the street.

Printers

Realizing that the paperless office still lies several years down the road, Microsoft made sure that Windows can shake hands and make enthusiastic gestures with more than 200 different types of printers. When you install Windows, you need to type in your printer's name. Windows checks its dossiers, finds your printer, and immediately begins speaking to it in its native language.

That's all there is to it. Unless, of course, your printer happens to be one of the several hundred printers *left off* the Windows master list. In that case, cross your fingers that your printer's manufacturer is still in business. You have to get a *driver* from the manufacturer before your prose can hit the printed page. (For information on printers, see Chapter 10.)

✔ You need to know the name and model number of your printer when you install Windows, or Windows snubs it. Windows can figure out what brands of computer parts are inside your case, but it can't figure out what's connected to the end of your printer cable.

✔ Printers must be turned on before Windows can print to them. (You'd be surprised how easily this little fact can be forgotten in the heat of the moment.)

> ✔ Windows prints in a WYSIWYG (what you see is what you get) format, which means that what you see on the screen is reasonably close to what you'll see on the printed page.

Networks

Only die-hard computer geeks have a computer network at home, and they deserve what they get. Ordinary people deal with networks only in business settings, where the networks can be safely ignored except when they crash, which is usually right before it's your turn at the next available teller.

Networks connect PCs so that employees can share information. They can all send stuff to a single printer, for example, or send messages to each other asking whether Marilyn has passed out the paychecks yet.

> ✔ You're probably on a network if you can answer yes to any of these questions: Can your coworkers and you share a printer, data, or messages without standing up or yelling across the room? Do you ever *log in* or *log out* on your computer? When your computer stops working, does everybody else's computer stop working, too?

> ✔ You can safely ignore networks. Most networks require a paid human attendant, usually that person with drained-looking eyes, slumped shoulders, and a mouth that's slightly open on one side.

> ✔ Another common name for network is *not work*.

> ✔ When they work, you need to deal with networks only when you first turn Windows on. For a description of this frivolity, see the section on networks in Chapter 4. And for even more frivolity, check out Chapter 20, "Windows on a Network," for information about Windows for Workgroups.

Sound Cards (Making Barfing Noises)

For years, PC owners looked enviously at Macintosh owners — especially when their Macs ejected a disk. The Macintosh would simultaneously eject a floppy disk from its drive and make a cute barfing sound. Macs come with sound built in; they can barf, giggle, and make *really* disgusting noises that won't be mentioned here. (Any Mac owners will be happy to play them back for you.)

But the tight shirts at IBM decided there was no place for sound on a Serious Business Machine. Windows fixes that mistake, so now the accounting department's computers can barf as loudly as the ones in the art department down the hall.

✔ Before your computer can barf, it needs a *sound card*. A sound card looks just like a video card. In fact, all cards look alike: long, green, flat things that nestle into long flat slots inside the computer. Speakers plug into a sound card like a monitor plugs into a video card.

✔ Just as computers mimic IBM's original computer design, sound cards mimic the designs of three popular sound cards: AdLib, Sound Blaster, and Roland MPU-401. The AdLib and Roland cards are standards for playing music; the Sound Blaster design is a standard for playing music *and* for making noises.

✔ Windows works with these three standard sound cards. It works with other sound cards, as well, as long as you get the right driver. Refer to the section in Chapter 17 on installing a driver.

✔ Windows comes with a pleasant chimes sound already included, but it doesn't have any barf noises. Most computer gurus can either find a copy for you or personally record one.

✔ Just like the Macintosh, Windows enables you to assign cool sounds to various Windows functions. For example, you can make your computer scream louder than you do when it crashes. For more information, refer to the section in Chapter 10 on making cool sounds with multimedia.

Parts Required by Windows

Table 2-4 compares what Windows asks for on the side of the box with what you *really* need before it works well.

Table 2-4	What Windows Requires
Windows' Ethereal Requirements	*Normal, Human Requirements*
MS-DOS 3.1 or later	Buy MS-DOS 6.2 or later
286 or later microprocessor	At least a 386SX microprocessor; a 486 is better still
1MB total memory	4MB total memory; 8MB is better still
One high-density disk drive/ 10MB of space on a hard disk	One high-density disk drive/ *at least* 40MB of space on a hard disk; 200MB is better still
EGA or better card and monitor	Super VGA (800 x 600 resolution or better) card and monitor
Options: mouse	*Required:* mouse, preferably Microsoft-compatible

Your Computer's Parts

Use this handy list to write down all the parts of your computer. You'll probably need to know them later on, if only to read this list to the technical support person on the other end of the phone:

My IBM-compatible computer runs DOS version number _____.

(With your computer on, type **VER** at the DOS prompt and press Enter to find out.)

It has a _____ CPU brain.

(80286, 80386, 386SX, 486, and so on)

It has _____ of memory, or RAM.

(256K, 512K, 1MB, 2MB, 4MB, 8MB, or more)

Its monitor displays _____ graphics.

(Hercules, Monochrome, CGA, EGA, VGA, SVGA, or XGA)

Its disk drive can handle _____ -density, _____ -inch disks.

(This can be high- or low-density and 3½-inch or 5¼-inch disks.)

My mouse is made by _____.

(This can be Genius, Logitech, Microsoft, Disney, or a bunch of others.)

My hard drive can store _____ megabytes of important stuff.

(This is the total capacity of your hard drive, usually listed on your sales receipt: 40MB, 80MB, 120MB, 240MB, or more.)

My hard drive currently has _____ megabytes of space available.

(Type **DIR** at the DOS prompt, ignore the stuff that races by, and write down the last line that appears on the screen. It'll probably say something like 20162048 bytes free because computers usually leave off commas to confuse people. Chop off the last six numbers to round it off to megabytes, so 20162048 is 20 megabytes. DOS 6.2 finally starts adding commas, by the way.)

I will print stuff on my _____ model of printer made by
_____.

(For example, this can be a Laserjet II made by Hewlett-Packard, a Silentwriter2 90 by NEC, or a Panasonic 1180 by Panasonic.)

I have a _____ brand of sound card made by _____.

(For example, this can be a Sound Blaster Pro by Creative Labs or a Pro AudioSpectrum by Media Vision.)

Chapter 3
Out of the Box and onto the Hard Drive (Installation Chores)

*I*nstalling software means copying the program from the disks in the box onto the hard drive inside your PC. Unfortunately, it usually also means hours of tinkering until the newly installed software works correctly with your particular computer, printer, disk drives, and internal organs. Because of the frustration potential, installation chores should usually be left to a computer guru. Gurus like that sort of stuff. (They even like the smell of freshly copied floppy disks.)

Luckily, Microsoft took mercy on Windows beginners. It created Windows to install itself. Just slide the first disk into the disk drive and type a magic word. After that, keep feeding disks into the computer when it asks for a new one.

Remove the first floppy disk before trying to slide in the next one, and you'll be fine.

This chapter walks you through the installation process. You see how easy Microsoft made this chore, and you find out where else in the book you can turn if you need further information.

Turning On the Computer

The first step is to look for the computer's *on* switch. It's usually the largest switch on the computer. Sometimes it's red and important looking.

 ✔ Put your ear next to the computer's case: If the computer is not making any noise, it's either turned off or broken. Flip its power switch to the opposite direction, and it will either jump to life or stay broken (or stay unplugged, which is why it always works in the repair shop).

 ✔ When a computer is first turned on, it makes a grinding sound, several clicking noises, and a whirring sound. Then it flashes long strings of code words on the screen. You can safely ignore the words unless you're reading them to a technical support person over the telephone.

Turning the computer off and then turning it on again can send devastating jolts of electricity through the computer's tender internal organs. Turn the computer on in the morning and off when you're through for the day. Some sensitive people even leave their computers turned on all the time to spare them that morning power jolt.

And never turn the computer off while it's running Windows or any other program. Doing so can destroy data and damage your programs. If the computer is doing something weird, like freezing up solid, try the less disastrous disciplinary measures described in Chapter 17.

Getting to the DOS Prompt

Depending on who set up your computer, it leaves you in one of three places after its initial *first-turn-on flurries* subside. Only one of these three places is proper for installing Windows. That place is the DOS prompt, which looks somewhat like this:

```
C:\>
```

The following sections tell you how to find that DOS prompt if the computer dumps you anywhere else.

If you're dumped at a menu

Some computers leave their owners at a *menu,* or list of options displayed on the screen. For example, a menu may say, "To run WordPerfect press 1."

To leave the menu, look for the choice that says, "Exit to DOS" or something similar. If there's no such thing, then holler for the person who set up your computer and say that you need access to a DOS prompt.

While you're talking to the person who set up your computer, ask that guru to install Windows for you. If the answer is no, continue reading this chapter.

If you're dumped in a program

If you do most of your computing with one program — say, Microsoft Works — the computer may conveniently deposit you in that program each morning. Just as with a menu, you need to find a way out to the DOS prompt. Press the keys you usually press to exit the program, and you should be left at the DOS prompt.

✔ If you can't figure out how to quit the program, try pressing the F1 key in the upper left corner of the keyboard. That key often brings up a help screen with pertinent suggestions.

✔ If the program stubbornly refuses to leave the screen, call the person who set up your computer and ask what that program's Exit command is.

✔ If Windows already leaps to the screen each morning, it's probably an early version that you're trying to replace. Bring the Program Manager to the screen and either double-click on its upper left corner or hold down Alt and press F4. Then click on the OK button when you're asked whether you really want to leave.

If you're dumped at the DOS prompt (you're already there)

If the computer normally leaves you at a nearly blank screen with a C:\> in its top left corner, you're ready to roll. That C:\> is the DOS prompt, and it's your first step toward installing Windows. Congratulations! Pop the champagne!

✔ You must be looking at the DOS prompt before you can install Windows.

✔ That's the last time you have to look at the DOS prompt, however. After you install Windows on the hard drive, you can install your other Windows programs directly from Windows.

✔ Keep the champagne away from the keyboard.

Removing the Wrapper from the Box

Now pick up the box that contains the Windows software and look for where the plastic bunches up in the corners. With your incisors, bite into that little chunk of bunched-up plastic and give it a good tug. Repeat this procedure a few times until you've created a finger-sized hole. Then peel back the plastic until the box is free.

Inside the box, hunt around for the most boring-looking piece of paper with the finest print. It's the Hardware Compatibility List and Driver Library, and you'll need it later if things go wrong.

Installing Windows the Simple Way

Forget those awkward experiences setting up metal Christmas trees or listening to your car make funny noises. Windows caters to beginners with an installation program that checks under your PC's hood and sets itself up automatically, adjusting the fluid levels as needed.

Legal gibberish that lunges at you when you open the box

In the normal world, people sign contracts to make things official. In the computer world, they tear open little packages with their teeth. By opening the little plastic wrapper holding the Windows disks, you're saying that you've read the legal stuff in the manual and that you've earnestly nodded your head in acceptance.

Basically, Microsoft's full page of fine print says four things:

- You don't *own* the software you've just purchased. Microsoft does, so it can say what you can and can't do with it. If you don't like that arrangement, take Windows back to the software store for a refund.

- You can't give away free copies of Windows to your friends. Make those freeloaders buy their own copies.

- Bought a new laptop? Then you have to buy a new copy of Windows to go with it. Microsoft says that you can't use the same copy of Windows on your desktop computer and your laptop.

- If Windows messes up your computer or your work, it's not Microsoft's fault.

Welcome to Windows!

Here's how to pull into the full-service lane:

1. **Pull the six floppy disks out of the box and remove their thin protective wrappers.**

   (No teeth are necessary for this one, but keep them around, just in case.)

2. **Find the disk labeled *Disk 1* and put it into the disk drive.**

   Don't know how to put a disk into a disk drive? Turn to Chapter 2 and read the section on disks and disk drives.

3. **If you put the disk into drive A on the computer, type the following:**

```
C:\> A:
```

   That is, you press the letter A, type a colon, and then press Enter. The computer then pays attention to drive A, where you've placed the disk.

   Alternatively, if you put the disk into drive B, then type this stuff instead:

```
C:\> B:
```

   You press B, type a colon, and then press Enter. The computer then looks at the disk in drive B.

   Note: Windows comes on two sizes of disks: big (5 ¼ inches wide) and small (3 ½ inches wide). If the first disk doesn't nestle snugly into the disk drive, you've bought the wrong size. Take the stuff back to the store and ask the sales person for the Windows box with the other-sized disks.

4. **Rub your palms together gleefully and type your first Windows command, SETUP, like this:**

```
A:\> SETUP
```

   You type **SETUP** (a single word with no space in the middle) and press Enter. If you're installing from drive B, you see B:\>, but everything else is the same.

   When Windows sees the code word SETUP, it begins to leap from the disk, ready for action. You hear it rummaging around inside the computer. The drives whirl and make clunking noises, and your first taste of Windows appears on the screen.

   The first screen is an anticlimactic *welcome* screen saying that you're installing Windows.

5. **If you've lost your nerve at this point, press F3 to exit. Otherwise, press Enter and Windows proceeds.**

   The second screen asks you a simple question: Do you want to use the express setup (quick and easy), or do you want to struggle through the custom setup (designed for experienced users who want or need control over how Windows is set up)?

6. **Press that Enter key to choose the express setup.**

   The Setup program then rumbles around inside the computer, searching for any old versions of Windows. If you're already using Windows, the Setup program asks to overwrite the old version with the new one.

7. **If you're already using Windows, press Enter for the Setup program to overwrite the old version.**

   The new version of Windows is copied over the old version. (If you're suspicious of this overwrite activity, check out this chapter's sidebar about this practice.)

   Now Windows takes over. It asks you to type in your own name and your company's name.

8. **Type in your name and press Tab; then type in your company's name and press Enter.**

   Congratulations. You've made it around the bend, and you're heading for the home stretch.

Should I let the new Windows version wipe out the old version?

Should you copy this foreign, unproved version of Windows 3.1 over your older, faithful version of Windows 3.0 — a version that serves you so well except when it crashes?

Yeah, go ahead. The new version won't wipe out the important parts of the old version. The desktop will look the same as before. The new version just adds a few new features and cleans out a few trouble spots in the old version.

To be on the safe side, copy your important data files to floppy disks before you begin. You've probably been backing up your work anyway, so doing it shouldn't take long.

✔ If you *haven't* been copying your important files to floppy disks for safekeeping, head to the store and ask for a hard disk backup package.

✔ If you're the extra-cautious sort, you can install the new version of Windows into a separate directory and try it out for a while. I did. After 15 minutes or so, I deleted the old version because it was just cluttering up my hard drive.

✔ If you *do* decide to keep both versions of Windows on the hard drive, be sure to remove the Windows Version 3.0 from the PATH setting in the AUTOEXEC.BAT file, if you know what that means. It's a chore best left to computer gurus who get most of their exercise from opening software boxes.

Installing Windows the Hard Way

You're joking, right? Leave the Custom Setup option to people who enjoy fussing with their computers and do so for hours on end (or at least until their spouses get home).

Introducing Windows to Your Printer

After the Setup program huffs and puffs for a while, it drops a box on the screen that lists various printer names. Windows nerds classify this box as a *list box* within a *dialog box*. Everybody else says that it's just a list of printer names on the screen with some button things next to it. Either way, Figure 3-1 shows you what it looks like.

If your printer begins with the letter *A*, you may be in luck. The list is in alphabetic order, and your printer's name may be at the top of the screen.

If you have a WangLDP8 or another tail-ender, you have to look farther down the list. Windows, the over-accommodating helper that it is, gives you seven different ways to move down that list.

But why mess around? Just use the *cursor-control keys,* that huddled cluster of arrow-wearing keys on the right side of the keyboard. Press the down-arrow key to move down the list and the up-arrow key to go back up.

When the black line rests on your printer's name, press Enter and you're on your merry way. If you're curious about the other ways to move down the list, check out the field guide to boxes, buttons, and bars in Windows, which you'll find in Chapter 6.

Figure 3-1:
The first dialog box you'll encounter. Scientific name: Liboxus Dialogicus. Common name: box with button things.

```
┌──────────────────── Printer Installation ────────────────────┐
│                                                               │
│  Select a printer from the following list. Press the UP and DOWN │
│  Arrow keys to move the highlight and scroll through the list. │
│                                                               │
│  Then press ENTER to install the printer.                     │
│                                                               │
│  ┌────────────────────────────┐▲      ┌──────────────┐        │
│  │No Printer Attached         ││      │    Install   │        │
│  │Generic / Text Only         ││      └──────────────┘        │
│  │Agfa 9000 Series PS         ││      ┌──────────────┐        │
│  │Agfa Compugraphic 400PS     ││      │    Cancel    │        │
│  │Agfa Compugraphic Genics    ││      └──────────────┘        │
│  │Apple LaserWriter           ││      ┌──────────────┐        │
│  │Apple LaserWriter II NT     ││      │     Help     │        │
│  │Apple LaserWriter II NTX    ││▼     └──────────────┘        │
│  └────────────────────────────┘      ┌──────────────┐        │
│                                       │  Exit Setup  │        │
│  To see more printers, use the UP and DOWN Arrow keys.        │
│                                                               │
│  Selected Printer: No Printer Attached                        │
└───────────────────────────────────────────────────────────────┘
```

This tip is too cool to wait for another chapter. Press the first letter of your printer's name — W for WangLDP8, for example. The black line jumps down to the name of the first printer starting with that letter, making your printer's name much quicker to locate. This press-the-first-letter trick works any time you're facing a long list in a Windows box.

After you choose your printer's name, a slightly more confusing-looking box appears, asking you to choose a port. Press Enter and choose the LPT1: port. Almost everybody uses that port. If Windows complains later, saying that it can't find your printer, head for the section in Chapter 10 on changing to a different printer.

✔ Windows provides a gigabillion different ways for you to accomplish the same task. Although this feature increases the chances that your random pecks will be correct, it also makes Windows seem more complicated than it really is.

✔ In the Printer Installation dialog box you just barreled through (see Figure 3-1), you didn't need to mess with all those buttons and bars. You certainly didn't have to know that they're called *command buttons* by Microsoft's button-labeler crew. Most of Windows is like that: simpler than it first appears.

✔ Back to the printer business: If your printer *isn't* listed in the master list, look for the printer it *emulates*. Most laser printers, for example, can emulate either a Hewlett-Packard LaserJet II printer or something called PostScript, so you can choose one of those two. Or both. You can choose as many printers as you want and see which one works. Windows doesn't mind.

✔ If your printer isn't listed and you don't know what the heck it's supposed to emulate, then choose the first option, No Printer Attached. Windows is casual enough to let you set it up later. When you've figured out what's on the end of your printer cable, head for the section in Chapter 10 on changing to a different printer.

Installing a few other fancy nonexistent printers

After you've installed your printer, and while the Printer Installation dialog box is still sitting there, you may want to select two other printers — even if you don't own them.

First, you may want to select the second printer option on the list: Generic/Text Only. This option lets Windows send text to nearly any printer on the market. It won't print any fancy text or pictures. Instead, it just puts your words on paper, using the same font as a standard office typewriter. But, because it's so simple, it's often the quickest way to print out a grocery list on a slow printer.

On the other hand, you may want to create slick-looking newsletters for the Homeowners Association or Jenny's Girl Scout troop. If you may be tackling some of this desktop publishing stuff, you should install another printer you don't own: PostScript.

PostScript is a fancy language that enables expensive printers to create fancy, expensive-looking graphics. Most copy shops have PostScript printers in the back room. After making Windows print PostScript to a file, you can hand the floppy disk to the people at the copy shop down the street. The copy shop people will print the stuff on their printer, and you'll be able to say, "Aw, it was nothing," when everybody says how classy your newsletter looks.

Whenever you want Windows to print to these nonexistent printers, click on the word File from any Windows program and click on the words Print Setup when the menu drops down. From there, click on the name of the printer you want to use: your normal printer, Generic/Text Only, or PostScript. (Put a check mark in the Print to Encapsulated PostScript File box to send your PostScript stuff to a file.)

When you're through playing with printers you don't own, head back to the Print Setup menu and click on your own printer's name so things will return to normal.

Sniffing Out Your DOS Programs

Windows snoops through your hard drive almost as professionally as Joey snooped through your locker in the third grade. In the process, Windows tries to create *icons* (little on-screen pictures) for your programs. You then can click on these icons to start your programs. The icon with little blue *WP* letters automatically starts WordPerfect, for example.

Windows sometimes runs into problems when snooping through your old DOS programs, however. Sometimes two programs have the same name. If Windows comes across the file WP.EXE, for example, Windows doesn't know whether WP stands for WordPerfect or WoolPull, Grandma's knitting program. So it asks for help by displaying the dialog box shown in Figure 3-2.

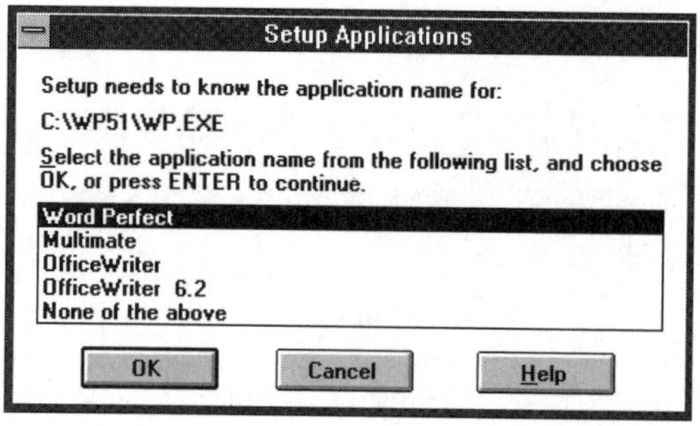

Figure 3-2:
Windows
hopes that
you'll know
the names
of your
programs
because it
doesn't
know them.

Setup Applications

Setup needs to know the application name for:

C:\WP51\WP.EXE

Select the application name from the following list, and choose OK, or press ENTER to continue.

Word Perfect
Multimate
OfficeWriter
OfficeWriter 6.2
None of the above

[OK]   [Cancel]   [Help]

If you know that you have WordPerfect on your hard drive and you're pretty sure that Windows has found that file, then go ahead and press Enter. That's it. Windows handles the rest. (Again, there's no need to play with those buttons along the bottom of the dialog box. If you're curious, though, you can point the mouse arrow to OK and then click the mouse button. It's the same as pressing Enter.)

✔ Windows comes with special instructions for most popular DOS programs. These special instructions are called *PIFs,* and they're weirder than a Shriner's hat. If a DOS program behaves strangely, you'll probably have to change the settings in its PIF, a procedure cautiously outlined in Chapter 16.

✔ If Windows *did* find Grandma's knitting program and not WordPerfect, then press the down arrow until the black bar rests over the None of the above option in the dialog box and press Enter.

Taking the Tutorial

Windows comes with a tutorial program that introduces you to such banalities as Control menus, scroll bars, menu bars, and other absurdities. Feel free to take the tutorial if you have ten minutes to spare.

✔ When you get bored in the middle of the tutorial, press the Esc key on the keyboard to quit the tutorial. If only we'd had that button in high school!

✔ The best part of the tutorial is a little animation of an energetic finger clicking a mouse button. After that, it's rather dry.

✔ Don't feel guilty for not immediately finishing the tutorial (or not even trying it out). It's always waiting for you in the Windows Program Manager. For information on going back to school, check out the section in Chapter 11 on going back to the tutorial.

Leaving the Setup Program

When the tutorial slides off the screen, the Windows Setup program sputters around for a while, and then it leaves a single box on the screen with three buttons: Restart, Reboot, or Return to MS-DOS.

If you want to start playing with Windows immediately, click on the Restart button. The screen goes blank, Windows fiddles around for a few seconds, and then Windows reappears, ready for action.

But if you've had quite enough Windows for one day, remove any disk you may have lurking in drive A and click on the button labeled Reboot. The computer beeps, makes some grinding sounds, and brings the C:\> prompt back to the screen.

At this point, turn off the monitor and get a glass of water. You've accomplished an awful lot today.

Turning Off the Computer

If you're through computing for the day, turn off the computer. Find that switch you used to turn it on and flick it the other way. (Or, if it's a push button, give it another push.)

Never turn off the computer while Windows is running. Make sure that you're at the C:\> prompt and that Windows isn't running in the background.

To make sure that Windows isn't lurking back there somewhere, type **EXIT** at the DOS prompt and press Enter. If Windows pops up on the screen, breathe a sigh of relief. The computer wasn't ready to be turned off. If the DOS prompt says something rude, like Bad command or file name, shut it up by turning off the computer.

Installing Windows for Workgroups

Chances are, you'll never have to install the networking version of Windows, Windows for Workgroups. Described in Chapter 20, Windows for Workgroups is designed for offices in which people link their computers together with cables; all the computers can then share information and things like printers. Most offices come with haggard computer gurus to install networking software.

Windows for Workgroups can run on a computer that doesn't use a network, too. That capability, plus its cool new game of Hearts, tempts some people to install Windows for Workgroups in place of their old version of Windows — even if they don't have a network.

- ✔ The good news: Installing Windows for Workgroups is almost identical to installing plain old Windows — the version described in this chapter. Plus, Windows for Workgroups runs fine on computers that will *never* be connected to a network.

- ✔ The bad news: Windows for Workgroups eats up about 5MB more space than the ordinary version of Windows. That's about all the bad news, though. You just have to stick a few more disks into your computer and twiddle your thumbs a little bit longer while everything's being installed.

- ✔ More good news: Windows for Workgroups comes with a great Hearts game. You can play against your computer or anybody else on your network. Fun!

Chapter 4
Windows Stuff Everybody Thinks You Already Know

In This Chapter

▶ Explanations of terms you need to understand in order to use Windows

▶ Information on where to look for more details on the topics that are introduced

*W*hen Windows first hit the market in 1985, it failed miserably. The weakling computers of the day burst a pectoral over its fancy graphics. In addition, Windows was slow and dorky looking with ugly colors.

Today's computers have Jean-Claude Van Damme arms: They can easily whip Windows into shape. With faster computers, perseverance, and 20 fashionable new color schemes, like Pastel, Wingtips, and Black Leather Jacket, Windows has turned into a trendy best-seller.

But because it has been around for so long, a lot of computer geeks have had a head start. To help you catch up, this chapter is a coffee-shop guide to those Windows words the nerds have been batting around for ten years.

Backing Up a Disk

Computers store *bunches* of files on their hard drives. And that can be a problem. When the computer's hard drive eventually dies, it takes all your files down with it. Pffffft. Nothing left.

Computer users who don't like anguished *Pfffft* sounds *back up* their hard drives religiously. They do so in two different ways.

Some people copy all their files from the hard disk to a bunch of floppy disks. Although custom-written backup programs make this task easier, it's still a time-consuming chore. Who wants to spend half an hour backing up computer files *after* finishing work?

Other people buy a *tape backup* unit. This special, computerized tape recorder either lives inside your computer like a floppy disk or plugs into the computer's rear. Either way, the gizmo tape records all the information on your hard disk. Then, when your hard disk dies, you still have all your files. The faithful tape backup unit plays back all your information onto the new hard drive. No scrounging for floppy disks.

✔ DOS 6 comes with Microsoft's Backup, a program that automatically copies files from your hard disk to floppy disks. Unfortunately, you need to feed floppy disks to the computer until it's through copying everything. Yawn.

✔ If you installed DOS 6, you'll find the Backup program listed in Program Manager's Microsoft Tools window. Not there? Then look for the word *Tools* along the top of File Manager. Click on Tools, and Backup should appear in the drop-down menu.

✔ The average cost of a tape-backup unit runs from $200 to $800, depending on the size of your computer's hard drive. Some people back up their work every day, using a new tape for each day of the week. If they discover on Thursday that last Monday's report had key concepts, they can pop Monday's tape into the backup unit and grab the report.

✔ Backing up a *floppy* disk is a little easier. Head to Chapter 12 for information.

✔ You'll find the DOS 6 Backup program covered completely in this book's sequel, *MORE Windows For Dummies* (IDG Books Worldwide).

Clicking

Computers make plenty of clicking sounds, but only one click counts: the one that occurs when you press a button on a mouse. You'll find yourself clicking the mouse hundreds of times in Windows. For example, to push the on-screen button marked Push Me, you'd move the mouse until the pointer rested over the Push Me button and click the mouse.

✔ When you hear people say, "Press the button on the mouse," they leave out an important detail: *Release* the button after pressing it. Press the button with your index finger and release it, just as you press a button on a touch-tone phone.

✔ Most mice have 2 buttons; some have 3, and some esoteric models for traffic engineers have more than 32. Windows listens only to clicks coming from the button on the *left* side of your mouse. It's the one under your index finger if you're right-handed (or if you're left-handed and lucky enough to find a left-handed mouse). Refer to Chapter 10 for more mouse button tricks.

✔ A few Windows applications that are sold separately, notably Word for Windows, listen to clicks coming from the *right* button as well as from the *left* button.

✔ Don't confuse a *click* with a *double-click*. For more rodent details, see "The Mouse," "Double-Clicking," and "Pointers/Arrows" later in this chapter. The insatiably curious can find even more mouse stuff in Chapter 2.

The Command Line

The *command line* is a macho place where you can type stern code words to boss the computer around. The most famous command line comes with DOS, and it looks like this:

```
C:\> MYPROGRAM
```

When you type a program's name at the command line, DOS rummages around, looking for that program. If DOS succeeds, it loads the program and brings it to the screen for your working pleasure. If it doesn't find it, it burps back with the following bit of ugliness:

```
Bad command or file name
```

✔ The most common reason DOS burps back is because you've spelled the file's name wrong. It's more critical than an English teacher with a hair bun. You must be exact.

✔ Don't confuse the command line with the DOS prompt, although the two usually go hand in hand. The *command line* is the information you type next to the DOS prompt. The *DOS prompt* is the thing you'll find described if you move your eyes to the section "The DOS Prompt."

✔ For the most part, Windows replaces typing stuff at the command line with a more pleasant way of computing: pressing buttons or clicking on pictures. You'll find command lines hidden in the Program Manager and the File Manager, however, if you want to boss your computer around that way. For more information, see "Graphical User Interfaces."

The Cursor

Typewriters have a little mechanical arm that strikes the page, creating the desired letter. Computers don't have little mechanical arms (except in science fiction movies), so they have *cursors:* little blinking lines that show where that next letter will appear in the text.

- ✔ Cursors appear only when Windows is ready for you to type text, numbers, or symbols — usually while you're writing letters or reports.

- ✔ The cursor and the mouse pointer are different things that perform different tasks. When you start typing, text appears at the cursor's location, not at the pointer's location.

- ✔ You can move the cursor to a new place in the document by using the keyboard's *cursor-control keys* (the ones with little arrows). You also can point to a spot with the mouse pointer and click the button. The cursor leaps to that new spot.

You can distinguish between the cursor and the mouse pointer with one look: Cursors always blink steadily; mouse pointers never do.

For more information, check out "Pointers/Arrows" in this chapter or Table 2-3 in Chapter 2.

Defaults (and the Any Key)

Finally, a computer term that can be safely ignored. Clap your hands and square dance with a neighbor! Here's the lowdown on the, er, hoedown: Some programs present a terse list of inexplicable choices and casually suggest that you choose the only option that's not listed: the *default option.*

Don't chew your tongue in despair. Just press Enter.

Those wily programmers have predetermined what option works best for 99 percent of the people using the program. So, if people just press Enter, the program automatically makes the right choice and moves on to the next complicated question.

- ✔ The default option is similar to the oft-mentioned *Any key* because neither of them appears on your keyboard (or on anybody else's, either, no matter how much money they paid).

✔ *Default* can also be taken to mean *standard option* or *what to select when you're completely stumped.* For example, "Strangers riding together in elevators will stare at their shoes by default."

✔ When a program says to press any key, simply press the spacebar. (The Shift keys don't do the trick, by the way.)

The Desktop (and Wallpapering It)

To keep from reverting to revolting computer terms, Windows uses familiar office lingo. For example, all the action in Windows takes place on the Windows *desktop*. The desktop is the background area of the screen where all the windows pile up.

Windows comes with a drab gray desktop. To jazz things up, you can cover the desktop with pictures, or *wallpaper.* Windows comes with several pictures you can use for wallpaper (and Chapter 10 can help you hang it up).

You can customize the wallpaper to fit your own personality: pictures of little kittens, for example, or egg-beaters. You can draw your own wallpaper with the built-in Windows Paintbrush program. Paintbrush saves your work in the required wallpaper format: a special bitmap file ending in the letters BMP.

Directories

In your everyday paper world, files are stored in folders in a cabinet. In the computer world, files are stored in a *directory* on a disk. Dusty old file cabinets are boring, but directories are even more dreadfully boring: They'll *never* hold any forgotten baseball cards.

Maintaining files and working with directories are painful experiences that are explained in Chapter 12. In the meantime, just think of a directory as a separate work area to keep files organized. Different directories hold different projects; you move from directory to directory as you work on different things with your computer.

A file cabinet's Vegetables folder can have an Asparagus folder nested inside for organizing material further. Directories can have several nested *subdirectories* to keep related files from getting lost.

The DOS Prompt

Depending on whom you bribed to set up your computer, it leaves you at one of three places when you first turn it on.

For some people, the computer flashes mumbo jumbo on the screen, loads your favorite program, and leaves you there gracefully. The best computers leave you in Windows automatically — right there at the familiar-looking Program Manager that's been set up to run all your favorite programs at the click of a mouse.

For other people, the computer stops short at a menu — a list of options, such as WordPerfect, Tetris, or Windows.

For people who didn't use the right bribe, the computer flashes mumbo jumbo on the screen and then dumps them at another piece of mumbo jumbo: the DOS prompt.

The DOS prompt rhymes with *the boss chomped,* and it's a symbol that looks somewhat like this:

```
C:\>
```

If you've been rudely dumped at the DOS prompt, you can scoot quickly to Windows by typing the following friendly, positive word:

```
C:\> WIN
```

That is, you type **WIN** and follow it with a press of the Enter key.

To appease the DOS hounds, Windows waits in the background while you run a DOS session. All you see on your screen is the eerie DOS prompt, which can be confusing. Are you running Windows, or are you running DOS? To find out what's going on, type **EXIT** and press Enter. If Windows was waiting for you, it welcomes you back. If Windows wasn't there, DOS angrily snaps back at you with the following:

```
Bad command or file name
```

Double-Clicking

Windows places a great significance on something pretty simple: pressing a button on the mouse and releasing it. Pressing and releasing the button once is known as a *click.* Pressing and releasing the button twice in rapid succession is a *double-click.*

Windows watches carefully to see whether you've clicked or double-clicked on its more sensitive parts. The two actions are completely different.

> ✔ A click and a double-click mean two different things to Windows programs. They're not the same.

> ✔ A double-click can take some practice to master, even if you have fingers. If you click too slowly, Windows thinks you're clicking twice — not double-clicking. Try clicking a little faster next time, and Windows will probably catch on.

> ✔ Can't click fast enough for Windows to tell the difference between a mere click and a rapid-fire double-click? Then grab the office computer guru and say that you need to have your Control Panel called up and your clicks fixed. If the guru is at the computer store, tiptoe to the section on tinkering with the Control Panel in Chapter 10.

Dragging and Dropping

Although the term *drag and drop* sounds as if it's straight out of a *Hitman's Handbook,* it's really a nonviolent mouse trick in Windows. Dragging and dropping is a way of moving something — say, a picture of an egg — from one part of your screen to another.

To *drag,* put the mouse pointer over the egg and *hold down* the mouse button. As you move the mouse across your desk, the pointer drags the egg across the screen. Put the pointer/egg where you want it and release the mouse button. The egg *drops,* uncracked.

For more mouse fun, see "Clicking," "Double-Clicking," "The Mouse," "Pointers/ Arrows," and, if you're not yet weak at the knees, the information on the parts of your computer in Chapter 2.

Drivers

Although Windows does plenty of work, it hires help when necessary. When Windows needs to talk to unfamiliar parts of your computer, it lets special *drivers* do the translation. A driver is a piece of software that enables Windows to communicate with parts of your computer.

Hundreds of computer companies sell computer attachables, from printers to sound cards to sprinkler systems. Microsoft requires these companies to write drivers for their products so Windows knows the polite way to address them.

✔ Sometimes computer nerds say that your *mouse driver* is all messed up. They're not talking about your hand, even though your hand is what steers the mouse. They're talking about the piece of software that helps Windows talk and listen to the mouse.

✔ New versions of Windows often require new drivers. If you send a begging letter to the company that made your mouse, the company may mail you a new, updated driver on a floppy disk. Occasionally, you can get these new drivers directly from Microsoft or from the wild-haired teenager who sold you your computer. Find a computer guru to install the driver, however, or check out the section on installing drivers in Chapter 17.

Files

A *file* is a collection of information in a form that the computer can play with. A *program file* contains instructions telling the computer to do something useful, like adding up the number of quarters the kids spent on Sweet Tarts last month. A *data file* contains information you've created, like a picture of a steak knife you drew in the Windows Paintbrush program.

✔ Files can't be touched or handled; they're invisible, unearthly things. Somebody figured out how to store files as little magnetic impulses on a round piece of specially coated plastic, or *disk.*

✔ A file is referred to by its *filename.* DOS makes people call files by a single word containing no more than eight letters. For example, FILENAME could be the name of a file, as could REPORT, SPONGE, or X.

✔ Yes, it's difficult to think up descriptive filenames.

✔ Filenames have optional *extensions* of up to three letters that usually refer to the program that created them. For example, the Windows Write word processor saves files with the extension WRI. DOS puts a period between the two parts of the file's name. For example, PITTANCE.WRI, TOFU.JOE, and O.MY are all proper filenames.

> ✔ Filenames have more rules and regulations than the Jacuzzi at the condo's clubhouse.
>
> ✔ For more information than you'll ever want to know about filenames, flip to Chapter 12.

Graphical User Interfaces

The way people communicate with computers is called an *interface*. For example, the Enterprise's computer used a *verbal interface*. Captain Kirk just told it what to do.

DOS uses a *command line interface*. People type *commands* into the computer, and the computer either digests them or tosses them back in confusion.

Windows uses a *graphical user interface*. People talk to the computer through *graphical symbols*, or pictures. A graphical user interface works kind of like Travel Kiosks at airports. You select some little button symbols right on the screen to find out which hotels offer free airport shuttles.

> ✔ A graphical user interface is called a *GUI*, pronounced *gooey*, as in *Huey, Dewey, Louie, and GUI*.
>
> ✔ Despite what you read in Microsoft's full-page ads, Windows isn't the only GUI for a personal computer. Geoworks, OS/2 and Deskmate are all GUIs (pronounced *gooeys*, as in *Those are Huey's GUIs*).
>
> ✔ The little graphical symbols or buttons in a graphical user interface are called *icons*.
>
> ✔ Sooner or later, computers will be capable of speaking to us. A few of today's more expensive computers can actually speak a few words, but even they stumble when asked to comment on the sacrifice of Isaac in Kierkegaard's *Fear and Trembling*.

Hardware and Software

Alert! Alert! Fasten your seat belt so you don't slump forward when reading about these two particularly boring terms: hardware and software.

Your CD player is *hardware;* so are the stereo amplifier, speakers, and batteries in the boom box. By itself, the CD player doesn't do anything but hum. It needs music to disturb the neighbors. The music is the *software,* or the information processed by the CD player.

✔ Now you can unfasten your seat belt and relax for a bit. Computer *hardware* refers to anything you can touch, including hard things like a printer, a monitor, disks, and disk drives.

✔ Software is the ethereal stuff that makes the hardware do something fun. A piece of software is called a *program.* Programs come on disks (or CDs, too, if you've anted up for the latest computer gear).

✔ Software has very little to do with lingerie.

✔ When somber technical nerds (STNs) say, "It must be a hardware problem," they mean that something must be wrong with your computer itself: its disk drive, keyboard, or central processing unit (CPU). When they say, "It must be a software problem," they mean that something is wrong with the program you're trying to run from the disk.

Here's how to earn points with your computer gurus: When they ask you the riddle "How many programmers does it take to change a lightbulb?" pretend that you don't know this answer: "None; that's a hardware problem."

Icons

An *icon* is a little picture. Windows fills the screen with little pictures, or icons. You choose among them to make Windows do different things. For example, you'd choose the Printer icon, the little picture of the printer, to make your computer print something. Icons are just fancy names for cute buttons.

✔ Windows relies on icons for nearly everything, from opening files to releasing the winged monkeys.

✔ Some icons have explanatory titles, like Open File or Terrorize Dorothy. Others make you guess that the Little Juggling Man icon opens the network mail system.

✔ For more icon stuff, see "Graphical User Interfaces."

Kilobytes, Megabytes, and So On

Figuring out the size of a file folder is easy: Just look at the thickness of the papers stuffed in and around it. But computer files are invisible, so their size is measured in *bytes* (which is pronounced like the thing Dracula does).

A byte is pretty much like a character or letter in a word. For example, the word *sodium-free* contains 11 bytes. (The hyphen counts as a byte.) Computer nerds picked up the metric system a lot more quickly than the rest of us, so bytes are measured in kilos (1,000), megas (1,000,000), and gigas (way huge).

A page of double-spaced text is about 1,000 bytes, known as *1 kilobyte,* which is often abbreviated as 1K. One thousand of those kilobytes is a megabyte, or 1MB. Your computer's hard drive is full of bytes; most hard drives today contain between 40MB and 500MB.

✔ Depending on how much money you paid, your floppy disks can hold from 360 kilobytes to 2.8 megabytes (2,800 kilobytes).

✔ All files are measured in bytes, regardless of whether they contain text. For example, that leafy background art some people put on their Windows desktop takes up 15,118 bytes. (For information on changing to a leafy desktop, see Chapter 10.)

✔ The Windows File Manager can tell you how many bytes each of your files consumes. To learn more, check out the information on the File Manager in Chapter 12.

One kilobyte doesn't really equal 1,000 bytes. That would be too easy. Instead, this byte stuff is based on the number two. One kilobyte is really 1,024 bytes, which is 2 raised to the 10th power, or 2^{10}. (Computers love mathematical details, especially when there's a 2 involved.) For more byte-size information, see Table 4-1.

Table 4-1	Ultra-Precise Details from the Slide-Rule Crowd		
Term	*Abbreviation*	*Rough Size*	*Ultra-Precise Size*
Byte		1 byte	1 byte
Kilobyte	K or KB	1,000 bytes	1,024 bytes
Megabyte	M or MB	1,000,000 bytes	1,048,576 bytes
Gigabyte	G or GB	1,000,000,000 bytes	1,073,741,824 bytes

Loading, Running, Executing, and Launching

Files are yanked from a file cabinet and placed onto a desk for easy reference. On a computer, files are *loaded* from a disk and placed into the computer's memory so you can do important stuff with them. You can't work with a file or program until it has been loaded into the computer's memory.

When you *run, execute,* or *launch* a program, you're merely starting it up so you can use it. *Load* means pretty much the same thing, but some people fine-tune its meaning to describe when a program file brings in a data file.

 ✔ The Windows Program Manager enables picture lovers to start programs by using icons. The Windows File Manager enables text-and-word lovers to start programs by clicking on their names in a list.

 ✔ If you're feeling particularly bold, you can load programs by using the command line hidden in File Manager and Program Manager. For the full dirt, check out the information on the Program Manager in Chapter 11 and the information on the File Manager in Chapter 12.

Memory

Whoa! How did this ugly memory stuff creep in here? Just read the next sentence and then check out the memory stuff in Chapter 15 for the gory, dripping details.

The sentence: The more memory the computer has, the more pleasantly Windows behaves.

 ✔ Memory is measured in bytes, just like a file. Most computers have at least 640 kilobytes, or 640K, of memory.

 ✔ Windows requires 386-class computers to have at least 2 megabytes, or 2MB, of memory or it won't even bother to come out of the box. A 286 computer can squeak by with a little less memory, but just barely.

Memory and hard drive space are both measured in bytes, but they're two different things: *Memory* is what the computer uses for quick, on-the-fly calculations when programs are up and running on the screen. *Hard disk space* is what the computer uses to store unused files and programs.

Everybody's computer contains more hard disk space than memory because hard drives are a great deal cheaper. Also, a hard disk remembers things even when the computer is turned off. A computer's memory, on the other hand, is washed completely clean whenever someone turns it off or pokes its reset button.

The Mouse

A *mouse* is a smooth little plastic thing that looks like Soap on a Rope. It rests on a little roller, or *ball,* and its tail plugs into the back of the PC. When you push the mouse across your desk, the mouse sends its current location to the PC through its tail. By moving the mouse around on the desk, you move a corresponding arrow across the screen.

You can wiggle the mouse in circles and watch the arrow make spirals. Or, to be practical, you can maneuver the on-screen arrow over an on-screen button and click the mouse button to boss Windows around. (Refer to "Clicking," "Double-Clicking," and "Pointers/Arrows," and, if you haven't run out of steam, turn to Chapter 2 for information on the parts of your computer.)

Multitasking and Task Switching

Windows can run two programs at the same time, but computer nerds take overly tedious steps to describe the process. So skip this section because you'll never need to know it.

Even though the words *task switching* and *multitasking* often have an exclamation point in computer ads, there's nothing really exciting about them.

When you run two programs, yet switch back and forth between them, you're *task switching.* For example, if Jeff calls while you're reading a book, you put down the book and talk to Jeff. You are task switching: stopping one task and starting another. The process is similar to running your word processor and then stopping to look up a phone number in the handy Windows Cardfile.

But, when you run two programs simultaneously, you're *multitasking.* For example, if you continue reading your book while listening to Jeff talk about the Natural History Museum's new Grecian urns, you're multitasking: performing two tasks at the same time. In Windows, multitasking can be playing its Solitaire game while you print something in the background.

These two concepts differ only subtly, and yet computer nerds make a big deal out of the difference. Everybody else shrugs and says, "So what?"

For more information on multitasking, check out the memory stuff in Chapter 15.

Networks

Networks connect PCs with cables so employees can share information and equipment. They can all send stuff to one printer, for example, or they can send messages back and forth talking about Jane's new hairstyle.

Just be glad that you, as a Windows beginner, are safely absolved from knowing anything about networks. Leave network stuff to that poor person in charge.

And if you *are* using a network, check out Chapter 20. It's filled with information about networking and the networking version of Windows, called Windows for Workgroups.

Pointers/Arrows

This one sounds easy at first. When you roll the mouse around on your desk, you see a little arrow move around on the screen. That arrow is your *pointer,* and it is also called an *arrow.* (Almost everything in Windows has two names.)

The pointer serves as your *electronic index finger.* Instead of pushing an on-screen button with your finger, you move the pointer over that button and click the left button on the mouse.

So what's the hard part? Well, that pointer doesn't always stay an arrow. Depending on where the pointer is located on the Windows screen, it can turn into a straight line, a two-headed arrow, a four-sided arrow, a little pillar, or a zillion other things. Each of the symbols makes the mouse do something slightly different. Luckily, you'll find these and other arrowheads covered in Chapter 2.

Programs/Applications

Most people call a computer program a *program.* In Windows, programs are called *applications.*

✔ I dunno why.

✔ Those free programs that came with Windows (Program Manager, File Manager, Write, and so on) aren't called programs or applications. They're called *Windows Applets.*

✔ For the record, DOS programs are *programs.* Windows programs are *applications.* And the programs that came with Windows are *Applets.*

✔ This book uses the terms *program* and *application* interchangeably. And it hardly uses the name *Applet* at all because it sounds so funny.

Quitting, Exiting, and Returning to DOS

When you're ready to throw in the computing towel and head for greener pastures, you need to stop, or quit, any programs you've been using. The terms *quit, exit,* and *return to DOS* mean pretty much the same thing: making the current program on your screen stop running so you can go away and do something a little more rewarding.

Luckily, exiting Windows programs is fairly easy because all of them use the same special exit command. You hold down the Alt key (either one of them, if you have two) and press the key labeled F4. (The F4 key is a *function key;* function keys are either in one row along the top of your keyboard or in two rows along its leftmost edge.)

Don't quit a program by just flicking off your computer's power switch. Doing so can foul up your computer's innards. Instead, you must leave the program responsibly so that it has time to perform its housekeeping chores before it shuts down.

✔ When you press Alt+F4, the program asks whether you want to save any changes you've made to the file. Normally, you click on the button that says something like "<u>Y</u>es, by all means save the work I've spent the last three hours trying to create." (If you've muffed things up horribly, click on the <u>N</u>o button. Windows disregards any work you've done and lets you start over from scratch.)

✔ If, by some broad stretch of your fingers, you press Alt+F4 by accident, click on the button that says Cancel, and the program pretends that you never tried to leave it. You can continue as if nothing happened.

✔ The Alt+F4 trick doesn't work for a DOS program — even if it's running in its own window. You must exit the DOS program by using its own exit keys. Complicated? Well, yes. That's why people are switching to Windows.

✔ You can also exit a Windows program through its uppermost left corner, where you'll see a square button that looks like an aerial view of a single-slot toaster. Double-clicking on that toaster also exits the program.

✔ When you exit the Program Manager, you quit Windows and return to DOS.

Save your work before exiting a program or turning off your computer. Computers aren't smart enough to save it automatically.

The Save Command

Save means to send the work you've just created on your computer to a disk for safekeeping. Unless you specifically save your work, your computer thinks you've just been fiddling around for the past four hours. You need to specifically tell the computer to save your work before it will safely store the work on a disk.

Thanks to Microsoft's snapping leather whips, all Windows programs use the same Save command, no matter what company wrote them. Press and release the Alt, F, and S keys in any Windows program, and the computer saves your work.

If you're saving something for the first time, Windows asks you to think up a filename for the work and pick a directory to stuff it into. Luckily, this stuff's covered in the section in Chapter 5 on saving something.

✔ Files can be saved to a hard disk or a floppy disk.

✔ Choose descriptive filenames for your work. For example, JOHN0692.TXT is more descriptive than LETTER. DOS gives you only 11 letters to work with, however, and these inelegant restrictions are poked around in Chapter 12.

✔ Some programs, like Microsoft's Word for Windows, have an *autosave* feature that automatically saves your work every five minutes or so.

The Save As Command

Huh? Save as *what?* A chemical compound? Naw, the Save As command just gives you a chance to save your work with a different name and in a different location.

Dump those leftover temp files

If you come across a file ending in TMP, like ~DORK4U.TMP, you can safely delete it by typing the following command and pressing the Enter key:

```
C:\> DEL ~DORK4U.TMP
```

That is, type **DEL,** followed by a space and the name of the file (including the period and the **TMP** that follows it). Then press Enter. The little ~ is on the key in the upper left corner of your keyboard.

Don't ever delete a TMP file unless you're absolutely positive that you're not still running Win-dows. If you think Windows may be running in the background, type **EXIT** at the prompt, like this:

```
C:\> EXIT
```

Then press Enter. If Windows is running in the background, typing **EXIT** brings Windows back to the forefront. If you delete a TMP file while Windows is running, you lose your current work, causing much anguish.

For example, suppose that you open the OHGOLLY.TXT file in your STUFF directory and change a few sentences around. You want to save the changes, but you don't want to lose the original stuff. So you select Save As and type in the new name, OHGOLLY2.TXT.

- ✔ The Save As command is identical to the Save command when you're first trying to save something new: You can choose a fresh name and location for your work.

- ✔ Female armadillos have exactly four babies at a time, and they're always the same sex.

Temp Files

Like children who don't put away the peanut butter jar, Windows also leaves things lying around. They're called *temp files* — secret files Windows creates to store stuff in while it's running. Windows normally deletes them automatically when you leave the program. It occasionally forgets, however, and leaves them cluttering up your hard drive. Stern lectures leave very little impression.

- ✔ Temp files usually (but not always) end with the letters TMP. Common temp filenames include ~DOC0D37.TMP, ~WRI3F0E.TMP, the occasional stray ~$DIBLCA.ASD, and similar looking files that start with the wavy ~ thing. (Some people call it a *tilde.*)

> ✔ If you exit Windows the naughty way — by just flicking the computer's off switch — Windows won't have a chance to clean up its temp file mess. If you keep doing it, you'll eventually see hundreds of TMP files lying around your hard drive. Be sure to exit Windows the Good Bear way: by quitting the Program Manager and clicking on OK when Windows says, `This will end your Windows session.`

The Windows

DOS programs completely fill your screen; only one fits on the screen at one time. Windows, however, enables you to run several programs at the same time by placing them in *windows*. A window is just a little box.

You can move the boxes around. You can make them bigger or smaller. You can make them fill your entire screen. You can make them turn into little icons at the bottom of your screen. You can spend hours playing with them. In fact, most frustrated new Windows users do.

> ✔ You can put as many windows on the screen as you want, peeping at all of them at the same time or just looking into each one individually. This activity appeals to the voyeur in all of us.

> ✔ For instructions on how to retrieve a lost window from the pile, head immediately to Chapter 8.

> ✔ When a DOS program runs *as a window* in Windows, it won't fill the whole screen. Windows shrinks it a little so you can see other windows sitting around it.

Part II
Making Windows
Do Something

The 5th Wave   By Rich Tennant

"OH, I'VE GOT IT BOOTED ALL RIGHT—JUST DON'T ASK ME TO DOUBLE KNOT IT!"

In this part...

Windows is more fun than a plastic snap-together stegosaurus from the bottom of a Cracker Jack box. It's especially fun to show friends the built-in screen savers, like the one that straps you into a starship and cruises toward the fifth quadrant's snack shop at warp speed. You can even adjust the ship's speed through Windows' Control Panel.

Unfortunately, some spoil-sport friend will eventually mutter the words that bring everything back to Earth: "Let's see Windows do something useful, like balance a checkbook or teach the kids to rinse off their plates and put them in the dishwasher."

Toss this eminently practical part at them to quiet 'em down.

Chapter 5
Starting Windows

*H*old on to your hat! Then try to type at the same time. No, let the hat fly by the wayside because this is a hands-on Windows chapter that demonstrates some dazzling special effects. First, you make Windows leap to your screen, carrying a program along with it!

Then, at the click of the mouse, you launch a second program, running at the same time as the first! Plus, you learn secret magic tricks to bypass the mouse and use the keyboard instead!

Finally, you learn how to print your work so you'll have some hard copy to show those doubting friends of yours.

Oh, and you learn to save your work so you can find it again the next day. So warm up those fingers, shake out your sleeves, and get ready for action. . . .

Revvin' Up Windows

If your PC came with Windows already installed, Windows probably leaps to your screen automatically when you first turn on the computer. If not, you must open the cage door manually by typing the following word at the C:\> prompt:

```
C:\> WIN
```

That is, you type **WIN** and follow it with a deft press of the Enter key.

Your screen goes blank for a few seconds, only to fill up with a bright blue advertisement for Windows. Finally, Windows hefts itself to the screen, bringing along something called the *Program Manager.* The Program Manager runs in its own *window,* a box-like container that keeps its insides from spilling over the screen.

Windows is like an elevator that moves around your computer, and the Program Manager is like its panel of buttons. By pushing the buttons on the Program Manager, you tell Windows where to go and what to do.

- ✔ When you first start Windows, you hear a triumphant *Ta-Da!* sound coming from the computer's sound card. If you don't have a sound card, you don't hear anything but a strong inner urge driving you toward the computer store's sound-card aisles. (Sound cards range in price from $75 to $250.)

- ✔ Microsoft chose the program name WIN because it's such an eager, positive-sounding command, like something from a best-selling *You Can Be a Success Despite Your Chin* paperback.

TIP

Dumping the advertisement

When you first type **WIN** and press Enter, a Windows *logo,* or advertisement, fills the screen for a few moments. (It's a little late for an ad, seeing as how you've already bought the package, but Microsoft's marketing department was hard to stifle.)

The impatient Microsoft programmers didn't want to be slowed down by an ad for their own product, so they added a secret command:

```
C:\> WIN :
```

By typing **WIN,** followed by a space and a colon, as shown above, *everyone* can skip the ad! Pretty sneaky, huh? If only televisions had something similar. . .

Playing on a network

If you're part of a computer network, talk to your network administrator about *logging in* and *out*. Then write it all down here before you forget:

To start my computer, I type _____ .

To start Windows, I type _____ .

You have to memorize a password, too, but don't write it here. (You can carry it in your wallet, just in case.)

If you're not part of a network, wipe the sweat from your forehead, breathe a sigh of relief, and move on. If you're using Windows for Workgroups, you can find more information in Chapter 20.

Starting your favorite program

When Windows first takes over your computer, it fills the screen with a big square box called the Program Manager. Although the Program Manager looks and sounds imposing, it's merely a plate of buttons with labels underneath them. Push a button, and that program hops to the screen in its own little window. Figure 5-1 gives you a look at the buttons that Program Manager offers when it first comes to the screen.

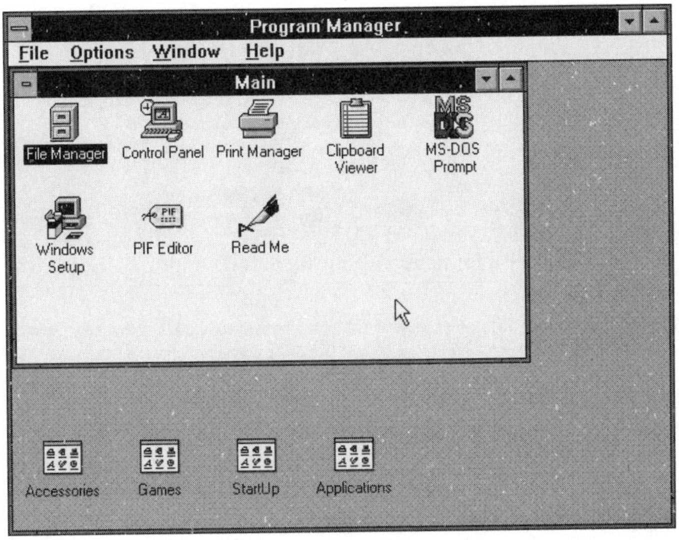

Figure 5-1: The Program Manager holds "picture buttons" called icons.

Because the buttons have little pictures on them, they're called *icons.* (No relation to the icons favored by the Byzantine emperors in the eighth and ninth centuries A.D. They still used DOS back then.)

Icons offer clues as to the program they represent. For example, the icon of the file cabinet stands for the Windows *File Manager,* a program that copies files, deletes them, and moves them around.

See the dark bar shading the File Manager icon's title in Figure 5-1? The bar means that File Manager is *highlighted:* It's queued up and ready to go. If you press the Enter key while the File Manager is highlighted, File Manager hops to the forefront. (Don't press Enter, though, because File Manager is too boring to play with right now. Besides, you can start the program another way, and the other way is more fun.)

Look at the little arrow sitting by itself in the corner of your screen. Roll your mouse around until that arrow hovers over the Quill Pen icon that says Read Me. (Those sly folks at Microsoft hope the insatiably curious will want to read that file, so they called the icon *Read Me* and left it in a conspicuous place.)

Double-click your mouse button, and the Windows word processor, a program called Write, pops up on the screen. The screen looks like Figure 5-2.

Write is the second window. By double-clicking on its icon, you've told Program Manager to load the Write program and bring it to the top of the screen. It's now covering up part of Program Manager, unfortunately, but you'll get used to

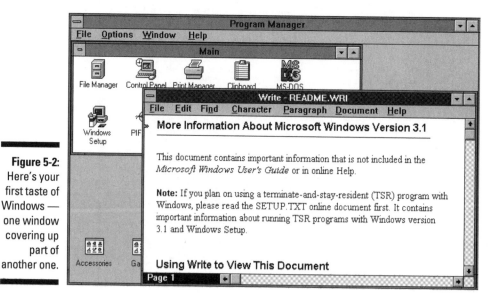

Figure 5-2:
Here's your
first taste of
Windows —
one window
covering up
part of
another one.

it. All the windows tend to overlap. Luckily, they're mobile. You can move them around until you can see everything.

But check this out. You've not only loaded Write; you've loaded a file (the Read Me file) into Write at the same time, all with one double-click.

Congratulations! You've not only opened your first program in Windows, but you've opened a file, as well. See, you can open both programs and files in the Program Manager.

Now comes the hard part: reading the Read Me file. It's full of undigestibles, like "Solving Memory Conflicts by Excluding an Address Range." Sheesh! And they wonder why nobody bothers to read the documentation!

- ✔ The Program Manager is just a panel of buttons. When you press a button, the program assigned to that button heads for the top of the screen and appears in a little window.

- ✔ Icons can stand for files as well as for programs. When you double-clicked on the Write icon in Program Manager, you not only started the Write program, but you also opened the Read Me file automatically.

- ✔ Microsoft has already set up Program Manager to include icons for the most popular programs and files on your computer — stuff like 1-2-3 and WordPerfect. If you want to add some other programs and files, however, check out the section in Chapter 11 on creating your very own program group.

- ✔ If you're kind of sketchy about all this *double-click* stuff, head back to the section in Chapter 2 on your mouse and that double-click stuff.

- ✔ If the icon you're after in Program Manager has a little black bar around its name, then it's *highlighted*. If you just press the Enter key, the highlighted program will load itself into a little window. Or you can still double-click on it to load it. Windows lets you do things in a bunch of different ways.

- ✔ This chapter gives you just a quick tour of Windows. You'll find glowing descriptions of Program Manager in Chapter 11.

- ✔ If you want to test your patience with the Read Me file, you can press the PgDn key to make Write move down to the next page of text. The PgUp key will move it back up a page if you want to read it again.

What's really in that Read Me file, anyway?

The stuff in the Read Me file is pretty dry. It describes ways to coax Windows into working with various brands of video cards, mice, sound cards, and third-party utility programs. Basically, it's a file for computer gurus to chew on if Windows isn't working right.

And, if Windows isn't working right on your computer, Read Me is probably the first file your computer guru will head for — after wolfing down a handful of the M&Ms you've thoughtfully left next to your monitor.

Finding the Secret Pull-Down Menus

Windows, bless its heart, makes an honest effort toward making computing easier. For example, Program Manager puts a bunch of options on the screen in front of you. You just choose the one you want, and Windows takes it from there.

But, if Windows put all its options on the screen at the same time, it would look more crowded than a 14-page menu at the House of Hui restaurant. To avoid resorting to fine print, Windows hides some menus in special locations on the screen. When you click the mouse in the right place, more options leap toward you like Sparky, the friendly Dalmatian.

Here's where some of those menus hide: in a row of words beginning with the word File that rests along the top edge of just about every Windows window. Move your mouse pointer over the word File and click once (no double-click this time).

A menu opens from beneath the word File. It is called a *pull-down menu,* if you're interested, and it looks like what you see in Figure 5-3.

 ✔ Pull-down menus open from any of those key words along the top of a window. Just click the mouse on the word, and the menu tumbles down like shoeboxes falling off a closet shelf.

 ✔ To close the menu, go back up and click the mouse again, but click it someplace away from the menu.

 ✔ Different Windows programs have different words across the menu bar, but almost all of the bars begin with the word File. The File pull-down menu contains file-related options, like Open, Save, Print, and Push Back Cuticles.

 ✔ You'll find pull-down menus sprinkled liberally throughout Windows.

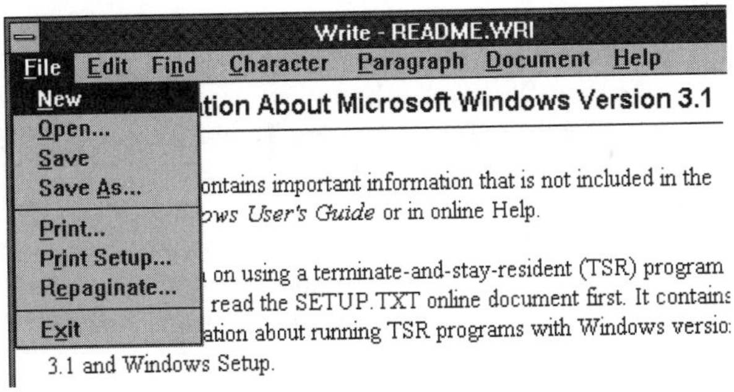

Figure 5-3:
Click on a
word along
the top of
any window
to reveal a
secret *pull-
down menu.*

Loading a file

First, here's the bad news: Loading a file into a Windows program can be a mite complicated sometimes. Second, *loading* a file means the same thing as *opening* a file.

Now that those trifles have been dispensed with, here's the good news: All Windows programs load files in the exact same way. So, after you've learned the proper etiquette for one program, you're prepared for all the others!

Here's the scoop: To open a file in any Windows program, look for the program's *menu bar,* that row of important-looking words along its top. Because you're after a file, click on the word File.

A most-welcome pull-down menu descends from the word File. The menu has a list of important-looking words. Because you're trying to open a file, move the mouse to the word Open and click once again.

Yet another box hops onto the screen, as shown in Figure 5-4, and you'll see this box over and over again in Windows.

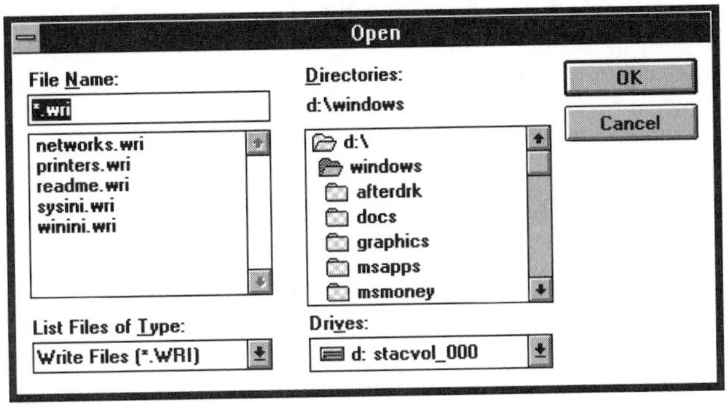

Figure 5-4:
Every
Windows
program
tosses this
box at you
when you
load or save
a file.

See the list of files in the box called File Name? Those files are ready to be pulled into Write and displayed on the screen. Double-click on the file named printers.wri, and Write loads it and displays it on the screen. (Write tosses its earlier file, Read Me, to the wayside.) If you don't have a mouse, press the down arrow until the printers.wri file is highlighted and press Enter.

You've done it! You've loaded a file into a program! Those are the same stone steps you'll walk across in any Windows program, whether it was written by Microsoft or by the teenager down the street. They all work in the same way.

✔ When the big, lunky Open box appears, you can load a new file by double-clicking on its name. Or you can click on the name once to highlight it (it turns black) and then press the Enter key or click on the OK button to load it. Windows is full of multiple options like that. (Different strokes for different folks and all.)

✔ If you've changed an open file, even by an accidental press of the spacebar, Write takes it for granted that you've changed the file for the better. When you try to load another file, Write cautiously asks whether you want to save the changes you've made to the current file. Click on the No button unless you do, indeed, want to save that version you've haphazardly changed.

✔ The Open box has a bunch of options in it. You can open files that are stored in directories or on other disk drives. You can also call up files that don't end with the letters WRI. All this Open box stuff is explained in Chapter 6.

✔ If you're still a little murky on the concepts of *files, directories,* and *drives,* flip to Chapter 12 for an explanation of the File Manager.

Putting two programs on the screen simultaneously

After spending all your money for Windows and a computer powerful enough to cart it around, you're not going to be content with only one program on your screen. You want to fill the screen with programs, all running in their own little windows.

How do you put a second program on the screen? Well, if you've opened Write by double-clicking on its icon in Program Manager, then you're already running two programs at the same time: Program Manager is sitting behind Write.

✔ This section is intentionally short. When working in Windows, you almost always have two or more programs on the screen at the same time. There's nothing really special about it, so there's no need to belabor the point here.

✔ The special part comes when you move information between the two programs, which is explained in Chapter 9.

✔ Or, if you want to move multiple windows around on the screen, then move yourself to Chapter 7.

✔ If you've inadvertently clicked on the Program Manager window, you're probably wondering where the Write window disappeared to. It's now hidden behind the Program Manager window. To get it back, check out the information on retrieving lost windows in Chapter 8.

✔ To switch between windows, just click on them. When you click on a window, it immediately becomes the *active* window — the window where all the activity takes place. For more information on switching between windows, switch to Chapter 7.

Using the Keyboard

It's a good thing Microsoft doesn't design automobiles. Each car would have a steering wheel, a joystick, a remote control, and handles on the back for people who prefer to push. Windows offers almost a dozen different ways for you to perform the most simple tasks.

For example, check out the top of any window, where that important-looking row of words hides above secret, pull-down menus. Some of the words have certain letters underlined. What gives? Well, it's a secret way for you to open their menus without using the mouse. This sleight of hand depends on the Alt key, that dark key resting next to your keyboard's spacebar.

Press (and release) the Alt key and keep an eye on the row of words in the *menu bar*. The first word, File, turns black immediately after you release the Alt key. You haven't damaged it; you've selected it, just as if you'd clicked on it with the mouse. The black color means that it's highlighted.

Now, see how the letter P in Paragraph is underlined? Press the letter P, and the pull-down menu hidden below Paragraph falls recklessly down, like a mushroom off a pizza.

That's the secret underlined-letter trick! And pressing Alt and P is often faster than plowing through a truckload of mouse menus — especially if you think that the whole mouse concept is rather frivolous, anyway.

✔ You can access almost every command in Windows by using the Alt key rather than a mouse. Press the Alt key and then the underlined letter from the option you're after. That option, or command, then begins to work.

✔ If you've accidentally pressed the Alt key and find yourself trapped in Menu Land, press the Alt key again to return to normal. If that doesn't work, try pressing the Esc key.

✔ As pull-down menus continue to appear, you can keep plowing through them by selecting underlined letters until you accomplish your ultimate goal. For example, pressing Alt and then P brings down the Paragraph pull-down menu. Pressing D subsequently activates the Double-space option from the Paragraph menu and immediately double-spaces your current paragraph.

When you see a word with an underlined letter in a menu, press and release your Alt key. Then press that underlined letter to choose that menu item.

Printing Your Work

Eventually, you'll want to transfer a copy of your finely honed work to the printed page so you can pass it around. Printing something from any Windows program (or application or applet, whatever you want to call it) takes only three keystrokes. Press and release the Alt key and then press the letters F and P. What you see on your screen will be whisked to your printer.

Pressing the Alt key activates the words along the top, known as the *menu bar*. The letter F wakes up the File menu, and the letter P tells the program to send its stuff to the printer — pronto.

✔ Alternatively, you can use the mouse to click on the word File and then click on the word Print from the pull-down menu. Depending on the RPM of your mouse ball and the elasticity of your wrist, both the mouse and the keyboard method can be equally quick.

✔ If nothing comes out of the printer after a few minutes, try putting paper in your printer and making sure that it's turned on.

✔ When you print something in Windows, you're actually activating yet another program. Called the Print Manager, it just sits around and feeds stuff to your printer. You may see it as a little icon at the bottom of your screen. If you're curious about the Print Manager, check out the section in Chapter 9 that covers it.

Saving Your Work

Any time you've created something in a Windows program, be it a picture of a spoon or a letter to the *New York Times* begging for a decent comics page, you'll want to save it to disk.

Saving your work means placing a copy of it onto a disk, be it the mysterious hard disk inside your computer or a floppy disk, one of those things you're always tempted to use as beverage coasters. (Don't try it, though.)

Luckily, Windows makes it easy for you to save your work. You need only press three keys, just as if you were printing your work or opening a file. To save your work, press and release the Alt key, then press the letter F, and then press the letter S.

If you prefer to push the mouse around, click on the word File from the Windows menu bar. When the secret pull-down menu appears, click on the word Save. Your mouse pointer turns into an hourglass, asking you to hold your horses while Windows shuffles your work from the program to your hard disk or a floppy disk for safekeeping.

That's it!

✔ If you're saving your work for the first time, you'll see a familiar-looking box: It's the same box you saw when opening a file. See how the letters in the File Name box are highlighted? The computer is always paying attention to the highlighted areas, so anything you type will appear in that box. Type in a name for the file and press Enter.

✔ If Windows throws a box in your face saying something like "This filename is not valid," then you haven't adhered to the ridiculously strict filename guidelines discussed in Chapter 4.

✔ Just as files can be loaded from different directories and disk drives, they can be saved to them as well. You can choose between different directories and drives by clicking on various parts of the Save box. All this stuff is explained in Chapter 6.

Quitting Windows

Ah! The most pleasant thing you'll do with Windows all day could very well be to stop using it. And you do that the same way you started: through the Program Manager, that boxy thing that popped up the first time you started Windows.

Figure 5-5:
Windows
wants to
know
whether you
really want
to exit.

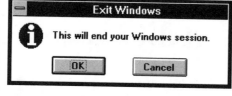

Other Windows programs come and go, but the Program Manager is always on your screen somewhere. When you exit Program Manager, you're also exiting Windows.

First, make the Program Manager pop to the forefront by clicking on it. Just put the mouse pointer over it somewhere and click. Keyboard buffs can hold down the Alt key and press the F4 key at the same time. Windows, tearful that you're leaving, sends out one last plea, as shown in Figure 5-5.

If you mean business, click on the OK button or press Enter. Windows starts to put all of its parts away, preparing to leave the screen of your computer. If, by some bizarre mistake, you've pressed the Alt+F4 combination in error, click on the Cancel button, and Windows ignores your *faux pas.* (Keyboard users must press Tab to highlight the Cancel button and then press Enter.)

Mouse motorists can exit Windows in a different way: by double-clicking on that little square with the doohickey in the top left-hand corner of the Program Manager. It's called the Control-menu box, and it looks like this:

✔ When you tell Windows you want to quit, it searches through all your open windows to see whether you've saved all your work. If it finds any work you've forgotten to save, it tosses a box your way, letting you click on the OK button to save it. Whew!

✔ If you happen to have any DOS programs running, Windows stops and tells you to quit your DOS programs first. See, Windows knows how to shut down Windows programs because they all use the same command. But all DOS programs are different. You have to shut the program down manually, using whatever exit sequence you normally use in that program.

✔ If you have a sound card, you hear a pleasant wind-chimes sound telling you that it's time to go home and relax. (Or time to buy a sound card if you haven't yet succumbed to the urge.)

Chapter 6
Examining All Those Buttons, Bars, and Boxes

• •

In This Chapter

▶ Looking at a typical window

▶ Getting into bars

▶ Changing borders

▶ Getting to know the button family

▶ Disregarding the dopey Control-menu box

▶ Dialog box stuff: text boxes, drop-down list boxes, list boxes, and other gibberish

▶ Just tell me how to open a file!

▶ Hey! When do I click, and when do I double-click?

• •

As children, just about all of us played with elevator buttons until our parents told us to knock it off. An elevator gave such an awesome feeling of power: Push a little button, watch the mammoth doors slide shut, and feel the responsive push as the spaceship floor begins to surge upward. . . . What fun!

Part of an elevator's attraction still comes from its simplicity. To stop at the third floor, you merely press the button marked 3. No problems there. OK, the parking levels sometimes get a little weird — especially when they're named after fruits or vegetables. Still, the push-and-stand-back-while-the-door-closes concept is classic in its simplicity.

Windows takes the elevator button concept to an extreme, unfortunately, and it loses something in the process. First, some of the Windows buttons don't even *look* like buttons (unless you're heading down to the parking garage). Most of the Windows buttons have ambiguous little pictures rather than clearly marked labels. And the worst of it comes with their terminology: The phrase *push the button* becomes *click the scroll bar above or below the scroll box on vertical scroll bars*. Yuck!

When braving your way through Windows, don't bother learning all these dorky terms. Instead, treat this chapter as a field guide, something you can grab when you stumble across a confusing new button or box that you've never encountered before. Just page through until you find its picture. Read the description to see whether that particular creature is deadly or just mildly poisonous. Then read to see where you're supposed to poke it with the mouse pointer.

You'll get used to the critter after you've clicked on it a few times. Just don't bother remembering the scientific name *vertical scroll bar,* and you'll be fine.

A Typical Window

Nobody wants a field guide without pictures, so Figure 6-1 shows a typical window with its parts labeled.

Just as boxers grimace differently depending on where they've been punched, windows behave differently depending on where they've been clicked. The following sections describe the correct places to click and, if that doesn't work, the best places to punch.

> ✔ Windows is full of little weird-shaped buttons, borders, and boxes. You don't have to remember their Latin or Greek etymologies. The important part is just learning what part you're supposed to click on. Then you can start worrying about whether you're supposed to single-click or double-click. (And that little dilemma is explained at the end of this chapter.)

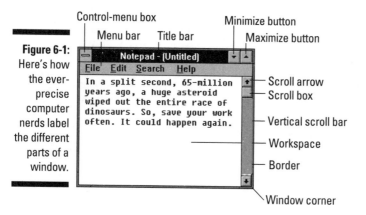

Figure 6-1: Here's how the ever-precise computer nerds label the different parts of a window.

> ✔ After you've clicked on a few windows a few times, you'll realize how easy it really is to boss them around. The hard part is learning everything for the first time, just like when you stalled the car while learning how to use the stick shift.

Bars, Bars, and More Bars

Windows is filled with bars; perhaps that's why some of its programs seem a bit groggy and hung over. Bars are simply thick stripes along the edges of a window. You'll find three types of bars.

The title bar

The title bar is that topmost strip in any window (see Figure 6-2). It lists the name of the program, as well as the name of any open file. For example, the title bar in Figure 6-2 comes from the Windows Notepad. It contains an untitled file because you haven't had a chance to save the file yet. (For example, the file may be full of notes you've jotted down from an energetic phone conversation with Ed McMahon.)

Figure 6-2:
A title bar
lists the
program's
name along
the top of a
window.

You choose a name for that file when you save it for the first time. That new filename then replaces the admittedly vague (Untitled) in the title bar.

> ✔ The title bar merely shows the name of the current program and file. If you've just started to create a file, the title bar refers to that file's name as (Untitled).

> ✔ The title bar can serve as a *handle* for moving a window around on the screen. Point at the title bar, hold down the mouse button, and move the mouse around: An outline of the window moves as you move the mouse. When you've placed the outline in a new spot, let go of the mouse button. The window leaps to that new spot and sets up camp.

✔ When you're working on a window, its title bar is *highlighted,* meaning that it's a different color from the title bar of any other open window. By glancing at all the title bars on the screen, you can quickly tell which window is currently being used.

To enlarge a window so that it completely fills the screen, double-click on its title bar. It expands to full size, making it easier to read and covering up everything else. No mouse? Then press Alt, the spacebar, and then X.

The menu bar

Windows has menus *everywhere.* But if menus appeared all at once, everybody would think about deep-fried appetizers instead of computer commands. So Windows hides its menus in something called a *menu bar* (see Figure 6-3).

Figure 6-3:
A menu bar
provides a
handy place
for Windows
to hide its
cluttersome
menus.

| File | Edit | Search | Appetizers | Help |

Lying beneath the title bar, the menu bar keeps those little menus hidden behind little words. To reveal secret options associated with those words, click on one of those words.

If you think mice are for milksops, then use the brawny Alt key instead. A quick tap of the Alt key activates the menu words across the top of the window. Press the arrow keys to the right or left until you've selected the word you're after and then press the down-arrow key to expose the hidden menu. (You can also press a word's underlined letter to bring it to life, but that tip is explained later in more detail.)

For example, to see the entrees under the word Edit, click your mouse button on Edit (or press Alt and then E). A secret menu tumbles down from a trap door, as shown in Figure 6-4, presenting all sorts of *edit-related* options.

✔ When you select a key word in a menu bar, a menu comes tumbling down. The menu contains options related to that particular key word.

✔ Just as restaurants sometimes run out of specials, a window sometimes isn't capable of offering all its menu items. Any unavailable options are *grayed out,* as are the Cut, Copy, Paste, and Delete options in Figure 6-4.

- ✔ If you've accidentally selected the wrong word, causing the wrong menu to jump down, just sigh complacently. (S-i-i-i-i-igh.) Then select the word you *really* wanted. The first menu disappears, and the new one appears below the new word.

- ✔ If you want out of Menu Land completely, click the mouse arrow back down on your work in the windows *workspace.* (Or press your Alt key, whichever method comes to mind sooner.)

- ✔ Some menu items have *shortcut keys* listed next to them, like the Ctrl+Z key combination next to the Undo option in Figure 6-4. Just hold down the Ctrl key and press the letter Z to undo your last effort. The Undo option takes place immediately, and you don't have to wait for the menu to tumble down.

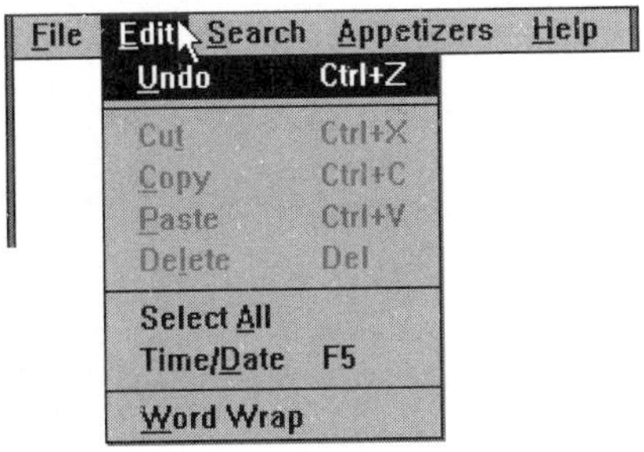

Figure 6-4:
Select any
word in the
menu bar to
reveal its
secret
hidden
menu.

File	Edit	Search	Appetizers	Help
	Undo	Ctrl+Z		
	Cut	Ctrl+X		
	Copy	Ctrl+C		
	Paste	Ctrl+V		
	Delete	Del		
	Select All			
	Time/Date	F5		
	Word Wrap			

If you find yourself performing the same task on a menu over and over, check to see whether there's a shortcut key next to it. By pressing the shortcut key, you can bypass the menu altogether, performing that task instantly.

The scroll bar

The scroll bar, which looks like an elevator shaft, is along the edge of a window (see Figure 6-5). Inside the shaft, a little freight elevator (the scroll box) travels up and down as you page through your work. In fact, by glancing at the little elevator, you can tell whether you're near the top of a document, the middle, or the bottom.

For example, if you're looking at stuff near the *top* of a document, the elevator box is near the top of its little shaft. If you're working on the bottom portion of your work, the elevator box dangles near the bottom. You can watch the little box travel up or down as you press the PgUp or PgDn key. (Yes, it's easy to get distracted in Windows.)

Figure 6-5:
Scroll bars
enable you
to page
through
everything
that's in the
window.

Here's where the little box in the scroll bar comes into play: By clicking in various places on that scroll bar, you can quickly move around in a document without pressing the PgUp or PgDn key.

✔ Instead of pressing the PgUp key, click in the elevator shaft *above* the little elevator (the *scroll box*). The box jumps up the shaft a little bit, and the document moves up one page, too. Click *below* the scroll box, and your view moves down, just as with the PgDn key.

✔ To move your view up line by line, click on the boxed-in arrow *(scroll arrow)* at the top of the scroll bar. If you hold down the mouse button while the mouse pointer is over that arrow, you see more and more of your document, line by line, as it moves you closer to its top. (Holding down the mouse button while the pointer is on the bottom arrow moves you closer to the bottom, line by line.)

✔ Scroll bars that run along the *bottom* of a window can move your view from side to side rather than up and down. They're handy for viewing spreadsheets that extend off the right side of your screen.

✔ Some scroll bars don't have a little scroll box inside them, and then you have to use the little arrows to move around. There's no little elevator to play with. Sniff. Sniff.

✔ Want to move around in a hurry? Then put the mouse arrow on the little elevator box, hold down the mouse button, and *drag* the little elevator box up or down inside the shaft. For example, if you drag the box up toward the top of its shaft and release it, you can view the top of the document. Dragging it and releasing it down low takes you near the end.

✔ Clicking or double-clicking on the little elevator box itself doesn't do anything, but that doesn't stop most people from trying it anyway.

✔ If you don't have a mouse, you can't play on the elevator. To view the top of your document, hold down Ctrl and press Home. To see the bottom, hold down Ctrl and press End. Or press the PgUp or PgDn key to move one page at a time.

Undoing what you've just done

Windows offers a zillion different ways for you to do the same thing. Here are three ways to access the <u>U</u>ndo option, which unspills the milk you've just spilled:

✔ Click on the word <u>E</u>dit and then click on the word <u>U</u>ndo from the menu that falls down. (This approach is known as *wading through the menus.*) The last command you made is undone, saving you from any damage.

✔ Press and release the Alt key, then press the letter E (from <u>E</u>dit), and then press the letter U (from <u>U</u>ndo). (This *Alt key method* is handy when you don't have a mouse.) Your last bungle is unbungled, reversing any grievous penalties.

✔ Hold down the Ctrl key and press the Z key. (This little quickie is known as the *shortcut key method.*) The last mistake you made is reversed, sparing you from further shame.

Don't feel like you have to learn all three methods. For example, if you can remember the Ctrl+Z key combination, you can forget about the menu method or the Alt key method.

Or, if you don't want to remember *anything,* then stick with the menu method. Just pluck the <u>U</u>ndo command as it appears on the menu.

Finally, if you don't have a mouse, you'll have to remember the Alt key business until you remember to buy a mouse.

Borders

A border is that thin edge enclosing a window. Compared with a bar, it's really tiny.

✔ You use borders to change a window's size. You can learn how to do that in Chapter 7.

✔ You can't use a mouse to change a window's size if the window doesn't have a border.

✔ If you like to trifle in details, you can make a border thicker or thinner through the Windows Control Panel, which is discussed in Chapter 10. In fact, laptop owners often thicken their windows' borders to make them a little easier to grab with those awkward trackballs.

✔ Other than that, you won't be using borders much.

The Button Family

Three basic species of buttons flourish throughout the Windows environment: command buttons, option buttons, and minimize/maximize buttons. All three species are closely related, and yet they look and act quite differently.

Command buttons

Command buttons may be the simplest to figure out — Microsoft labeled them! Command buttons are most commonly found in *dialog boxes,* which are little pop-up forms that Windows makes you fill out before it will work for you.

For example, when you ask Windows to open a file, it sends out a form in a dialog box. You have to fill out the form, telling Windows what file you're after, where it's located, and other details that vary according to time zone.

Table 6-1 identifies some of the more common command buttons that you encounter in Windows.

Table 6-1	Common Windows Command Buttons	
Command Button	*Habitat*	*Description*
OK	Found in nearly every pop-up dialog box	A click on this button says, "I'm done filling out the form, and I'm ready to move on." Windows then reads what you've typed into the form and processes your request. (Pressing the Enter key does the same thing as clicking on the OK button.)
Cancel	Found in nearly every pop-up dialog box	If you've somehow loused things up when filling out a form, click on this Cancel button. The pop-up box disappears, and everything returns to normal. Whew! (The Esc key does the same thing.)
Help	Found in nearly every pop-up dialog box	Stumped? Click on this button. Yet another box pops up, this time offering help on your current situation. (The F1 function key does the same thing.)
Setup... Settings... Pizza...	Found less often in pop-up dialog boxes	If you encounter a button with ellipsis dots (...) after the word, brace yourself: Selecting that button brings yet *another* box to the screen. From there, you must choose even *more* settings, options, or toppings.

✔ By selecting a command button, you're telling Windows to carry out the command that's written on the button. (Luckily, no command buttons are labeled Explode.)

✔ See how the OK button in Table 6-1 has a slightly darker border than the others? That darker border means that the button is *highlighted.* Anything in Windows that's highlighted takes effect as soon as you press the Enter key; you don't *have* to select it.

✔ Some command buttons have underlined letters that you don't really notice until you stare at them. An underlined letter tells you that you can press that command button by holding down the Alt key while pressing the underlined letter. (That way you don't have to click or double-click if your mouse is goofing up.)

✔ Instead of scooting your mouse to the Cancel button when you've goofed in a dialog box, just press your Esc key. It does the same thing.

If you've clicked on the wrong command button but *haven't yet lifted your finger from the mouse button,* stop! There's still hope. Command buttons take effect only *after* you've lifted your finger from the mouse button. So keep your finger pressed on the button and scoot the mouse arrow away from the button. When the pointer no longer rests on the button, gently lift your finger. Whew. Try *that* trick on any elevator.

Option buttons

Sometimes Windows gets ornery and forces you to choose just a single option. For example, you can elect to *eat* your brussels sprouts or *not* eat your brussels sprouts. You can't choose both, so Windows won't let you select both of the options.

Windows handles this situation with an *option button.* When you choose one option, the little dot hops over to it. If you choose the other option, the little dot hops over to it instead. You'll find option buttons in many dialog boxes. Figure 6-6 shows an example.

Figure 6-6:
When you
choose an
option, the
black dot
hops to it.

✔ Although Windows tempts you with several choices in an option box, it lets you select only one of them. It moves the dot (and little dotted border line) back and forth between the options as your decision wavers. Click on the OK button when you've reached a decision. The *dotted* option then takes effect.

✔ If you *can* choose more than one option, Windows won't present you with option buttons. Instead, it offers the more liberal *check boxes,* which are described in a separate section later in this chapter.

✔ Option buttons are round. Command buttons are rectangular.

Minimize/maximize buttons

All the little windows in Windows often cover each other up like teenage fans in the front row of a Guns 'n' Roses concert. In order to restore order, you need to separate the windows by using their minimize/maximize buttons.

These buttons enable you to enlarge the window you want to play with or shrink all the others so they're out of the way. Here's the scoop.

The minimize button is in the upper right corner of every window. It looks like this:

A single-click on the *minimize button* makes its window disappear and reappear as a tiny icon along the bottom of your screen. (Double-click on the icon to return the window to its normal size.) Keyboard users can press Alt, the spacebar, and then N to minimize a window.

✔ Minimizing a window doesn't destroy its contents; it just transforms the window into a little icon at the bottom of the screen.

✔ To make an icon turn back into an on-screen window, double-click on it. It reverts to a window in the same size and location as before you shrank it. (Keyboard users can press Alt, the spacebar, and then R.)

✔ Closing a window and turning a window into an icon are two different things. Closing a window purges it from the computer's memory. In order to reopen it, you need to load it off your hard drive again. Turning a window into an icon keeps it handy: loaded into memory and ready to be used at an instant's notice.

The maximize button is in the upper right corner of every window, too. It looks like this:

A single-click on the *maximize button* makes the window swell up something fierce, taking up as much space on the screen as possible. Keyboard users can press Alt, the spacebar, and then X to maximize their windows.

 ✔ If you're frustrated with all those windows that are overlapping each other, click on your current window's maximize button. The window muscles its way to the top, filling the screen like a *real* program.

 ✔ Immediately after you maximize a window, its little maximize button turns into a *restore button* (described momentarily). The restore button lets you shrink the window back down when you're through giving it the whole playing field.

You don't *have* to click on the maximize button to maximize a window. Just double-click on its *title bar,* the thick strip along the window's top bearing its name. That double-click does the same thing as clicking on the maximize button, and the title bar is a lot easier to aim for.

In the upper right-hand corner of every *maximized* window is the restore button, which looks like this:

When a window is maximized, a click on this button returns it to the size it was before you maximized it. (Keyboard users can press Alt, the spacebar, and then R.)

 ✔ Restore buttons appear only in windows that fill the entire screen (which is no great loss because you need a restore button only when the window is maximized).

 ✔ On a 386-class computer, DOS programs can run in a window. But, when they're in a window, they can't fill the entire screen, even if you click the maximize button. DOS windows just can't grow as large as normal windows. Perhaps they smoked cigarettes in their youth. (Or maybe they didn't read the "Changing Fonts in a DOS Window" trick, described in Chapter 16.)

 ✔ When DOS programs *aren't* running in a window, they can fill the entire screen. Windows hides in the background, tapping its toe until they finish and it can grab the screen again. For more information on this confusing DOS stuff, troop to Chapter 16.

The Dopey Control-Menu Box

Just as all houses have circuit breakers, all windows have *Control-menu boxes.* These boxes sit in the top left-hand corner of every window, where they look like an aerial view of a single-slot toaster:

Don't bother with this Control-menu box stuff

The Control-menu box provides a quick exit from any window: Just give the little square a quick double-click. Other than that feature, however, the Control-menu box is pretty useless, redundant, and repetitive.

For example, by clicking once on the Control-menu box, you get a pull-down menu with a bunch of options. Choose the Move option, and you can move around the window with the keyboard's arrow keys. (But it's much easier to move a window by using the mouse, as you'll see in Chapter 7.)

Choosing the Size option lets you change a window's size. (But that's much easier with a mouse, too, as you'll find out in Chapter 7.)

Don't bother with the menu's Minimize and Maximize options, either. Those two options have their own dedicated buttons, right in the window's other top corner. Click on the minimize button (downward arrow) to minimize the window; click on the maximize button (upward arrow) to maximize the window. Simple. There's no need to bumble through a menu for the Minimize and Maximize options when minimize and maximize buttons are already staring you in the face.

The Close option is redundant. You could have closed the window by double-clicking on the Control-menu box in the first place and avoided the hassle of going through a menu.

The Switch To option brings up the Task List, which is more easily called up by double-clicking anywhere in your Windows background, on that *wallpaper* stuff. Or you can just hold down the Ctrl key and press Esc to bring up the Task List. Either way, the Task List is also covered in Chapter 7.

So don't bother messing with the Control-menu box because it's just a waste of time.

(You may need to play with it if you're using a laptop and don't have a mouse, however. But even then, you should invest in a trackball, as described in Chapter 2. Until then, press Alt and the spacebar to bring up the Control menu and then press any of the underlined letters to access the function.)

That toaster provides a whole bunch of functions, but they're all pretty dopey, so ignore them all except for this one here: Double-click on the Control-menu box whenever you want to leave a window.

- ✔ You can get by without using the Control-menu box at all. Just hold down the Alt key and press the F4 key to exit a window.

- ✔ If you click once on the Control-menu box, a secret hidden menu appears, but it's pretty useless. So ignore it, skip the technical chatter in the sidebar about the Control-menu box, and move along to the more stimulating dialog boxes that follow.

Dialog Box Stuff (Lots of Gibberish)

Sooner or later, you'll have to sit down and tell Windows something personal. You'll want to tell Windows the name of a file to open, for example, or the name of a file to print. To handle this personal chatter, Windows sends out a *dialog box.*

A dialog box is merely another little window. But, instead of containing a program, it contains a little form or checklist for you to fill out. These forms can have up to five parts, which are discussed in the following sections. Don't bother trying to remember the names of the parts, however. It's more important to figure out how they work.

Text boxes

A text box works just like a fill-in-the-blanks test in history class. You can type anything you want into a text box — even numbers. For example, Figure 6-7 shows a dialog box that pops up when you want to move to a specific page in Write.

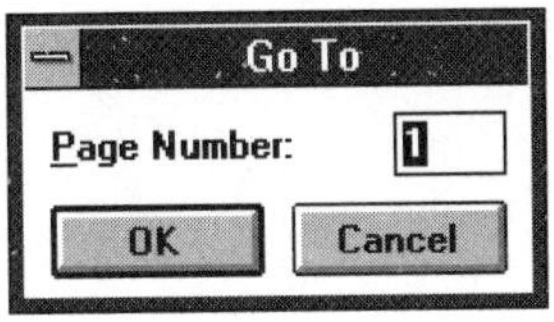

Figure 6-7:
This dialog box from Write contains a *text box.*

When you type a page number into this box and press the Enter key, Write tries to turn to that page. If that page doesn't exist, Write sends out a reprimanding dialog box, telling you to try again.

- ✔ Two clues let you know whether a text box is *active,* or ready for you to start typing stuff into it: The box's current information is highlighted, or a cursor is blinking inside it. In either case, just start typing the new stuff. (The older highlighted information disappears as the new stuff replaces it.)

- ✔ If the text box *isn't* highlighted, or there *isn't* a blinking cursor inside it, then it's not ready for you to start typing. To announce your presence, click inside it. Then start typing. Or press Tab until the box becomes highlighted or has a cursor.

- ✔ If you click inside a text box that already contains words, you must delete the information with the Delete or Backspace key before you can start typing in new information. (Or you can double-click on the old information; that way the incoming text will automatically replace the old text.)

Regular list boxes

Some boxes don't let you type stuff into them. They already contain information. Boxes containing lists of information are called, appropriately enough, *list boxes.* For example, the Windows Clock brings up a list box if you're bored enough to want to change its screen font (see Figure 6-8).

✔ See how the Caligula font is highlighted? It's the currently selected font. Press Enter (or click on the OK command button), and the Windows Clock displays the time using that font.

✔ See the scroll bars along the side of the list box? They work just as they do anywhere else: Click on the little scroll arrows (or press the up or down arrow) to move the list up or down, and you'll be able to see any names that don't fit in the box.

✔ Most list boxes have a text box above them. When you click on a name in the list box, that name hops into the text box. Sure, you could type the name into the text box yourself, but it wouldn't be nearly as much fun.

✔ When confronted with a bunch of names in a list box, type the first letter of the name you're after. Windows immediately scrolls down the list to the first name beginning with that letter.

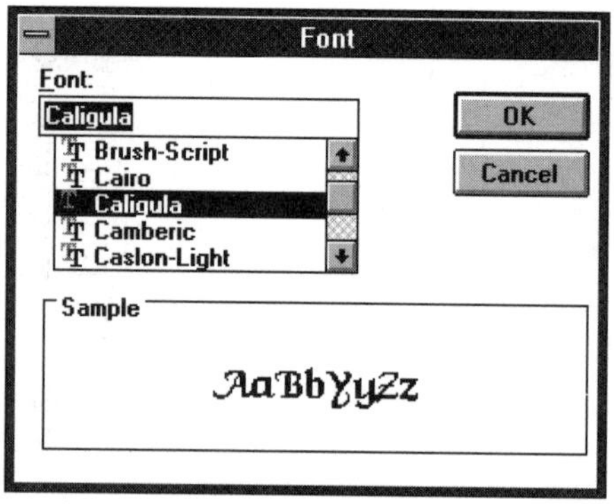

Figure 6-8:
By selecting a font from the list box, you change the way the numbers look in the Windows Clock.

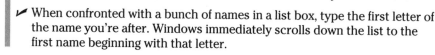

Drop-down list boxes

List boxes are convenient, but they take up a lot of room. So Windows sometimes hides list boxes, just as it hides pull-down menus. Then, if you click in the right place, the list box appears, ready for your perusal.

When one just isn't enough

Because the Windows Clock can display only one font at a time, you can select only one font from the Clock's list box. Other list boxes, like those in File Manager, let you choose a bunch of names simultaneously. Here's how:

✔ To select more than one item, hold down the Ctrl key and click on each item you want. Each item stays highlighted.

✔ To select a bunch of *adjacent* items from a list box, click on the first item you want. Then hold down Shift and click on the last item you want. Windows immediately highlights the first item, last item, and every item in between. Pretty sneaky, huh?

✔ Finally, to select every single item in the list, hold down the Ctrl key and press the forward slash (/) key. Fun!

So, where's the right place? It's that downward-pointing arrow button, just like the one shown next to the box beside the Font option in Figure 6-9.

Figure 6-10 shows the drop-down list.

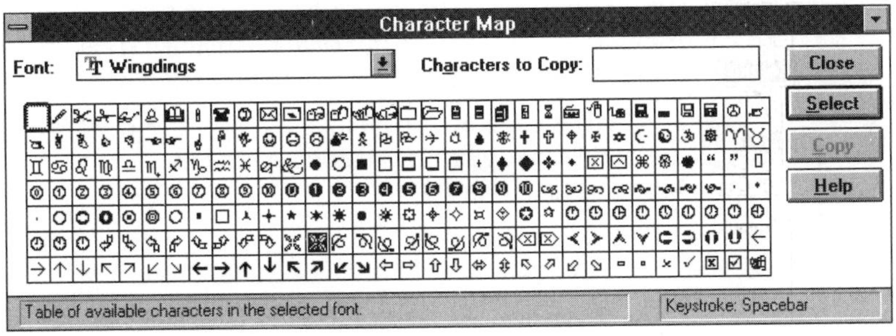

Figure 6-9:
Click on the downward-pointing arrow next to the Font box to see a drop-down list box.

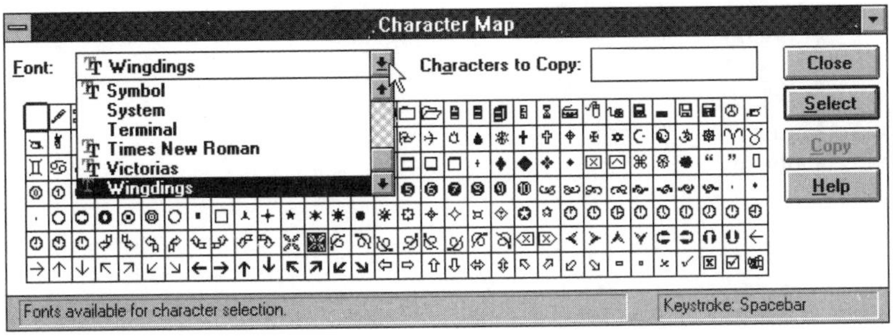

Figure 6-10:
A list box drops down to display all the fonts that are available.

To make a drop-down list box drop down without using a mouse, press the Tab key until you've highlighted the box next to the little arrow. Hold down the Alt key and press the down-arrow key, and the drop-down list starts to dangle.

- Unlike regular list boxes, drop-down list boxes don't have a text box above them. That thing that *looks* like a text box just shows the currently selected item from the list; you can't type anything in there.

- To scoot around quickly in a drop-down list box, press the first letter of the item you're after. The first item beginning with that letter is instantly highlighted. You can press the up- or down-arrow key to see the ones nearby.

- Another way to scoot around quickly in a drop-down list box is to click on the scroll bar to its right. (Scroll bars are discussed earlier in this chapter, if you need a refresher.)

- You can choose only *one* item from the list of a drop-down list box.

Check boxes

Sometimes you can choose from a whopping number of options in a dialog box. A check box is next to each option, and if you want that option, you click in the box. If you don't want it, you leave the box blank. (Keyboard users can press the up- or down-arrow key until a check box is highlighted and then press Enter.) For example, with the check boxes in the dialog box shown in Figure 6-11, you pick and choose what you'll see in the File Manager.

- By clicking in a check box, you change its setting. A click in an empty square turns on that option. If the square already has an X in it, a click turns off that option, removing the X.

- You can click next to as many check boxes as you want. With *option buttons,* those things that look the same but are round, you can select only *one* option.

Figure 6-11:
An X appears in each check box you've chosen.

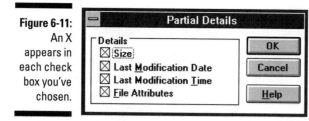

Just Tell Me How to Open a File!

Enough with the labels and terms. Forget the buttons and bars. How do you load a file into a program? This section gives you the scoop. You follow these same steps every time you load a file into a program.

Opening a file is a *file-related* activity, so start by finding the word File in the window's menu bar (see Figure 6-12).

Figure 6-12:
To open a file, you first select the word File in the window's menu bar.

Then simply do the following:

1. **Click on the word File (or press Alt and then F) to knock down that word's hidden little menu.**

   Figure 6-13 shows the File pull-down menu.

2. **Click on the word Open (or press O) to bring up the Open dialog box.**

   You can predict that the word Open will call up a dialog box because of the trailing ... things beside the word Open on-screen. (Those ... things are called an *ellipsis* or *three dots*, depending on the tightness of your English teacher's hair bun.)

Figure 6-13:
When you select File, the File pull-down menu appears.

Figure 6-14 shows the Open dialog box, which leaps to the front of the screen. In fact, you see a similar dialog box almost any time you mess with the File pull-down menu in any program.

✔ If you see your filename listed in the first list box, in this case, the one listing the orange.wri file, you're in luck. Double-click on the file's name, and it automatically jumps into the program. Or hold down Alt and press N; then press the up- or down-arrow key until the file's name is highlighted and press Enter.

✔ If you don't see the file's name, it's probably in a different directory. Click on the little folders in the list box to the right. Each time you click on a different folder, that folder's contents appear in the first list box.

✔ Can't find the right directory? Then perhaps that file is on a different drive. Click on the Drives drop-down list box (or hold down Alt and press V) to search in a different drive.

✔ Could the file be named something strange? Then click on the List Files of Type drop-down list box (or hold down Alt and press T) to choose a different file type. To see *all* the files in a directory, choose the All Files (*.*) option. Then all the files in that directory show up.

✔ This stuff is incredibly mind-numbing, of course, if you've never been exposed to directories, drives, wild cards, or other equally painful carryovers from Windows' DOS days. For a more rigorous explanation of this scary file-management stuff, troop to Chapter 12.

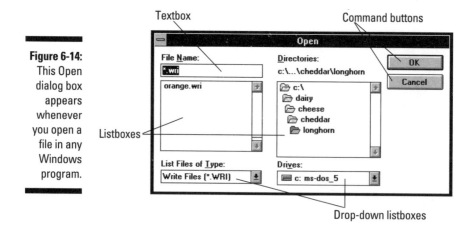

Textbox

Command buttons

Figure 6-14:
This Open
dialog box
appears
whenever
you open a
file in any
Windows
program.

Listboxes

Drop-down listboxes

Hey! When Do I Click, and When Do I Double-Click?

That's certainly a legitimate question, but Microsoft only coughs up a vague answer. Microsoft says that you should *click* when you're *selecting* something in Windows and you should *double-click* when you're *choosing* something.

Huh?

Well, you're *selecting* something when you're *highlighting* it. For example, you may select a check box, an option button, or a filename. You click on it to *select* it, and then you look at it to make sure that it looks OK. If you're satisfied with your selection, you click on the OK button to complete the job.

To *select* something is to set it up for later use.

When you *choose* something, however, the response is more immediate. For example, if you double-click on a filename, that file immediately loads itself into your program. The double-click says, "I'm choosing this file, and I want it now, buster." The double-click alleviates the need to confirm your selection by clicking on the OK button.

You *choose* something you want to have carried out immediately.

✔ All right, this is still vague. So always start off by trying a single-click. If that doesn't do the job, then try a double-click. It's usually a lot safer than double-clicking first and asking questions later.

✔ If you accidentally double-click rather than single-click, it usually doesn't matter. But, if something terrible happens, hold down the Ctrl key and press the letter Z. You can usually undo any damage.

✔ If Windows keeps mistaking your purposeful double-click as two disjointed single-clicks, then head for the section in Chapter 10 on tinkering with the Control Panel. Adjusting Windows so that it recognizes a double-click when you make one is pretty easy.

Chapter 7
Arranging Things (Moving Windows Around)

. . . .

In This Chapter

▶ Moving a window to the top of the pile

▶ Moving a window from here to there

▶ Making windows bigger or smaller

▶ Shrinking windows to icons

▶ Making icons back into windows

▶ Switching from window to window

▶ Using the way-cool Task List

▶ Organizing your desktop

. . . .

*A*h, the power of Windows. Using separate windows, you can put a spreadsheet, a drawing program, and a word processor on the screen *at the same time.*

You can copy a hot-looking graphic from your drawing program and toss it into your memo. Stick a chunk of your spreadsheet into your memo, too. And why not? All three windows can be on the screen *at the same time.*

You have only one problem: With so many windows on the screen at the same time, you can't see anything but a confusing jumble of programs.

This chapter shows how to move those darn windows around on the screen so you can see at least *one* of them.

Moving a Window to the Top of the Pile

Take a good look at the mixture of windows on the screen. Sometimes you can recognize a tiny portion of the window you're after. If so, you're in luck. Move the mouse pointer until it hovers over that tiny portion of the window and click the mouse button. Shazam! Windows immediately brings the clicked-on window to the front of the screen.

That newly enlarged window probably covers up strategic parts of other windows. But at least you'll be able to get some work done, one window at a time.

✔ Windows places a lot of windows on the screen simultaneously. But only one of them can be used at a time; the others just sit there. The one that's on top, ready to be used, is called the *active* window.

✔ The active window is the one with the most lively title bar along its top. The title bar is a brighter color than all the others.

✔ The last window you've clicked on is the *active* window. All your subsequent keystrokes and mouse movements will affect that window.

Although many windows may be on the screen, you can enter information into only one of them: the active window. To make a window active, click on any part of it. It rises to the top, ready to do your bidding.

Another way to move to a window is by using the Windows Task List. See "The Way-Cool Task List" section later in this chapter.

Moving a Window from Here to There

Sometimes you want to move a window to a different place on the screen (known in Windows parlance as the *desktop*). Maybe part of the window hangs off the edge of the desktop, and you want it centered. Or maybe you want to put two windows on the screen side by side so you can compare their contents.

In either case, you can move a window by grabbing its *title bar,* that thick bar along its top. Put the mouse pointer over the window's title bar and hold down the mouse button. Now use the title bar as the window's handle. When you move the mouse around, you tug the window along with it.

When you've moved the window to where you want it to stay, release the mouse button to release the window. The window stays put and on top of the pile.

✔ The process of holding down the mouse button while moving the mouse is called *dragging*. When you let go of the mouse button, you're *dropping* what you've dragged.

✔ Sometimes you drag and drop a window to a new spot, but it just won't stay put. It moves over a fraction of an inch before coming to rest. You try to drop a window where *you* want it to be, and the computer yanks it back to the place where *it* wants it to be. It's aggravating, but you probably have to live with it, even if you bother reading the technical sidebar in this chapter about granularity and the Windows internal grid.

✔ When placing two windows next to each other on the screen, you usually need to change their size as well as their location. The very next section tells how to change a window's size, but don't forget to read "The Way-Cool Task List" later in this chapter. It's full of tips and tricks for resizing windows as well as moving them around.

✔ Stuck with a keyboard and no mouse? Then press Alt, the spacebar, and M. Then use the arrow keys to move the window around. Press Enter when it's in the right place.

What's the granularity of your grid?

Windows don't always stay where you drop them. When you let go of the mouse button, the window doesn't lie exactly where you've moved its border. It jumps a fraction of an inch to the right or the left, up or down.

Sometimes just clicking on the title bar can cause the same weird jump: When you click on the title bar, the window's border lights up, anticipating a move. But, if instead of moving the window you just release the mouse button, the window *still* moves itself over a fraction of an inch and comes to rest.

Microsoft says that this quirk is not a bug; it's a design feature. Apparently, Windows works a little bit faster when all the windows are lined up according to an *invisible internal grid*. So, if you don't drop the window exactly on that grid, Windows picks the window up and shuffles it over for you.

This design feature is aggravating, and it's annoying as all get out when you're trying to position two windows next to each other. But Microsoft says that Windows is supposed to work that way, especially when running in VGA mode.

Some people, however, *like* the grid. In fact, they want to make it more pronounced. To adjust the invisible grid, see the section of Chapter 10 on sizing the grid. You need to change something called *granularity*. (No relation to healthy breakfast cereals.)

You'll still have that subtle shifting movement, however, even if you set the granularity to zero.

Making a Window Bigger or Smaller

Sometimes moving the windows around isn't enough. They still cover each other up. Luckily, you don't need any special hardware to make them bigger or smaller. See that thin little border running around the edge of the window? Use the mouse to yank on a window's corner border, and you can change its size.

First, point at the corner with the mouse arrow. When it's positioned over the corner, the arrow turns into a two-headed arrow. Now hold down the mouse button and drag the corner in or out to make the window smaller or bigger. The window's border expands or contracts as you tug on it with the mouse, so you can see what you're doing.

When you're done yanking and the window's border looks about the right size, let go of the mouse button. The window immediately redraws itself, taking the new position.

Here's the procedure, step by step:

1. **Point the mouse pointer at the edge of the corner.**

    It turns into a two-headed arrow, as shown in Figure 7-1.

Figure 7-1:
When the mouse points at the window's bottom corner, the arrow grows a second head.

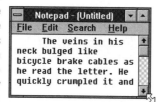

2. **Hold down the mouse button and move the two-headed arrow in or out to make the window bigger or smaller.**

    Figure 7-2 shows how the new outline takes shape when you pull the corner inward to make the window smaller.

3. **Release the mouse button.**

    The window shapes itself to fit into the border you've just created (see Figure 7-3).

That's it!

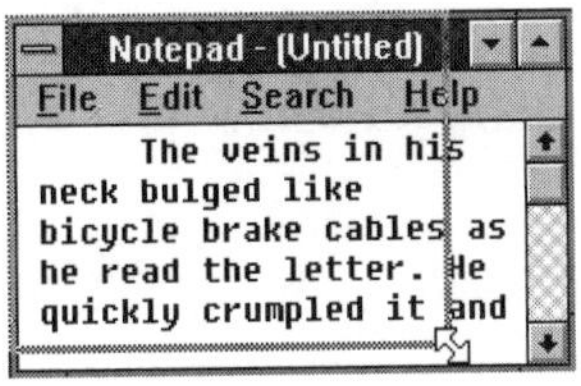

Figure 7-2:
As you move the mouse, the window's border changes to reflect its new shape.

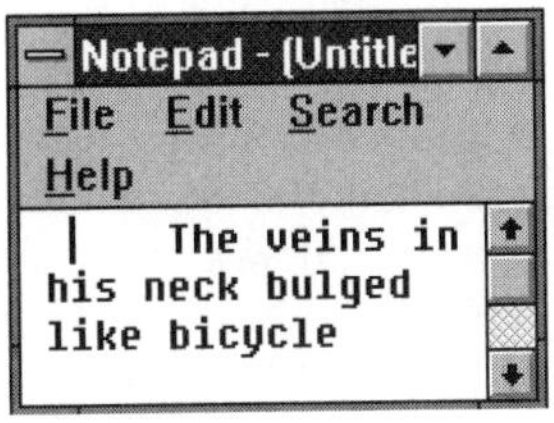

Notepad - [Untitled]
File   Edit   Search   Help

    The veins in his
neck bulged like
bicycle brake cables as
he read the letter. He
quickly crumpled it and

Figure 7-3:
Let go of the mouse button, and the window fills its newly adjusted border.

Notepad - [Untitle
File   Edit   Search
Help

| The veins in
his neck bulged
like bicycle

- ✔ This procedure may seem vaguely familiar because it is. You're just *dragging and dropping* the window's corner to a new size. That *drag and drop* concept works throughout Windows. For example, you can *drag and drop* a title bar to move an entire window to a new location on the screen.

- ✔ You can grab the side border of a window and move it in or out to make it fatter or skinnier. You can grab the top or bottom of a window and move it up or down to make it taller or shorter. But grabbing for a corner is always easiest because then you can make a window fatter, skinnier, taller, or shorter, all with one quick flick of the wrist.

If a window is hanging off the edge of the screen and you can't seem to position it so that all of it fits on the screen, try shrinking it first. Grab a visible corner and drag it toward the window's center. Release the mouse button, and the window shrinks itself to fit in its now-smaller border. Then grab the window's title bar and hold down the mouse button. When you drag the title bar back toward the center of the screen, you can see the whole window once again.

Making a Window Fill the Whole Screen

Sooner or later you get tired of all this New Age, multiwindow mumbo jumbo. Why can't you just put *one* huge window on the screen? Well, you can.

To make any window grow as big as it gets, double-click on its *title bar,* that topmost bar along the top of the window. The window leaps up to fill the screen, covering up all the other windows.

To bring the pumped-up window back to normal size, double-click on its title bar once again. The window shrinks to its former size, and you can see everything that it was covering up.

> ✔ When a window fills the entire screen, it loses its borders. That means you can no longer change its size by tugging on its title bar or dragging its borders. Those borders just aren't there anymore.

> ✔ If you're morally opposed to double-clicking on a window's title bar to expand it, you can expand it another way. Click on its *maximize button,* that upward-pointing arrow in its top right corner. The window hastily fills the entire screen. At the same time, the maximize button turns into a two-headed *restore* button; click on the restore button when you want the window to return to its previous size.

> ✔ Refer to Chapter 6 for more information on the maximize, minimize, and restore buttons.

> ✔ If you don't have a mouse, you can make the window bigger by holding down the Alt key, pressing the spacebar, and pressing X. But for goodness sake, buy a mouse so you don't have to try to remember these complicated commands!

> ✔ DOS programs running in on-screen windows can't fill the screen. When you double-click on their title bars, they get bigger, but Windows still keeps 'em relatively small. If you take them out of the window, however, they fill the screen completely and shove Windows completely into the background. To take a DOS program out of a window, click on the DOS window to make it active and then hold down the Alt key and press Enter. The DOS program suddenly lunges for the entire screen, and Windows disappears. To bring it back, hold the Alt key and press Enter again. (For more of this DOS stuff, see Chapter 16.)

Shrinking Windows to Icons

Windows spawn windows. You start with one window to write a letter to Mother. You open another window, to check her address, for example, and then yet another to see whether you've forgotten any recent birthdays. Before you know it, four more windows are crowded across the desktop.

To combat the clutter, Windows provides a simple means of window control: You can transform a window from a screen-cluttering square into a tiny button at the bottom of the screen.

Click on the downward-pointing arrow in any window's top right-hand corner. Whoosh! The window disappears, and a little *icon* appears at the bottom of the screen. That icon is a special button that enables you to call the window back into instant action.

If your desktop is messy, however, you may not be able to see that new little icon; another window may be covering the bottom of the screen. Keep clicking those downward-pointing arrows. Eventually, you'll turn all the open windows into icons, and you'll be able to see what's going on.

The difference can be dramatic. Figure 7-4 shows a desktop with a bunch of open windows.

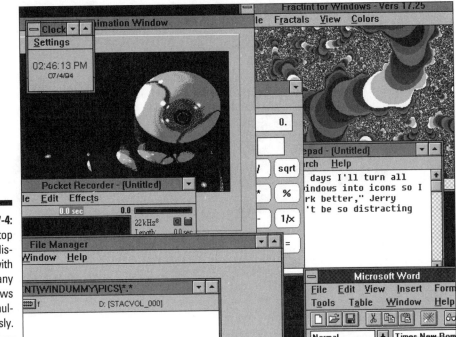

Figure 7-4: A desktop can be distracting with too many windows open simultaneously.

Figure 7-5 shows that same desktop after all but one window have been turned into icons. Those other windows are still readily available, mind you. Just double-click on a window's icon, and it instantly leaps back to its former place on the screen.

✔ To turn an open window into an icon, click on the downward-pointing arrow in its top right-hand corner. The window *minimizes* itself into an icon and lines itself up at the bottom of the screen.

✔ Icons come with little titles so that you can tell which program each of them represents.

✔ When you minimize a window, you neither destroy its contents nor close it. You merely change its shape. It is still loaded into memory, waiting for you to play with it again.

✔ To put the window back where it was, double-click on its icon. It hops back up to the same place it was before.

Figure 7-5:
Here's the same desktop that you saw in Figure 7-4. Seeing what is going on is easier when the open windows are turned into icons.

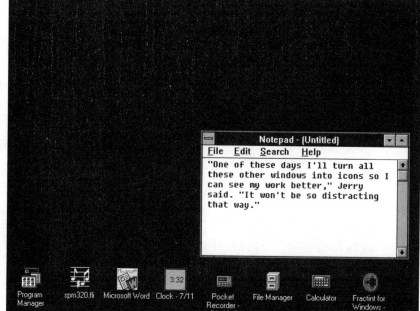

✔ When you load a program by using Program Manager or File Manager, you can make it start up as an icon rather than as a full-sized window. Information about this little triviality appears in Chapter 11 and Chapter 12.

✔ To keep your icons lined up nice and neat, check out the Task List in "The Way-Cool Task List" section later in this chapter.

✔ Keyboard users can press Alt, the spacebar, and N to minimize a window. Press Alt, the spacebar, and R to restore it to its former glory.

Turning Icons Back into Windows

To turn an icon at the bottom of the screen back into a useful program in the middle of the screen, just double-click on it. Pretty simple, huh?

✔ If you prefer wading through menus, then just click on an icon *once*. A Control menu shoots out the top of its head. Click on the menu's Restore option, and the icon disappears as its program leaps back to its former window position.

✔ In addition to using a swift double-click, you can use a few other methods to turn icons back into program windows. The very next section describes one way, and "The Way-Cool Task List" later in this chapter describes another.

Keeping your icons straight

Don't be confused by a program icon at the bottom of the screen and a program icon in the Program Manager. They're two different things. The icon at the bottom of the screen stands for a program that has already been loaded into the computer's memory. It's ready for immediate action. The icon in the Program Manager stands for a program that is sitting on the computer's hard disk waiting to be loaded.

If you mistakenly click on the icon in the Program Manager rather than the icon at the bottom of the screen, you load a *second* copy of that program. Two versions of the program are loaded: one running as a window and the other running as an icon waiting to be turned back into a window.

Running two versions can cause confusion — especially if you start entering stuff into both versions of the same program. You won't know which window has the *right* version!

Switching from Window to Window

Sometimes switching from window to window is easy. If you can see any part of the window you want — a corner, a bar, or a piece of dust — just click on it. That's all it takes to bring that window to the front of the screen, ready for action.

If the window you want is an icon, you have to double-click on it, but even that isn't so rough. Things get murky only when windows aren't in plain sight. The following sections give a few tricks for switching from window to window to window.

The Alt+Tab trick

This trick is so beautiful that Microsoft should have plastered it across the front of the Windows box instead of hiding it on page 56 of a 650-page manual.

Hold down the Alt key and press the Tab key. A most-welcome box pops up in the center of the screen, naming the last program you've touched (see Figure 7-6).

Figure 7-6:
When you hold down the Alt key and press Tab, Windows displays the name of the last program you used.

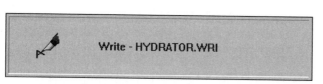

Write - HYDRATOR.WRI

If the program you're after is named, rejoice! And remove your finger from the Alt key. The window named in that box leaps to the screen.

If you're looking for a *different* program, keep your finger on the Alt key and press the Tab key once again. At each press of Tab, Windows displays the name of another open program. When you see the one you want, release the Alt key, hoot, and holler. The program leaps to the screen, ready for your working pleasure.

> ✔ Sometimes the Alt+Tab trick doesn't bring a box to the screen. Instead, it cycles through all the open windows by highlighting their title bars, which isn't nearly as much fun. If Windows isn't giving you cool boxes, then check out the section on tinkering with the Control Panel in Chapter 10. (You need to click in the Fast "Alt+Tab" Switching check box, which is in the Desktop dialog box.)

✔ The Alt+Tab trick works even if you're running a DOS program with Windows lurking in the background. The pop-up box doesn't look quite as cool, but, hey, it's there.

✔ As the Alt+Tab trick cycles through the open programs, it includes the names of icons along the bottom of the screen, even though their windows are not currently visible. When you release the Alt key, the program listed in the window leaps to the forefront, even if it's currently an icon.

✔ The *first* time you press the Tab key, the little pop-up window lists the name of the program you last accessed. If you prefer to cycle through the program names in the *opposite* direction, then hold down the Shift key *and* the Alt key while pressing the Tab key. If you agree that this is a pretty frivolous option, then rub your stomach and pat your head at the same time.

The Alt+Esc trick

The concept is getting kind of stale with this one, but here goes: If you hold down the Alt key and press the Esc key, Windows cycles through all the open programs but in a slightly less efficient way.

Instead of bringing their names to a big box in the middle of the screen, Windows brings the entire program to the forefront. Sometimes this method can be handy, but usually it's a little slower.

If Windows is currently cycling through an icon, it highlights only the icon's name at the bottom of the screen. That's not much of a visual indicator, and most of the time it won't even catch your eye.

When you see the window you want, release the Alt key. If it's an open window, it becomes the active window. But, if you release the Alt key while an icon's name is highlighted, you need to take one more step: You need to double-click on the icon to get the window on the screen.

The Alt+Esc trick is a little slower and a little less handy than the Alt+Tab trick described in the preceding section. And you won't want to bother with it at all once you read about the way-cool Task List in the very next section.

The Way-Cool Task List

This section introduces one of the handiest tricks in Windows, so pull your chair in a little closer. Windows comes with a special program that keeps track of all the open programs. Called the *Task List,* it always knows what programs are running and where they are. To call up the Task List, look for part of the desktop's *background* — any section that isn't currently covered with a window.

Double-click on that uncovered part of the background and stand back. (If you can't see any of the background, then hold down the Ctrl key and press the Esc key. That key combination does the same thing as double-clicking.) The Task List hops into action (see Figure 7-7).

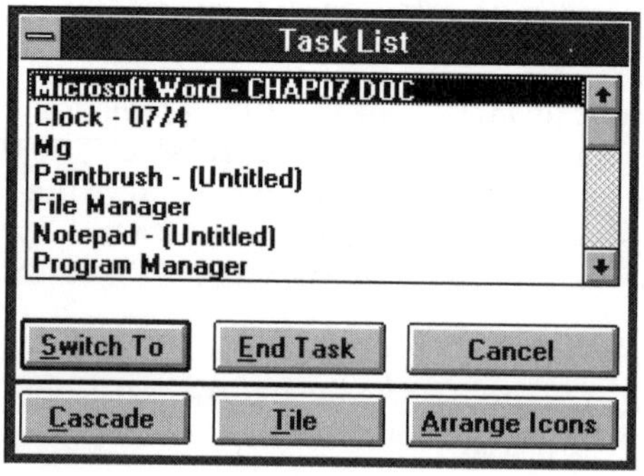

Figure 7-7:
Double-click
anywhere
in the
background
to call up
the Task
List.

Task List

Microsoft Word - CHAP07.DOC
Clock - 07/4
Mg
Paintbrush - (Untitled)
File Manager
Notepad - (Untitled)
Program Manager

Switch To   End Task   Cancel

Cascade   Tile   Arrange Icons

The Task List names all the windows that currently clutter the screen. If you're running a whole bunch of programs, you see a scroll bar along the Task List's right side. Just click on the up or down arrows in the scroll bar to see the other programs on the list.

From the Task List, you can perform powerful magic on your open windows.

Switching to another window

The currently active window, the one you were playing with immediately before calling up the Task List, is the dark, highlighted name at the top of the list. In the example shown in Figure 7-7, it's Microsoft Word. To switch immediately to a different window, just double-click on that window's name. The window instantly leaps to the front of the fray. It hops up there even if it's an icon.

(Double-clicking on a program's name is the same as single-clicking on a name and then selecting the Switch To command button or pressing Enter. Both actions accomplish the same thing, but the double-click is faster. The slowest method is for keyboard users: Press the down arrow until you've highlighted the program you're after. Then press Enter.)

Ending a task

Mad at a program? Then kill it. Highlight the program's name on the Task List and select the End Task command button (or hold down Alt and press E). The highlighted program quits, just as if you'd chosen its Exit command from within its own window.

The departing program gives you a chance to save any work before it quits and disappears from the screen.

Cascading and tiling windows

Sometimes those windows are scattered *everywhere*. How can you clean up in a hurry? By using the Cascade and Tile commands. Both commands organize all your open windows but in drastically different ways. Figure 7-8 shows what your screen looks like when you click on the Cascade button.

Talk about neat and orderly! The Task List grabs all the windows and deals them out like cards across the desktop. When you click on the Cascade button (or hold down Alt and press C), all the open windows are lined up neatly on the screen with their title bars showing.

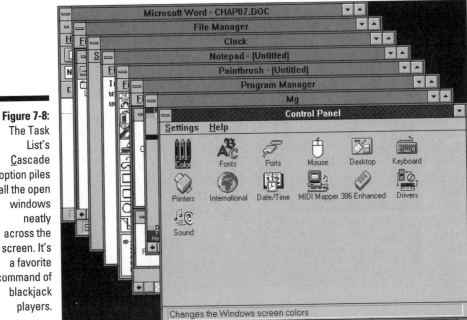

Figure 7-8: The Task List's Cascade option piles all the open windows neatly across the screen. It's a favorite command of blackjack players.

The Tile command rearranges the windows, too, but in a slightly different way (see Figure 7-9).

The Tile command arranges all the currently open windows across the screen, giving each one the same amount of space. This arrangement helps you find one that has been missing for a few hours. (You can select this command by clicking on the Tile button or by holding down Alt and pressing T.)

Note: Both the Tile and Cascade commands arrange only open windows. They straighten up the icons into an orderly row along the bottom of the screen, but they don't open those icons and display their contents on the screen.

If you have only two open windows, the Tile command arranges them side by side, making it easy for you to compare their contents. The Tile command places them side by side *vertically,* however, which makes them useless for comparing text. All you can see is the first few words of each sentence. So hold down the Shift key while you click on the Tile command, and Windows arranges the two open windows side by side *horizontally,* which makes a lot more sense. You can see complete sentences.

Figure 7-9:
The Task List's Tile command organizes the open windows like tiles on the shower floor. You can see them all, but they're too small to be of much use.

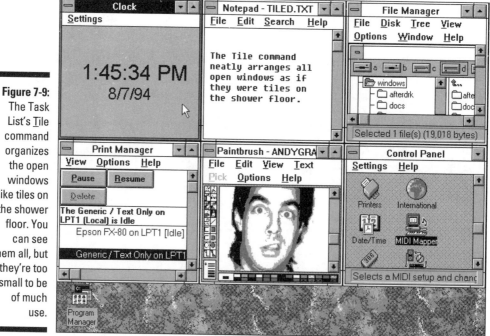

Arranging icons

The Task List can be considered a housekeeper of sorts, but it *only* does windows. It arranges the open windows neatly across the screen, but it just tidies up the icons along the bottom. It doesn't show their contents.

If the open windows look fine, but the icons look a little shabby along the bottom, click on the Task List's A̱rrange Icons button (or hold down Alt and press A). The Task List ignores any open windows, but it makes sure that all the icons are evenly spaced and orderly along the bottom row.

The Task List is an easily accessible helper. Take advantage of it often when you're having difficulty finding windows or when you want to clean up the desktop so you can find things.

Exiting the Task List

Unfortunately, it's easy to call up the Task List by mistake. For example, if you get sloppy when trying to double-click on an icon, you can end up double-clicking in the background, and then the heroic Task List leaps into action. Quietly click on the Task List's Cancel command button (or just press Esc), and the Task List will sneak off, pretending not to notice your overshoot.

Organizing Your Desktop

Although Windows lets you organize your desktop in a zillion different ways, from disgustingly messy to retentively natty, only one method *really* works the best. But, because Microsoft wants to stress how *flexible* Windows can be, you won't see this method pictured very often.

So here's the secret: Leave only one window open at a time, if you can help it, and leave the rest of your programs as icons beneath that window. You can access everything, and your desktop looks like Figure 7-10.

The layout shown in Figure 7-10 is the most efficient layout for several reasons:

1. **It's quick and easy to set up.**

    Turn all your windows into icons by clicking on their minimize button, that downward-pointing arrow in their upper right corner. Then double-click on the window you currently want to use. Next, double-click in the background to call up the Task List and click on its Ṯile command button.

    The Task List neatly aligns the open window in the center of the screen and systematically aligns all the icons beneath it. That's it! If only vacuuming the living room were that quick and easy!

Figure 7-10:
This
arrangement
is the most
efficient
way to
organize the
windows on
your
desktop.

2. You can *really* see what's going on in your main window.

Sure, you can put your programs in tiny windows and constantly click on their scroll bars to see any information inside them. But most people would rather get their work done than diddle around with scroll bars all day.

3. You can easily access all your open windows.

When you're done with one window, you turn it into an icon and double-click on the icon of the next program you want to work with.

Never let open windows cover up the bottom part of the screen. If you don't keep that bottom strip of the desktop free and clear, you can't find any icons you've stashed down there.

When the desktop is getting too messy for comfort, shrink all the windows to icons except for the one you want to work on. Then use the Task List's <u>T</u>ile command to organize the work area automatically.

If your computer is using something other than VGA mode — and you can fit more than one window on-screen simultaneously — go for it. But if you're having trouble finding the window you want, keep only one open at a time.

Chapter 8
Retrieving a Lost Window from the Pile

· ·

In This Chapter

▶ Plucking a lost window from the Task List

▶ Finding a window that's off the edge of the screen

▶ Cascading and tiling windows

▶ Returning to Windows from DOS

· ·

*S*ooner or later, Windows gives you that head-scratching feeling. "Golly," you say, as you frantically tug on your mouse cord. "That window was *right there* a second ago. Where did it go?"

When your windows start playing hide and seek, this chapter tells you where to search and how to make them stop playing foolish games. Then, when you find your Solitaire window, you can get back to work.

Plucking a Lost Window from the Task List

Forget about that huge, 1940s roll-top mahogany desk in the resale shop window. The Windows peewee *desktop* can't be any bigger than the size of your monitor.

In a way, Windows works more like those spike memo holders than like an actual desktop. Every time you open a new window, you're tossing another piece of information onto the spike. The window on top is relatively easy to see, but what's lying directly underneath it?

If you can see a window's ragged edge protruding from any part of the pile, click on it. The window magically rushes to the top of the pile. But what if you can't see *any* part of the window at all? How do you know it's even on the desktop?

You can solve this mystery by calling up your helpful Windows detective: the Task List. The Task List keeps a master list of everything that's happening on your screen (even the invisible stuff).

To call up the Task List, double-click on any bare area of your desktop — any place that's not covered by a window or an icon. If your desktop is so cluttered that you can't find a bare spot, or if you don't have a mouse, then just hold down your Ctrl key and press the Esc key. The Task List pops into action (see Figure 8-1).

See the list of programs in the center of the Task List? Your missing window is *somewhere* on the list. Press the up- or down-arrow key to move up or down the list. When the name of your window is highlighted, press Enter.

The Task List instantly tosses your newfound window to the top of the pile.

✔ If you see the window's name on the list, just double-click on it to retrieve it. You don't have to use your arrow keys if you don't want to.

✔ Most of the time, the Task List performs admirably in tracking down lost windows. If your window isn't on the list, then you've probably closed it. Closing a window, also known as *exiting* a window, takes it off your desktop and out of your computer's memory. To get that window back, you need to open it again, using the services of the Program Manager (see Chapter 11) or the File Manager (see Chapter 12).

✔ I lied. Sometimes a window can be running and yet *not* listed on the Task List. Some utility programmers figure that people don't *need* to see their programs or their icons. Berkeley Systems' After Dark screen saver, for example, can be running on your screen and yet not show up on the Task List or as an icon at the bottom of your screen. It simply works in the background. To access a background program like this one, you double-click on its icon in the Program Manager (see Chapter 11).

✔ Sometimes you see your missing program listed in the Task List, and you double-click on its name to dredge it from the depths. But, even though Task List brings it to the top, you *still* can't find it on your desktop. The program may be hanging off the edge of your desktop, so check out the very next section.

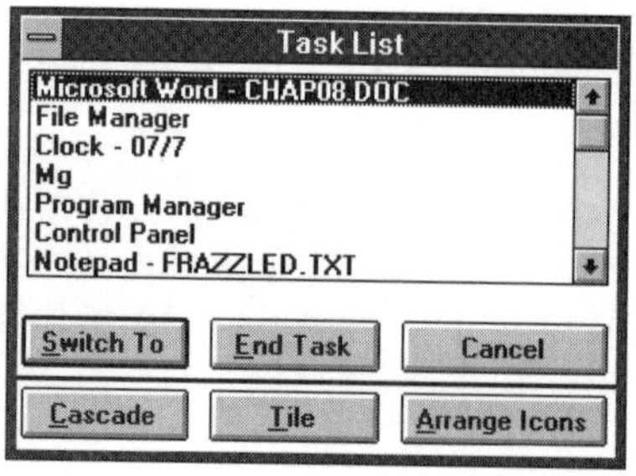

Figure 8-1:
The mighty
Task List
always
contains an
up-to-date
list of all
open
windows.

Task List
Microsoft Word - CHAP08.DOC
File Manager
Clock - 07/7
Mg
Program Manager
Control Panel
Notepad - FRAZZLED.TXT

Switch To	End Task	Cancel
Cascade	Tile	Arrange Icons

Finding a Window That's off the Edge of the Screen

Even a window at the top of the pile can be nearly invisible. A window can be moved anywhere on the Windows desktop, including off the screen. In fact, you can inadvertently move 99 percent of a window off the screen, leaving just a tiny corner showing (see Figure 8-2).

- ✔ If you can see any part of the rogue window's *title bar,* that thick strip along its top, hold the mouse button down and *drag* the traveler back to the center of the screen.

- ✔ Sometimes a window's title bar can be completely off the top of the screen. How can you drag it back into view? Start by clicking on any part of the window that shows. Then hold down your Alt key and press the spacebar. A menu appears from nowhere. Select the word <u>M</u>ove, and a mysterious four-headed arrow appears. Press your arrow keys until the window's border moves to a more manageable location and then press Enter. Whew! Don't let it stray that far again!

- ✔ For an easier way to make Windows not only track down all your criminally hidden windows but also line them up on the screen in *mug shot* fashion, check out the next two sections.

Figure 8-2:
Microsoft Word, in the top right-hand corner, is almost completely off the screen, making the window difficult for you to find.

Cascading Windows (The "Deal All the Windows Out in Front of Me" Approach)

Are you ready to turn Windows into a personal card dealer who gathers up all your haphazardly tossed windows and deals them out neatly on the desktop in front of you?

Then turn the Task List into a card dealer. Double-click in any windowless area of your desktop or hold down the Ctrl key and press the Esc key. The Task List leaps to the forefront. Select the Cascade button, and the Task List gathers all your open windows and deals them out in front of you, just like in a game of blackjack.

Each window's title bar is neatly exposed, ready to be grabbed and repri-manded with a quick click of the mouse.

- ✔ If the missing window doesn't appear in the stack of neatly dealt windows, then perhaps it's an icon. The Cascade command gathers and deals only the open windows; it leaves the icons resting along the bottom of the screen.

- ✔ For more about the Cascade command, check out Chapter 7.

Tiling Windows (The "Stick Everything on the Screen at Once" Approach)

Windows can stick all your open windows onto the screen at the same time. You'll finally be able to see all of them. No overlapping corners, edges, or menu flaps. Sound too good to be true? It is. Windows *shrinks* all the windows so they fit on the screen. But, hey, at least you can see them all.

Call up the Task List with a double-click in the background (or hold down Ctrl and press Esc) and then select its Tile command button.

- ✔ The Tile command pulls all the open windows onto the screen at the same time. If you have two open windows, each of them takes up half the screen. With three windows, each window gets a third of the screen. If you have 12 windows, each window takes up one-twelfth of the available space. (They're *very* small.)

- ✔ If you *still* don't see the missing window, consider another possibility: If icons already fill the bottom of your screen, Windows starts stacking a second row of icons right above the first row. Start clicking the minimize buttons of the windows that are tiled near the bottom to see whether they're covering up any icons. (If you don't have a mouse, press Alt, the spacebar, and N.)

- ✔ You can learn more about the Tile command in Chapter 7. The minimize button is covered in Chapter 6.

Running DOS without Getting Lost

Windows gets tricky when you start running DOS programs. Unlike Windows programs, hoggy DOS programs expect to have the entire computer to themselves. Windows has to trick them into thinking everything is normal.

As part of one trick, Windows enables you to run a DOS program so that it takes up the whole screen, just as if you weren't using Windows at all. All you see on the screen is the DOS program. Windows gives no clue that it is lurking somewhere in the background.

This trick makes the DOS program happier, but it can cause headaches for you. You can have a hard time remembering exactly what's happening. Are you running a DOS program under Windows? Or are you just running a plain old DOS program by itself? Sometimes Windows waits in the background while a DOS prompt sits on the screen with no program showing at all. With all these options, getting lost is easy.

- ✔ If you think that you may be lost at the DOS prompt, type the following command and then press Enter:

```
C:\> EXIT
```

That is, type **EXIT** and then press the Enter key. If Windows is waiting in the background, it lurches back to life, banishing the DOS prompt in the process. If you want to return to the DOS prompt for some bizarre reason, double-click on the DOS icon in Program Manager (or highlight the icon and press Enter).

- ✔ If you're stuck in a DOS program and want to get back to another window, hold down the Alt key and press Esc. If Windows is lurking in the background, it leaps back to the screen, turning your DOS program into an icon. Then, because you're back to Windows, you can grab the window you *really* want.

- ✔ For more soothing salves to treat DOS-program confusion, check out Chapter 16.

Chapter 9
Sharing Information (Moving Words, Pictures, and Sounds Around)

*U*ntil Windows came along, IBM-compatible computers had a terrible time sharing anything. Their programs were rigid, egotistical things, with no sense of community. Information created by one program couldn't always be shared with another program. Older versions of programs passed down this selfish system to newer versions, enforcing the segregation with *proprietary file formats* and *compatibility tests.*

To counter this bad trip, the Windows programmers created a communal workplace where all the programs could groove together peacefully. In the harmonious tribal village of Windows, programs share their information openly in order to make a more beautiful environment for all.

In the Window's co-op, all the windows can beam their vibes to each other freely, without fear of rejection. Work created by one Windows program is accepted totally and lovingly by any other Windows program. Windows programs treat each other equally, even if one program is wearing some pretty freaky threads or, in some gatherings, *no threads at all.*

This chapter shows you how easily you can move those good vibes from one window to another.

Examining the Cut and Paste Concept (and Copy, Too)

Windows took a tip from the kindergartners and made *cut and paste* an integral part of all its programs. Information can be electronically *cut* from one window and *pasted* into another window with little fuss and even less mess.

Just about any part of a window is up for grabs. You can highlight an exceptionally well-written paragraph in your word processor, for example, or a spreadsheet chart that tracks the value of your Indian-head pennies. After *highlighting* the desired information, you press a button to *copy* or *cut* it from its window.

At the press of the button, the information heads for a special place in Windows called the *Clipboard.* From there you can paste it into any other open window.

The beauty of Windows is that with all those windows on the screen at the same time, you can easily grab bits and pieces from any of them and paste all the parts into a new window.

- ✔ Unlike DOS programs, Windows programs are designed to work together, so taking information from one window and putting it into another window is easy. Sticking a map onto your party fliers, for example, is *really* easy.

- ✔ Cutting and pasting works well for the big stuff, like sticking big charts into memos. But don't overlook it for the small stuff, too. For example, copying someone's name and address from your Cardfile is quicker than typing it by hand at the top of your letter. Or, to avoid typographical errors, you can copy an answer from the Windows Calculator and paste it into another program.

- ✔ Cutting and pasting is different from that new *Object Linking and Embedding* stuff you may have heard people raving about. That more powerful (and, naturally, more confusing) *OLE* stuff gets its own section later in this chapter.

- ✔ When you cut or copy some information, it immediately appears in a special Windows program called the *Clipboard.* From the Clipboard, it can be pasted into other windows. The Clipboard has its own bag of tricks, so it gets its own section later in this chapter.

Highlighting the Important Stuff

Before you can grab information from a window, you have to tell the window exactly what parts you want to grab. The easiest way to tell it is to *highlight* the information with a mouse.

You can highlight a single letter, an entire novel, or anything in between. You can highlight pictures of water lilies. You can even highlight sounds so you can paste belches into other files (see the OLE section later in this chapter).

In most cases, highlighting involves one swift trick with the mouse: Put the mouse arrow at the beginning of the information you want and hold down the mouse button. Then move the mouse to the end of the information and release the button. That's it! All the stuff lying between your mouse moves is highlighted. The information usually turns a different color so that you can see what you've grabbed. An example of highlighted text is shown in Figure 9-1.

If you're mouseless, use the arrow keys to put the cursor at the beginning of the stuff you want to grab. Then hold down the Shift key and press the arrow keys until the cursor is at the end of what you want to grab. You see the stuff on the screen become highlighted as you move the arrow keys. This trick works with almost every Windows program. (If you're after text, hold down the Ctrl key, too, and the text is highlighted word by word.)

Some programs have a few shortcuts for highlighting parts of their information:

✔ To highlight a single *word* in Notepad, Write, or most text boxes, point at it with the mouse and double-click. The word turns black, meaning that it's highlighted. (In Write you can hold down the button on its second click, and then, by moving the mouse around, you can quickly highlight additional text word by word.)

✔ To highlight a single *line* in Write, click next to it in the left margin. Keep holding down the mouse button and move the mouse up or down to highlight additional text line by line.

✔ To highlight a *sentence* in Write, hold down the Ctrl key and click anywhere within that sentence. Keep holding down the mouse button and move the mouse to highlight additional text sentence by sentence.

✔ To highlight a *paragraph* in Write, double-click next to it in the left margin. Keep holding down the mouse button on the second click and move the mouse to highlight additional text paragraph by paragraph.

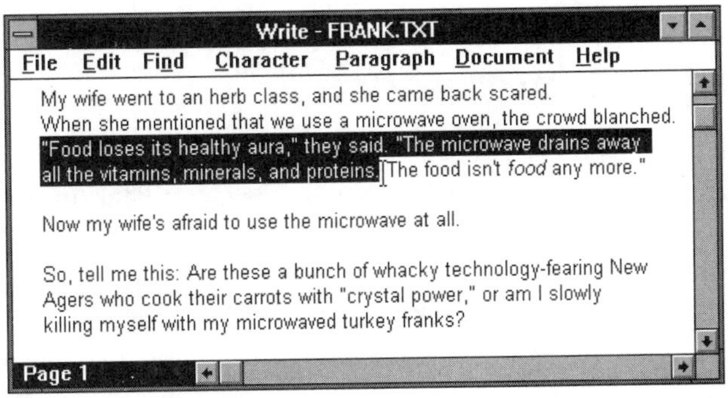

Figure 9-1: Highlighted text turns a different color for easy visibility.

```
                     Write - FRANK.TXT
 File   Edit   Find   Character   Paragraph   Document   Help
 My wife went to an herb class, and she came back scared.
 When she mentioned that we use a microwave oven, the crowd blanched.
 "Food loses its healthy aura," they said. "The microwave drains away
 all the vitamins, minerals, and proteins. The food isn't food any more."

 Now my wife's afraid to use the microwave at all.

 So, tell me this: Are these a bunch of whacky technology-fearing New
 Agers who cook their carrots with "crystal power," or am I slowly
 killing myself with my microwaved turkey franks?

 Page 1
```

✔ To highlight an entire *document* in Write, hold down the Ctrl key and double-click anywhere in the left margin. (To highlight the entire document in Notepad, press and release the Alt key and then press the letters E and A. So much for consistency between Windows programs. . . .)

✔ To highlight a portion of text in just about any Windows program, click at the text's beginning, hold down the Shift key, and click at the end of the desired text. Everything between those two points becomes highlighted.

✔ To highlight part of a picture or drawing while in Paintbrush, click on the *second* scissors icon near the top left corner. Then, while holding down the mouse button, slide the mouse over the desired part of the picture.

After you've highlighted text, you must either cut it or copy it *immediately*. If you do anything else, like absentmindedly click the mouse someplace else in your document, all your highlighted text reverts to normal, just like Cinderella after midnight.

Be careful after you highlight a bunch of text. If you press any key — the spacebar, for example — Windows immediately replaces your highlighted text with the character that you type — in this case, a space. To reverse that calamity and bring your highlighted text back to life, hold down Alt and press the Backspace key.

DOS windows have their own methods of highlighting information. Check out the section "Using Copy and Paste with a DOS Program," later in this chapter, for the real dirt.

Deleting, Cutting, or Copying What You Highlighted

After you've highlighted some information (which is described in the preceding section, if you've just entered the classroom), you're ready to start playing with it. You can cut it, copy it, or delete it. All three options differ drastically.

Deleting the information

Deleting the information just wipes it out. Zap! It just disappears from the window. To delete highlighted information, just press the Delete or Backspace key.

✔ If you've accidentally deleted the wrong thing, panic. Then hold down the Ctrl key and press the letter Z. Your deletion is graciously undone. Any deleted information pops back up on the screen. Whew!

✔ Holding down the Alt key and pressing the Backspace key also undoes your last mistake. (Unless you've just said something dumb at a party. Then use Ctrl+Z.)

Cutting the information

Cutting the highlighted information wipes it off the screen, just as the Delete command does, but with a big difference: When the information is removed from the window, it is copied to a special Windows storage tank called the *Clipboard.*

When you're looking at the screen, cutting and deleting look identical. In fact, the first few times you try to cut something, you feel panicky, thinking that you may have accidentally deleted it instead. (This feeling never really goes away, either.)

To cut highlighted stuff, hold down the Shift key and press the Delete key. Whoosh! The highlighted text disappears from the window, scoots through Windows' underground tubes, and appears on the Clipboard. From there it's ready for further action.

✔ One way to tell whether your Cut command actually worked is to paste the information back into your document. If it appears, you know that the command worked, and you can cut it out again right away. If it doesn't appear, you know that something has gone dreadfully wrong. (For the Paste command, discussed a little later, hold down the Shift key and press the Insert key, that 0 on the numeric keypad.)

✔ Microsoft's lawyers kicked butt in the Apple lawsuit, so Windows now uses the same cut keys as the Macintosh. You can hold down the Ctrl key and press the letter X to cut. (Get it? That's an *X,* as in *you're crossing,* or *X-ing, something out.*)

Copying the information

Compared with cutting or deleting, *copying* information is quite anticlimactic. When you cut or delete, the information disappears from the screen. But, when you copy information to the Clipboard, the highlighted information just sits there in the window. In fact, it looks as if nothing has happened, so you repeat the Copy command a few times before giving up and just hoping it worked.

To copy highlighted information, hold down the Ctrl key and press the Insert key (the 0 on the numeric keypad or INS on some keyboards). Although nothing seems to happen, that information really will show up on the Clipboard.

✔ Windows now uses the same Copy keys as the Macintosh does. If you don't like the Ctrl+Insert combination, you can hold down the Ctrl key and press the letter C to copy. That combination is a little easier to remember, actually, because *C* is the first letter of *copy*.

✔ To copy an image of your entire Windows desktop (the *whole screen*) to the Clipboard, press the Print Screen key, which is sometimes labeled PrtSc or something similar. (Some keyboards make you hold down the Shift key simultaneously.) A snapshot of your screen appears on the Clipboard, ready to be pasted someplace else. Computer nerds call this snapshot a *screen shot.* All the pictures of windows in this book are screen shots. (And, no, the information doesn't also head for your printer.)

✔ To copy an image of your currently active window (just one window — nothing surrounding it), hold down the Alt key while you press your Print Screen key. The window's picture appears on the Clipboard. (You usually don't have to hold down the Shift key with this one, even for wacky keyboards. But if Alt+Print Screen doesn't work, hey, try holding down the Shift key anyway.)

Finding out more about cutting, copying, and deleting

Want to know more about cutting, copying, and deleting? Read on (you really should read this stuff):

✔ The cut, copy, and paste process works differently in DOS windows. See "Using Copy and Paste with a DOS Program" in this chapter for a dose of DOS details.

✔ If you prefer to use menus, the Cut, Copy, and Paste commands tumble down when you select the word Edit on any menu bar.

✔ When you're using the Print Screen key trick to copy a window or the entire screen to the Clipboard (see the preceding section), one important component is left out: The mouse arrow is *not* included in the picture, even if it was in plain sight when you took the picture. In fact, you can tell that the Print Screen command works because the arrow disappears for a split second as the image heads for the Clipboard. (Are you asking yourself how all the little arrows got in this book's pictures? Well, I draw 'em all in by hand!)

✔ Sometimes figuring out whether the Cut or Copy commands are really working is difficult. To know for sure, keep the Windows Clipboard showing at the bottom of the screen. Then you can watch the images appear on it when you press the buttons. (To open the Clipboard, double-click on its icon in the Program Manager. If you're mouseless, hold down Alt and press Esc until the Clipboard icon is highlighted; then press Enter.)

✔ Some Windows programs, like Microsoft Word for Windows, have an *autosave feature.* This feature automatically saves your work every few minutes, so if your computer dies suddenly, you won't lose much of your work. Be forewarned, however: If the Autosave command kicks in immediately *after* you've deleted some highlighted work, the Undelete command won't work.

✔ Don't keep screen shots or large graphics on the Clipboard any longer than necessary. They consume a lot of memory that your other programs could be using. To clear off any memory-hogging detritus, copy a single word to the Clipboard or call up the Clipboard Viewer and press Del.

Pasting Information into Another Window

After you've cut or copied information to the special Windows Clipboard storage tank, it's ready for travel. You can *paste* that information into just about any other window.

Compared with highlighting, copying, or cutting, pasting is relatively straight-forward: Click the mouse anywhere in the destination window and click in the spot where you want the stuff to appear. Then hold down the Shift key and press the Insert key (the 0 key on the numeric keypad). Presto! Anything that's sitting on the Clipboard immediately leaps into that window.

✔ Another way to paste stuff is to hold down the Ctrl key and press V. That combination does the same thing as Shift+Insert. (It also is the command those funny-looking Macintosh computers use to paste stuff.)

✔ You also can choose the Paste command from a window's menu bar. Select the word <u>E</u>dit and then select the word <u>P</u>aste. But don't select the words Paste <u>S</u>pecial. That command is for the Object Linking and Embedding stuff, which gets its own section later in this chapter.

✔ The Paste command inserts a *copy* of the information that's sitting on the Clipboard. The information stays on the Clipboard, so you can keep pasting it into other windows if you want. In fact, the Clipboard's contents stay the same until a new Cut or Copy command replaces them with new information.

Using Copy and Paste with a DOS Program

DOS programs all behave a little strangely under Windows. Likewise, the Copy and Paste commands work a little differently. It gets kind of complicated, so you should really think about ditching your DOS programs and switching to Windows programs if you're serious about copying and pasting.

You must remember certain rules when you use the Copy and Paste commands with DOS programs:

Rule 1: You can't cut text or anything else from a DOS program in Windows. You can only *copy* stuff. The original information always remains in your DOS program.

Rule 2: You can't paste anything but text into most DOS programs.

Rule 3: You can't paste text into a DOS program when it's running in *full-screen mode,* meaning that it's taking up the entire screen.

Rule 4: When copying information from a DOS program, you need to decide beforehand if you want to copy a *picture* from the DOS window or copy *text* — actual words. You can't copy a picture out of a DOS program unless you have a 386, 486, or Pentium computer and the DOS program is running in a window. The following two sections explain the procedures for copying pictures and text from a DOS program.

Rule 5: Copying and pasting from DOS programs is decidedly complicated and tedious, as evidenced by rules 1 through 4.

Copying a picture from a DOS program

If you have a 386, 486, or Pentium computer, place the DOS program in its own window on the screen. Then hold down the Alt key while pressing the Print Screen key.

The Alt+Print Screen key trick copies a *graphics image* of the DOS window to the Windows Clipboard. From there you can paste the picture into the Windows graphics program, Paintbrush, and clean it up a little before copying it to its final destination.

- ✔ If you don't have a 386, 486, or Pentium computer, go buy one. Otherwise, you can't run a DOS program in a window.

- ✔ This method gives you a snapshot of the DOS program that is running in the window. It is surrounded by typical window dressing, like menu bars, title bars, scroll bars, and the like. You can erase these extraneous elements in Paintbrush to make the picture look better.

- ✔ If you use this trick to copy a DOS program that's showing only text, you get just a *picture* of that text. You can't copy the text into a word processor or arrange it into paragraphs. It's just a picture, like a Polaroid snapshot of an open book.

Copying text from a DOS program

If the DOS program is running full screen, then press your Print Screen key. (Some keyboards make you hold down the Shift key simultaneously.) Even though Windows is running invisibly in the background, it dredges all the text showing in the DOS program and copies it onto the Clipboard. (Not to the printer, though. Print Screen doesn't do that in Windows.)

If the DOS program is running in a *window* on the screen, here's how to grab that text:

1. Click in the DOS program's Control-menu box, that little gray square in its top left-hand corner. (Or press Alt and the spacebar if you don't have a mouse.)

The big Control menu lunges toward you, as shown in Figure 9-2.

Figure 9-2:
A swift click on the box in a DOS program's top left corner brings down its Control menu.

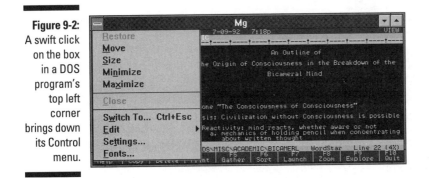

2. From the Control menu, select the word Edit.

The word Edit has a little arrow next to it, telling you that more menu options are hidden. Additional options shoot out from the side, as shown in Figure 9-3. Notice that the word Mark is already highlighted, ready for you to choose it.

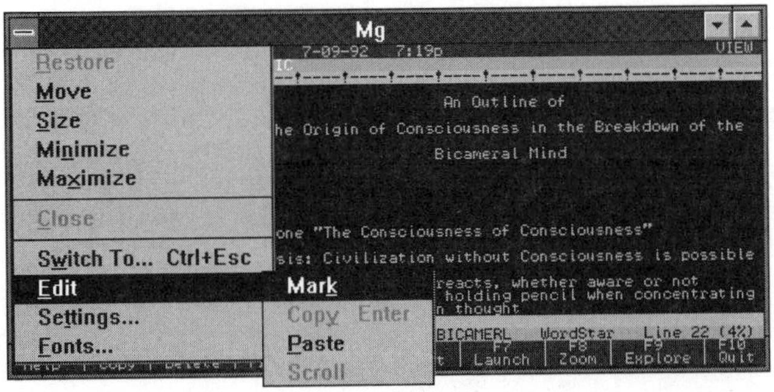

Figure 9-3:
When you select Edit, more options shoot out the side.

3. **Either click on the word Mar_k_ or press Enter to move into Mark mode.**

   The pull-down menu bails, and you can select the text from the window, just as you do in any other Windows application.

4. **Hold down the mouse button when you're at the beginning of what you want to grab, move the mouse to the end of the text, and then release the mouse button.**

   (If you don't have a mouse, use the arrow keys to move the cursor to the beginning of what you want to grab. Then, while holding down Shift, move the cursor to the end of the text.)

   Your screen looks similar to the one shown in Figure 9-4.

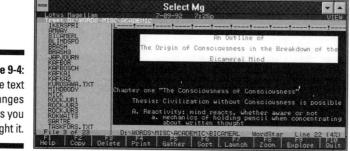

Figure 9-4:
The text
changes
color as you
highlight it.

5. **When the information you're after changes color, press Enter.**

   Wham! Windows copies that highlighted text to the Clipboard.

   ✔ When grabbing text from a DOS application in a window, you can grab it only in square- or rectangular-sized chunks. That limitation is not as bad as it seems, though, because Windows tosses out any extraneous spaces at the ends of lines.

   ✔ You can't retain any of the special formatting the DOS text may have had, like boldface or underline. Any adjacent graphics are also left out. In addition, if the text itself is in graphics form, like fancy letters or something, you can't grab it as text.

   ✔ *Select mode* can be confusing: Your DOS application is frozen on the screen and doesn't respond. It's frozen because you're picking chunks out of it. And you can tell that you're picking chunks out of it by looking at the title bar: The word Select is in front of the program's name.

   ✔ If you change your mind and don't want to grab information out of there, press Esc, and everything goes back to normal. As normal as a computer can be, anyway.

Instead of clicking your way through all those Control menus, try this: Click on the Control menu but *hold down the mouse button.* Then, as you move the mouse down to the word <u>E</u>dit, the second menu magically appears. Let go of the mouse when you're over the Mar<u>k</u> command, and you'll be in Select mode. You can do all that quickly and easily, without lifting your finger. Really!

Pasting text into a DOS program

Most DOS programs are text-based critters. You can't copy any graphics into most of them. You can dump some words into them, however, by following steps 1 through 3 in the preceding section. But, instead of choosing the Mar<u>k</u> command, choose the <u>P</u>aste command.

Any text on the Clipboard is instantly poured into the DOS program, starting where you've left the cursor sitting.

Note: You'll probably have to reformat the text after you pour it into the DOS program. The sentences usually break in all the wrong places. Plus, you lose any special formatting, like boldface or underline. Hey, that's what you get for still clinging to your stubborn old DOS programs!

Stuck with an anemic 286 machine? It can't run a DOS program in a window, but it can still paste some text into it. When the program is running full screen, click where you want the text to appear. Then hold down the Alt key and press the Esc key. The DOS program turns into an icon at the bottom of your screen. Next, click once on the DOS program's icon and watch its Control menu rise eerily from the top of its head. Click on the word <u>E</u>dit and then on the word <u>P</u>aste. Presto! The text on the Clipboard jumps into your DOS program, right where you left the cursor sitting.

Using the Clipboard

Windows employs a special program to look after all the stuff that's being slung around by cutting and copying. Called the *Clipboard,* it's merely a window that hangs onto anything that has been cut or copied.

From the Program Manager, double-click on the Clipboard icon, which looks like this:

Clipboard

The Clipboard pops up on the screen. Inside the Clipboard, you see any information you've cut or copied recently. Figures 9-5, 9-6, and 9-7 show some examples.

Figure 9-5:
This Clipboard contains a recently copied picture of a chip.

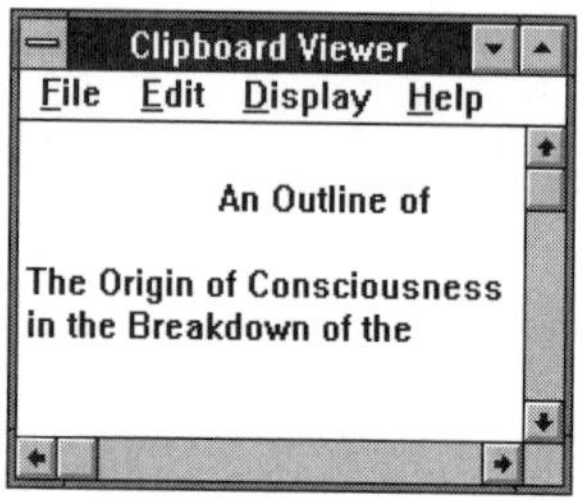

Figure 9-6:
This Clipboard displays text recently copied from a DOS program.

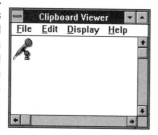

Figure 9-7:
This Clipboard contains a sound copied from the Windows Sound Recorder.

> ✔ Sometimes the Clipboard can't show you exactly what you've copied. For example, if you copy a sound from the Windows Sound Recorder, you just see a picture of the Sound Recorder's icon. And, at the risk of getting metaphysical, what does a sound look like, anyway?

✔ The Clipboard functions automatically and transparently. Unless you make a special effort, you don't even know it's there.

✔ To better track what's being cut and pasted, some people leave the Clipboard sitting open at the bottom of the screen. Then they can actually _see_ what they've cut or copied. (To open the Clipboard, or any other program, double-click on its icon in the Program Manager. Or use the Tab and arrow keys to highlight the icon and press Enter.)

✔ Most of the time the Clipboard is used just for temporary operations — a quick cut here, a quick paste there, and then on to the next job. But you can save a Clipboard's contents for later use. Select the word File from the menu bar and then select Save As from the pull-down menu. Type in a filename and click on the OK command button (or just press Enter).

✔ The Clipboard can hold only one thing at a time. Each time you cut or copy something else, you replace the Clipboard's contents with something new. If you want to collect a bunch of _clips_ for later pasting, use the Save As option described in the preceding paragraph. The Clipboard also starts up empty each time you start Windows.

✔ Windows for Workgroups, the networking version of Windows, uses a slightly different version of the Clipboard — it lets people look at the Clipboards on other computers in the office. Windows for Workgroups is covered in Chapter 20.

Keeping the Clipboard clear

Whenever you cut or copy something, that information heads for the Clipboard. And it stays there, too, until you cut or copy something else to replace it. But, while that information sits there on the Clipboard, it uses up memory.

Windows needs all the memory it can get, or it begins running slowly or balking at opening more windows. Big chunks of text, pictures, and sounds can consume a lot of memory, so clear off the Clipboard when you're through cutting and pasting, to return the memory for general Windows use.

To clear off the Clipboard quickly, just copy a single word to the Clipboard: Double-click on a word in a text file, hold down the Ctrl key, and press C.

Or, if the Clipboard is up on the screen, click on it to bring it to the forefront and then press your Delete key. You clear the Clipboard off, enabling Windows to use the memory for more pressing matters. (No mouse? Then hold down Alt and press Esc until you've highlighted the Clipboard and press Delete.)

Looking at Cool Object Linking and Embedding Stuff

Because the concepts of cutting and pasting are so refreshingly simple, Microsoft complicated them considerably with something called *Object Linking and Embedding,* known as *OLE.* It sounds complicated, so I'll start with the simple part: the object.

The *object* is merely the information you want to paste into a window. It can be a sentence, a road map, a sneeze sound, or anything else that you can cut or copy from a window.

Normally, when you paste an object into a window, you're pasting the same kind of information. For example, you paste text into a word processor and pictures into the Windows Paintbrush program. But what if you want to paste a sound into Write, the Windows word processor?

That's where Object Linking and Embedding come in, offering subtle changes to the paste concept. You'll probably never use them, but they can be fun to fiddle around with on cloudy days. Beware, however: OLE awareness is the first step down those ever spiraling stairs toward computer-nerd certification.

Embedding

On the surface, *embedding* an object looks just like pasting it. The object shows up in the window. Big deal. But, when you embed an object, you're also embedding the name of the program that created that object. When you double-click on the object, poof! The program that created it jumps to the top of the screen, ready to edit it.

For example, you can embed a spreadsheet chart showing your current net worth in a letter you're writing to an old high-school friend. Then, if the stock market changes before you mail the letter, you can easily update the letter's chart. Just call up the letter in your word processor and double-click on the chart. The spreadsheet that created the chart pops up, ready for you to make the changes. When you're done, you close the spreadsheet. The spreadsheet disappears, leaving the updated chart in your letter.

Embedding is really pretty handy. You don't have to remember the chart's filename. You don't even have to call up your spreadsheet. Windows does all that grunt work automatically. Just double-click on the chart, make the changes when your spreadsheet appears, and then quit the spreadsheet to return to the letter.

As with most things in Windows, the OLE concept is easier to use than its name implies.

Linking

Linking looks just like embedding or pasting. Your chart appears in your letter, just as before. But here's where things get weird: You're not really pasting the chart. You're pasting the chart's *filename*.

The word processor runs over to the file containing the chart, sees what the chart looks like, and then puts a copy of it in the letter.

What's the point? Well, unlike with pasting or embedding, you're keeping only one copy of the chart around. When you call up the chart in your spreadsheet and change it, those changes are automatically reflected in your word processor the next time you load that letter. With only one *real* version of the object lying around, every copy is always the right version.

> ✔ Not all Windows programs can handle object linking and embedding. In fact, of the programs that come in the Windows box, only Paintbrush, Write, Sound Recorder, Cardfile, and Object Packager are OLE savvy.

> ✔ *Dynamic Data Exchange* was an earlier method for sharing information between Windows programs. It never really worked all that well, and OLE pretty much replaces it. So don't bother trying to learn what it was or, actually, used to be.

> ✔ Object Linking and Embedding is new to Windows 3.1, providing yet another reason for Windows 3.0 owners to shell out the extra bucks.

Should you paste, embed, or link your important objects? Here's what to do:

> ✔ Use *Paste* for objects you'll never want to change.

> ✔ *Embed* objects if you want to be able to edit them easily at a later date.

> ✔ Choose the *Link* option if you want several programs to share the same version of a single object.

What's That Object Packager Thing?

As if the Object Linking and Embedding concept weren't complicated enough, Microsoft added a few more features. The Windows Object Packager provides even more ways for you to cut and paste stuff from window to window.

The Object Packager is one of those fancy multimedia toys. Its icon looks like this:

Packager

The Object Packager enables you to dump a *package* into a window. A *package* is simply an icon that represents a file. Instead of pasting actual information into your window, you're pasting an icon, or picture, that *represents* that information. Then, when somebody double-clicks on the icon, the information pops up in a window.

This description makes it sound more complicated than it really is, so here's a simple example: You write a letter to your brother by using Write. Your kid writes a letter to your brother's kid by using Notepad. Using Object Packager, you import your kid's letter into a package and then paste that package into your own letter.

You copy your letter to a disk and mail it to your brother. Your brother reads your letter by using Write. There, in the middle of the Write document, he sees an icon for Notepad. He calls over his kid, who double-clicks on the Notepad icon. Shazam! Your kid's letter pops to the top of the screen in Notepad.

Whew! The miracles of modern technology!

✔ What's the point? Well, Object Packager enables you to mix different types of data. In the preceding scenario, for example, you mixed data created by Write with data created by Notepad. Yet the Object Packager kept the two types of data separate.

✔ If you have a sound card, you can package sounds with Object Packager and insert them into documents. For example, you can send a thank-you letter to a friend who invited you over to dinner and package the sound of applause along with your kind words. When your friend double-clicks on the icon representing the applause, the grateful sound will fill the room.

✔ Object Packager lets you *pretty up* your package in several ways. You can choose the little icon, or picture, you'd like to represent your package, for example. You can type in a descriptive title to be displayed beneath the icon.

✔ Yeah, this Embedding and Linking stuff's a little too large to fit in a normal beginner's pocket. That's why it's covered more fully in this book's sequel, *MORE Windows For Dummies*. (And if you're embedding or linking sound, pictures, or videos, check out *Multimedia and CD-ROMs For Dummies* for answers.)

Controlling the Print Manager

Many of the Windows programs work in the background. You know that they're there only when something is wrong and weird messages start flying around. The Print Manager is one of those programs.

Normally, you never encounter the Print Manager. When you choose the Print command in a program, you may see the Print Manager icon appear at the bottom of your screen. When your printer stops spitting out pages, the Print Manager icon disappears and so does the Print Manager.

When everything is running smoothly, the Print Manager icon looks like this at the bottom of your screen:

Printman

Your printer can print only one thing at a time. If you try to print a second memo before the first one is finished, Print Manager jumps in to help. It intercepts all the requests and lines them up in order, just like a harried diner cook.

To check up on what is being sent to the printer, double-click on the Print Manager icon, and you see the Print Manager in all its glory, as shown in Figure 9-8.

✔ If your computer is hooked up to more than one printer, each one is listed in the Print Manager's window. They are listed regardless of whether they're turned on. In fact, they are listed even if you sold them to George through a classified ad last weekend. They don't disappear until you tell your computer to remove them through the Control Panel, which is discussed in Chapter 10.

✔ The CHAP09.DOC file in Figure 9-8 is highlighted because it is currently being printed. If you change your mind and don't want to print CHAP09.DOC after all, click on the Delete command button at the top of the window (or hold down Alt and press D). Print Manager stops sending that file to the printer. (Your printer may spit out a page or two before it stops.)

Figure 9-8:
In this example, the Print Manager has sent 9 percent of a Microsoft Word file to the NEC Silentwriter2 90 printer.

				Print Manager	▼ ▲

View   Options   Help

Pause	Resume	Delete	Microsoft Word - CHAP09.DOC current on local LPT1 (NEC Silentwriter2 90)

Generic / Text Only on LPT1 [Idle]

HP LaserJet IIP on LPT1 [Idle]

NEC Silentwriter2 90 on LPT1 [Printing]
    Microsoft Word - CHAP09.DOC   9% of 289K 8:02 PM 7/9/1992
  2 Microsoft Word - CHAP10.DOC   14K 8:03 PM 7/9/1992
  3 Microsoft Word - CHAP13.DOC   119K 8:08 PM 7/9/1992

Panasonic KX-P1180 on LPT1 [Idle]

- When the printer is through with CHAP09.DOC, it moves to the second file in the lineup, which, in this case, is CHAP10.DOC.

- Some printers let you change the order in which the files are printed. For example, to scoot Chapter 13 ahead of Chapter 10, click on its name and hold down the mouse button. Then *drag* the file up so it cuts in front of Chapter 10. Release the button, and the Print Manager changes the printing order. (The printing order is called a *queue*, pronounced *Q*.)

- To cancel a print job, select the filename of the one you don't like and then choose the <u>D</u>elete command button at the top of the window.

- If the boss is walking by the printer while you're printing your party flier, select the filename of the flier and choose the <u>P</u>ause command button. The printer will stop. When the boss is out of sight, choose <u>R</u>esume to continue.

- If you're on a network (shudder), you may not be able to change the order in which files are being printed. You may not even be able to pause a file.

- If your printer is not hooked up, or you *did* sell it to George last weekend, Print Manager tries to send it to that printer anyway. When it doesn't get a response, it sends you a message that your printer is not responding. Plug the printer in, turn it on, and try again. Or delete that file from the queue, go back to the program you're printing from, and select another printer to send the stuff to. Then head to Chapter 10 to see how to take your recently sold printer off the menu for good.

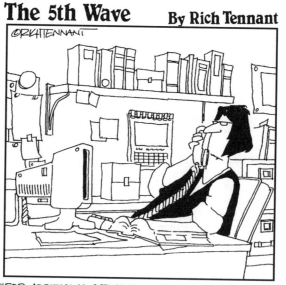

The 5th Wave By Rich Tennant

"FOR ADDITIONAL SOFTWARE SUPPORT, DIAL "9", "POUND" THE EXTENSION NUMBER DIVIDED BY YOUR ACCOUNT NUMBER, HIT "STAR", YOUR DOG, BLOW INTO THE RECEIVER TWICE, PUNCH IN YOUR HAT SIZE, PUNCH OUT YOUR LANDLORD,..."

Chapter 10
Customizing Windows (Fiddling with the Control Panel)

. . . .

In This Chapter

▶ Exploring the Control Panel

▶ Getting around the desktop

▶ Changing colors

▶ Understanding TrueType fonts

▶ Making Windows recognize your double-click

▶ Setting the computer's time and date

▶ Changing to a different printer

▶ Making cool barf sounds with multimedia

▶ Looking at the 386 Enhanced mode and swap files

▶ Playing with new modes

. . . .

*I*n a way, working with Windows is like remodeling a bathroom. You can spend time on the practical things, like calculating the optimum dimensions for piping or choosing the proper brand of caulking to seal the sink and tub. Or you can spend your time on the more aesthetic options, like adding an oak toilet-paper holder, a marble countertop, or a rattan cover for the Kleenex box.

You can remodel Windows, too, and in just as many ways. On the eminently practical side, head for the Windows Control Panel, call up the 386 Enhanced options, and spend hours optimizing the Virtual Memory settings.

Or check out the Control Panel's more refined options: Change the menu bars to mahogany, for example, cover the Windows desktop with marble, or cover the background with rattan patterns.

This chapter shows you how to turn Windows into that program you've always dreamed of owning someday. (Although you *still* can't have bay windows...)

Looking at the Control Panel

The Control Panel is the cupboard that holds most of the Windows switches. Flip open the Control Panel, and you can while away an entire workday adjusting all the various Windows options.

To get to the action, double-click on the Control Panel icon in the Program Manager's Main window. The Control Panel's icon looks like this:

Control Panel

When the Control Panel opens on the screen, as shown in Figure 10-1, you see even more icons. Each one hides switches that control different parts of the computer.

Mouseless users can choose an icon by pressing the cursor-control keys until they have highlighted the icon they want; then press Enter.

Everybody's Control Panel looks different because everybody can afford different computer toys. For example, some people have special icons for *MIDI keyboards,* those synthesizers you see hooked up to laptops at rock concerts. Others have icons that help them agonize over their network settings. Table 10-1 takes a look at what each icon hides.

Each of these options is discussed in more glowing detail later in this chapter.

You don't have to keep referring to this chapter to find out what each icon does. When you select an icon, its job description appears at the bottom of the window.

When Windows refers to 386 Enhanced mode, it's talking about 486 and Pentium computers, too.

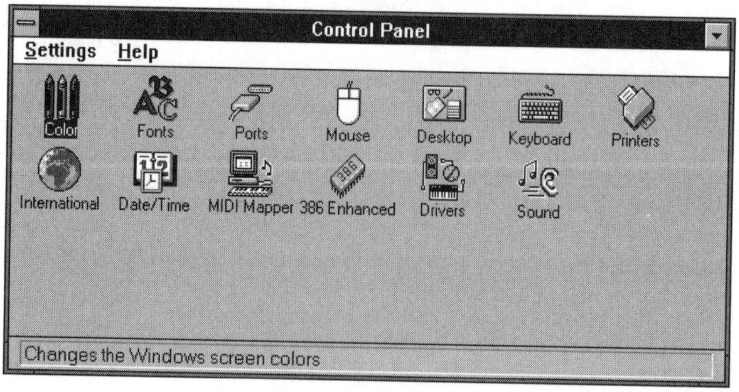

Figure 10-1:
Double-click
on an icon in
the Control
Panel to
reveal
hidden
switches
for that
particular
area.

Control Panel
Settings Help
Color Fonts Ports Mouse Desktop Keyboard Printers
International Date/Time MIDI Mapper 386 Enhanced Drivers Sound
Changes the Windows screen colors

Table 10-1	Deciphering the Control Panel Icons
This Icon	*Does This*
Color	Windows installs boring colors at first. You use the Color icon to liven things up by changing the colors of the bars, buttons, background, and everything else. Fun!
Fonts	Windows comes with fonts like Arial and Courier. If you head back to the software store and buy more, like Lucida Blackletter and Lucida Handwriting, you install them by double-clicking on this icon.
Ports	If you have a *modem* or a *serial printer* plugged into the computer's rump, they're actually plugged into *ports.* This icon changes those port settings. (If your stuff already works, don't ever click here.)
Mouse	Make that mouse scoot faster across the screen, change it from right-handed to left-handed, and change all sorts of other things.
Desktop	This one provides a plethora of options to while away the day. Change the wallpaper, screen saver, and other fun stuff.
Keyboard	You can change how long the keyboard takes to repeat a letter when you hold down a key. Yawn. Rarely used.
Printers	Bought a new printer? You have to fiddle around in here to let Windows know about it.
International	Packed up the computer and moved to Sweden? Then click around in here to get those funny foreign characters.
Date/Time	Does the Windows clock tell the right time? If not, double-click here to bring things up to date.
Network	Yech. Let your network folks mess with this one. They're getting paid extra for it.
386 Enhanced	Like race-car mechanics, computer gurus with 386-class computers can fiddle around in here for hours. Don't play in here unless a nearby computer guru can serve as Safety Patrol. This is scary stuff.
Drivers	Opened your wallet for a sound card? Then open this icon to install its driver. It tells Windows what brand of sound card you decided on.
MIDI Mapper	It's used mostly by musicians with synthesizers. And it's ugly, technical stuff. Toss in a Lou Reed CD for an attitude boost before entering the grim world of Source Channels and Patch Names.
Sound	The most fun! Make Windows play different sounds for different events. For example, hear a cool Pink Floyd riff whenever a Windows error message pops up on the screen.

Customizing the Desktop

By far, the most often-used part of the Control Panel is the Desktop icon, which looks like this:

By opening this door, you can change the wallpaper, screen saver, and other visual aspects of the Windows desktop (see Figure 10-2).

Unlike other switches in the Control Panel, the Desktop icon doesn't control anything too dangerous. Feel free to fiddle around with all the settings. You can't cause any major harm. If you do want to play, however, be sure to write down any original settings. Then you can always return to normal if something looks odd.

Changing the wallpaper

When Windows first installs itself, it paints a dull gray background across the screen and then starts sprinkling windows and icons over it. Windows *has* to choose that dull gray in the beginning, or nobody would think it's a *serious business application.*

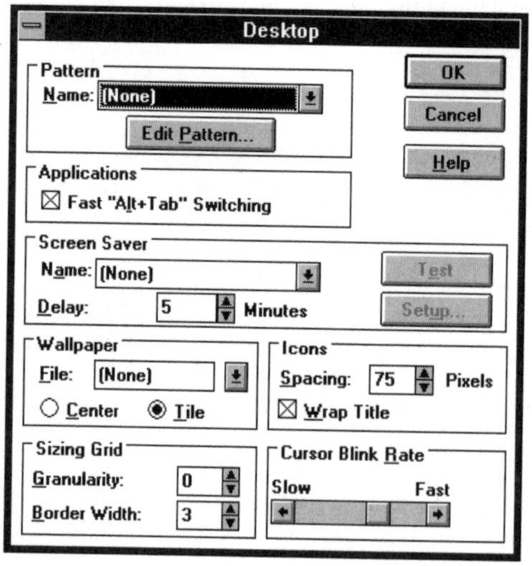

Figure 10-2:
The Desktop
dialog box
offers a
plethora of
options to
fiddle with.

However, Microsoft snuck more than a dozen other backgrounds, known as *wallpaper,* into the Windows box. Those pieces of wallpaper are hiding on the hard drive, just waiting to be installed. Different wallpaper can reflect different personalities (see Figure 10-3). For example, you can turn the window's background into of pile of fallen autumn leaves. You can choose an argyle pattern that matches your socks. Or you can create your own wallpaper in Paintbrush and hang it yourself.

To change the wallpaper, double-click on the Desktop icon. A rather large dialog box appears (see Figure 10-2). Look for the word Wallpaper next to a drop-down list box and click on the downward-pointing arrow by the box (see Figure 10-4).

If you aren't using a mouse, you can select an item in a list box by using the arrow keys to highlight the item you want and then pressing Enter. (In a long list, you can get to the item more quickly by pressing the first letter in the item's name.)

Click on the scroll bar to see all the possible wallpaper files. When you see the filename of the wallpaper you want, select it. Then choose the OK command button. The dialog box disappears, and you are back at the Control Panel (with the new wallpaper displayed proudly in the background). Double-click on the Control Panel's top left-hand corner (its Control-menu box), and it disappears as well.

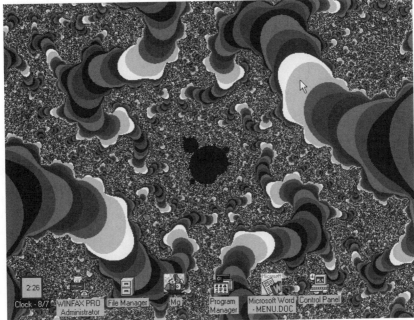

Figure 10-3:
Windows wallpaper, that backdrop beneath all the windows and icons, can match your mood for the day.

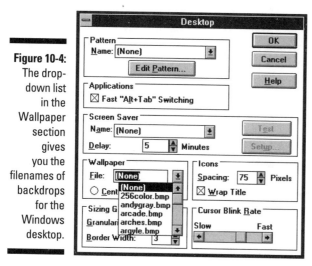

Figure 10-4:
The drop-
down list
in the
Wallpaper
section
gives
you the
filenames of
backdrops
for the
Windows
desktop.

Wallpaper can be *tiled* across the screen or *centered.* Small pictures should be *tiled,* or painted repeatedly across the screen. Larger pictures look best when they're centered. Select the option button next to your preference. Or try them both and then choose the one you like best.

Wallpaper files are merely *bitmaps,* or files created in Windows Paintbrush. (Bitmap files end with the letters BMP.) Anything you create in Windows Paintbrush can be used as wallpaper. In fact, you can even use Paintbrush to alter the wallpaper Microsoft provided with Windows.

Windows can use only wallpaper that's stored directly in the Windows directory. If you create a potential wallpaper in Paintbrush, you have to move the file to the Windows directory before it shows up in the Desktop dialog box's master list. If this concept seems strange, foreign, confusing, or all three, then check out Chapter 12 for more information about directories and moving files between them.

Wallpaper looks like a lot of fun, but it may be *too much* fun if your computer doesn't have at least 2MB of RAM. Wallpaper can use up a great deal of the computer's memory, consistently slowing Windows down. If you find yourself running out of memory, change the wallpaper to the (None) option. The screen won't look as pretty, but at least Windows will work.

Small files that are *tiled* across the screen take up much less memory than large files that are *centered* on the screen. If Windows seems slow or it sends you furtive messages saying it's running out of memory, try tiling some smaller bits of wallpaper. Also try black-and-white wallpaper; it doesn't slow down Windows as much.

Adding or changing patterns

The Pattern option sprinkles tiny lines and dots across the screen. To add or change those sprinkles, click on the downward-pointing arrow in the Pattern section, the topmost section in the Desktop dialog box (see Figure 10-2). Choose from the patterns Microsoft provided or, if you're desperate for something to do, click on the Edit Pattern button to create your own little patterns.

> ✔ I'm not going to discuss patterns much because they're just plain dumb. Patterns obscure the titles underneath the icons, making them difficult to read at the bottom of the screen. Try it out yourself. Then click on the (None) option in the Name drop-down list to get rid of them.

> ✔ In order to see patterns across the back of the desktop, you need to change the wallpaper option to (None). Otherwise, the patterns just show up behind the icon titles at the bottom of the screen (making them difficult to read).

Choosing the Fast "Alt+Tab" Switching option

By all means, turn on the Fast "Alt+Tab" Switching option listed in the Applications section of the Desktop dialog box. (You see it near the top half of Figure 10-4.) If there is no X in that option's box, click in the box. If the box has an X, the option is already turned on.

This option enables you to easily switch between windows by holding down the Alt key and pressing Tab. Each press of Tab brings the name of another window to the screen. When you see the name of the window you want, let go of the Alt key and watch as the window magically appears. It's fast and convenient.

Using the Screen Saver option

In the dinosaur days of computing, computer monitors were permanently damaged when an oft-used program burned its image onto the screen. The program's faint outlines showed up even when the monitor was turned off.

To prevent this *burn-in*, people installed a *screen saver* to jump in when a computer hadn't been used for a while. The screen saver would either blank the screen or fill it with wavy lines to keep the program's display from etching itself into the screen.

Today's monitors don't really have this problem, but people use screen savers anyway — mainly because they look cool.

✔ Windows comes with several screen savers built in, although none of them is activated at first. To set one up, click on the downward-pointing arrow in the Screen Saver box and then select the screen saver you want. (***Hint:*** Starfield Simulation looks cool.)

✔ Immediately after choosing a screen saver, click on the T<u>e</u>st command button to see what the screen saver looks like. Wiggle the mouse or press the spacebar to come back to Windows.

✔ Fiddlers can click on Set<u>u</u>p for more options. For example, you can set a password, and then when the screen saver kicks in, you won't be able to see the screen again until you type in the password. When you've forgotten your password, turn to Chapter 17 for help.

✔ Click on the up or down arrows next to Minutes to tell the screen saver when to kick in. If it's set to 5, for example, Windows waits until you haven't touched the mouse or keyboard for 5 minutes before letting the screen saver out of its cage.

Arranging icons

Sometimes the icons along the bottom of the screen or in Program Manager can overlap. To change their distance from each other, click on the arrows next to the word <u>S</u>pacing in the Icons section of the Desktop dialog box. The bigger the number of pixels, the farther apart they'll sit from each other.

✔ Click on the <u>W</u>rap Title check box to keep icons with long titles from banging into each other.

✔ The new spacing doesn't take place until you call up the Task List and click on the <u>A</u>rrange Icons option, which is described in the Task List section of Chapter 7. (If you've clicked on the Program Manager's <u>A</u>uto Arrange option from its <u>O</u>ptions menu, the icons update themselves immediately, too. If not, click on <u>W</u>indow on the Program Manager's menu bar and then click on <u>A</u>rrange Icons to see the change.)

Sizing the grid

Normally, Windows lets you drop the windows wherever you put them. If you want Windows to keep things rigidly aligned, however, increase the number in the <u>G</u>ranularity box, which is in the Sizing Grid section of the Desktop dialog box. Windows creates an invisible *grid* based on that number. The bigger the number, the more pronounced the grid.

Then, when you release a window on the desktop, Windows forces the window to line up with the grid.

> ✔ The grid can be very confusing if you don't know what's going on. The windows won't drop where you want them to drop.

> ✔ Even when the grid is set to 0, a tiny grid is still in effect, so some of the windows move just a tiny bit when you drop them. You can't do anything to combat this feature, even if you find it annoying as all get out.

> ✔ In the Sizing Grid section, you also can adjust the window's *border,* that skinny edge you can drag to change the window's size. Most people just leave it at 3. No sense messing with something that isn't broken (unless you're using a laptop and think that a wider border would be easier to handle with that clunky old trackball).

Determining the cursor blink rate

Don't like the way the cursor blinks? Then either speed it up or slow it down by sliding the scroll box toward the words Fast or Slow in the Cursor Blink Rate section of the Desktop dialog box.

> ✔ If you don't know what a *scroll box* is, reach for your back pocket and pull out your field guide, Chapter 6.

> ✔ Laptop users may want to increase the blink rate to make the cursor a little easier to spot.

Getting Better Colors

If you paid extra for a fancy color monitor, the time has come to put it to use. You can make Windows appear in any color you want by clicking on the little crayons in the Control Panel:

Color

The Color dialog box opens up, enabling you to choose between several Microsoft-designed color schemes or to create your own. (Tell your boss that a more pleasant color scheme will enhance your productivity.) Figure 10-5 shows the Color dialog box.

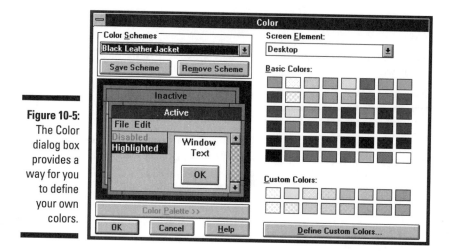

Figure 10-5:
The Color dialog box provides a way for you to define your own colors.

To choose between previously designed color schemes, click on the drop-down list box beneath the words Color Schemes and then click on the scheme you want to try out. Each time you select a new one, the sample window below the Color Schemes section shows you how it looks. If you want to change a color scheme slightly, click on the Color Palette command button, and you can assign different colors to different sections.

And, if you want even more choices, you can mix your *own* colors by clicking on the Define Custom Colors command button.

Feel free to play around with the colors, trying out Black Leather Jacket and Hot Dog Stand. Or design your own combinations. Playing with the colors is an easy way to learn the different window components by name. It's also a fun way to work with dialog boxes. But if you goof something awful, and all the letters suddenly disappear, click the Cancel button. (It's the button on the bottom, second from the left.)

  ✔ Windows continues to display the newly chosen colors until you head back to the Colors icon and change them again.

  ✔ Laptop users should try the color schemes beginning with the letters *LCD*. They are designed especially for visibility on a laptop's monochrome screen.

Understanding the Fuss about TrueType Fonts

In the first few versions of Windows, the *fonts,* or sets of letters, numbers, and other characters, produced individual letters and numbers that looked kind of jagged. A capital A, for example, didn't have smooth, diagonal lines. Instead, the sides had rough ridges that stuck out. They usually looked fine on the printer but pretty awful on the screen, especially when the headlines were in large letters.

Windows 3.1 introduced a new font technology called TrueType fonts to eliminate the jaggies and make the screen more closely match what comes out of the printer.

Double-click on the Control Panel's Fonts icon to check out the Windows fonts, install additional fonts, or delete the ugly ones:

Note: You'll probably never need to fiddle with the Fonts icon. Just know it's there in case you ever want to get fancy and install more fonts on your computer. So pretend the technical sidebar about TrueType stuff doesn't even exist.

Fonts take up a great deal of space on the hard drive. If you installed some that you no longer use, delete them. Double-click on the Control Panel's Fonts icon, click on the name of the font you no longer use, and then click on the Remove option button. A box appears, asking whether you're *sure* that you want to remove it. Before clicking on the Yes button, click on the check box marked Delete Font File From Disk. Otherwise, Windows removes that font only from the program's font menus, and the font file still clogs up the hard drive.

Just what is this TrueType stuff, anyway?

In early versions of Windows, people with fancy fonts had a problem. They could create some fine-looking documents that would have raised a smile from Gutenberg himself. But, when they copied a document to a disk and gave it to somebody else, that person couldn't see those same fancy fonts. Only people who had those same fancy fonts already installed on their computer could see the document the way it was supposed to look.

TrueType fixes that problem handily by embedding the font in the document itself. You can create a letter in Write by using fancy TrueType fonts; when you give a disk with the letter on it to a friend, that person can see the same fonts in the letter even if those fonts aren't installed on their computer.

At least, the True Type fonts included with Windows will work that way; sometimes other True Type fonts won't embed themselves.

Also, TrueType fonts are *scalable.* You can make them bigger or smaller, and they still look nice. Earlier font technology required a different set of fonts for each size. The files were pretty hoggy compared with TrueType technology.

Most people get along fine with the fonts that are included with Windows, so they never have to worry about TrueType or how it works.

Making Windows Recognize Your Double-Click

Clicking twice on a mouse button is called a double-click; you do a lot of double-clicking in Windows. But sometimes you can't click fast enough to suit Windows. It thinks your double-clicks are just two single-clicks. If you have this problem, head for the Control Panel's Mouse icon:

Mouse

When you double-click the Mouse icon, the Mouse dialog box pops up (see Figure 10-6). If your Mouse dialog box doesn't look like the one in Figure 10-6, the company that made your mouse slipped its own box into the Control Panel. The following instructions may not work for you, but you can generally access the same types of options for any mouse. For help, try pressing F1.

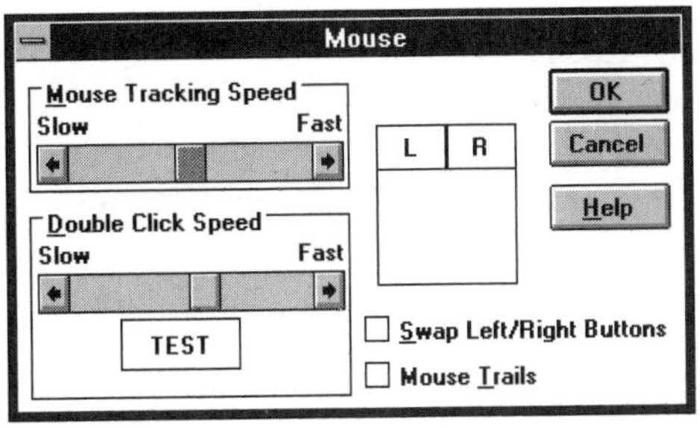

Figure 10-6:
You can use the Mouse dialog box to change the mouse's work habits.

To check the double-click speed, double-click in the box marked TEST. Each time Windows recognizes your double-click, it changes the box's color.

Slide the scroll box above the TEST box toward the words Fast or Slow until Windows successfully recognizes your double-click efforts. Click on the OK command button when you're through, and you're back in business.

- For a psychedelic experience, click in the Mouse Trails box to see *ghost arrows* follow the mouse pointer. Laptop users can spot the arrow more easily when it is followed by ghosts.

- The mouse arrow doesn't have to move at the same speed as the mouse. To make the arrow *zip* across the screen with just a tiny push, click on the Fast side of the Mouse Tracking Speed scroll bar. To slow it down, click on the Slow side.

- If you're left-handed, click on the Swap Left/Right Buttons check box. Then you can hold the mouse in your left hand and yet still click with your index finger.

- The instant you click on the Swap Left/Right Buttons check box, Windows switches the buttons. To reverse that selection, you need to click on it with the *left* button.

Setting the Computer's Time and Date

Many computer users don't bother to set the computer's clock. They just look at their wristwatches to see when it's time to stop working. But they're missing out on an important computing feature: Computers stamp new files with the current date and time. If the computer doesn't know the correct date, it stamps files with the *wrong* date. Then how can you find the files you created yesterday? Last week?

Also, Windows does some funny things to the computer's internal clock, so you may want to reset the date and time when you notice that the computer is living in the past.

To reset the computer's time or date, choose the Control Panel's Date/Time icon:

A double-click on the Date/Time icon brings a simple dialog box to the screen. Click on the number you'd like to change and then click on the up or down arrows to make the number bigger or smaller. When the time is set correctly, click on the OK command button.

✔ You need to keep the date and time set correctly if you plan to use the Windows Clock or Calendar programs.

✔ Most computers have an internal clock that automatically keeps track of the time and date. Nevertheless, Windows can slow down that clock considerably, especially when running in 386 Enhanced mode.

Adding or Removing a Printer

Most of the time, the printer will work fine. Especially after you turn it *on* and try printing again. In fact, most people will never need to read this section.

Occasionally, however, you may need to tweak some printer settings. You'll need to install a new printer or remove one that you've sold (so it won't keep cluttering up the list of printers). Either way, start by choosing the Control Panel's Printers icon:

The Printers dialog box surfaces, as shown in Figure 10-7.

If you're installing a new printer, then grab the Windows setup disks that came in the box; you'll need them during the installation. Now, to add a new printer, click on the Add command button.

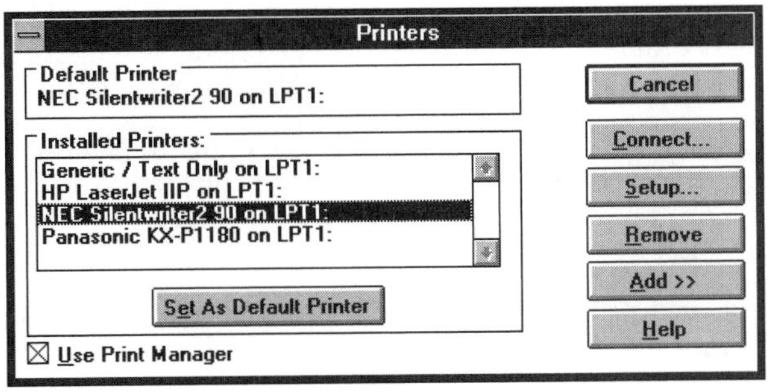

Figure 10-7:
Install new
printers in
the Printers
dialog box or
fiddle with
the ones you
already
have.

Déjà vu! You see the same list of printers as when you first installed Windows. Now, just as before, press the PgUp or PgDn key until you see the new printer listed. Press Enter or double-click on the printer's name. Windows asks you to stick one of the setup disks into a drive, and the drive makes some grinding noises.

After a moment, you see the new printer listed in the box. Choose the Set As Default Printer command button and then click on the Close button. If you're like most people, your printer will work like a charm. If it doesn't, then you may have to wade through the technical stuff in the sidebar about printer ports and such.

Printer ports and configuration nonsense

Windows shoots information to printers through ports, little metal outlets on the computer's rump. Most printers connect to a port called *LPT1:*, or the first *line printer port.*

Always choose this option first. If it works, then skip the rest of this technical chatter. You've already found success!

Some people, however, insist on plugging computers into a second printer port, or *LPT2:*. (If you meet one of these people, ask them why.) Still other people buy *serial* printers, which plug into *serial ports* (also known as *COM ports*).

Different brands of printers work with Windows in different ways, but here are a few tips: To connect a printer to a different port, click on the Connect command button. From there, you can select the

port you want. Look to see what port you're plugging the printer into and select that port from the menu. (Computer ports are rarely labeled, so you'll probably have to bribe a computer guru to help you out. Start tossing Cheet-os around your chair and desk; they're attracted by the smell.)

If you're connecting a printer to a serial port, you need to do one more little chore: configure the serial port. Click on the Settings box and make sure that the following numbers and characters appear, in this order: 9600, 8, N, and 1.

The printer should be all set. If not, call over a computer guru. At least you only have to go through all this printer hassle once — unless you buy another printer.

✔ To remove a printer you no longer use, click on its name and then click on the <u>R</u>emove command button. That printer's name will no longer appear as an option when you try to print from a Windows program.

✔ You can change most of the printer options in the program you're printing from. Click on <u>F</u>iles in the menu bar and then click on P<u>r</u>int Setup. From there, you can access the same box of printer options as you find in the Control Panel.

✔ Some fancy laser printers offer a wide variety of options, like printing from different paper trays or printing at different resolutions. To play with these options, click on the <u>S</u>etup button. Yet another box appears, listing the settings for that particular printer. You can go even further with some of the fancier printers by clicking on an <u>O</u>ptions button for a second box and then deeper still by clicking on an <u>A</u>dvanced button.

✔ If the printer isn't listed in the Windows master list, then you'll have to contact the printer's manufacturer for a *driver*. When it comes in the mail, repeat the process for adding a printer but select the first listed option that comes up: Install Unlisted or Updated Printer. Windows asks you to stick in the manufacturer's disk so it can copy the *driver* onto the hard disk. (For more information, check out the section in Chapter 17 on installing a new driver.)

✔ Working with printers can be more complicated than trying to retrieve a stray hamster from under the kitchen cupboards. Feel free to use any of the Help buttons in the dialog boxes. Chances are they'll offer some helpful advice, and some are actually customized for your particular brand of printer. Too bad they can't catch hamsters.

Making Cool Barf Sounds with Multimedia

The term *multimedia* means mixing two or more mediums — usually combining sound and pictures. A plain old television, for example, could be called a *multimedia tool,* especially if you're trying to impress somebody.

Windows can mix sound and pictures if you have a *sound card:* a gizmo costing about $100 that slips inside the computer and hooks up to a pair of speakers or a stereo.

Macintosh computers have had sound for years. And for years, Mac owners have been able to *assign sounds to system events.* In lay language, that means having the computer make a barfing sound when it ejects a floppy disk.

In Windows, you can't assign sounds to the floppy drives, but you can assign noises to other *events* by double-clicking on the Control Panel's Sound icon:

The Sound dialog box appears, as shown in Figure 10-8. Windows comes with sounds for seven system events. An event can be anything as simple as when a dialog box pops up or when Windows first starts up in the morning.

Windows lists the events on the left side of the box and the sounds on the right. Click on the event first and then click on the sound you want to hear for that event. In the preceding example, Windows makes a barfing sound whenever it sends out an urgent dialog box with an exclamation point in it.

> ✔ To take advantage of this multimedia feature, you have to buy and install a sound card. Then you have to install a *driver,* so you need to turn to the section in Chapter 17 on installing a new driver.

> ✔ To hear a sound before you assign it, click on its name and then click on Test.

> ✔ You can record your own sounds for most sound cards. You can probably pick up a cheap microphone at Radio Shack; most sound cards don't include one.

> ✔ Be forewarned: Sound consumes a *lot* of disk space, so stick with short recordings — pertinent B.B. King guitar riffs, for example, or the sound of a doorbell ringing.

> ✔ Several third-party companies sell cool sound stuff for Windows. Check out Chapter 23 for more sound tricks.

Figure 10-8:
You can use the Sound dialog box to assign sounds to seven system events.

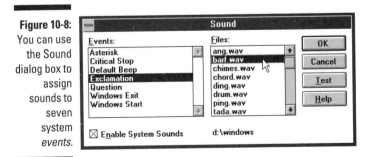

Learning Which Icons to Avoid

Unless you have a very pressing reason, avoid these icons in the Control Panel:

Network   International   Ports   Keyboard

- ✔ The Network icon controls how Windows talks to other computers through your office's network — those cables meandering from PC to PC. Talk to your network administrator before playing with this icon *just to see what it does.*

- ✔ The International icon changes the keyboard layout to the one used by people in other countries. It doesn't make the Windows dialog boxes appear in German (although you can order the German version of Windows from Microsoft). Instead, a foreign keyboard layout makes certain keys produce foreign characters. It also changes the way currency appears and stuff like that. You can easily leave the keyboard set for Taiwan by accident, and then you wonder why the time and date look funny.

- ✔ If you're into the Dvorak keyboard layout, it is listed here as well.

- ✔ The Ports icon changes the way Windows sends and receives data from the COM port. Chances are it's already set up correctly unless you're installing a network.

- ✔ The Keyboard icon doesn't do any major damage, but it doesn't do any major good, either. It just controls how fast a key repeats if you hold it down. Big deal. If the keyboard isn't mmmaking characters repeat, then don't messssssss with it.

Examining Scary 386 Enhanced and Swap Files Stuff

When Windows installed itself, it took a gander at the parts inside the computer and then set itself up to work with them in the most efficient way. So, unless smoke is coming out of the exhaust pipe, don't mess with the 386 Enhanced icon:

386 Enhanced

Windows treats 386, 486, and Pentium computers the same way. If Windows mentions 386, it *really* means 386, 486, and Pentium computers.

Windows enthusiasts with 386-class computers tinker with this icon to fine-tune the way Windows uses memory and connects to modems and printers. Everybody else leaves it alone. So you should skip past the ruggedly technical drivel in the sidebar about 386 Enhanced stuff.

What's this 386 Enhanced stuff?

Computers with a 386-class microprocessor can handle programs slightly differently from computers with the earlier breed of chips. Older chips could run only one program at a time. But the 386-class computers can jump into a special 386-protected mode, where they can run a bunch of programs at the same time. (You can read more about that protected stuff in Chapter 15.)

When Windows runs a bunch of programs at the same time, they often fight over who gets to play with different parts of the computer. Sometimes two programs want to use the printer at the same time, for example, and then the settings in the 386 Enhanced area come in. Windows has to play day-care worker and dish out the computer's resources so everybody gets a chance at them.

Windows probably chose the correct settings when it installed itself. But here's what the 386 Enhanced area does anyway:

Device Contention

Windows decides who gets what and when. Windows can handle *sharing* problems in one of the following ways:

1. **It can always warn you when two programs want the same device.**

2. **It can never warn you when two programs want the same device.**

3. **It can turn the device over to a second program when the first one is finished or hasn't used it for a while.**

Different settings apply to different computers, but here's my experience: The <u>N</u>ever Warn option is dumb. You want to know about fights so you can break them up. The <u>A</u>lways Warn option works better. Still, I've had the best luck with the <u>I</u>dle option set to 2 seconds. At that setting, if one program hasn't touched the device for the past 2 seconds, Windows lets the other program use it. It has worked well for me, but, as they say on TV, your mileage may vary.

Scheduling

When Windows runs in the special 386 Enhanced mode, it's running several programs at the same time. In a way, what it is doing is similar to what a mother baboon does when she has eight nipples and 12 babies. The mother baboon decides who gets which nipple, and for how long, before moving on to the next baby. Windows decides which program gets processor time, and how much time it gets, before moving on to the next program.

Minimum timeslice: This option specifies how many milliseconds of processor time each program gets before Windows moves to the next program. If the number is small, Windows moves more quickly. A larger number gives each program more time. If you set the number too low, the programs look as if they're running more smoothly, but watch out: Windows spends too much time shifting its attention between the programs, and everything slows down. If the number is set too high, the programs run jerkily as Windows switches its attention back and forth between them.

(continued)

(continued)

Windows in Foreground: This option specifies the proportion of processor time parceled out when a *Windows* program is the active window.

Windows in Background: This option specifies the proportion of processor time parceled out when a *DOS* program is the active window.

Exclusive in Foreground: If you check this box, the Windows active program gets *all* the processor time, and any DOS programs in the background don't run (not good if you're running Procomm in the background to grab your e-mail).

The moral? Don't mess with these settings unless you have a good reason to mess with them or too much time on your hands.

Virtual Memory

When Windows runs in 386 Enhanced mode, it can use more memory than the computer actually owns. How? It grabs some of the hard drive and stashes memory information there. This method is slower than using RAM, but, hey, it works. This chunk of hard drive space is called a *swap file*.

Permanent/temporary: Windows works faster if you choose a *permanent* swap file. Windows then grabs a large chunk of the hard drive for its exclusive use. Unfortunately, that permanent swap file *stays* permanent, even when you're not using Windows. But it's faster. When Windows works with a *temporary* swap file, it runs more slowly. But Windows creates the file when it starts and erases it when it's finished. Windows chooses the optimum size for the swap drive, so don't bother changing the settings. It usually won't even let you try.

The Windows temporary swap file is called WIN386.SWP. You can delete it if Windows happens to leave it lying around. (Make sure that you're *really* out of Windows before you delete it, however, and not just *shelled* to DOS.)

The permanent swap file consists of two different files, SPART.PAR and 386SPART.PAR. The first file sits in the Windows directory; the second file is hidden on the root directory. Don't mess with either of them.

Finally, you can't put a swap file on a disk that's compressed by Stacker or other third-party compression programs.

Use 32-Bit Disk Access: Most newer hard drives can handle 32-bit access, which makes Windows run a little faster. But, if you have a laptop with a battery-powered hard drive, don't select this option! Windows can't understand what's happening when the rechargeable batteries start to drain. Also, some older hard drives don't work with this option. Moral? Back up everything on the hard drive and try it out. If it works, keep it there. If it doesn't work, then reinstall everything on the hard drive.

The point to all this? You can spend hours fiddling with this stuff, just as you can spend hours tuning your car. I sure did. And, after the novelty wore off, I came to the conclusion that the Windows default settings were probably just as good as any other settings. (I take my car in to the shop to be tuned now, too.)

Playing with New Video Modes

Just as Windows can print to hundreds of different brands of printers, it can accommodate zillions of different monitors, too. It can even display different *video modes* on the same monitor.

For example, Windows can display different amounts of color on-screen or it can shrink the size of everything, packing more information onto the screen. The number of colors and the size of the information on-screen comprises a *video mode.*

Some Windows programs only work in a specific video mode, and they casually ask you to switch to that mode. Huh?

Here's what's happening: Monitors plug into a special jack on the back of the computer. That jack connects to a *video card* — the gizmo that translates your computer's language into something you can see on the monitor. That card handles all the video mode switches. By making the card switch between modes, you can send more or fewer colors to your monitor or pack information onto the screen.

To make a video card switch to a different video mode, call the Windows Setup program into service. Start by double-clicking on the Windows Setup icon; it's in the Main window of the Program Manager:

The Setup program leaps to the screen. Click on Options from its menu bar and then click on Change System Settings. Finally, click on the downward-pointing arrow next to the Display box. After all that clicking, you see the screen shown in Figure 10-9.

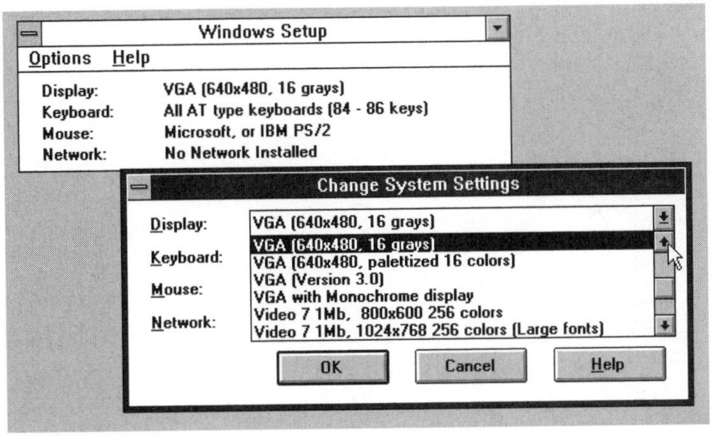

Figure 10-9:
The Setup program enables most monitors to display Windows in different video modes.

Windows Setup

Options   Help

Display: VGA (640x480, 16 grays)
Keyboard: All AT type keyboards (84 - 86 keys)
Mouse: Microsoft, or IBM PS/2
Network: No Network Installed

Change System Settings

Display: VGA (640x480, 16 grays)

Keyboard: VGA (640x480, 16 grays)
             VGA (640x480, palettized 16 colors)
Mouse: VGA (Version 3.0)
             VGA with Monochrome display
Network: Video 7 1Mb, 800x600 256 colors
             Video 7 1Mb, 1024x768 256 colors (Large fonts)

OK   Cancel   Help

Here, you can select the video mode you want to see on-screen. Make sure that the card and monitor are physically capable of displaying that mode, however, before you start playing around in here.

Windows comes with drivers for many popular video cards and monitors — not all of them work with your particular computer. If you choose a video mode that your card or monitor can't support, you can't see Windows anymore. You're safest when choosing modes that say "VGA" and "640 × 480" somewhere in their names.

✔ Monitors and cards can display Windows in different *resolutions*. The higher the resolution, the more information Windows can pack onto the screen. (And the smaller the windows become, too.) For more information about this monitor/card/resolution stuff, troop over to Chapter 2 and read the section about computer parts that I told you to ignore.

✔ New video cards usually come with a disk that contains special information called a *driver*. Windows should ask you to insert this disk when you're changing video modes by using the Windows Setup program.

✔ The more colors you ask Windows to display, the slower it runs. Usually, it's best to stick with 16 or 256 colors unless you have a fancy video card and a fancy monitor to go with it.

If you'll be looking at pictures by using Kodak's PhotoCD technology, you'll probably want Windows to display as many colors as possible — often 65,000 or 1.6 million. Switch back to fewer colors when you're done, however, if Windows starts running too slowly.

If Windows refuses to load after you choose a new video mode, you're stuck in DOS. Switch to your Windows directory and type the command **SETUP.** When the DOS version of the Windows Setup program arises, choose VGA from among the various Display options. Doing so should bring Windows back to the screen.

Part III
Using Windows Applications (Those Free Programs)

The 5th Wave

By Rich Tennant

"IT'S AMAZING HOW MUCH MORE SOME PEOPLE CAN GET OUT OF A PC THAN OTHERS."

In this part...

Did you know that

- ✔ Kleenex were called *Celluwipes* back in 1924?

- ✔ Fred MacMurray's face was the model for comic book hero Captain Marvel?

- ✔ Smokey the Bear's first name was *Hot Foot Teddy?*

- ✔ Windows comes with a bunch of *free* programs that aren't even mentioned on the outside of the box?

This part takes a look at all the stuff you're getting for nothing. Well, for the price on your sales receipt, anyway.

Chapter 11
The Ever-Present Program Manager

*I*n the old days of computing, pale technoweenies typed disgustingly long strings of code words into computers to make them do something. *Anything.*

Windows brings computers to the age of modern convenience: To start a program, click a button. Just one obstacle remains — which button? Welcome to the ultimate elevator panel: the Windows Program Manager and its layers of nested buttons.

This chapter tells you how to make the Program Manager more helpful so you can get into your programs faster.

The Program Manager's Reason to Live

The Program Manager may look complicated, but it's really just a big panel of buttons. Each button, called an *icon,* is connected to one of your programs by an invisible wire. By double-clicking on an icon, you tell a program to jump to the screen and get ready for action.

To choose an icon, double-click on it. That icon's program begins running.

Mouseless users can choose an icon by pressing the cursor-control keys until they have highlighted the desired icon; then press Enter.

About all Program Manager is good for, really, is starting programs. But, boy, it sure lets you set up those little buttons in a bunch of different ways. For example, you can create a separate panel, or *window,* of icons for each of your projects. To work on a project, call up that project's window of buttons. Every program you need for that project is right there, ready to be turned on.

The Program Manager is the first Windows program to appear on the screen. It's also the last: When you close the Program Manager, you're also telling Windows to shut down for the day.

My Program Manager looks like the one shown in Figure 11-1. But just as my car's back seat looks different from yours, your Program Manager is probably arranged a little differently to reflect your different computing tasks.

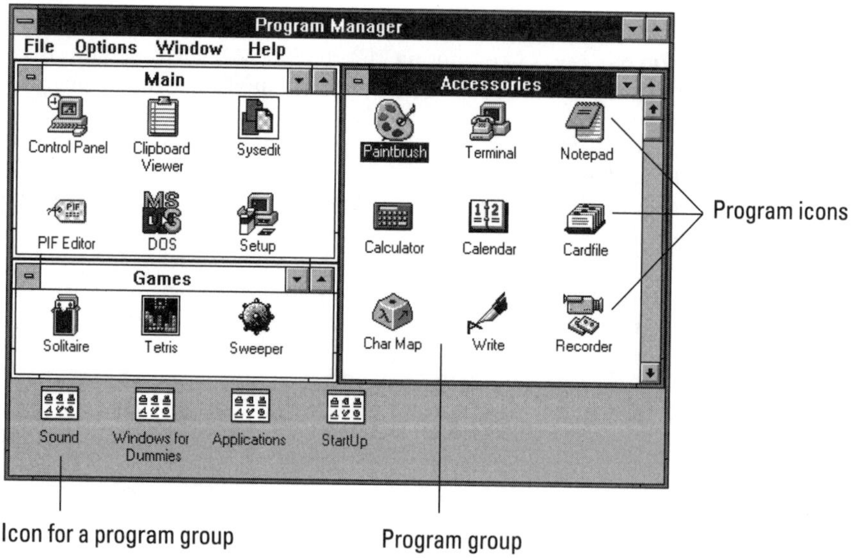

Figure 11-1:
Each button, or icon, in the Program Manager stands for one of your programs.

Icon for a program group   Program group

See the icons for games stored in the window called Games? That Games window is called a *program group*. It's just a fancy name for a panel, or window, that contains a bunch of related buttons.

Program group windows work just like any other kind of window, with one major exception: They're stuck inside the Program Manager, never to escape. You really wouldn't want them to escape, though. You'd never find your icons again.

- ✔ At first glance, the Program Manager seems foreign and scary, like something stuck beneath the table at a fancy restaurant. Just think of the Program Manager as something simple: a panel of buttons that can start your programs.

- ✔ The Program Manager's buttons are called *icons*. (No relation to the stuff hanging on church walls.) Icons sometimes look like their programs. An icon for a paint program looks like an artist's palette, for example.

- ✔ You can arrange the icons any way you like. You can put icons for similar programs or projects in their own separate windows, or *program groups*.

- ✔ Some program group windows have so many icons stuffed in them, you can't see them all. If some icons are hanging outside the edge of a window, that window will have scroll bars along an edge. Click on the scroll bar, and the icons *scroll* into view. Don't know what a scroll bar is? Then reach into your back pocket and pull out Chapter 6, your field guide to the buttons, bars, and boxes in Windows.

- ✔ The icons in the Program Manager are not *programs*. They're just *buttons* that access those programs. If you delete an icon, you haven't deleted the actual *program*, just as the fourth floor isn't wiped out if its button falls off in the elevator. To put the button back on, see the section "Putting a Favorite Program's Icon into the Program Manager" or see the building superintendent.

- ✔ Like any other window, the Program Manager can be shrunk to an icon and left at the bottom of the screen until you want it back. The icon looks like this:

Program
Manager

When you need to see the Program Manager again, double-click on its icon, and it jumps back up to its former size.

Turning Program Groups into Icons and Back Again

Hurrah! There's nothing new and complicated in this section. That's because the windows *inside* the Program Manager work just like the windows *outside* the Program Manager.

For example, you can shrink a program group window into an icon to keep it handy, just as you can shrink a normal window. Click on the program group window's downward-pointing arrow, or *minimize button,* in its top right-hand corner. The window vanishes and reappears as a handy icon at the bottom of the Program Manager's main workspace.

Unlike most icons, though, program group icons all look the same when they're lined up at the bottom of the Program Manager. Luckily, the icons are labeled so that you can tell which one is which.

To bring the program group window back up when you need it, double-click on its icon. It faithfully returns to its position as a window in the Program Manager.

✔ The Program Manager's windows behave like any other window: They have *minimize* and *maximize* buttons to make them smaller and bigger. They have *title bars* that display their names, and you can tug at their borders with a mouse to change their size. In fact, almost all the stuff about moving windows around that is covered in Chapter 7 works with the Program Manager's windows.

✔ If you try to close a Program Manager's window by double-clicking in its top left-hand corner, it doesn't close. Instead, it turns into an icon. To get rid of a window permanently, check out the "Getting Rid of Icons and Program Groups" section later in this chapter.

✔ To confuse people more efficiently, the Program Manager displays two different kinds of icons. The colorful ones in the windows launch programs. The drab ones along the Program Manager's bottom are shrunken program groups. Choose the drab icons to bring up more windows full of colorful program icons.

✔ Sometimes all the icons in the Program Manager pile up on top of each other. To align them neatly, click on one of the icons, click on Window from the menu bar, and select Arrange Icons from the pull-down menu. If you were fiddling with the program icons in a program group, they snap to attention in orderly rows. If you were working with program group icons, those icons snap to attention. But Windows won't tidy up both kinds of icons at the same time. Weird, huh?

✔ To keep your program icons orderly *all* the time, select <u>O</u>ption from the Program Manager's menu bar and then select <u>A</u>uto Arrange. (A check mark will appear next to it.) The <u>A</u>uto Arrange option makes all the program icons organize themselves automatically. Unfortunately, this trick doesn't affect the program group icons along the bottom of the Program Manager. Those icons usually stay pretty organized by themselves, but occasionally you have to use the <u>A</u>rrange Icons trick described in the preceding paragraph.

Starting a Program from the Program Manager

The Program Manager offers a zillion different ways for you to run a program, from super easy to incredibly elaborate. In this section, the different techniques are arranged from the easiest to the most challenging, with their difficulty level spelled out along the way. An IQ rating of 100 requires a little Windows know-how; the lower the IQ number, the easier the method is.

Keep the Program Manager big and bold on your screen so you can see everything inside it. (Shrink all your other programs to icons and *tile* the Program Manager across the top of the screen, as conveniently described in the section of Chapter 7 on organizing your desktop.)

Press Enter (IQ: 70)

Sometimes, you get lucky. You spot a program's icon right off the bat. Look at the icon's title; if it's highlighted with a dark bar, press Enter. The program jumps to action.

✔ When you call the Program Manager to the screen, it highlights the name of the last program you started. Just press Enter to run it again.

✔ The terms *loading, launching, starting, opening, running,* and *revvin' up a program* all mean the same thing: making a program jump up in a window on the screen so you can get some work done.

The easy double-click (IQ: 80)

Sometimes you see the icon for the program you're after, but its title isn't highlighted. Point the mouse arrow at the icon and double-click. (*Double-click* is computer-geek code talk meaning *click the mouse's left button twice in rapid succession.*) The program receiving the double-click immediately hops to the screen.

Sometimes you want a program to load itself as an *icon* at the bottom of the screen — not as a window. Hold down a Shift key while double-clicking, and the program appears as an icon at the bottom of the screen.

This technique enables you to load several programs quickly and easily: Just double-click on each icon while holding down the Shift key. Each program loads as an icon, ready to spring into action when needed.

✔ A variation of the double-click method is to click *once* and then press Enter. That technique works, but golly! It's easier to just double-click on the icon in the first place!

✔ Sometimes the icon isn't sitting in front of you. Look for *scroll bars* along the edges of the windows in the Program Manager. Click in the scroll bar, and the windows shift their contents around, letting you see more of their icons.

✔ If you *still* can't find an icon for the program, perhaps it's in a window that has been shrunk to an icon at the bottom of the Program Manager. Try double-clicking on those icons to turn them back into windows and then ferret through them to see whether the program is there. Figure 11-2 shows how the screen looks when three program group windows are open. Four more program groups are icons along the bottom.

Figure 11-2:
Double-click on
a program
group icon to
see what icons
it contains.

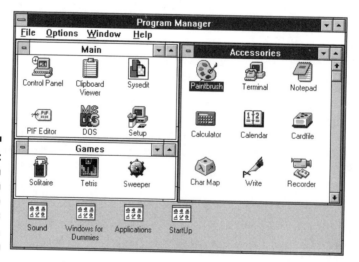

The menu launch (IQ: 100)

Highlight the title of the program you want to load by clicking once on its icon. Then select File from the Program Manager's menu bar and click on Open. The program jumps to the screen.

This method is easy enough but rarely worth bothering with. So why mention it? Because it's there. And it proves that Windows offers *so* many different ways to do the same thing that there's no point in trying to remember them all.

The keyboard launch (IQ: 120)

If you don't have a mouse, you're stuck with the awkward keyboard method. Start by holding down the Ctrl key and pressing the Tab key. With each press of the Tab key, a different program group window comes to the surface. When you see the icon you want, let go of the Ctrl key and head for the arrow keys. Press the right- or left-arrow key until you've highlighted the icon of the program you're after. Then press Enter, and that program loads.

- ✔ The mouse method is so much easier that it's ridiculous. Buy a mouse. If you have a laptop, head back to the store and buy a trackball.

- ✔ Don't see the program you want? Maybe it's in one of those program groups sitting at the bottom of the Program Manager as an icon. When the Ctrl+Tab combination highlights one of the program group icons, leggo of both keys and press Enter. That icon turns into a program group, letting you see what's inside.

- ✔ Are icons hiding outside the boundaries of a window? Press those arrow keys, and any icons outside the window move into view.

You can make the Program Manager turn itself into an icon after it launches a program so that it's out of the way and yet conveniently accessible. Click on Options in the menu bar and then select Minimize on Use from the pull-down menu. A check mark appears. The Program Manager will now squat as an icon immediately after you load any program. (If you hold down Shift while double-clicking in order to load a program as an icon, the Program Manager stays on the screen; it doesn't squat, even if you've checked the Minimize on Use option.)

The Command Line (IQ: 120)

DOS holdouts love this method. Click on File from the Program Manager's menu bar and then select Run. A frightful object called the Command Line box appears like a bad dream. Figure 11-3 shows the empty Command Line box.

Type the name of the program you're after and press Enter. If Program Manager can find the program, it loads the program.

Microsoft added the Command Line to placate die-hard DOS fans. Icon clickers never even know it's there.

The browse (IQ: 120)

Sooner or later, you'll want to run a program that's not listed on the Program Manager. Its icon just isn't listed.

If you want to put an icon for that program on the Program Manager, head for the section "Putting a Favorite Program's Icon into the Program Manager."

But, if you want to load a program *just this once,* then click on File from the Program Manager's menu bar and then select Run. When the Command Line box appears, click on its Browse button. Shazam! Yet another box appears, this time listing the programs by name.

Pick your way through the dialog box until you see the program and then select its name. The program pops to the screen.

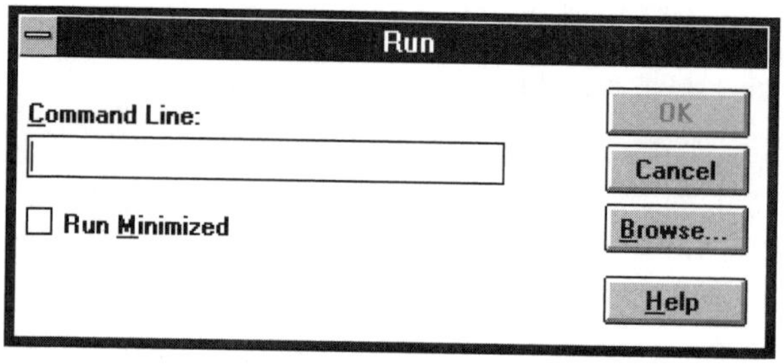

Figure 11-3:
The
Program
Manager's
Command
Line box
makes DOS
holdouts
happy.

Run

Command Line:

☐ Run Minimized

OK

Cancel

Browse...

Help

TECHNICAL STUFF

Is it a *real* DOS command line?

For the most part, Windows treats the Command Line like a regular ol' DOS command line. When you type in the name of a Windows or DOS program, Windows tries to run it. Windows first searches the current directory, and then it looks along the path. If Windows can't find the program, you see the deadly sounding "application execution error" message. (This situation is not as serious as it sounds. Choose the OK button and everything returns to normal.)

If Windows didn't find the program, you have to type in the pathname along with the program's name. For example, to load WordPerfect, you type something like this:

```
C:\WORDS\WP\WP
```

The Program Manager's Command Line differs from the DOS command line in one key area: It can't handle DOS commands like DIR and TYPE.

If you're salivating at the thought of a command line, you shouldn't be running Windows. If you're looking for a quick, menuless way to call up a program, though, you may give the Command Line a shot.

- ✔ If you don't know how to *pick your way through* this particular dialog box, head to the section of Chapter 6 on opening a file. (This dialog box rears its head every time you open or save a file.)

- ✔ Picking your way through the dialog box takes the same amount of time as slapping an icon for that program onto the Program Manager. You should probably avoid this browse method and put the icon on the Program Manager instead. You can find the program more easily the next time you want to use it, and you can see what its icon looks like. (See the "Putting a Favorite Program's Icon into the Program Manager" section later in this chapter.)

Creating Your Very Own Program Group

Sooner or later, you'll want to create your own program group. Perhaps you want to keep your adventure game icons in a separate window from your arcade game icons.

Start by clicking on File from the Program Manager's menu bar and then the word New, directly beneath it. As Figure 11-4 shows, Windows asks you to make a choice.

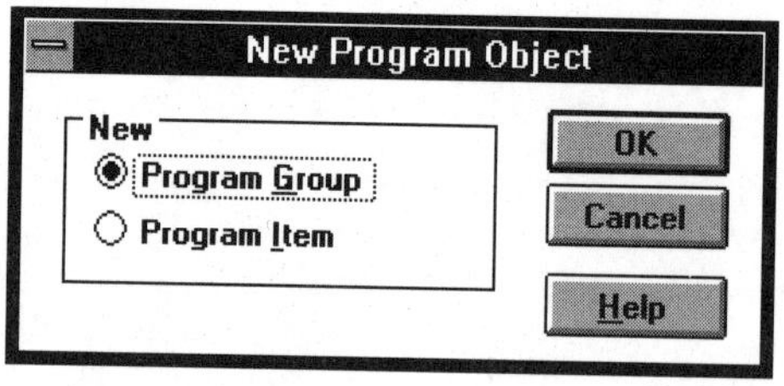

Figure 11-4:
Click on the
Program
Group
option to
create a
new
program
group.

Click on the circle next to Program Group. (The Program Item option enables you to add a single icon — not a group.) The box shown in Figure 11-5 appears.

Type in a name that describes the new program group — something like **Adv. Games**. The name will sit at the top of the new program group window.

Ignore the Group File box. In fact, you can get into more trouble by filling it out than by leaving it alone.

Press the Enter key at the end of the description, and the new, empty program group appears at the top of the Program Manager.

✔ Don't make the program group descriptions too long. When you turn a program group into an icon, the description becomes its title. Extra-long titles beneath icons bump into each other, like knees of people on airplanes.

✔ Although creating different program groups for different projects is fun, having too many program groups slows Windows down. Try dragging the icons from several program groups into one program group and then delete the old, empty ones. If you want some empty, technical talk explaining why you shouldn't have many program groups, head for Chapter 15. Otherwise, toss some salt over your shoulder and move on.

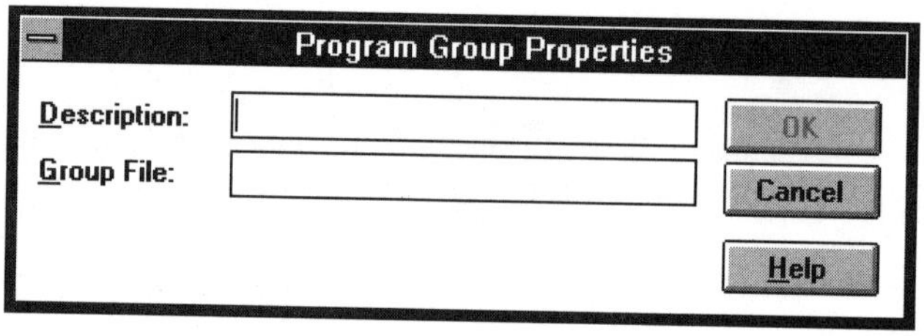

Figure 11-5:
In the
Description
box, type a
name for
the new
program
group.

Putting a Favorite Program's Icon into the Program Manager

When Windows installs itself, it snoops through your computer's hard drive to see how much software you can afford to buy. When it spots a Windows program, it automatically sticks an icon for that program into the Program Manager. When Windows sees a DOS program it recognizes, it pops an icon for that program in there, too.

Most new Windows programs automatically pop their new icon into the Program Manager when you install them. But if a program doesn't come with an installation program, you're stuck doing two steps on your own.

First, you need to copy the new program to its own directory on your hard drive. (Creating directories and copying files are covered in Chapter 12.) Next, you need to put that program's icon into Program Manager so that it will be ready for easy clicking. Windows offers a zillion different ways to add an icon to the Program Manager, but stick with the following two: Make Windows do most of the work or tackle the job yourself.

Making Windows do all the grunt work

Why bother working hard? Here's how to make Windows snoop around your hard drive, find *all* your Windows programs, and put an icon for each one into the Program Manager:

1. **Double-click on the Windows Setup icon.**

   The icon lives in the Program Manager's Main window; it's a picture of a little computer next to an open box of disks. A double-click makes the Windows Setup program rise to the screen.

2. **Click on Options from the menu and then select Set Up Applications.**

   Figure 11-6 shows what the menu looks like.

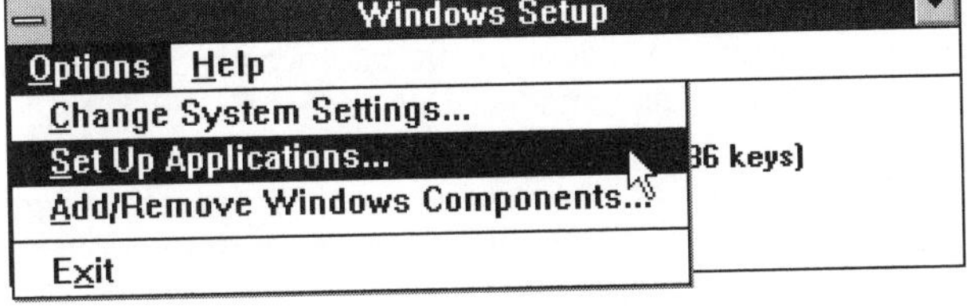

Figure 11-6:
The Windows Setup program enables you to put more icons on the Program Manager.

3. Select Search for applications and click on OK.

Chances are, your Search for applications option is already selected, as shown in Figure 11-7. If so, just click on the OK button.

4. Select the drives that Windows should search.

A box pops up, listing the word *Path* and all your computer's hard drives, as shown in Figure 11-8. Don't know which drives to search? Then make Windows search everywhere by choosing *all* the drives: Click on Path and the other listed drives until they're all highlighted.

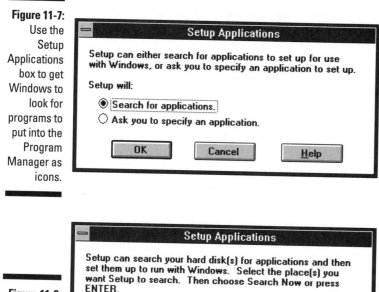

Figure 11-7:
Use the Setup Applications box to get Windows to look for programs to put into the Program Manager as icons.

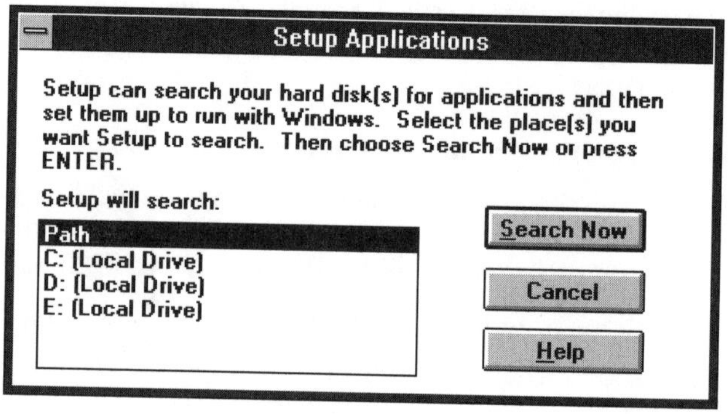

Figure 11-8:
Windows asks which drive you want it to search.

5. Click on the Search Now button.

Windows starts poking around inside your computer, looking for any Windows programs it recognizes. (It may even recognize a popular DOS program or two as well, just as it does in the "Sniffing Out Your DOS Programs" section of Chapter 3.) When Windows finishes looking, it displays a message that looks something like the one in Figure 11-9. Your screen may look different because your computer probably has different programs.

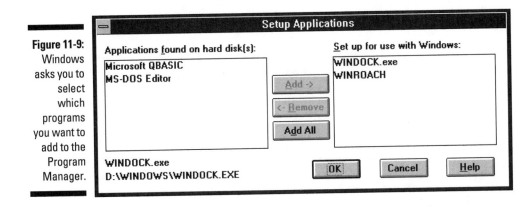

Figure 11-9:
Windows
asks you to
select
which
programs
you want to
add to the
Program
Manager.

6. Click on the programs you'd like to see as Program Manager icons.

If Windows finds several pages of program names, use the arrow keys to scroll up or down the list, clicking on the names of the programs you'd like to see listed as icons in Program Manager. Don't recognize the program names? Then click on the A̲dd All button. Doing so puts icons for *all* of those programs into Program Manager. (You can weed out the icons you don't want later.)

7. Click on the A̲dd button and then click OK.

After a flurry of activity, Windows puts icons for all your chosen programs into the Program Manager's Applications window. Finally.

✔ This process makes Windows handle the grunt work of finding programs and sticking their icons in Program Manager. However, you're still stuck with the drudgery of wading through all those boring menus.

✔ Windows finds all your Windows programs, but it can find only the most popular DOS programs. If your particular DOS program hasn't sold at least half a million copies, you probably have to install it yourself, as described in the next section.

Doing the grunt work yourself

You can stick a program's icon into the Program Manager a lot faster than Windows can. Unfortunately, you have to know exactly where that program is hiding on the hard drive. You need to know the name of the program's *directory* — its special home on your hard drive.

If you know your new program's name and directory, here's how to put its icon into Program Manager:

1. **Hold down Alt and double-click on a bare spot in the program group window.**

   For example, if you want to put your new program's icon in Program Manager's Applications window, hold down Alt and double-click on a little white spot in the Applications program group. Be careful not to click on an icon that's already living there — aim for a blank spot, like the space *between* two icons. A box leaps into action, as shown in Figure 11-10.

2. **Click on the Browse command button.**

   Yet another box leaps to the forefront, as shown in Figure 11-11. The box may look familiar; it's the same box that appears when you load a file into a program. This time, however, the box lists the names of *programs*, not data files.

3. **Double-click on the program's name and click on OK.**

   When you see the program's name listed in the File Name box, double-click on it. Don't see it? Click on the Drives box to search different drives; click on the folders in the Directories box to search other directories.

   A double-click on the program's name followed by a click on the OK button puts that particular program's icon into Program Manager.

Figure 11-10:
You can fill out the Program Item Properties form or click on Browse to avoid it.

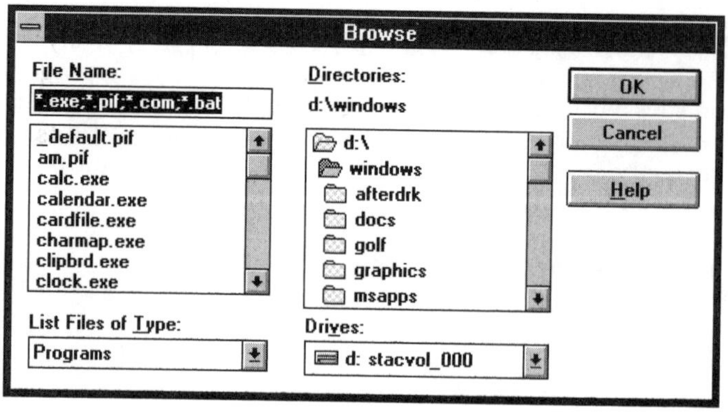

Program Item Properties

Description:
Command Line:
Working Directory:
Shortcut Key: None
☐ Run Minimized

OK
Cancel
Browse...
Change Icon...
Help

Figure 11-11:
You can use the Browse box to tell Windows what to put into the Program Manager.

Browse

File Name:
`*.exe;*.pif;*.com;*.bat`

_default.pif
am.pif
calc.exe
calendar.exe
cardfile.exe
charmap.exe
clipbrd.exe
clock.exe

Directories:
d:\windows

d:\
windows
afterdrk
docs
golf
graphics
msapps

List Files of Type:
Programs

Drives:
d: stacvol_000

OK
Cancel
Help

✔ If you're not sure how to navigate the files listed in the Browse box, check out the section in Chapter 6 on opening a file.

✔ Select a data file — say, a letter to Grandma — to give it an icon on the Program Manager. Your word processor's icon appears with the data file's name as a title beneath it. When you double-click on its icon, your word processor hops to the screen, bringing your letter to Grandma along with it.

✔ Windows automatically sticks a file's name under its icon as a title. If you want a different title, type it into the Description box in that boring Program Item Properties form. For example, you can type in *WordPerfect* rather than *WP,* the name Windows uses.

✔ Click on the Run Minimized option if you want a program to always load as an icon at the bottom of the screen — not as a full-fledged window.

✔ If you usually use a program with files in a particular directory, type the directory's name in the Working Directory box. If you don't know what a directory is, head for Chapter 12.

✔ Windows enables 386-class computer owners to type a shortcut key for a program. When you press the shortcut key, the program leaps to the top of the stack. For example, if you type a Q into the Shortcut Key box, then the program jumps to the screen when you simultaneously hold down the Ctrl and Alt keys and press Q. Shortcut keys can conflict with each other, however, so choose them carefully. Or just don't bother with them at all, like me.

✔ Don't ever try to use Ctrl+Alt+Delete as a shortcut key. Pressing those keys simultaneously tells Windows something is drastically wrong with the computer. Don't ever press that combination unless the computer is acting awfully weird — a program is frozen on the screen, for example, or the sound card is stuck in an endless screaming loop.

✔ Sick of all the dumb boxes that pop up for something as simple as adding a new icon? Then there's a quicker way: Put both the Program Manager and File Manager on the screen and then *drag* the file's name from the File Manager to a window in the Program Manager. It looks *way* cool, it's easy, and it's explained in Chapter 12.

You can change a program's settings in Program Manager at any time. Hold down Alt and double-click on its icon. Instead of loading the program, the Program Manager tosses the program's Program Item Properties form onto the screen. You can then change the program's icon, its directory, its title, and a host of other fun things.

Getting Rid of Icons and Program Groups

Tired of looking at a Program Manager icon you never use? Then dump it. Click once on the tired old icon and press Delete. Then click on the Yes button when the ever-cautious Windows asks whether you're *sure* that you want to delete it. Poof! The icon disappears.

To delete an entire program group, turn it into an icon. Then press the Delete key. Click on Yes when Windows asks whether you're sure. Schwing! The entire program group disappears.

Windows will delete a program group even if it's full of icons. Make sure that you're not deleting an entire program group when you really just want to delete one of the icons inside it.

- The undo command, Ctrl+Z, doesn't work when you've deleted an icon or a program group. You have to re-create them from scratch if you've goofed up somehow.

- You can't delete a program group as an icon when its little menu is sticking out of its head. Press Esc to make the menu disappear and then press the Delete key to vaporize the icon.

- When you delete an icon, you're not deleting the *program.* You're just deleting the button that activates the program. You need to delete the program manually if you want to remove it permanently from the hard drive. To delete the program, head for the File Manager (and Chapter 12).

Windows sets up five program groups when it first installs itself: Main, Accessories, Games, StartUp, and Applications. If you accidentally delete some of these groups, or the icons inside them, you can make Windows put them back by following the instructions in the next section.

Restoring Your Original Program Manager

Has your Program Manager lost some of the icons and program groups that it started out with? Try this trick to make Program Manager add its original icons and program groups. (Unfortunately, this trick doesn't work in Windows for Workgroups, just in plain ol' Windows.)

From the Program Manager's File menu, choose Run. Then type the following in the Command Line box:

```
SETUP /P
```

That is, you type **SETUP,** a space, a forward slash, and **P.**

Windows puts the original five groups back into the Program Manager, complete with the icons they originally contained. It may toss in a few duplicate icons, but that's probably better than not having them at all.

Tiling, Cascading, and Piling Up Program Groups

The Program Manager has its own cleaning crew that whips haphazard windows into neatly organized rows.

To *cascade* the windows, click on <u>W</u>indow from the menu bar and then select <u>C</u>ascade from the pull-down menu. Program Manager deals the program groups across the Program Manager like cards in a game of blackjack.

To *tile* the windows, click on <u>W</u>indow and then select <u>T</u>ile. All the program group windows are tiled across the screen, each one taking up the same amount of space.

✔ I don't like either command because neither one takes into account the number of icons filling a window. For example, a window with only one icon is given as much space as a window with 43 icons. I prefer to set up the windows meticulously by hand, keeping lesser used categories as icons along the bottom.

✔ When you start Windows, Program Manager doesn't remember how you last organized the program groups, even if you spent hours lining everything up just so. To force Program Manager to remember your handiwork, choose the <u>S</u>ave Settings on Exit option from the <u>O</u>ptions menu. Then Program Manager starts up with everything looking the same way it did when you last used it.

✔ You have another option: Set up the Program Manager the way you always want it to look, save the settings, and then don't choose the <u>S</u>ave Settings on Exit option. The Program Manager starts up nice and orderly, even if you left it a mess when you last used Windows. How do you save the settings? By reading the following tip.

✔ To make the Program Manager remember the current setup of its windows, hold down the Shift key and double-click on its Control-menu box, that little square in its top left-hand corner. (This trick doesn't work in most other programs. In fact, if you try it, the program thinks that you're trying to close it down.)

I Want a Better Icon!

Some icons, like the one for WinRoach, look pretty darn cool. (WinRoach acts cool, too, making random roaches scurry beneath your open windows.) The WinRoach icon looks like this:

WINROACH

Other icons, like the one for DOS programs that Windows can't recognize, are decidedly drab:

VDE

To change a boring icon to something more fancy, hold down the Alt key and double-click on the icon. A box pops up. Click on the Change Icon button. Yet another box pops up. Yawn and then click on the Browse button.

You see a list of program names. Almost all the names contain at least one icon, but one program has a bunch of icons it's willing to share. Select PROGMAN.EXE. It's the name of the Program Manager, which is the Nordstrom of icons. Figure 11-12 shows some of the icons that you see when you select PROGMAN.EXE.

Select the icon you want to use and then click on the OK button to get rid of the box. The new icon replaces the old one in the Program Manager.

- ✔ Near the PROGMAN.EXE file is the MORICONS.DLL file. Look in there for even *more* icons.

- ✔ Unfortunately, you can't create your own icons in Paintbrush. If you're desperate for some new icons, head back to the software store and ask for an *icon designer program.* (They can be fun, but your friends will want to know why you're spending so much time in front of the computer.)

Figure 11-12:
In the Change Icon box, you can select a new icon to replace a boring old icon.

Change Icon
File Name: D:\WINDOWS\PROGMAN.EXE
Current Icon:
OK   Cancel   Browse...   Help

Moving an Icon into Another Window

Finally! Something that doesn't require a button, box, bar, or menu!

To move an icon from one window into another, just drag it with the mouse: Put the pointer over the icon, hold down the mouse button, and move the pointer to the new window. Leggo of the mouse button. Presto! The icon has moved out of the first window and is already putting up drapes in the second.

To *copy* the icon, hold down Ctrl while doing the same thing. A copy of the icon appears in the second window.

- ✔ If you keep Auto Arrange selected under the Options menu, the icons space themselves out neatly to make room for the incoming icons.

- ✔ You can move icons to another program group even if that program group is shrunk down to an icon itself. Just drag them there and let go.

Making Programs Run Automatically When You Start Windows

I like the Windows Clock to sit at the bottom of the screen, so I told the Program Manager to load the Clock automatically whenever I start Windows.

Whenever Windows starts, it also starts any program with its icon in the StartUp program group. This feature is a great time-saver. To put an icon in the StartUp group, just drag it there, as described in the preceding section.

- ✔ If you don't have a StartUp group for some reason, create one. See the section "Creating Your Very Own Program Group" and type **STARTUP** in the Description box.

- ✔ You can hold down the Alt key and double-click on the icons in the StartUp group and then click on their Run Minimized box. They'll appear as icons at the bottom of the screen, ready for action each time you start Windows.

- ✔ If you suddenly change your mind and don't want Windows to load the programs in your StartUp group, try this: Hold down the Shift key when loading Windows and then release the key when Program Manager comes to the screen. Holding down the Shift key tells Windows to ignore the StartUp group's contents.

Help! Everything Turned into One Huge Program Group!

One simple mistake can make Windows look as if everything is messed up permanently. For example, you're clicking away in Program Manager when, all of a sudden, everything disappears. Program Manager turns into one big, borderless window, with just a few icons in the corner. All the other windows in Program Manager have disappeared.

You accidentally did one of two things:

1. You clicked on the program group's *maximize button,* that upward-pointing arrow in its top right-hand corner.

2. You double-clicked on its *title bar,* that thick strip holding its name along the top.

Both actions make the program group fill the entire screen; it's supposed to happen.

To restore order, double-click on the title bar again. Or click on the *restore button,* that funny two-headed arrow in the window's upper right-hand corner. Either way, the window returns to normal size, and everything looks the way it used to.

Everybody does this at least once. Although it's scary at first, there's no harm done.

Going Back to the Tutorial

When you first installed Windows, it offered you a chance to take a Windows tutorial. If you blew it off but can't get rid of the nagging feeling that you've missed something, take the tutorial now. Or anytime you like. It's always waiting for you in the Program Manager.

Click on <u>H</u>elp from the menu bar along the top of the window and then click on <u>W</u>indows Tutorial. When the tutorial gets too boring, press Esc and it will vanish.

Don't worry if you can't get through the tutorial in one sitting. It's always waiting for your return, perhaps during a particularly long-winded phone call.

Chapter 12

That Scary File Manager

*T*he File Manager is where people wake up from the Windows dream, clutching a pillow in horror. They bought Windows to make their computers easier to use, to lift them from the DOS psychobabble of *subdirectories* and *pathnames* and *hidden/system files*.

But open the File Manager, and those ugly DOS terms leer up at you. You not only have to keep that painfully technical DOS stuff straight, but you also have to do it while bouncing from button to button.

This chapter explains how to use the File Manager, and along the way it dishes out a big enough dose of DOS for you to get your work done. But, if you're really into file management (heaven knows why), consider picking up this book's forefather, *DOS For Dummies*, published by IDG Books Worldwide. It goes into just enough detail (yet keeps the dirge-level gratefully low).

Why Is the File Manager So Scary?

The File Manager is an awkward mixture of two wildly different computing worlds — DOS and Windows. It's as if somebody tried to combine an automobile with a bathtub. Then everybody's confused when they open the door and the water pours out.

To join in the confusion, double-click on the little filing cabinet icon in the Main program group to root through the File Manager's drawers. If you don't have a mouse, do the same old stuff you always do to choose an icon: Press the arrow keys until you highlight the File Manager icon and then press Enter. The File Manager icon looks like this:

File Manager

Everybody organizes his or her computer differently. Some people don't organize their computers at all. So your File Manager looks a little different from the one shown in Figure 12-1.

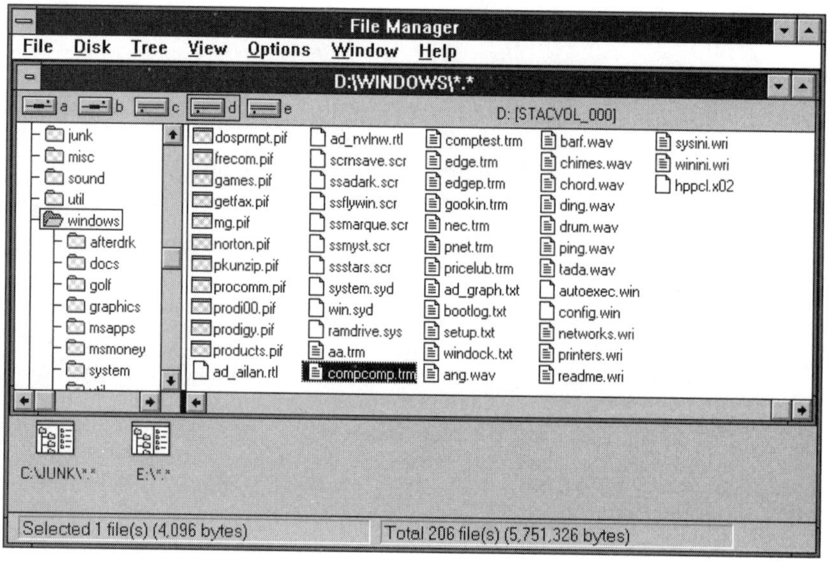

Figure 12-1:
You use the
Windows
File
Manager to
print, copy,
delete,
move,
rename, and
undelete
files.

In a way, the File Manager is a lot like the Program Manager. The Program Manager is a big panel of buttons, and the File Manager is a big panel of filenames. In fact, some people like the File Manager's *text-based* system of names better than the Program Manager's *picture-based* system. (It's that *right-brained* versus *left-brained* stuff.)

Both manager programs organize their contents into bunches of little windows. The File Manager, for example, enables you to open a window into each of your disk drives so you can see the contents of each one simultaneously. You also can shrink those windows into icons, just as in the Program Manager.

The File Manager and the Program Manager have many similarities, but they have one monstrous difference: The Program Manager's icons are just buttons that stand for your programs. The names and icons in the File Manager are your actual programs and subdirectories. In the Program Manager, you're target shooting. In the File Manager, you're shooting the actual ducks.

 ✔ If you accidentally delete an important file, turn to the "How to undelete a file" section later in this chapter. If you haven't saved many files since your mishap, you should be able to retrieve the deleted file from the hard disk's deleted files purgatory.

 ✔ In a way, learning how to use the File Manager is like learning how to play the piano. Neither is intuitively obvious, and you'll hit some bad notes with both. Don't be frustrated if you don't seem to be getting the hang of it. Liberace would have hated the File Manager at first, too.

Saved by the check box

If you're a newcomer to all this file stuff, install the File Manager's safety net.

Select Options at the top of the File Manager and then select Confirmation from the pull-down menu. When the box shown in Figure 12-2 appears, click in every empty check box until they all have an X. Then select the OK button.

The File Manager will keep an eye out for any potentially dangerous activities. For example, if you accidentally try to delete all the files on the hard drive, the File Manager clutches your wrist and sends out a box asking whether you're *sure* that you want to do that. Select No, and the File Manager doesn't delete them.

After you become more familiar with the File Manager, you can dismantle that safety net by clicking in the check boxes to remove those Xs. However, even hard-core Windows users should keep the Directory Delete option checked. Just one slip of the Delete key can wipe out the entire Windows directory.

Figure 12-2:
The
Confirmation
box provides
a safety net
for the File
Manager.

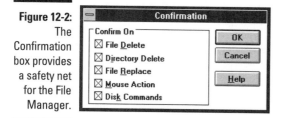

Getting the Lowdown on Subdirectories

This stuff is really boring, but if you don't read it, you'll be just as lost as your files.

A *subdirectory* is a workplace on a disk. Hard drives are divided into many subdirectories to separate your many projects. You can work with the spreadsheet, for example, without having all the word processing files get in the way.

Any disk can have subdirectories, but hard drives need them the most because they need a way to organize their thousands of files. By dividing a hard drive into little subdirectory compartments, you can more easily see where everything sits.

The File Manager enables you to move around to different subdirectories and peek at the files you've stuffed inside each one. It's a pretty good organizational scheme, actually. Socks never fall behind a subdirectory and jam the drawer.

- ✔ Subdirectories and directories are really the same thing: a work/storage area on a disk. A *subdirectory* is a name for a directory that's a subset of another directory. It's a deeper level of organization, like adding drawer partitions to sort your socks by color. Each sock color partition is a subdirectory of the larger, sock-drawer directory.

- ✔ Of course, you can ignore subdirectories and keep all your files in the Windows directory. That's like tossing everything into the back seat of the car and pawing around to find your Kleenex box a month later. Stuff you've organized is a lot easier to find.

- ✔ If you're eager to create a subdirectory or two, page ahead to this chapter's "Creating a Subdirectory" section.

- ✔ Windows created two subdirectories when it installed itself on your computer. It created a WINDOWS directory to hold most of its programs and a SYSTEM subdirectory to hold its internal engine parts.

- ✔ Computers use a *tree metaphor,* as shown in Figure 12-3, to display the wacky world of directories.

TECHNICAL STUFF

What's all this path stuff?

Often Windows can't find a file, even if it's sitting right there on the hard disk. You have to tell Windows where the file is sitting, and in order to do that, you need to know that file's *path*.

A path is like the file's address. A typical mailing address uses generalities (your home state) before getting specific (your Apt. #). A computer path does the same thing. It starts with the letter of the disk drive and ends with the name of the file. In between, the path lists all the subdirectories the computer must travel through in order to reach the file.

For example, look at the SOUNDS folder in Figure 12-3. For Windows to find a file stored there, it starts from the d : \ folder, travels through the WINDOWS folder, and then goes through the GOLF folder. Only then does it reach the SOUNDS folder.

Take a deep breath. Exhale. Quack like a duck, if you like. Now, the *d* in d : \ stands for disk drive D. (In the path, disk drive letters are always followed by a colon.) The disk drive letter and colon make up the first part of the path. All the other folders are subdirectories, so they're listed after the d : part. DOS separates subdirectories with something called a backslash, or \ . The name of the actual file — let's say GRUNT.WAV — comes last.

D:\WINDOWS\GOLF\SOUNDS\GRUNT.WAV is what you get when you put it all together, and that's the official path of the GRUNT.WAV file in the SOUNDS directory.

This stuff can be tricky, so here it is again: The letter for the drive comes first, followed by a colon and a backslash. Then come the names of all the subdirectories, each separated by a backslash. Last comes the name of the file (with no backslash after it).

When you click on folders, the File Manager puts together the path for you. While you're clicking away, you can see the File Manager piece together the current path and display it at the top of the window.

In the tree system shown in Figure 12-3, all the subdirectory folders branch out sideways from the d : \ folder, at the top of the chart. Each branching folder is a subdirectory of that first d : \ folder. Because the d : \ folder is the root of all things, it's called the *root directory:* All the other directories branch out from it, like branches on a tree. Or at least like a tree growing out the side of a cliff. Subdirectories can branch out as far as you want them to.

Most users have a c : \ directory. Others have a d : \ directory as well. Fanatics can create a z : \ directory, too.

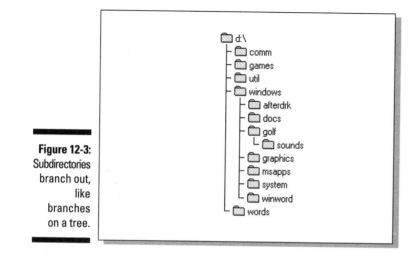

Figure 12-3:
Subdirectories
branch out,
like
branches
on a tree.

Peering into Your Drives and Directories

Knowing all this subdirectory stuff can impress the people at the computer store. But what counts is knowing how to use the File Manager to get to a file you want. Never fear. Just read on.

Seeing the files on a disk drive

Like everything else in Windows, disk drives are represented by buttons, or icons:

Those disk drive buttons live atop every window in the File Manager. See the box around the icon for drive D? The box indicates that those buttons were sitting atop a window displaying the contents of drive D before they were ripped out and stuck in this book.

✔ If you're kinda sketchy on those disk drive things, then you probably skipped Chapter 2. Trot back there for a refresher course.

✔ Click on a drive button, and the window displays the drive's contents. For example, put a disk in drive A and click on a window's drive A icon. The window's view changes to show what files and directories live on the disk in drive A.

Sometimes having two open windows makes it easier to compare the contents of two disk drives or subdirectories. To open a second window, double-click on any disk drive icon. A brand new window pops up, showing the contents of that particular disk drive.

A second window comes in handy when you want to move or copy files from one directory or drive to another, as discussed in the "Copying or Moving a File" section.

- ✔ The first two icons stand for the floppy drives, drive A and drive B. If you click on a floppy drive icon when no disk is in the drive, Windows stops you gently, suggesting that you insert a disk before proceeding further.

- ✔ If you're on a network, you see a network icon that lets you grab at the same stuff as everybody else on the network.

Seeing what's inside subdirectories

Because subdirectories and directories are really little storage compartments, the File Manager puts a picture of a little folder next to each subdirectory's name.

The subdirectories line up along the left side of a window, known as the *tree* side. One subdirectory, the one you're currently viewing, has a little box around its name.

The files inside the current subdirectory appear on the right side of the window, known as the *directory* side.

Finally, the subdirectory lives on a disk drive. Its home disk drive has a little box around it, too, at the top of the window.

It all looks somewhat like Figure 12-4.

To peek inside a subdirectory, double-click on its folder in the left side of the window. You see two things: That folder's next level of subdirectories appears beneath it on the left side of the window, and that folder's filenames spill out into the right side of the window.

- ✔ As you keep climbing farther out on a branch and more subdirectories open up, you're moving toward further levels of organization. If you climb back inward, you reach files and subdirectories that have less in common.

- ✔ Yeah, this stuff is really confusing, but keep one thing in mind: Don't be afraid to double-click, or even single-click, on a folder just to see what happens. Clicking on folders just changes your viewpoint; nothing dreadful happens, and no tax receipts fall onto the floor. You're just opening and closing file cabinet drawers, peeking into folders along the way.

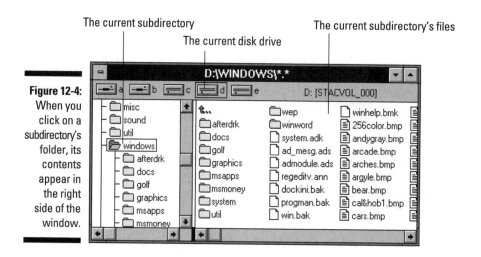

The current subdirectory   The current subdirectory's files

The current disk drive

Figure 12-4:
When you
click on a
subdirectory's
folder, its
contents
appear in
the right
side of the
window.

D:\WINDOWS*.*

- ✔ To climb farther out on the subdirectory branch, keep double-clicking on new folders as they appear.

- ✔ To move back up the subdirectory branch, double-click on a folder closer to the left side of the window. Any subdirectories beneath that folder will be hidden from view.

- ✔ If you're tired of this *hidden folders* foolishness, you can make the File Manager display *all* the subdirectories, no matter how far they branch out. Click anywhere in the window of the drive you want to expand, hold down Ctrl, and press * (the asterisk key). Whoosh! A folder for every subdirectory on the *tree* side opens up. The screen may be a little crowded, but, hey, at least all the subdirectories are out in the open.

- ✔ How can you tell whether a folder has any subdirectories branching from it? Well, you can double-click on it and watch to see whether any appear. If you want an easier way, select Tree from the menu bar and then select the Indicate Expandable Branches option. A plus sign then appears on any folders that have subdirectories. Folders on the end of the branch, the ones without any subdirectories beneath them, have a minus sign on them.

- ✔ Sometimes a subdirectory has too many files to fit in the window. To see more files, click on that window's scroll bars. What's a scroll bar? Time to whip out your field guide, Chapter 6.

Move the mouse pointer over the bar separating a subdirectory on the left from its filenames on the right. When the pointer turns into a mutant two-headed arrow, hold down the mouse button. Then move the bar to the left to give the filenames more room. Move the mouse to the right to give the subdirectory folders more room. Let go of the mouse when the split is adjusted just right, and the window reshapes itself to the new dimensions.

Loading a Program or File

A *file* is a collection of information on a disk. Files come in two basic types: program files and data files.

Program files contain instructions that tell the computer to do something: balance the national budget or ferret out a fax number.

Data files contain information created with a program, as opposed to computer instructions. If you write a letter to the grocer complaining about his soggy apricots, you're creating a data file.

To open either kind of file in the File Manager, double-click on its name. A double-click on a program file's name brings the program to the screen. If you double-click on a data file, the File Manager loads the file *and* the program that created it. Then it brings both the file and the program to the screen at the same time.

The File Manager sticks little icons next to the filenames so you know whether they're program or data files. In fact, even subdirectories get their own icons so you won't confuse them with files. Table 12-1 is a handy reference for those icons.

✔ Because of some bizarre New School of Computing mandate, Windows refers to any data file that it recognizes as a *document*. A document doesn't have to contain words; it can have pictures of worms or sounds of hungry animals. Documents get icons of dog-eared pieces of paper with little lines on it, like the one in Table 12-1.

✔ To load a program as an icon rather than as a full-fledged window, hold down the Shift key while you double-click. The program's icon appears at the bottom of the screen, ready for action.

✔ To make the File Manager turn into an icon when it launches a program, select <u>M</u>inimize on Use in the <u>O</u>ptions menu. Then, when you load a program, the File Manager turns into an icon and waits at the bottom of the screen — out of the way but ready to play.

Table 12-1	Subdirectory and File Icons
What It Looks Like	*What It Is / What It Does*
📂	A subdirectory. The folder is *open,* so this subdirectory is currently spilling its contents onto the right side of the window so you can see all its files.
📁	A subdirectory. This folder is *closed,* so it's just sitting there. Double-click on it, and it opens, showing you what's inside.
▭	A file. This is a *program.* Double-click on this thing to bring the program to the screen.
📄	A file. This is a *data file.* Double-click here and the File Manager loads the file, along with the program that created it. Fast and automatic.
📄	A file. Windows doesn't know *what* this file is, so clicking on it just causes confusion. Don't mess with the file, though; another Windows program may be using it on the sly.
📄	A file. This is a hidden file. Windows tried to hide this file from you so you wouldn't mess with it. (So *don't* mess with it.)
📁..	This isn't a file, but you'll see it anyway. If you click here, the File Manager shifts your view to the directory above the one you're currently looking at.

Don't bother reading this hidden technical stuff

Sometimes programs store information in a data file. They may need to store information about the way the computer is set up, for example. To keep people from thinking those files are trash and deleting them, the program hides those files.

For example, sometimes Windows creates a permanent swap file on the hard drive to speed things up on 386 and 486 computers. Windows uses this swap file, not you, so Windows hides it. You normally don't see the file's name or even know it exists.

You can view the names of these hidden files, however, if you want to play voyeur. Select View from the menu bar and then choose the By File Type option from the pull-down menu. Select the Show Hidden/System Files check box and then select the OK button.

The formerly hidden files appear alongside the other filenames. Be sure not to delete them, however. The programs that created them will gag, possibly damaging other files.

You can hide your own files by holding down Alt, double-clicking on a filename, and clicking on Hidden when the box pops up. You can even hide entire directories this way.

Why bother? Well, you can keep people from snooping through your private journal by making it a hidden file. However, anybody who has nosed through this technical stuff knows how to find your journal, so you're probably better off hiding it on a floppy disk somewhere. Better yet, name it something innocuous — not something like PRIVATE.TXT. Then your innermost thoughts are safe from everybody but the most click-happy computer nerd.

Deleting and Undeleting Files

Sooner or later, you'll want to delete a file that's not important anymore — yesterday's lottery picks, for example, or something you've stumbled on that's too embarrassing to save any longer. But then, hey, suddenly you realize that you've made a mistake and deleted the wrong file. Not to worry. The File Manager can probably resurrect that deleted file if you're quick enough.

Getting rid of a file or directory

To permanently remove a file from the hard drive, click on its name. Then press the Delete key. This surprisingly simple trick works for files, programs, and even subdirectories.

The Delete key deletes entire directories, as well as any subdirectories beneath them. Make sure that you've selected the file that you want to delete before you press the Delete key.

- ✔ When you press Delete, Windows tosses a box in your face, asking whether you're sure. If you are, select the <u>Y</u>es button.

- ✔ Don't delete any files that have an exclamation point in their icon. These files are hidden files, and the computer wants you to leave them alone. (Other than that, they're not particularly exciting, despite the exclamation point.)

- ✔ As soon as you learn how to delete files, you'll want to read the very next section, "How to undelete a file."

Deleting an icon from the Program Manager just deletes a button that loads a program. You can always put the button back on. Deleting a file from the File Manager permanently removes that file from the hard disk.

How to undelete a file

Sooner or later, your finger will push the Delete key at the wrong time, and you'll delete the wrong file. A slip of the finger, the wrong nudge of a mouse, or, if you're in Southern California, a small earthquake at the wrong time can make a file disappear. Zap!

Scream! When the tremors subside, open File Manager, and click on <u>F</u>ile from the row of words along its top. A menu drops down from the heavens and leaves you with two options, both described here.

If you're using DOS 6 or 6.2 ...

Using DOS 6 or higher? Then look on the File Manager's File menu for the word Undelete and click on it. The Windows Undelete program opens, ready to search your hard drive or floppy disk for a deleted file.

Click on the program's Drive/Dir button to look for deleted files in different directories and drives. Spot the accidentally deleted file? Then click on its name and click on the Undelete button.

Prepare yourself: The Undelete program asks you to type in the first letter of the file's name. If you remember, type that letter. If you don't remember, type any letter; the program isn't picky.

Click the OK button after typing the letter, and the program drags the file back to safety.

If you're not using DOS 6 or 6.2 ...

Even if you're not using the latest version of DOS, you may still be able to retrieve your file. If you don't see the word Undelete on File Manager's File menu, choose Run from the menu instead. Then, when the box shown in Figure 12-5 pops up, type the word **UNDELETE** and press Enter.

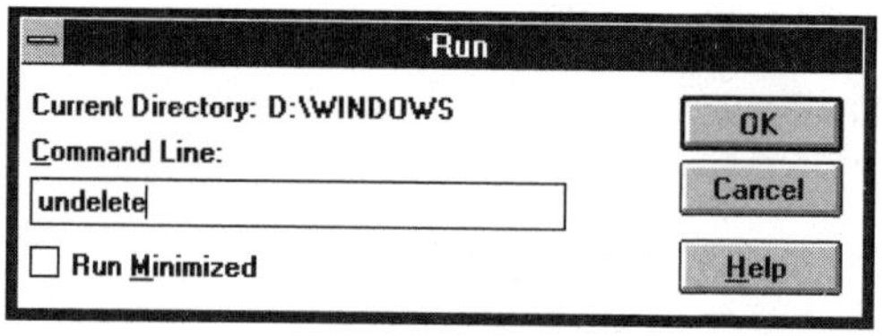

Figure 12-5:
Type
UNDELETE
in the Run
box to
undelete a
file you've
just deleted.

```
┌─────────────────────────────────────────────────┐
│ ═                     Run                         │
├─────────────────────────────────────────────────┤
│ Current Directory: D:\WINDOWS          ┌────────┐ │
│ Command Line:                          │   OK   │ │
│ ┌───────────────────────────────────┐  └────────┘ │
│ │undelete│                          │  ┌────────┐ │
│ └───────────────────────────────────┘  │ Cancel │ │
│ ☐ Run Minimized                        └────────┘ │
│                                        ┌────────┐ │
│                                        │  Help  │ │
│                                        └────────┘ │
└─────────────────────────────────────────────────┘
```

Even if some other words are already in the box, type **UNDELETE** anyway; it replaces the other words. When you hit Enter, File Manager hems and haws, the screen flashes to black, and you see something similar to the following words:

```
Directory: D:\WINDOWS
File Specifications: *.*

Deletion-tracking file not found.

MS-DOS directory contains    1 deleted files.
Of those,    1 files may be recovered.

Using the MS-DOS directory.
?VDINNER TXT      3835  7-16-92  7:24a  ...A  Undelete (Y/N)?
```

If this is the file you want to retrieve, press Y and Enter.

✔ The Undelete program then tosses you a real stumper: It asks you to type the first letter in that file's name. If you don't remember, just make one up. After you type a letter, your file will be retrieved from purgatory.

✔ To see which version of DOS you're running, click on the MS DOS icon in the Program Manager's main window. Then type the word **VER** following the wacky C:\> thing and press Enter:

```
C:\> VER
```

DOS tells you what version you're using. If it's not DOS 5, DOS 6, or newer, trot back to the software store, credit card in hand. That Undelete feature comes in handy.

✔ After you delete a file, every new file you subsequently save to disk decreases your chances of retrieving the deleted one.

✔ The File Manager's Undelete trick works even if File Manager didn't delete the file. Whether the file died in your word processor or any other program, File Manager's a good way to bring it back to life.

✔ For even more information about the Undelete software that comes with DOS 6, check out *MORE Windows For Dummies*.

Moving Windows around in File Manager

Windows loves to fill your screen with windows, and File Manager's no exception. File Manager can display the contents of your hard disk's directories in several different ways. For example, you can see a drive's directories and files within File Manager's *own* window, as in Figure 12-6.

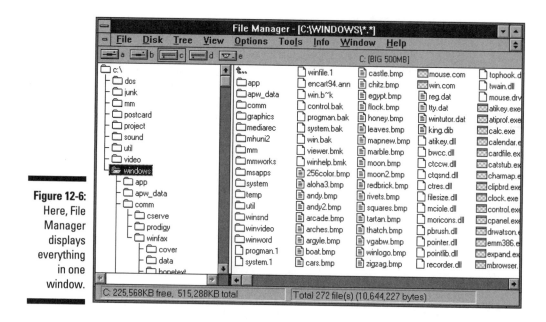

Figure 12-6:
Here, File
Manager
displays
everything
in one
window.

Alternatively, you can make File Manager put that drive's directories and files into their own, separate windows. Just click on the restore button — that button in the upper right corner with two arrows, one pointing up, the other pointing down — to put that drive's contents into their own window, as shown in Figure 12-7.

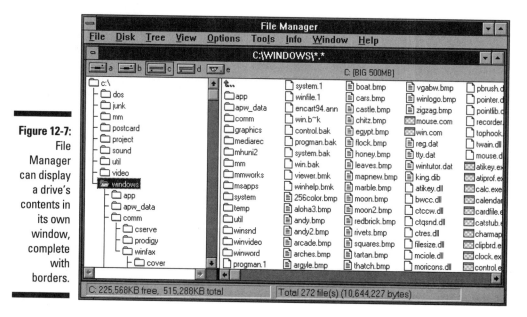

Figure 12-7:
File
Manager
can display
a drive's
contents in
its own
window,
complete
with
borders.

Perhaps you want File Manager to display more than one window on-screen, showing a different drive's contents in each window, as in Figure 12-8.

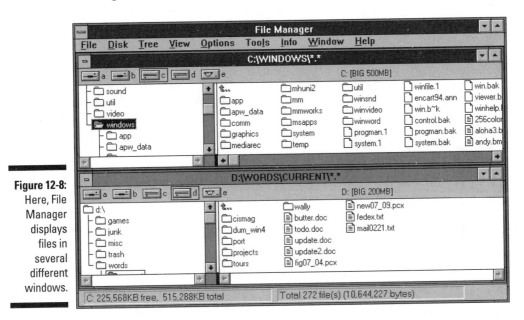

Figure 12-8:
Here, File
Manager
displays
files in
several
different
windows.

File Manager can even put icons on-screen, as shown in Figure 12-9.

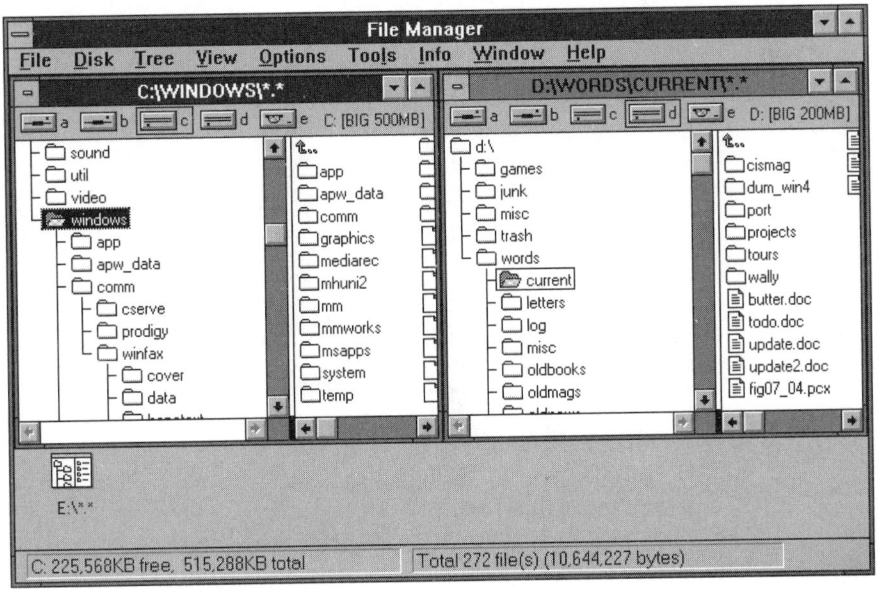

Figure 12-9:
Here, File
Manager
displays
several
different
windows,
with icons
beneath
them.

Why should you bother shuffling windows around? Sometimes you *want* to see the two different drives or directories on-screen simultaneously. That makes it easy to copy or move files back and forth between them, as described in the next section. Or perhaps you want to compare the sizes of files living in two different directories.

Luckily, File Manager shuffles its windows in the same way as Program Manager or any other part of your desktop. Its windows can be moved, resized, or turned into icons, just like any other windows. (Window rearranging gets its due in Chapter 7.)

Here are the main tips for moving windows around in File Manager:

- ✔ If File Manager won't display more than one window, hold down Shift and press F4. File Manager switches to window mode and arranges all your currently open windows across its screen.

- ✔ To change the current window's view to a different drive, *click* on that drive's icon from the drives listed along the top of File Manager.

- ✔ To open a *second* window that shows a different drive, *double-click* on that drive's icon from among the drives listed along the File Manager's top.

- ✔ To see which windows File Manager has open, click on <u>W</u>indow from its top menu. A list of currently open windows appears at the bottom of the screen.

- ✔ Just like Program Manager, File Manager can cascade or tile all the open windows across its screen. Just choose <u>T</u>ile or <u>C</u>ascade from the File Manager's <u>W</u>indow menu.

- ✔ File Manager's windows turn into icons just like any other windows; just click on the downward-pointing arrow in the upper right corner. No downward-pointing arrow? Then hold down Shift and press F4 — that brings the downward-pointing arrows into view.

- ✔ Too many windows open in File Manager? Then start closing down the superfluous ones. Hold down Shift and press F4, and then double-click in the unwanted window's upper left corner. (The Close button looks like an aerial view of a square toaster.)

- ✔ Basic window manipulation techniques are covered in Chapter 7.

Copying or Moving a File

To copy or move files to different directories on your hard drive, use your mouse to *drag* them there. For example, here's how to move a file to a different directory on your hard drive:

1. **Move the mouse pointer until it hovers over the file you want to move and then press and hold down the mouse button.**

2. **While holding down the mouse button, point at the directory to which you'd like to move the file.**

   The trick is to hold down your mouse button *the whole time*. As you move the mouse, its arrow drags the file along with it. For example, Figure 12-10 shows how File Manager looks when I drag the ZIGZAG.BMP file from my WINDOWS directory to my JUNK directory.

3. **Release the mouse button.**

   When the mouse arrow hovers over the place to which you'd like to move the file, take your finger off the mouse button. To make sure that you've pointed correctly, Windows asks whether you're *sure* you want to move that file, as shown in Figure 12-11. If you're sure, click on the Yes button; otherwise, click on the No button to cancel everything.

Moving a file by dragging its name is pretty easy, actually. The hard part often comes when trying to put the file and its destination on-screen at the same time. You often need to make File Manager put two windows on-screen, as described in the preceding section. When you can see the file and its destination, start dragging.

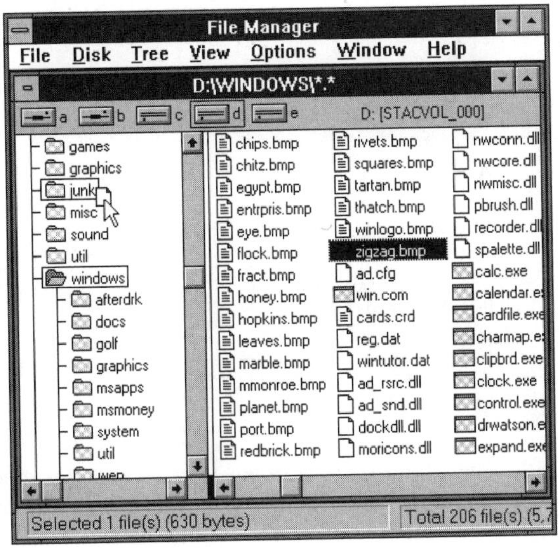

Figure 12-10: The ZIGZAG.BMP file is being dragged to the JUNK directory on the left side of the window.

Figure 12-11:
Click on Yes
and the File
Manager
carries out
your mouse-
dragging
instructions.

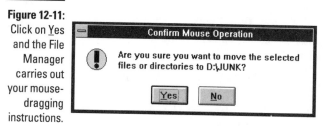

However, File Manager does something awfully dumb to confuse people. When you drag a file from one directory to another on the same drive, you move the file. When you drag a file from one directory to another on a different drive, you copy that file.

I swear, I didn't make up these rules. And it gets more complicated: You can hold down either Ctrl or Alt to reverse the rules. Table 12-2 can help you keep these oafish oddities from getting too far out of control.

Table 12-2	Moving Files Around
To Do This	*Do This*
Copy a file to another location on the *same* disk drive	Hold down Ctrl and drag it there.
Copy a file to a *different* disk drive	Drag it there.
Move a file to another location on the *same* disk drive	Drag it there.
Move a file to a *different* disk drive	Hold down Alt and drag it there.
Remember these *obtuse* commands	Refer to the handy cheat sheet at the front of this book.

Instead of dragging files between open windows, try this: Open a window that shows the file's destination and then minimize it — click on the downward-pointing arrow in its upper right corner. Doing so turns the window into an icon along the File Manager's bottom. Then drag your file to that icon, as shown in Figure 12-12.

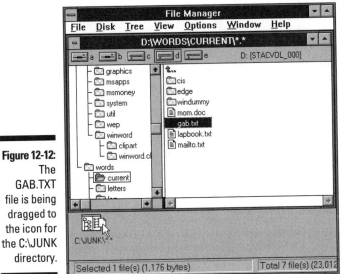

Figure 12-12:
The
GAB.TXT
file is being
dragged to
the icon for
the C:\JUNK
directory.

- To copy or move files to a floppy disk, drag those files to the icon for that floppy disk, which you should find along the top of the File Manager window.

- If you know what a *path* is, you can use the Copy command from the File Manager's File menu. In the To box, type the path of the file's destination. If you don't know what a *path* is, just drag the files over there with the mouse.

- Personally, I can never remember whether to hold down Ctrl or Alt or to just drag a file. So I try dragging first and wait for the File Manager to say whether I'm copying or moving. If I didn't get it right, I drag the file back and try again, this time holding down Ctrl or Alt. Eventually, I stumble onto the right combination. Welcome to the File Manager.

When dragging a file someplace in File Manager, look at the icon attached to the mouse pointer. If the document icon has a *plus sign* in it, you're *copying* the file. If the document icon is blank, you're *moving* the file. Depending on where the file's being dragged, pressing Ctrl or Alt toggles the plus sign on or off, making it easier to see whether you're currently copying or moving the file.

After running a program's installation program to put it on your hard drive, don't move it around.

Selecting More Than One File

The File Manager lets you grab an armful of files at one swipe; you don't always have to piddle around, dragging one file at a time.

To pluck several files from a list, hold down Ctrl as you click on the filenames. Each name stays highlighted as you click on the next filename.

To gather several files sitting next to each other, click on the first one. Then hold down the Shift key as you click on the last one. Those two files are highlighted, along with every file between them.

- ✔ You can drag these armfuls of files in the same way as you drag one.

- ✔ You can delete these armfuls, too.

- ✔ You can't rename or print an armful of files all at once. To do those things, you have to go back to piddling around with one file at a time.

Renaming a File

If you're a He-Man stuck with a name like Pink Gardenia, you can petition the courts to change it to Blue Gardenia. Changing a filename requires even less effort: Click on the file's name, select File from the File Manager's menu bar, and then select Rename when the menu tumbles down.

Type the file's new name in the box beneath its old name, click on OK, and you're off.

- ✔ When you rename a file, only its name changes. The contents are still the same, it's still the same size, and it's still in the same place.

- ✔ You can't rename groups of files this way. The File Manager spits in your face if you even try.

- ✔ You can rename directories this way, too. (Renaming a directory can confuse Windows, however, which grows accustomed to directories the way they're first set up.)

Using Legal Folders and Filenames

DOS is picky about what you can and can't name a file or directory, so Windows has to play along. If you stick to plain old letters and numbers, you're fine. But don't try to stick any of the following characters in there:

```
. : / \ [ ] : * | < > + = ; , ?
```

If you use any of those characters, DOS balks, Windows bounces an error message to the screen, and you have to try again. You can't use a space, either. Well, you can, but only through some weird, nerdy trick you don't want to hear about.

These are illegal filenames:

```
TIPPER GORE
JOB:2
ONE<TWO
OH DARN
```

These are legal names:

```
AL_GORE
JOB2
2BIGGER1
#@$%)
```

> ✔ You're allowed to tack a three-letter extension onto a filename, but don't bother. Windows programs *brand* files with their own extension so the File Manager knows what program created them. You'll run across extensions like SAVVY.WRI, README.TXT, NUDE.BMP, and ENEMIES.CRD across the hard disk. Those extensions are automatically added by the Windows programs Write, Notepad, Paintbrush, and Cardfile, respectively.

> ✔ Don't end a filename with a period. If you type a period at the end when naming a file, the program leaves off its automatic extension, greatly confusing matters.

Copying a Disk

To copy files from one disk to another, drag 'em over there. To copy an entire disk, however, use the File Manager's disk copying command.

What's the difference? When you're copying files, you're dragging specific filenames. But, when you're copying a disk, the File Manager duplicates the disk exactly: It even copies the empty parts! (That's why it takes longer than just dragging the files over.)

The File Manager's Copy Disk command has two main limitations:

First, it can copy only floppy disks that are the same *size* or *capacity*. Just as you can't pour a full can of beer into a shot glass, you can't copy one disk's information onto another disk unless they both hold the same amount of data.

Second, it can't copy the hard drive or a RAM drive. Luckily, you really have no reason to copy them, even if you know what a RAM drive is.

Here's how to make a copy of a floppy disk if your disk drives are of the same size and capacity:

1. **Place the original disk in drive A and the second disk in drive B.**

   Put your important disk — the one you want to copy — in drive A. The desired duplicate goes in drive B.

   The File Manager's Copy Disk command makes an *exact* copy of a disk. In the process, it wipes out *everything* on the disk that's receiving the information. Before proceeding, make sure that the second disk is either blank or doesn't contain anything important.

2. **From File Manager's Disk menu, select Copy Disk.**

   Click on the word Disk at File Manager's top and then select Copy Disk when the menu drops down. A Copy Disk box appears, listing your floppy drives.

3. **Make sure that the letter *A:* is in the Source in box and *B:* is in the Destination In box.**

   The letter *A:* is probably already in the Source In box. You may have to click on the Destination In box's downward-pointing arrow to bring up the B drive, however.

4. **Click on the OK button.**

   ✔ If you have only one disk drive, you can still copy a disk. Select drive A as both the source and the destination. Watch the File Manager's instructions: You have to remove the first disk and stick in the second disk from time to time, depending on the vigor of your computer.

   ✔ You can copy a disk in drive B, too, by choosing B as both the source and the destination.

   ✔ All this *capacity* and *size* stuff about disks and drives is slowly digested in Chapter 2.

Creating a Subdirectory

To store new information in a file cabinet, you grab a manila folder, scrawl a name across the top, and start stuffing it with information.

To store new information in Windows — a new program, for example — you tell File Manager to create a new subdirectory, think up a name for the new subdirectory, and start moving or copying files into it.

New, more organized subdirectories make finding information easier, too. For example, you can clean up a crowded LETTERS directory by creating two subdirectories: BUSINESS and PERSONAL.

Here's how to create a new directory — a subdirectory called BUSINESS — that lives in your LETTERS directory:

1. **Click on the directory in which you want the subdirectory to appear.**

   If you want a new GAMES directory in your WINDOWS directory, for example, you click on the WINDOWS directory. In this case, you would click on the LETTERS directory, as shown in Figure 12-13, because you want the BUSINESS subdirectory to appear in the LETTERS directory.

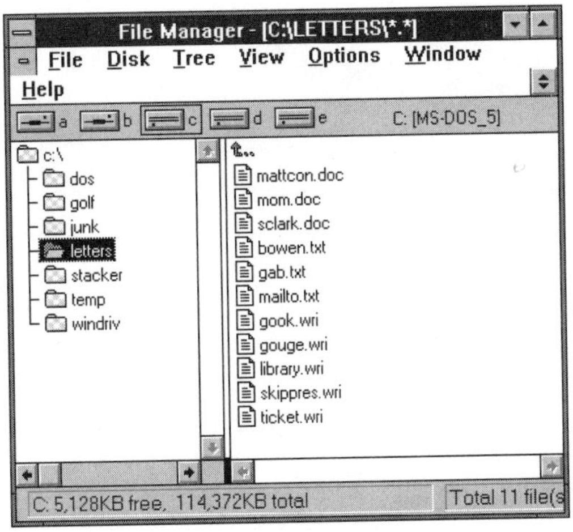

Figure 12-13:
You can clean out the crowded LETTERS folder by creating new sub-directories.

File Manager - [C:\LETTERS*.*]

File Disk Tree View Options Window
Help

C: [MS-DOS_5]

c:\
— dos
— golf
— junk
— letters
— stacker
— temp
— windriv

mattcon.doc
mom.doc
sclark.doc
bowen.txt
gab.txt
mailto.txt
gook.wri
gouge.wri
library.wri
skippres.wri
ticket.wri

C: 5,128KB free, 114,372KB total   Total 11 file(s

2. **Select Create Directory from File Manager's File command.**

   Click on the word File from the top of File Manager and choose Create Directory from the menu that drops down. A box pops up and asks you to think of a name for your new directory.

3. **Type the new directory's name and press Enter.**

   Windows is picky about names you give to directories and files. For the rules, check out the "Using Legal Folders and Filenames" section earlier in this chapter.

After you type the directory's name and press Enter, the new BUSINESS directory appears, ready for you to start moving your business letter files. For impeccable organization, follow the same steps to create a PERSONAL directory and move your personal files into there, as shown in Figure 12-14.

Figure 12-14:
You can
drag files
into the new
BUSINESS
and
PERSONAL
subdirectories
to organize
your work.

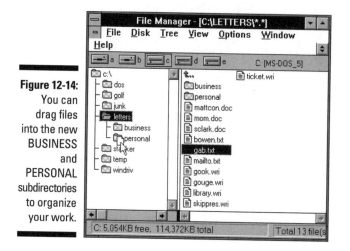

- ✔ Want to install a new Windows program? Create a new directory for it and copy its files there. Then head to Chapter 11 to see how to put the new program's icon in Program Manager for easy clicking.

- ✔ To move files into a new subdirectory, drag them there. Just follow the directions in the "Copying or Moving a File" section.

- ✔ When copying or moving lots of files, select them all at the same time before dragging them. You can chew on this stuff in the "Selecting More Than One File" section.

- ✔ Just as with naming files, you can use only certain characters when naming directories. Stick with letters and numbers, and you'll be fine.

Seeing More Information about Files

Whenever you create a file, DOS scrawls a bunch of secret hidden information on it: its size, the date you created it, and some even more trivial stuff. To see what DOS is calling files behind your back, select View from the menu bar and then select All File Details from the menu.

The File Manager fills the right side of the window with everything it knows about the files. If you select Partial Details, you can pick and choose what information you want displayed. For example, you can view the filenames and the dates they were created. Or perhaps the filenames and their sizes. Or any combination, actually.

- ✔ Although some of the file information is handy, it takes up a lot of space, limiting the number of files you can see in the window. Displaying only the filename is usually a better idea. Then, if you want to see more information about a file, try the following tip.

- ✔ Hold down Alt and double-click on a file to see its size, date, and other information.

- ✔ With the Alt+double-click trick (described in the preceding paragraph), you can change a file's attributes, as well. Attributes are too boring to be discussed further, so duck beneath the technical stuff coming up.

Normally, the File Manager displays filenames sorted alphabetically by name. But, by clicking on the Sort options in the View menu, you make the File Manager display them in a different order. It puts the biggest ones at the top of the list, for example, when you choose Sort by Size. Or you can choose Sort by Type to keep files created by the same application next to each other. Or you can choose Sort by Date to keep the most recent files at the top of the list.

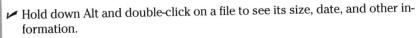

Who cares about this stuff, anyway?

MS-DOS gives each file four special switches called *attributes.* The computer looks at the way those switches are set before it fiddles with a file.

Read Only: Choosing this attribute allows the file to be read but not deleted or changed in any way.

Archive: The computer sets this attribute when a file has changed since the last time it was backed up with the special DOS BACKUP command.

Hidden: Setting this attribute makes the file invisible during normal operations.

System: Files required by a computer's operating system have this attribute set.

The File Manager makes it easy — perhaps too easy — to change these attributes. In most cases, you should leave them alone. They're just mentioned here so you'll know what computer nerds mean when they tell cranky people, "Boy, somebody must have set *your* attribute wrong when you got out of bed this morning."

Dragging, Dropping, and Running

You can drag files around in the File Manager to move them or copy them. But there's more: You can drag them outside of the File Manager and drop them onto icons to load them into other files and programs, as shown in Figure 12-15.

Drag the EGYPT.BMP file onto the Paintbrush icon and let go of the mouse button. Paintbrush loads the EGYPT.BMP file and then just sits there as an icon, the same as before. But, when you double-click on it, Paintbrush comes to the screen with EGYPT.BMP waiting inside.

This feature brings up all sorts of fun ideas. If you have a sound card, you can listen to sounds by dropping sound files onto icons for the Media Player or Sound Recorder. You can drop text files into Notepad to load them quickly. Or you can drop Write files into Write. You can even print files by dropping them onto the Print Manager.

- ✔ OK, the first thing everybody wants to know is what happens if you drag a sound file into Write? Or a Write file into Notepad? Or any other files that don't match? Well, Windows will probably send you a box saying that it got indigestion. Just click on the OK button, and things will return to normal. No harm done.

- ✔ The second question everybody asks is why bother? You can just double-click on a file's name to load it. That's true. But this way is more fun and occasionally faster.

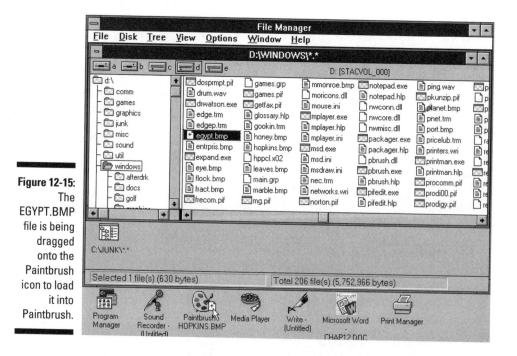

Figure 12-15: The EGYPT.BMP file is being dragged onto the Paintbrush icon to load it into Paintbrush.

✔ If you drag a file into an open window, the File Manager tries to *embed* that file. Embedding is part of that weird Object Linking and Embedding stuff discussed in Chapter 9.

✔ If you hold down Shift and Ctrl while dragging that file to an open window, your fingers turn into a square knot. You also *link* that file to the file in the open window. Linking is even more of that weird Object Linking and Embedding stuff discussed in Chapter 9.

✔ Never dragged and dropped before? Chapter 4 contains complete instructions.

Telling Windows What Program Made What File

If you see a lot of *blank* dog-eared icons in File Manager, Windows doesn't recognize a lot of the data files on your hard drive.

Most programs automatically add an extension to all data files they create. For instance, all Write files end with the extension WRI. Notepad files end with TXT.

If you double-click on a file ending in WRI, File Manager knows to load that file into Write and then bring it to the screen. Double-click on a file ending in TXT, and Windows loads *that* file into Notepad and brings it to the screen.

Windows doesn't automatically recognize every file, though. And it's not *supposed* to, either; some files shouldn't be messed with by man, beast, or Windows. Some files aren't even supposed to have extensions.

But it's OK to mess with some of those files, however, and for a handy reason. For example, if an icon-editor program automatically creates icon files ending in ICO, wouldn't it be nice to double-click on an ICO file and immediately have the icon editor bring that particular icon to the screen? To make this work, you need to tell Windows about the special relationship between your icon-editor program and the letters ICO.

Here's how to tell Windows which programs tack on certain letters to their file offspring:

1. **Click on one of the unrecognized filenames in File Manager.**

   Unrecognized files have blank, dog-eared icons, as shown way back in Table 12-1. A click on the file's name makes it turn dark.

2. **Click on File and choose Associate from the pull-down menu.**

   A box similar to the one in Figure 12-16 pops up.

3. **Type the name of the program in the Associate With box.**

   If you don't know that program's exact spelling, click on the Browse button and then click on the program's name. For example, click on the name of your icon-editor program if you'd like that program to be associated with ICO files.

4. **Click on the OK button.**

   Now Windows knows which program tacks the letters ICO onto its files' names. Double-click on a file ending in ICO, and Windows loads both that file and the program that created it — in this case, the icon editor.

   ✔ You can associate several different extensions with one program. For instance, Microsoft Word for Windows creates files ending in both DOC and DOT. A double-click on either kind of file brings Word to the screen, along with that file.

   ✔ If you want Notepad to pop up when you click on files ending in LOG, associate the letters LOG with the Notepad program. (The Notepad program is called NOTEPAD.EXE, by the way.)

   ✔ Joined the ICO hobbyists? Then keep your ICO files in your Windows directory. Otherwise, they don't appear on Program Manager's Change Icon menu.

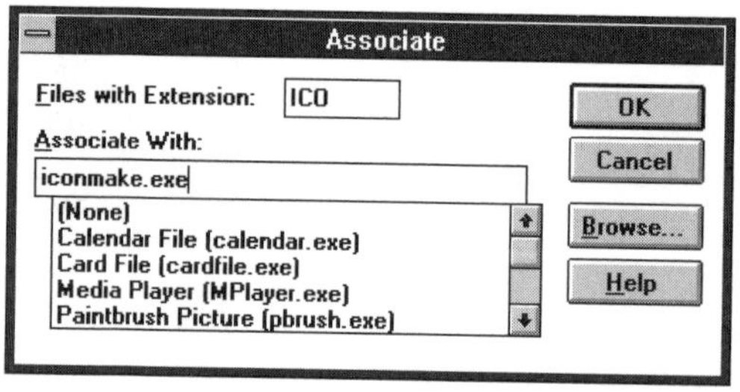

Figure 12-16:
You can use the Associate box to introduce Windows to a program's extension.

Associate	
Files with Extension: ICO	OK
Associate With: iconmake.exe	Cancel
(None) Calendar File (calendar.exe) Card File (cardfile.exe) Media Player (MPlayer.exe) Paintbrush Picture (pbrush.exe)	Browse... Help

Making File Manager Behave Itself

Sometimes File Manager acts just plain weird. It lists files that aren't there, doesn't list files that are there, or shows only half of the screen. When it starts to act up, whip it back into shape with the following sections.

It lists files that aren't there!

Sometimes the File Manager snoozes and doesn't keep track of what's *really* on the disk. Oh, it does pretty well with the hard drive, and it works pretty well if you're just running Windows programs. But it can't tell when you stick in a new floppy disk. Also, if you create a file from within a DOS program, the File Manager may not know that new file is there.

If you think the File Manager is holding out on you, tell it to *refresh,* or take a second look at what's on the floppy disk or hard drive.

You can click on <u>W</u>indow from the menu bar and choose <u>R</u>efresh from the pull-down menu, but a quicker way is to press the F5 key. (It's a function key along the top or left-side of the keyboard.) Either way, the File Manager takes a second look at what it's supposed to be showing and updates its list if necessary.

Press the F5 key whenever you stick in a different floppy disk. The File Manager then updates the screen to show that *new* floppy's files, not the files from the first disk.

It doesn't list files that are there!

The File Manager has so many options that you can easily click on the wrong one and then wonder why the lights went out. If all your files aren't showing up on the screen, you may have inadvertently told the File Manager to filter some of them out.

Select <u>V</u>iew from the menu bar and then click on By File <u>T</u>ype, the last option on the pull-down menu. The innocuous box shown in Figure 12-17 appears.

The File Manager shows only what has been checked off in the By File Type box. For example, if there isn't an X in the box next to <u>P</u>rograms, the File Manager doesn't list any program files.

Also, the *.* in the <u>N</u>ame box is a *wild card* standing for *all files.* If you see anything but *.* in this box, the File Manager isn't showing you all your files. Wild cards get their own section later in this chapter.

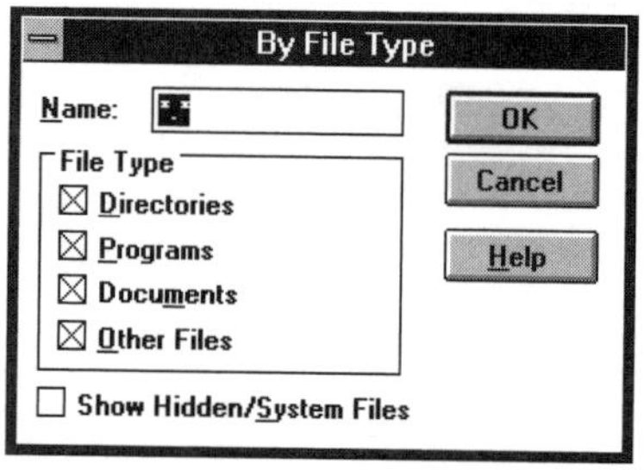

Figure 12-17:
If the File
Manager
isn't
showing all
your files,
your By File
Type box
probably
doesn't look
like this one.

- You probably shouldn't check the Show Hidden/System Files box. Windows keeps some files hidden so they won't be erased accidentally by unsuspecting computer users.

- Make sure that the *.* wild card (an asterisk, a period, and an asterisk) appears in the Name box.

- If you don't like seeing directory folders appear on both the right and left sides of the File Manager's windows, click in the check box next to Directories. When the check box is empty, the File Manager keeps directory folders off the right side of the screen.

- If File Manager still won't show some files that you know are there, press F5. That action tells File Manager to take another look at the disk and refresh the screen with an updated list of the disk's contents.

It shows only half of the screen!

Normally, the File Manager splits its windows neatly into two parts: a *tree* side showing the directories and a *file* side showing the names of files inside those directories. But sometimes you see only one or the other. Whoa. Where did the other half of the screen go?

The File Manager, in its painful struggle to be helpful, enables you to toggle those *side windows* on or off. To put things back to normal, choose View from the menu bar and then select the first option, Tree and Directory.

- Another cause for alarm is when a window is maximized, or filling the entire screen. It doesn't have any borders, so you can't move it around in the normal way. Yet it covers up every other window. The best cure is to click on the little two-headed arrow in the window's upper right corner to put everything back into a smaller window and restore order.

> ✔ The File Manager sometimes works best when one window sits on the screen and other directories or drives are kept as icons beneath it. Everything is easy to see, and dragging files from window to window is easy. (Just drag the files to the icons for the other windows.)

Playing with Wild Cards

A *wild card* is a holdout from the DOS days, so Windows has to play along. Luckily, the concept is pretty much the same as it is in poker.

In DOS and poker, a wild card can stand for anything. DOS uses two wild cards. One of them is a question mark, or *?*. The other is an asterisk, or *** thing.

The ? wild card is used for matching any single character in a filename. For example, if you type **P?G,** you're referring to any filename that starts with a P, ends with a G, and has a letter in between. The filename can be PIG, PEG, PUG, or even some nonsense word like POG.

You can use as many ? wild cards as you want. For example, H??? can stand for HELP, HYPE, HEEL, or any other word that has three letters following an H. You can even use the ? in a filename's extension. For example, CHOOCHOO.??T matches any occurrence of CHOOCHOO that has a T as the last letter in its extension.

The * wild card is more powerful. It refers to *anything.* For example, *.TXT refers to any file ending in TXT, like CHOOCHOO.TXT, O.TXT, or BEAR.TXT.

> ✔ Wild cards come in handy when you're telling the File Manager to do things with groups of files or to find files meeting certain specifications, as you can see in the "Finding the File You Saved Yesterday" section.

> ✔ You see the *.* wild card, pronounced *star dot star,* in many Windows boxes. It simply stands for *everything,* so it comes in handy.

> ✔ The * gets funny when it's used in the middle of words. For example, when searching for R*ESS, DOS just searches for filenames beginning with R. It ignores the ESS part. When DOS sees the *, it just takes off and doesn't bother looking any further. Kinda antsy, that DOS.

Finding the File You Saved Yesterday

Can't find a file you saved yesterday? Let the File Manager search for it while you grab a cool towel.

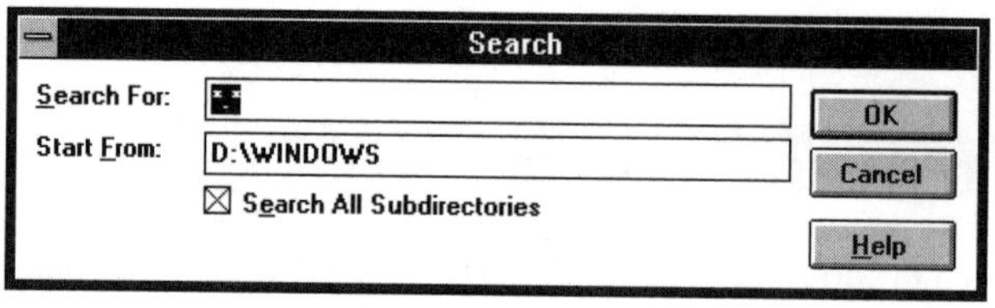

Figure 12-18:
When you
want to find
a file, you
can use the
Search box
to tell the
File
Manager
what to look
for and
where to
look.

Search	
Search For:	▓
Start From:	D:\WINDOWS
☒ Search All Subdirectories	

OK

Cancel

Help

Select File from the menu bar and then Search from the pull-down menu. The box shown in Figure 12-18 pops up.

The Search box shown in Figure 12-18 is set up to find any file in the WINDOWS directory on drive D. It also searches any subdirectories branching from the WINDOWS directory.

If you remember any part of the file's name, type it in the Search For box. For example, if you remember that it starts with B and ends with WRI, type **B*.WRI** in the Search For box. In the Start From box, type the name of the directory you think you put it in. If it's a Windows program, it's probably in the C:\WINDOWS or D:\WINDOWS directory or in one of their subdirectories.

Don't know what directory it's near? Then type in the disk drive's letter, followed by a colon (usually C: or D:), and the File Manager will search the entire disk drive.

Finally, be sure to click on the Search All Subdirectories box to make sure that the File Manager doesn't search just the current directory and give up.

✔ If you don't know what this ? and * stuff is all about, check out the wild card information in the section that precedes this one.

✔ If you don't know what subdirectories are all about, they're nailed down in their own section, earlier in this chapter.

✔ Finally, there's another way to search for yesterday's work: Select View and then select All File Details. Select View once again and choose Sort by Date. The File Manager lists all the files in the order they were created, with the most recent ones on top. Click in the directory where you last saw the file. Because you created it yesterday, it should be near the top. The dates are showing, making that file easier to find.

Formatting a Floppy Disk

New floppy disks won't work straight out of the box; your computer will burp out an error message if you even try. Floppy disks must be formatted, and unless you paid extra for a box of *preformatted* floppy disks, you must format them yourself. The File Manager handles this particularly boring chore quite easily. It's still boring, though, as you'll discover when repeating the process 12 times — once for each disk in the box.

Here's the procedure:

1. **Place the new disk into drive A or drive B and close the latch.**

2. **Select Disk from the File Manager's menu, and a Format Disk box will appear.**

3. **If you're formatting a high-capacity disk in drive A, then just select OK.**

   Your disk drives will whir for several minutes, and then File Manager will ask whether you'd like to format another.

4. **Keep saying Yes and keep feeding your computer the floppy disks until you've formatted the entire box.**

✔ You can format disks in your drive B by clicking on the little arrow in the Disk In: box. Likewise, you can change a disk's capacity by clicking on the little arrow in the Capacity: box. Don't know the capacity of your disks? Then head for the handy chart in Chapter 2.

✔ Don't get your hopes up. The Quick Format option won't speed things up unless your disk has already been formatted once before.

✔ If you want to able to "boot" your computer from a disk, check the Make System Disk option. These "System Disks" can come in handy if your hard drive ever goes on vacation.

Chapter 13
Big Free Programs

*I*f you can spell *potato,* you'll like Write, the Windows word processor. Write would be as good as any other word processor if only it had a spell checker. And maybe a thesaurus for people who like to aggrandize their vocabulary.

Paintbrush, the Windows drawing program, works great for drawing pictures, touching up charts, and creating posters that ask people to please rinse out the coffeepot in the lunchroom. The Windows Cardfile can finally replace the faithful Rolodex, if you don't mind typing in all the business cards you collected on that last trip. And Calendar? Well, it puts a calendar on the screen.

Surprisingly enough, most of these programs are relatively simple to figure out. This chapter just describes when the programs come in handy and how to handle those areas where Microsoft's *ease of use* formula lapses and things get weird.

Writing with Write

The icon for Write, found in Program Manager's Accessories window, looks pretty fancy: a distinguished-looking quill pen, like the ones that get ink on your hands:

Write

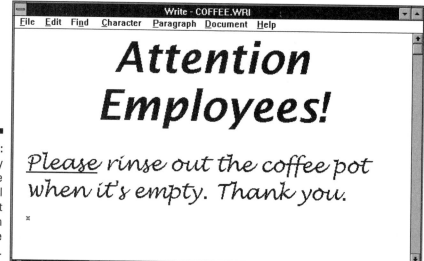

Figure 13-1:
Write may
not have
a spell
checker, but
it can churn
out some
fancy pages.

But, although the icon is fancy, Write isn't quite as fancy as some of the more expensive word processors on the market. You can't create multiple columns, for example, like the ones in newspapers or newsletters. But, if you don't need that frilly stuff, Write works fine for letters, reports, and other basic documents. You can change the fonts around to get pretty fancy, too, as Figure 13-1 shows.

Write also can handle the Windows *TrueType fonts,* that new technology that shapes how characters appear on the screen. You can create an elegant document by using some fancy TrueType fonts and mail it on a disk to somebody else. That person can view it in Write, just as you did. (Before TrueType, people could see only the fonts they'd laboriously installed onto their own computers.)

Plus, Write can handle all that embedding and linking stuff talked about in Chapter 9. Other word processors may take awhile to catch up with these nifty new Windows tricks.

✔ Write works well for most word processing needs: writing letters, reports, or term papers on somber philosophers with weird last names. Unless you're a lousy speller, you'll find Write easy to use, and you'll like its excellent price.

✔ If you're ditching your typewriter for Windows, remember this: On an electric typewriter, you have to push the Return key at the end of each line, or else you start typing off the edge of the paper. Computers, in contrast, are smart enough to sense when words are about to run off the end of the screen. They automatically drop down a line and continue the sentence. (Hip computer nerds call this phenomenon *word wrap.*)

Press Enter only when you're done typing a paragraph and want to start a new one. Press Enter twice to leave a blank line between paragraphs.

Opening and saving a file

In a refreshing change of pace, all Windows programs enable you to open and save a file in exactly the same way: Select the word File at the top of the program's window, and a menu tumbles down. Select Open or Save, depending on your whim.

A box pops up, listing the files in the current directory. Select the name of the file you want to open or type in the name of a new one. Then select the OK button. That's it.

- ✔ You can find more explicit instructions in the section of Chapter 6 on opening a file.

- ✔ Directories and equally mind-numbing concepts are browbeaten in Chapter 12.

- ✔ When you save a file for the first time, you have to choose a name for it, as well as a directory to put it in. Write subsequently remembers the file's name and directory, so you don't have to keep typing them in each time.

- ✔ Sometimes you open a file, change it, and want to save it with a different name or in a different directory. Choose Save As, not Save; Write then treats your work as if you were saving it for the first time; it asks you to type in a new name and a location.

- ✔ Although you can make up filenames on the fly in Write, you can't use Write to create new directories. That duty falls to the Windows File Manager, discussed in Chapter 12.

Saving a Write file as an ASCII file

Just as you can't drop a Ford engine into a Volvo, you can't drop a Write file into another company's word processor. All brands of word processors save their information in different ways in order to confuse the competition.

However, most brands of word processors can read plain old text: a document with no boldface type, italics, columns, or any other fancy stuff. These simple text files are called *ASCII* files (pronounced *ASK-ee*).

If somebody asks you to save a Write file as an ASCII file, choose Save As from the File menu. Click on the arrow next to Save File as Type and choose Text File (*.TXT) from the drop-down list. Type in a name for the file and press Enter. *Voilà!* You've created an ASCII file.

✔ The other Windows word processor, Notepad, can't handle anything *but* ASCII files. Notepad can't load Write's normal files — just the ones saved as ASCII files. (Write can handle Notepad's files, though.) Notepad is dissected in Chapter 14.

✔ Although most word processors can read and write ASCII files, problems still pop up. You lose any formatting, like italicized words, special indents, or embedded pictures of apples.

✔ ASCII stands for American Standard Code for Information Interchange. A bunch of technoids created it when they got tired of programmers saving their information in different ways. Today, most programs grudgingly read or write information using the ASCII format. In fact, ASCII files can even be exchanged with computers from different home planets, with only minor technical glitches.

Other Write stuff

✔ For some reason, Write's tabs don't work well with inexpensive printers known as *9-pin dot-matrix printers.* If the printer behaves erratically when it is trying to print a tab space in Write, buy a newer, more expensive printer. Or a newer, more expensive word processor.

✔ Write is always in the *Insert* mode: When you add something in the middle of a sentence, all the words move to the right to make room for the incoming stuff. Write doesn't support the *Overwrite* mode, where the incoming letters are written right over the old stuff. The Insert key on the keyboard won't do anything.

✔ After you've highlighted a block of text, you can copy it to another location by holding down the Alt key and clicking where you want that block to appear.

✔ A quicker way to open a file is to press and release the Alt key and then press the letters F and O. If you memorize the keyboard commands, you won't have to trudge through all the menus with the mouse. If you don't remember the key commands, check out the handy chart in Table 13-1. You'll find other time-savers listed, as well.

✔ Want to change your page margins? Click on Document and choose Page Layout when the menu drops down. The Page Layout box lets you specify top, bottom, and side margins.

✔ Write normally sets tab spaces for every half inch. To change them, click on Document and choose Tabs from the menu. When the Tabs box appears, type the number of inches you want for each tab. To make the first tab one inch but the second tab only a quarter-inch, for example, type **1** in the first tab box and **.25** in the second tab box.

✔ Saved a file in Write, but now you want to delete it? Head for File Manager and delete it there. Write's an overly sensitive program; it can only *create* files, not destroy them.

Table 13-1	Write Shortcut Keys
To Do This	*Do This*
Open a file	Press Alt, F, and O.
Save a file	Press Alt, F, and S.
Save a file under a new name	Press Alt, F, and A.
Print a file	Press Alt, F, and P.
Select the entire document	Hold down Ctrl and click in the left margin.
Select one word	Double-click on it.
Add *italics* to selected text	Hold down Ctrl and press the letter I (press Ctrl+I).
Add **boldface** to selected text	Hold down Ctrl and press the letter B (press Ctrl+B).
Add underline to selected text	Hold down Ctrl and press the letter U (press Ctrl+U).

Figuring Out the Calendar

Some cynics say that the free Windows programs aren't really programs. They're merely *demonstrations* of what Windows can do. Calendar fits in with that school of thought because it's too lame to be a *real* program. First, when Calendar is an icon, it always thinks the date is the 12th of the month. The icon never displays the current date (except on the 12th). The Calendar icon looks like this:

Calendar

Second, you can't list appointments that are longer than 80 characters. And the words start running off the page before you type even half that much, as you can see in Figure 13-2. This problem has no solution; even when Calendar fills the whole screen, its tiny calendar page stays the same size.

When you click on one of those appointments, the view gets even worse, as you can see in Figure 13-3.

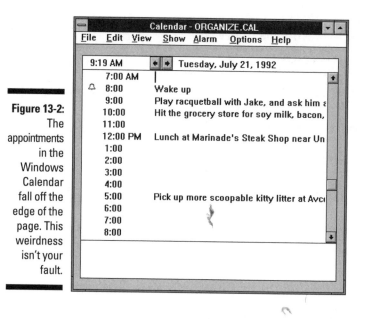

Figure 13-2:
The appointments in the Windows Calendar fall off the edge of the page. This weirdness isn't your fault.

Clicking on the *Lunch at Marinade's Steak Shop* appointment doesn't bring you to the word *Lunch.* Instead, Calendar jumps to the middle of the sentence, as shown in Figure 13-3, making it hard to tell what's going on. This strange behavior isn't your fault.

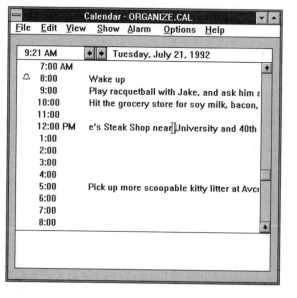

Figure 13-3:
With a single click, Calendar leaps to the middle of the appointment, making it difficult to read. This weirdness isn't your fault, either.

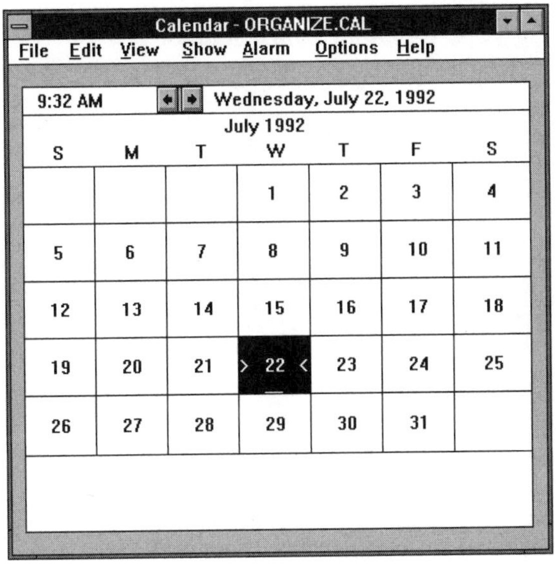

Figure 13-4:
A press of
the F9 key
makes
Calendar
display a
monthly
view.

Calendar works best when it's doing something simple, like displaying a monthly calendar. To see the monthly calendar, as shown in Figure 13-4, select View and then select Month from the pull-down menu. (Or just press F9, whichever comes to mind sooner. *Or* simply double-click inside the bar along Calendar's top, where the day and date are listed.)

The monthly view doesn't show any upcoming appointments, though. You have to mark important days yourself by clicking on them and pressing F6 (or choosing Mark from the Options pull-down menu).

Calendar doesn't search for upcoming appointments, either. You can't search for *Tina* to find out when you're next scheduled for lunch. You can only stumble across the information yourself by viewing appointments in the *Day* mode (press F8) and clicking on the little right- and left-pointing arrows at the top of the screen until you see the name. (And, if the name is off the edge of the page, you'll *never* see it.)

Calendar has one redeeming factor: You can set an alarm by clicking next to an appointment and pressing F5 (or choosing Set from the Alarm pull-down menu). You can set the alarm to go off ten minutes before the appointment, thank goodness.

Table 13-2	Calendar Shortcut Keys
To Do This	*Do This*
View an entire month	Press F9.
View a single day	Press F8.
Jump to a specific date	Press F4.
Set an alarm for a selected time	Press F5.
Add a special *mark* to a day	Press F6.
Enter an appointment on a specific time	Press F7.
Find help	Press F1.
Track your appointments	Buy a better program.

✔ If you find Calendar difficult to use, don't blame yourself. Everybody else does, too. It's fine for figuring out the date of the third Tuesday in a month, but it's terrible for planning appointments.

✔ Calendar always loads the day view first. If you want to see the current month, press F9.

✔ If you're looking for a program to help plan your day, check out some third-party scheduling programs, like PackRat by Polaris Software (1-800-PACKRAT).

✔ Try the shortcut keys in Table 13-2 before giving up on Calendar completely.

✔ Oh yeah — Calendar won't let you change your computer's time or date. If your computer's internal clock is off, head for the Windows Control Panel (or head to Chapter 10's "Setting the Computer's Time and Date" section).

Drawing Pictures with Paintbrush

Unlike Calendar, Paintbrush does what it sets out to do: It creates pictures and graphics to stick into other programs. The icon for Paintbrush is a picture of a palette:

Paintbrush

Paintbrush offers more than just a paintbrush. It has a can of spray paint for that *airbrushed* look, several pencils of different widths, a paint roller for gobbing on a bunch of paint, and an eraser for when things get out of hand. Figure 13-5 was drawn with Paintbrush.

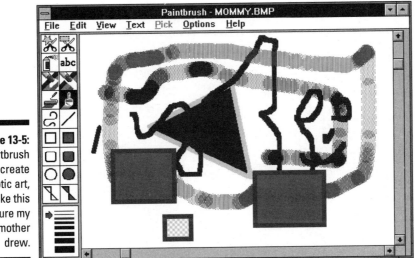

Figure 13-5:
Paintbrush
can create
exotic art,
like this
picture my
mother
drew.

In addition to capturing your artistic flair, Paintbrush can team up with a digital camera or scanner to touch up pictures in your PC. You can create a flashy letterhead to stick into letters in Write. You can even create maps to paste into your party fliers.

✔ Drawings and pictures can be copied from Paintbrush and pasted into just about any other Windows program.

✔ Remember that *cut and paste* stuff from Chapter 9? Well, you can cut out chunks of art from the Paintbrush screen using the *pick* or *scissors* tool described later in this section. The art goes onto the Clipboard, where you can grab it and paste it into any other Windows program.

✔ Paintbrush enables you to add text and numbers to graphics, so you can add street names to maps, put labels inside drawings, or add the vintage year to your wine labels.

✔ Paintbrush is showing its age; it often has problems saving or pasting pictures that contain 256 colors or more. Microsoft says that it's working hard on the problem.

Learning how to draw something

Paintbrush comes with a row of drawing tools along its left side. Not even Jeanne Dixon can figure out what they do, so Table 13-3 explains them.

Below the drawing tools panel lies the *palette,* which is shown in Figure 13-6. *Palette* is a fancy name for the colors you can dab onto your drawing.

Table 13-3	Paintbrush Tools
What It Looks Like	**What It's Called and What It Does**
	Pick: Grabs a rectangular chunk of the screen for cutting or copying to the Clipboard and pasting elsewhere.
	Scissors: Cuts irregular chunks of the screen for cutting or copying to the Clipboard and pasting elsewhere.
	Airbrush: Adds *spray paint* on the drawing. Good for touching up pictures of bus stop benches.
	Text: Enables you to add text, along with cool effects like *shadow* and *outline*.
	Eraser: Rubs out *everything,* leaving nothing but the current background color showing.
	Color eraser: Rubs out only the currently selected color, leaving everything else. (Handier than it seems.)
	Paint roller: It doesn't work like a paint roller. Instead, it *pours* color into an area, filling it up to its boundaries.
	Brush: It doesn't work like a brush. It's more like a pencil for drawing freehand. *Very* hard to use.
	Line: Draws a straight line between two points. (Hold down the Shift key to make vertical or horizontal lines.)
	Curve: Draws a line and then lets you bend it, twice. Truly weird.
	Boxes, rounded boxes, circles/ellipsis, and polygons: Click on these tools to create shapes that look just like the icons. The darker ones are shaded in with the foreground color.
	Line size box: Click on lines of different widths to change the width of the current brush, eraser, box, spray-paint stream, or whatever else you're fiddling with.

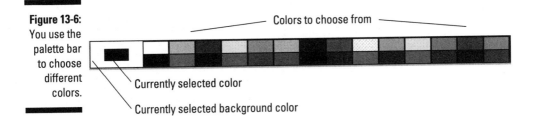

Colors to choose from

Currently selected color

Currently selected background color

The key to Paintbrush is to realize that you're always working with *two* colors: the color of the background and the color you're dabbing on top of it. Paintbrush starts out with the drab combination of black lines on a white background.

To change the color of the *foreground* — the color you use to draw things — click on one of the colors in the palette with the *left* mouse button. To change the color of the *background* — the color you're drawing *on* — click on that color in the palette with the *right* mouse button. You'll see your new background color when you start a new drawing.

After selecting colors, click on the tool you're after in the tool bar and then start slapping paint around. Here are a few tips to help you with some of the tools' less self-explanatory features:

Text: If you keep the colors set to *black on white,* the text's Outline or Shadow modes don't do anything. Paintbrush is outlining or shadowing the text with white on white, which doesn't show up. Click the right mouse button on a different color, say, red, to give words a red outline or shadow. Click the right mouse button back on white to return to normal.

Color eraser: This eraser doesn't really erase colors so much as it changes them. For example, if you don't like the yellow in a drawing, click on yellow in the palette. Then click on the preferred color in the palette, say, purple, with the right mouse button. When you hold down the mouse button and move the pointer over the drawing, all the yellow parts magically change to purple.

Scissors/pick: When you cut pieces out of a drawing, sometimes you leave white holes; at other times the holes are a different color. The trick? Holes take on the shade of the currently selected *background* color.

Brush: Although Paintbrush puts this tool in your hand when it first is loaded, the brush is the most difficult tool to use. Use the other tools to create shapes and then click on the brush for minor touch-ups.

Pasting stuff into Paintbrush

You can paste anything you want into Paintbrush, but there's a catch. If you're pasting something that's bigger than the size of the Paintbrush window, Paintbrush trims off the stuff that doesn't fit.

To paste some big, hunkering stuff, click on Zoom Out from the View menu. Paintbrush steps back to show the entire page. When you press the paste key combination, Ctrl+V, Paintbrush puts a big square on the screen to represent what you're pasting. Use the mouse to drag the square to where you want the big hunkering stuff to go and press Ctrl+V again. The big hunkering stuff appears.

Click on Zoom In from the View menu to return to normal. There it is!

Making new wallpaper in Paintbrush

Anything you make in Paintbrush can be turned into wallpaper and used as a backdrop. Just save your fun new file in the WINDOWS directory. When you head for the Control Panel, the new file is listed with the other potential wallpaper files.

More detailed wallpaper installation information awaits in Chapter 10.

Paintbrush tips and tricks

Not even the quickest art classes can teach you to paint a perfect rose in one day. The same truth applies to Paintbrush: You have to practice using all the tools before you can create something recognizable. Allow yourself several days of fiddling to familiarize yourself with how all the little tools work.

Here are a few tips for making Paintbrush a little more palatable:

- ✔ Before trying to change an important file in Paintbrush, make a copy of the file. Then make your changes to the copy, not the original.
- ✔ What to change something minuscule, like the eye color of somebody in the back row? Then choose Zoom In from the View menu; the mouse pointer turns into a little box. Point to the area you'd like to enlarge and click the mouse. Paintbrush blows up the area, leaving a postage-stamp-sized view of the big picture for perspective. Make your changes and then choose Zoom Out from the View menu to return to normal size. (Or, if you messed up horribly, choose Undo from the Edit menu instead; that cancels all your changes.)

✔ Is Paintbrush showing only black and white on-screen instead of color? Then choose Image Attributes from the Options menu and click on Colors in the Colors box. Paintbrush asks you if you're sure that you want to start over with color and then gives you the chance to save any work in progress to a file. When Paintbrush starts back up, you'll see color (provided your computer can display color, of course).

✔ Paintbrush normally saves files in a special Windows format ending in the letters BMP. But it can display PCX files, too, so if you come across a file ending in the letters PCX, just double-click on its name while in File Manager. In fact, Paintbrush can *save* files in the special PCX format as well. Choose Save As from Paintbrush's File menu, click on the down arrow in the Save File as Type box, and click on the up arrow from the menu that drops down. (Got all that?) The PCX file format now appears as an option, ready to be clicked on.

✔ Want to save a little piece of your current drawing as a small file? Then copy the little piece of art to the Clipboard using Paintbrush's Scissors tool, call up Write (the word processor), and press Ctrl+V to paste the art into Write. Then double-click on the art that you've just pasted into Write. A *second* copy of Paintbrush appears, this time containing just your snipped drawing. Choose Save As from Paintbrush's File menu and save your work. (Although this trick works great for saving little pieces of art in little files, it often chokes on more than 256 colors, unfortunately.)

Finally, if you don't have a color monitor and a mouse, you'll find Paintbrush unwieldy.

Tracking Friends and Enemies in Cardfile

The Cardfile works pretty much like the standard flip-through-the-business-cards gizmo organized people keep on their desks. Even the icon looks the same:

Cardfile

The actual program looks like a business card holder, too, as you can see in Figure 13-7.

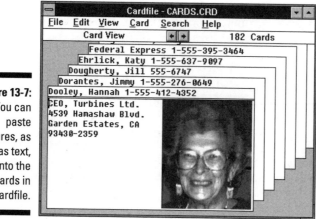

Figure 13-7:
You can paste pictures, as well as text, onto the cards in Cardfile.

To fit more names on the screen, Cardfile can display just the top line of each card. Select View and choose List when the menu falls down. Figure 13-8 shows a list made up of the top lines of several cards.

Cardfile provides you with a quick and easy way to keep track of people. It's simple, and yet it lets you add pictures, sounds, or even huge text files with that Object Linking and Embedding stuff from Chapter 9.

Figure 13-8:
In the List mode, when you type a single letter, Cardfile jumps to the first card starting with that letter.

```
 ═                 Cardfile - CARDS.CRD                ▼ ▲
 File   Edit   View   Card   Search   Help
          List View        ← →        180  Cards
Dooley, Hannah 1-555-412-4352                        ↑
Dorantes, Jimmy 1-555-276-0649
Dougherty, Jill 555-6747
Ehrlick, Katy 1-555-637-9097
Federal Express 1-555-395-3464
Figuracion, Inigo 1-555-234-5433
Filner, Bob City Council: 555-6688
Fire Dept tape 555-4444
Freasier, Roland attorney 555-7878
Freedman, Linda  1-555-562-6632
Gilmor, Gary: 225-1137
Golden, Judith: IRS 1-555-643-4069
Goodyear Blimp 1-555-770-0456
Gookin, Dan 1-555-233-5433
Gore, John: OEI Computers: 549-2199
Graves, Brad
Great Western Bank                                   ↓
```

Adding a new card

When you're ready to start typing in all your business cards, choose <u>A</u>dd from the <u>C</u>ard pull-down menu. (Or press the F7 key.) Cardfile gives you a blank line where you can type in the person's name and phone number. Press Enter and then fill out the rest of the card.

- ✔ After typing in the name, also type in the person's phone number and area code so Cardfile can automatically dial the phone number. (The upcoming *autodial* section explains how to make it dial the number.) Put a 1 in front of the number if it's long distance.

- ✔ To paste a picture into a card, click on Pictur<u>e</u> from the <u>E</u>dit menu. Then paste it from the Clipboard by pressing Ctrl+V (holding down Ctrl while pressing the letter V). Drag the picture until it's positioned just so and let go of the mouse button. (Use Paintbrush to copy the picture to the Clipboard.)

- ✔ If you try to paste in a picture that's too big to fit on the card, Cardfile automatically shrinks it for you. It doesn't shrink the picture when it's *printing* the cards, however. And it doesn't print in color, even if you shelled out the extra bucks for a color printer.

- ✔ You can't edit both the picture and the text at the same time. To switch Cardfile to the proper editing mode, choose either Pictur<u>e</u> or Te<u>x</u>t from the <u>E</u>dit menu. A check mark appears next to the one you can currently edit.

- ✔ To edit the picture, switch to the Edit Picture mode described earlier and double-click on the picture. Paintbrush appears with the image, ready for you to add a mustache. When you're through, close Paintbrush and the updated image appears in Cardfile.

Making Cardfile dial phone numbers automatically

If you have a computer gizmo called a *modem* connected to the computer, Cardfile automatically dials the number at the top of the card when you press F5. When Cardfile tells you to pick up the phone, pick it up and start talking.

- ✔ For this trick to work, you need a modem connected between the computer and the phone lines. You also need a plain old telephone plugged into the modem's phone jack. (Some expensive multiline phones can't handle this autodial stuff.)

✔ Cardfile dials any numbers it finds along the top of the card, so put a 1 in front of any long-distance numbers. (Don't put other numbers up there, like the person's shoe size, or the modem will dial those numbers, too.) Finally, if you need to dial a 9 for an outside line, press F5 and click on the Setup button. Click in the Use Prefix box and type the number 9 in the Prefix box.

✔ Cardfile lames out when autodialing phone numbers in the List mode, where all the names and numbers are showing on the screen. If you press F4 to jump to a person's name and then press F5 to dial that person's number, Cardfile doesn't come up with the right phone number. This problem is called a *bug,* meaning the responsible programmer is getting yelled at right now. It's not your fault.

Rooting through the cards for somebody's phone number

Cardfile complicated matters by offering two kinds of searches. It can search the names along the top of the cards, or it can search the information stored on the card itself. However, Cardfile can't be bothered to search *both* parts of the card at the same time.

✔ To search through the *names* at the top of the cards, select Search and then choose Go to (or just press F4). Type the name of the person you're after and press Enter. Cardfile dashes to the first card that matches that name. Not the right person? Then press F4 again and type in the name again. (You have to retype the name every time you repeat the process. It can take a *long* time to find the right Mr. Smith card. However, if you know Mr. Smith's first name — say, Pat — you can speed up the process by typing **Smith, Pat** in the box.)

✔ To search through the *information* stored on the cards, select Search and then select Find from the menu. Type in the word you're after and press Enter. Not the right card? Then press F3 to keep searching through the other cards.

Chapter 14
Little Free Programs

- -

- -

*T*his chapter is devoted to the insatiably curious. The ones who use one or two Windows programs but keep asking themselves one question whenever Windows comes to the screen: What do all those other icons do?

Just about everybody has already figured out that the playing card icon stands for Solitaire. The Calculator and Clock are easy enough to guess, too. But, in this chapter, you find out just what a double-click on the little movie camera or another icon does.

To get the heck back out of a program when your curiosity's sated, double-click on the program's *Control-menu box,* that square in its top left-hand corner.

Talking to Other Computers with Terminal

Terminal

Computer nerds have used modems for years, but they're only now becoming popular with normal, everyday people. Modems connect your computer with other computers through the phone lines so that you can read the latest news and weather or see how much money your neighbors owe on their credit cards.

If you have a modem, Terminal can make it dial up other computers and grab information from them.

✔ Installing and setting up a modem and flipping all the switches in the right direction are notoriously difficult. You need to worry about gross things like modem speed, parity, stop bits, and other buzz-word stuff. If you've just purchased a modem, lure a computer guru friend over to help install the thing and get it modulating in the right directions. When it has been tweaked in just the right way, a modem is pretty easy to use.

✔ Terminal is so difficult to use, in fact, that it fills a complete chapter in this book's sequel, *MORE Windows For Dummies.*

✔ Terminal works only with *text-based* on-line services, like CompuServe, GEnie, MCI Mail, or computer bulletin boards. It doesn't work with graphics-based bulletin boards like Prodigy and America Online.

✔ Terminal can't cruise the World Wide Web, either. It simply doesn't have enough horsepower to leave the curb of the Information Superhighway. It works with the text portions of the Internet, but don't count on anything fancy. (Warning of Upcoming Spousal Plug: For more information on modems and telecommunications programs, pick up *Modems For Dummies,* written by my wife, who now owes me one beer.)

Don't pick up the phone while the modem is using it to transmit information. Just picking up the handset can garble the signal and possibly break the connection.

Modems are computer gizmos that can translate the computer's digital information into sound and squirt it over the phone lines to other modems. They come in two types: internal and external. *Internal modems* plug into the nether reaches of the computer, and *external modems* have a cable that plugs into a serial port on the computer's rump. Both types do the same thing, but the external ones have little lights on them that blink as the sound flows back and forth.

Jotting Notes in Notepad

Notepad

Windows comes with two word processors, Write and Notepad. Write is for the letters you're sprucing up for other people to see. Notepad is for stuff you're going to keep for yourself.

Notepad is quicker than Write. Double-click on its icon, and it leaps to the screen more quickly than you could have reached for a notepad in your back pocket. You can type in some quick words and save them on the fly.

Understanding Notepad's limitations

Notepad's speed comes at a price, however. Notepad stores only words and numbers. It doesn't store any special formatting, like italicized letters, and you can't paste any pictures into it, as you can with Write. It's a quick, throw-together program for your quick, throw-together thoughts.

- Notepad tosses you into instant confusion: All the sentences head right off the edge of the screen. To turn one-line, runaway sentences into normal paragraphs, turn on the *word wrap* feature by selecting Word Wrap from the Edit menu. (You have to turn it on each time you start Notepad, strangely enough.)

- Notepad prints kind of funny, too: It prints the file's name at the top of every page. To combat this nonsense, select File and then choose Page Setup. A box appears, with a funny code word highlighted in the Header box. Press Delete to get rid of the word and click on the OK button. If you want to get rid of the automatic page numbering, clear out the Footer box as well.

- Here's another printing problem: Notepad doesn't print exactly what you see on the screen. Instead, it prints according to the margins you set in Page Setup under the File menu. This quirk can lead to unpredictable results.

- If you delete everything from a Notepad file and try to save the empty file, Windows tells you it won't bother saving sheer emptiness, and it deletes the file.

- Notepad saves everything in ASCII format, the bare-bones format almost all word processors can read. If some evil tech-head ever tells you to edit your AUTOEXEC.BAT or CONFIG.SYS files, use Notepad, not Write.

Turning Notepad into a log book

Although Notepad leans toward simplicity, it has one fancy feature that not even Write can match. Notepad can automatically stamp the current time and date at the bottom of a file whenever you open it. Just type **.LOG** in the very top, left-hand corner of a file and save the file. Then, whenever you open it again, you can jot down some current notes and have Notepad stamp it with the time and date. It looks similar to what you see in Figure 14-1.

- Don't try the .LOG trick by using lowercase letters and don't omit the period. It doesn't work.

- To stick in the date and time manually, press F5. The time and date appear, just as they do in the .LOG trick.

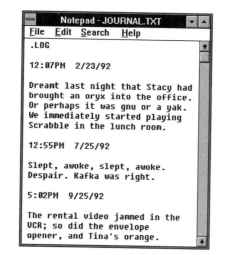

Figure 14-1:
Add the
word .LOG
to the file,
and
Notepad
stamps it
with the
time and
date
whenever
you open it.

Telling the Time with Clock

Clock

If you're not wearing a wristwatch, you may like the Windows Clock. A double-click on the Clock icon in Program Manager puts the current time at the bottom of the screen. In fact, I keep the Clock in my Program Manager's StartUp group so that it appears at the bottom of the screen automatically. (Make it start up as an icon, as explained in Chapter 11.)

The Clock is pretty easy to figure out, but here's one tip: Keep the Clock running as an icon, not as a window, or else it jumps around when you use the Task List's Tile or Cascade button to organize the desktop.

- ✔ Clock can display the time like a grandfather clock or like a digital watch. You tell it how you want the time displayed by selecting either Analog or Digital in the Settings menu (Clock's *only* menu).

- ✔ Although you can choose different fonts for Clock's digital display, don't get carried away. The one it is already using is pretty much the only one that's readable when Clock squats as an icon at the bottom of the screen.

- ✔ To make Clock stay visible, even when another window sits on it, click once on its icon at the bottom of the screen. When a menu shoots out the top of its head, select the Always on Top option. (You can find that option in its Control menu as well.)

Calculating Numbers with Calculator

Calculator

The Calculator is, well, a calculator. It looks simple enough, and it really is — unless you've mistakenly set it for Scientific mode and see some nightmarish logarithmic stuff. To bring it back to normal, select <u>V</u>iew and choose S<u>t</u>andard.

To punch in numbers and equations, click on the little buttons, just as if it were a normal calculator. When you press the = sign, the answer appears at the top. For an extra measure of handiness, you can copy the answers to the Clipboard by pressing Ctrl+C (holding down the Ctrl key while pressing C). Then click in the window where you want the answer to appear and press Ctrl+V. That method is easier than retyping a number like 2.449489742783.

✔ Unlike in other Windows programs, you can't copy Calculator's answer by running the mouse pointer over the numbers. You have to press Ctrl+C or choose <u>C</u>opy from the <u>E</u>dit menu.

✔ If the mouse action is too slow, press the Num Lock key and punch in numbers with the numeric keypad.

✔ Calculator lames out when you're typing in decimal numbers with zeros. If you enter the number 6.000002, the display doesn't show more than one zero until you type the 2. *Then* all the zeros finally show up. This quirk is called a *bug,* meaning that a programmer goofed up. It isn't your fault.

The programmer screwed up even worse, actually. When you subtract 2 from 2.01, Calculator responds with zero rather than .01, the real answer. In fact, Calculator messes up with several numbers ending in .01. Microsoft released a fixed version of Calculator in early 1995. The updated program is stored in a file called WW1138.EXE, and it can be downloaded from CompuServe (GO MSL) or Microsoft's BBS (206-936-6735).

Adding the à in Voilà (Character Map)

Char Map

To add weird foreign characters, like á, £, or even Ð, double-click on the Character Map icon, found in Program Manager's Accessories window. A box like the one shown in Figure 14-2 appears, listing every available character and symbol for the current font.

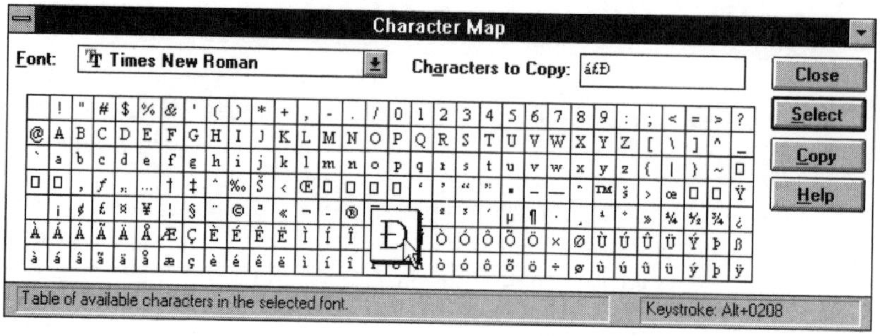

Figure 14-2:
You can use
the
Character
Map to find
foreign
characters
and stick
them in your
work.

Character Map
Font: ☐ Times New Roman ⬆ Characters to Copy: á£Ð

Table of available characters in the selected font.   Keystroke: Alt+0208

Close
Select
Copy
Help

Follow these steps to put a foreign character in your work:

1. **Make sure that the current font — the name for the style of the characters on the page — shows in the Font box.**

   Not showing? Then click on the down arrow and click on the font when it appears in the drop-down list.

2. **Scan the Character Map box until you see the symbol you're after; then pounce on that character with a double-click.**

   It appears in the Characters to Copy box.

3. **Click on Copy to send the character to the Clipboard.**

4. **Click on the Close button to close the Character Map.**

5. **Click in the document where you want the new symbol or character to appear.**

6. **Press Ctrl+V, and it pops right in there.**

   (Give it a second. Sometimes it's slow.)

The symbols in the Character Map box are easier to see if you hold down the mouse button and move the pointer over them.

 ✔ When working with foreign words, keep the Character Map handy as an icon, ready for consultation.

 ✔ For some fun symbols like ✎, 🖂, ✍, ✐, ✦, ♀, or ☑, switch to the Wingdings font. It's full of little doodads to spice up your work.

 ✔ You can grab several characters at a time by double-clicking on each of them and then copying them into your work as a chunk. You don't have to keep returning to the Character Map for each one.

That weird Alt+0208 stuff is too trivial to bother with

In the bottom right-hand corner, Character Map flashes numbers after the words `Keystroke: Alt+`. Those numbers hail back to the stone-tablet days of adding foreign characters when word processing. Back then, people had to look up a character's code number in the back of a boring manual.

If you remember the code numbers for your favorite symbols, however, you can bypass Character Map and add them directly to documents.

For example, the code number listed in the bottom corner for *é* is 0233.

Here's the trick: Press and release Num Lock, hold down Alt, and type **0233** with the numeric keypad. Let go of the Alt key, and the *é* symbol appears.

If you constantly use one special character, this method may be faster than using Character Map. (Press and release Num Lock when you're through.)

Repeating Keystrokes with Recorder

Recorder

Computers never tire of repeating things. To capture the computer's eagerness to repeat things ad nauseam, Windows includes Recorder (which is terribly complicated and has nothing to do with movies).

Recorder enables you to assign a whole bunch of keystrokes to a single key. Then, when you press the single key, Recorder plays back those keystrokes, saving you some time. Computer nerds call these recorded keys *macros,* and they play with them for hours until they get them right.

For everybody else, the concept is awkward, time-consuming, scary, and often dangerous. Frequently, setting up the Recorder takes more time than just typing in the stuff by hand. Don't bother with Recorder.

Using Sound Recorder and Media Player

Sound
Recorder

If you've bought and installed a sound card for your computer, you can play and record sounds with Sound Recorder. It looks and works pretty much like a tape recorder. Here's one warning, however: Don't get carried away when re-cording particularly long sounds. They take a *lot* of space on the hard drive.

Media Player

Media Player can't record, but it can play from a wide variety of devices. It can play sounds from a sound card, as well as connect to MIDI keyboards. It can access CD-ROM drives for both sound and data. It even plays videodiscs.

- ✔ Before these programs can work with your new hardware toys, you need to install *drivers* for the hardware toys. Flip to the section of Chapter 17 on installing a driver.

- ✔ Windows comes with a few drivers for the most popular sound cards. Other sound cards or CD-ROM drives come with drivers on a floppy disk that is boxed with the package.

- ✔ Sound cards and CD-ROM drives are covered in Chapter 2.

- ✔ *MORE Windows For Dummies,* this book's sequel, shows you how to use Sound Recorder and Media Player to play and record sounds, listen to compact discs, and even watch movies.

- ✔ Or if you're *really* entranced by flashing lights and screaming sounds, check out *Multimedia and CD-ROMs For Dummies.* It shows you how to buy, set up, and use all those cool multimedia gizmos everybody's talking about.

Playing Cards in Solitaire

Solitaire

Windows Solitaire works just like the card game, so here are just a few pointers for the computerized version:

- ✔ When the boss comes by, click on the minimize button, that downward-pointing arrow in the top right-hand corner. If you can't move the mouse quickly enough, hold down Alt and press the spacebar, followed by the letter N. In either case, Solitaire turns into an icon at the bottom of the screen. Double-click on the icon to resume play when the boss passes.

- ✔ Using Windows isn't easy on a laptop, and Solitaire can be a nightmare. You can play Solitaire with a keyboard by using an awkward combination of Tab, Enter, and the arrow keys. But a laptop's black-and-white screen makes it difficult to tell when a card is being placed on the right color.

- ✔ Sharp-eyed players will notice some background fun: The bats flap their wings, the sun sticks out its tongue, and a card slides in and out of a dealer's sleeve. These shenanigans only occur when you play in *timed* mode. To start the fun, choose <u>O</u>ptions from the <u>G</u>ame menu and make sure that there's an X in the T<u>i</u>med Game box.

- ✔ If you're using Windows for Workgroups, you may have noticed a game of Hearts lurking in your Games group. It's covered in Chapter 20.

Playing Minesweeper

Sweeper

Despite the name, Minesweeper does not cause any explosions, even if you accidentally uncover a mine. And it works better on laptops than Solitaire does. Minesweeper is more of a math game than anything else. No jumping little men here.

Start by clicking on a random square. If you click on a hidden mine, you lose on the first click. Otherwise, some numbers appear in one or more of the little squares. The number says how many mines are hidden in the squares surrounding that square.

Each square is surrounded by eight other squares. (Unless it's on the edge; then there are only five. And only three squares surround corner squares.) If, through the process of elimination, you're sure a mine exists beneath a certain square, click on it with the right mouse button to put a little flag there.

Eventually, through logical deduction (or just mindless pointing and clicking), you either accidentally click on a mine and are blown up, or mark all the mine squares with flags and win the game.

The key is to win it as fast as you can. The best time I've heard of at the beginner's level is 7 seconds.

Shortly after *Windows For Dummies* came out, Roger Segal of New York sent me a printout of his screen, showing his Minesweeper high score of only 6 seconds. A letter from Nessie in Maryland soon upped the ante to 5 seconds. And Bob Seidel in Virginia brought the record to 3 seconds.

Want to be in the same league? Then pick up *MORE Windows For Dummies*, head for Chapter 17, and read the step-by-step instructions on how to *cheat* — yep, the book shows you how to type a secret code and then amaze your friends by knowing in advance which squares contain bombs.

When you're done amazing friends, Chapter 15 of *MORE Windows For Dummies* shows you how to edit Minesweeper's secret High Score file. That lets you change the high score to anything you want. (Sniff. High scores won't mean anything anymore.)

Part IV

Looking at That Darn DOS Stuff

The 5th Wave   By Rich Tennant

"...AND TALK ABOUT MEMORY! THIS BABY'S GOT SO MUCH MEMORY, IT COMES WITH EXTRA DOCUMENTATION, A HARD DISK—AND A SENSE OF GUILT! I MEAN I'M TALKIN MEMORY!"

In this part...

*I*n the beginning, there was DOS, a cold, prickly Disk Operating System that poked anybody who tried to befriend it. Then Windows came to the rescue, bringing smooth, insulating layers of point-and-click friendliness to millions of computers.

Most of the time, Windows keeps things warm and fuzzy. Beneath it all, however, DOS boils and broods, rearing its head occasionally to take a nip.

This part of the book describes how Windows tries to keep DOS wrapped up and held down tight.

Chapter 15
Memory Stuff
You'll Want to Forget

*W*indows likes to play with lots of *memory*. Computer nerds refer to memory as *RAM* to make them feel bold: *RAM*. Shivers!

DOS dishes out the computer's memory, and it does a terrible job. Even Windows gets confused: It goes into special modes depending on the kind of memory Brad stuffed into your computer in the back room of the computer store.

This chapter explains all that memory stuff. You can probably skip it and ride off to greener pastures. But, if Windows keeps putting funny boxes on the screen that say something spiteful about memory, this is the chapter to wave in its face.

What Is Memory, Anyway?

Memory is like your teacher's chalkboard in math class. With a big chalkboard, the teacher could kick up some dust and complete some huge, complicated equations. With a smaller chalkboard, the teacher had to stop and erase all the old stuff to make room.

The computer uses memory as a sort of chalkboard, too. Computers turn everything — programs, data, and so on — into numbers. When you play Solitaire, the computer loads Solitaire's numbers into its memory — writes them on its memory chalkboard, so to speak — where it can perform the calculations needed to move those playing cards around.

When you write a letter, the words also head straight into the computer's memory. When the program saves your letter, it transfers your words from memory to disk. That disk is either the hard drive (the big disk inside the computer) or a floppy disk (those little coaster things).

The computer then wipes the slate clean, clearing the memory for other programs to use. One big difference between memory and a chalkboard is that the stuff on the chalkboard stays there until the janitor wipes it off, but all the information stored in the computer's memory vanishes the instant you flip the computer's off switch.

To keep from losing your new creations — letters, spreadsheets, or high scores — you have to save them to a disk before turning off the computer.

Don't turn off the computer while Windows is still running. Exit Windows by double-clicking in the little square in the Program Manager's top left-hand corner. When you double-click, Windows double-checks to make sure that you've saved your work. If everything is stowed away properly, Windows leaves the screen. Then it's OK to flip the off switch.

Why Does Windows Want So Much Memory?

Windows requires a lot of memory because so much is going on. Each open window needs memory just to show up on the screen. The programs in those windows want even *more* memory when they start to compute, whether they're moving playing cards around or balancing a budget.

Every time you open another window, Windows grabs for yet more memory from the computer's stockpile. If no memory is left, Windows lets you know. It pops up a message, asking you to please quit one or more applications to increase available memory and then try again. That message means you need to close some windows.

When Windows starts to run out of available memory, you notice that it is becoming sluggish. Unfortunately, there's really no cure. Either don't keep a bunch of windows open or take the computer back to the store and buy more memory. (Make them put it in for you.)

✔ On 386 or 486 computers, Windows puts on a cape and creates *virtual memory*. Windows grabs part of the computer's hard drive and uses it for memory. Windows runs more slowly, but you can do more stuff at once. This ruggedly technical bit of magic is discussed in Chapter 10's section on 386 Enhanced stuff.

✔ Windows needs more memory than ever when it's running DOS programs: programs that were never intended to be used with Windows. To make sure that these programs run correctly, you may need to piddle with their PIFs (I'm not kidding), a technique discussed in Chapter 16.

Metric Memory Terms to Ignore — Please

Instead of measuring the computer's memory in ounces or serving sizes, DOS measures it in *bytes*. One byte of memory can hold one character. For example, the word *flagrant* is 8 letters long, so it consumes 8 bytes of memory.

An entire page of text grabs about 1,000 bytes. Add in *kilobyte,* the metric term for 1,000, and that page consumes about 1 *kilobyte* of memory.

One thousand pages use about 1,000 kilobytes of memory, which brings in yet another metric term: *megabyte.* The 1,000 pages take up roughly 1 *megabyte* of memory.

✔ Kilobyte and megabyte are usually abbreviated as *K* and *MB*. For example, 4K means 4 kilobytes, and 120MB means 120 megabytes.

✔ RAM stands for *random-access memory*. Now that this term is on the table, you may as well know that a specific location in memory is called an *address*.

✔ The storage capacities of the hard drive and the memory are measured in megabytes. The hard drive needs a lot of megabytes because it stores all the programs and data, whether they're running or not. The memory, however, stores only programs that are currently running, so the hard drive is always bigger than the memory.

✔ Windows runs slowly if the computer has 2MB or less of RAM. The more RAM you can give it, the faster it runs.

✔ When two or more programs snatch for the same byte of memory, Windows belches. To dish out memory to impatient programs, Windows uses a memory manager, which is discussed later in this chapter.

Even More Memory Terms to Ignore

DOS divvies up the computer's available memory into four main parts: conventional, upper, expanded, and extended. (Windows sometimes divvies it up even more, but let's not get carried away.)

Conventional memory

Back in the good old days, computers used plain old conventional memory. The software box said how much memory the software needed — usually 512K or 640K. If the computer had that much conventional memory, it could cram the whole program into it, and you could get some work done.

Unfortunately, the DOS designers set aside only 640K of memory for running programs. As programs grew larger, they couldn't fit inside that 640K *barrier*. So the programmers started cheating — adding more memory and tricking DOS into thinking it was OK to use it.

Utterly trivial details about upper and expanded memory

Upper memory is a chunk of memory right above that 640K barrier that DOS can use. DOS can't run programs in it, but it can shove other stuff up there: instructions for displaying stuff on different brands of video cards and monitors, for example.

Expanded memory refers to memory chips on a special metal card that has been stuck inside the computer. Special software called an *expanded-memory manager* swaps some of the memory on the card with some memory in the 640K hot spot. By cycling chunks of memory back and forth, the software tricks the computer into using more memory.

Extended memory managers can also convert some of your computer's extended memory into expanded memory when a DOS program asks for it.

You don't have to worry about expanded or upper memory with Windows. And if you stick to running Windows programs exclusively, you can probably ignore this chapter. DOS programs cause the most problems.

Extended memory

Windows is huge. It doesn't fit inside the conventional DOS memory that all the DOS programs settle for. So Windows looks for something called *extended memory*.

Extended memory is a type of memory that comes with 286, 386, 486, and Pentium computers. DOS grabs the first 640K of that chunk and uses it as conventional memory to run plain old DOS programs. But, because DOS can't handle more than 640K of memory, it doesn't bother reaching for any of the other extended memory.

But Windows does. It comes with a special program called HIMEM that reins in the extended memory so Windows can use it for running programs.

✔ These trivial memory details surface and cause problems when you are running DOS programs under Windows. All DOS programs want that same 640K of memory, so Windows has to trick them into thinking they're getting it — even if more than one DOS program is running at the same time.

✔ The old-fashioned XT computers don't have any extended memory, so Windows doesn't run on them.

✔ Most 386, 486, and Pentium computers come with at least 1MB of memory installed. That's the bare minimum Windows requires to get out of bed.

What Mode Are You?

When you type **WIN** to get Windows moving, it looks at the computer's memory, kicks its tires, and starts up in one of two modes: Standard or 386 Enhanced. Windows automatically chooses the correct mode for the computer; you don't have to page through any tables and charts to find out which mode to use.

The *386 Enhanced mode* enables Windows to take advantage of the hot-rod capacities of 386, 486, and Pentium computers. In the 386 Enhanced mode, Windows lets DOS programs run in their own little windows, just like normal Windows programs do. Plus, Windows grabs part of the hard drive and uses it as memory, so you can run more programs at the same time.

In *Standard mode,* DOS programs can't run in their own windows. They get the full screen while Windows waits in the background. If you hold down Alt and press Esc, Windows leaps back onto the screen, transforming the DOS program into an icon at the screen's bottom. To get rid of the DOS program completely, just exit it normally.

Which mode is better? Well, Standard mode is almost always faster because Windows doesn't have to dilly-dally with DOS windows and converting hard drives into memory. If you're not running DOS programs, and Windows isn't shooting weird *out of memory* errors at you, Standard mode may work well for you.

If you need to run DOS programs in Windows so you can easily cut and paste information from them, you need the 386 Enhanced mode. Although it's slower, it offers more memory to run more and bigger programs.

To force Windows into Standard mode, type the following at the DOS prompt and then press Enter:

```
C:\> WIN /S
```

That is, type **WIN,** a space, a forward slash, and **S.** Then press Enter.

To force Windows into 386 Enhanced mode, type the following at the DOS prompt and then press Enter.

```
C:\> WIN /3
```

That is, type **WIN,** a space, a forward slash, and **3.** Then press Enter.

Windows automatically starts up in the mode that should serve the computer the best. If your computer doesn't have enough power to handle a particular mode, Windows doesn't run, even if you try forcing it.

- ✔ Windows automatically opts for Standard mode on 286 computers. No way to get around that one, even if you try forcing it with the */3* trick.

- ✔ Windows automatically goes into 386 Enhanced mode on 386, 486, and Pentium computers with 2MB of extended memory.

- ✔ Sometimes Windows dashes into Standard mode, even on a 386 computer with 2MB of extended memory. That's probably because the computer has a bunch of device drivers or terminate-and-stay-resident (TSR) programs hogging up some memory. Either get rid of the ones you don't need or use a memory manager to *load them high.*

- ✔ When Windows runs DOS programs in Standard mode, it creates little temporary files to help itself keep DOS under wraps. Normally, it deletes those little files when you close a DOS program. But, if something goes wrong, those files can end up hanging around on the hard drive. If you ever see them (they start with the characters ~*WOA*) when you're *not* running Windows, you can delete them.

- ✔ To see what mode Windows chose, click on <u>H</u>elp from the Program Manager's menu bar and select <u>A</u>bout. A box pops up, like the one shown in Figure 15-1, listing the mode on the third line from the bottom. The box also talks about *system resources,* a boring subject you can thankfully hop right over.

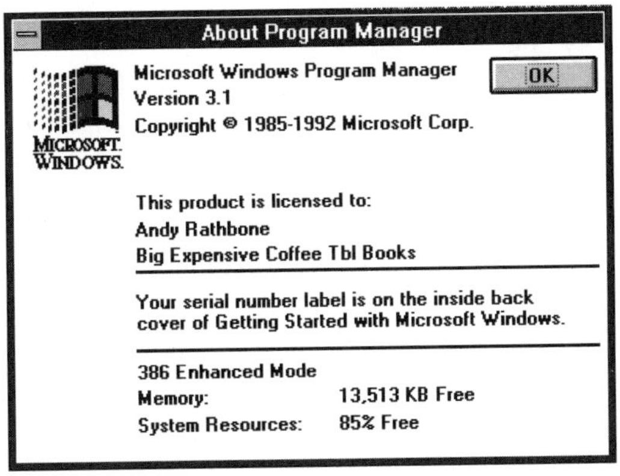

About Program Manager

Microsoft Windows Program Manager
Version 3.1
Copyright © 1985-1992 Microsoft Corp.

OK

MICROSOFT
WINDOWS

This product is licensed to:
Andy Rathbone
Big Expensive Coffee Tbl Books

Your serial number label is on the inside back
cover of Getting Started with Microsoft Windows.

386 Enhanced Mode
Memory: 13,513 KB Free
System Resources: 85% Free

Figure 15-1:
The About
Program
Manager
box shows
the mode
and the
*system
resources*
percentage.

System resources drivel

Windows can run a lot of programs at the same time. Anyone who has watched more than three kids knows what a strain it can be on one's resources. Instead of getting exasperated, Windows merely shows you its current stress level as a *system resources percentage*.

To see how strung out Windows has become, click on Help in the menu bar of just about any Windows program and then select About from the pull-down menu. Figure 15-1 shows what my box says in Program Manager.

The words at the box's bottom say that the computer's system resources are 85 percent free, meaning that Windows is devoting only 15 percent of itself to running the show. For Windows, system resources are never 100 percent free because the Program Manager always grabs a chunk right off the bat.

Windows starts to stumble when the system resources drop below 30 percent, and if the figure drops much lower than that, the program balks at opening any more windows. If Windows starts acting up, check the available system resources.

If the percentage is low, try closing some programs and reducing the number of program groups in the Program Manager. Both of these steps help bring the percentage back to a healthier level.

Even if you have plenty of available memory (Figure 15-1 shows that I have 13,513K), the system resources can still drop to a dangerous level. Windows sends you a message when it's too tired to work any more.

What's a Memory Manager?

Don't worry if you find the terms *conventional memory, expanded memory, extended memory, upper memory,* and *virtual memory* to be virtually confusing.

In fact, all this memory stuff confuses programs, too. Sometimes they all grab for the same piece and stagger away, stunned. You will, too, when their bounce freezes the computer up solid, forcing you to punch the reset button.

A memory manager makes sure that the right program grabs the right piece of memory at the right time. Windows comes with its own memory managers; when you installed Windows, Windows installed its memory managers as well.

Other people buy *third-party* memory managers to scrape every bit of memory from a system and place it at the Windows altar.

- Memory managers can do wonders. Sometimes they even make everything work better, right off the bat. Other times you have to tweak them incessantly, plugging in new numbers and just plain fiddling around.

- If you're going to buy a memory manager, buy a new computer game at the same time and invite a friendly computer guru to check the game out. When the guru shows up, casually let the memory manager box fall on the floor. Gurus love playing with that stuff just as much as with computer games.

Chapter 16
Those Hoggy DOS Programs

*W*indows programs are used to a communal lifestyle where they all eat from the same granola trough. They can share the computer's memory without bickering. DOS programs, however, hail from a different computing era. Windows must nurse DOS programs along, or the DOS programs won't run.

In fact, Windows keeps a special chart called a *PIF* (an acronym for *program information file*) for each problem-causing DOS program. A PIF (rhymes with *sniff*) contains the care and feeding instructions that Windows needs to make that particular DOS program happy.

The information in these PIFs can include some pretty meaty stuff. This chapter chops it into easily digestible chunks, but you may want to keep a napkin around, just in case.

Running DOS Programs under Windows

Some DOS programs are easy to run under Windows. Just head for the Program Manager, double-click on that program's icon, and stand back while it heads for the screen. Sometimes the program fills the entire screen while Windows waits in the background. Other times, the program runs happily in its own window.

But some DOS programs refuse to run under Windows at all. They were designed to use *all* of a computer's resources, so they balk if they think that Windows is just tossing them a few scraps.

To trick these DOS programs into feeling at home, Windows uses something called a PIF: a *program information file.* Each problem-causing DOS program gets its own PIF containing the special instructions needed to trick that program into running in Windows.

For example, a PIF may tell Windows to put the DOS program in a window or to make the program fill the entire screen. PIFs tell Windows the type of memory that the DOS program craves and how much of that memory it wants.

Microsoft wrote up some PIFs for the most popular DOS programs and tossed them in the Windows box. In fact, when you're double-clicking on a DOS program's icon in the Program Manager, you're *really* double-clicking on that program's PIF. Windows consults the PIF and then runs the program accordingly.

- When Windows installs itself, it searches to see what programs you've already installed on the computer. When it finds a DOS program it recognizes, it tosses a PIF for that program into the Windows directory and puts an icon for that PIF in the Program Manager.

- If you've installed a new DOS program and want to run it under Windows, check out the section about putting a favorite program into the Program Manager in Chapter 11. If Windows recognizes that new program, it pulls a PIF off the original Windows disks and everything is hunky dory.

- Some DOS programs come with their own Windows PIFs. When you install that program, it tosses its PIF onto the hard drive. PIFs usually start with the program's filename and end in the letters *PIF.* When Windows searches the hard drive, it sticks that PIF as an icon in the Program Manager, as described in the section about putting a favorite program into the Program Manager in Chapter 11.

- If you double-click on a DOS program that doesn't have a PIF, Windows uses a general-purpose PIF called _DEFAULT.PIF. This PIF contains settings that allow almost any DOS program to run without problem.

Making Your Own PIFs for DOS Programs

If a DOS program isn't working under Windows, call the company that made it and tell the company that you need its PIF for Windows. If the company doesn't have one, call your computer dealer or bribe a computer guru to make one for you.

Until then, simply exit Windows when you want to run that DOS program and then start Windows when you want to see Windows again. Don't bother trying to make your own PIF. This is heavy stuff, meant for advanced users who *enjoy* piddling with PIFs.

Besides, some DOS programs won't run under Windows no matter how much PIF coddling they get. Still, if you want to brave your way through creating a PIF, check out the books *MORE Windows For Dummies* or *Windows 3.1 SECRETS*, published by IDG Books Worldwide. They're full of techie tips for PIF hounds.

Until you become a PIF manufacturer, you're better off sticking with Windows programs when running Windows. Most companies are writing Windows versions of their DOS programs, so there's less need to run a DOS program in Windows, anyway.

Changing Fonts in a DOS Window

DOS programs are used to roaming free and wild, but Windows can force them to run inside a window, just like any other Windows program. A DOS window functions pretty much like any other window. You can move it around, tug on its borders to change its size, or shrink it into an icon if it's getting in the way.

If the DOS program normally fills the whole screen under Windows, try this: Hold the Alt key and press Enter. If the computer is running in 386 Enhanced mode, that DOS program hops into a window on the screen (see Figure 16-1).

Unfortunately, a DOS window is often too large to fit comfortably on the screen. To fix that oversight, change the size of the font used by the window. That action makes the letters smaller so more information will fit on the screen. Follow these steps to change the font size for a DOS window:

1. **Click once in the Control-menu box.**

   It is that square in the top left corner of the window. The Control menu appears.

2. **Click on Fonts.**

   The dialog box shown in Figure 16-2 appears. The little numbers on the left side of the dialog box, starting with 4 x 6, are the sizes of the fonts used by the current window.

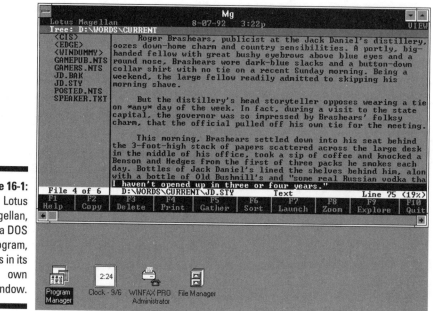

Mg

Lotus Magellan   8-07-92   3:22p   VIEW
Tree: D:\WORDS\CURRENT
<CIS>   Roger Brashears, publicist at the Jack Daniel's distillery,
<EDGE>   oozes down-home charm and country sensibilities. A portly, big-
<WINDUMMY>   handed fellow with great bushy eyebrows above blue eyes and a
GAMEPUB.NTS   round nose, Brashears wore dark-blue slacks and a button-down
GAMERS.NTS   collar shirt with no tie on a recent Sunday morning. Being a
JD.BAK   weekend, the large fellow readily admitted to skipping his
JD.STY   morning shave.
POSTED.NTS
SPEAKER.TXT   But the distillery's head storyteller opposes wearing a tie
              on *any* day of the week. In fact, during a visit to the state
              capital, the governor was so impressed by Brashears' folksy
              charm, that the official pulled off his own tie for the meeting.

                  This morning, Brashears settled down into his seat behind
              the 3-foot-high stack of papers scattered across the large desk
              in the middle of his office, took a sip of coffee and knocked a
              Benson and Hedges from the first of three packs he smokes each
              day. Bottles of Jack Daniel's lined the shelves behind him, alon
              with a bottle of Old Bushmill's and "some real Russian vodka tha
              I haven't opened up in three or four years."
File 4 of 6   D:\WORDS\CURRENT\JD.STY   Text   Line 75 (19%)
F1   F2   F3   F4   F5   F6   F7   F8   F9   F10
Help   Copy   Delete   Print   Gather   Sort   Launch   Zoom   Explore Quit

Program   Clock - 9/6   WINFAX PRO   File Manager
Manager   Administrator

Figure 16-1:
Lotus
Magellan,
a DOS
program,
runs in its
own
window.

3. Click on the different numbers and look in the Selected Font box to see how the words on the DOS program window will look in that font size.

The window's total size in relation to the desktop appears in the Window Preview box. Figure 16-2, for example, shows the font size 8 x 12 selected; the Window Preview box shows that a window of that size covers almost the entire desktop.

Smaller font-size numbers make for smaller words and a smaller DOS window. For example, the 6 x 8 font shrinks the DOS window to the more manageable size shown in Figure 16-3.

You can make the fonts larger, too, so that they're easier to read. If you're using a laptop on a plane, try some of the larger fonts so that the passenger sitting next to you won't have to strain so hard to see what you're doing.

✔ Windows can only force DOS programs into a window when running in 386 Enhanced mode, a special tweak reserved for 386, 486, and Pentium computers. If you're running Windows in Standard mode, DOS programs can't run in windows, even on a 386, 486, or Pentium computer. For more about this mode stuff, trot back to Chapter 15.

✔ The changing-fonts trick works only with DOS programs that display mostly text — like spreadsheets and word processors. DOS programs that use graphics don't work too well in windows. Their displays don't completely fit in a window, and the colors almost always look weird.

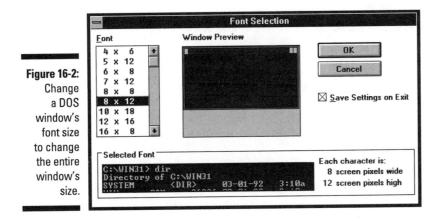

Figure 16-2:
Change
a DOS
window's
font size
to change
the entire
window's
size.

✔ You can change a DOS window's size by dragging the borders, but that's pointless. A DOS program's display doesn't shrink or grow in size like a Windows program does. If you drag the border in, you just cover up your view of the program.

✔ If you want to cut or paste anything from a DOS program in a window, head back to Chapter 9 for information about the DOS window versions of cut, copy, and paste.

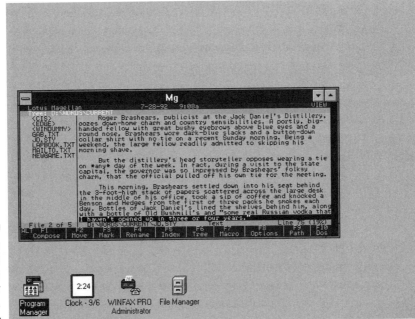

Figure 16-3:
Smaller DOS
fonts make
for smaller
windows.

Halting Runaway DOS Programs

Like startled Arkansas farmers who wake up in the belly of a space ship, some DOS programs simply freak out when they find themselves running under Windows. For example, some freeze up solid, stubbornly beeping each time you press a key.

First, look at the top of the DOS window. If it says Mark or Select, then Windows thinks that you're trying to copy information from it. Press Esc to restore order. If you really were trying to copy something, head for Chapter 9.

If pressing Esc didn't work, try holding the Alt key and pressing Enter. That action tells Windows to let the temperamental program have the entire screen. For example, if a program suddenly switches from text to graphics in a window, Windows freezes the program until you use the Alt+Enter trick.

That didn't work, either? Then things are getting serious. If the confused DOS program is in a window, follow these steps:

1. **Click on the Control-menu box in the upper left corner of the window.**

2. **Choose Settings from the menu that appears.**

3. **Click on the ominous-looking Terminate button from the box that appears.**

4. **When Windows asks whether you're sure, click on the OK button.**

Hopefully, these steps rip the DOS program from the computer's memory; use these steps pretty much as a last resort.

If the frozen DOS program is running full screen, hold the Ctrl key, press and hold Alt, and then press Delete (Ctrl+Alt+Delete). When Windows asks whether you're sure that you want to close the program, press Enter.

If you click on the Terminate button or press the Ctrl+Alt+Delete combination, you lose any unsaved work in the DOS program.

✔ Only use the Terminate or Ctrl+Alt+Delete method as a last resort. If at all possible, quit the DOS program in an orderly fashion. For some programs, you hold the Alt key and press X; in others, you press F10 or Esc. Almost all programs are different. (That's one reason why people are switching to Windows; its commands are more predictable.)

✔ After you use Terminate or Ctrl+Alt+Delete, save any work in the other windows. Then exit Windows and start it up again. That DOS program may have sabotaged things on its way out.

Part V
Getting Help

"HERE'S YOUR PROBLEM. SOME BOZO JAMMED YOUR KEYBOARD WITH A 4-LEAF CLOVER."

In this part...

Windows can do hundreds of tasks in dozens of ways. That means that approximately one million things can fail at any given time.

Some problems are easy to fix. For example, one misplaced double-click in Program Manager makes all your programs disappear. Yet one more click in the right place puts them all back.

Other problems are far more complex, requiring teams of computer surgeons to diagnose, remedy, and bill accordingly.

This part lets you separate the big problems from the little ones. You'll know whether you can fix it yourself with a few clicks and a kick. If your situation's worse, you'll know when it's time to call in the surgeons.

Chapter 17

The Case of the Broken Window

Sometimes you just have a sense that something's wrong: The computer makes quiet grumbling noises, or Windows starts running more slowly than Congress. Other times something's obviously wrong: Pressing any key just gives you a beeping noise, menus keep shooting at you, or Windows greets you with a cheery error message when you first turn it on.

Many of the biggest-looking problems are solved by the smallest-looking solutions. Hopefully, this chapter points you to the right one.

Geez, I Can't Even Get Windows to Install

When you're installing Windows, sometimes everything comes to a halt shortly after you stick the third disk in the drive. Any of the following suspects may be the culprit:

✔ You didn't remove the first and second disks from the disk drive before inserting the third.

✔ Windows isn't getting along well with some part inside the computer. To try to fix it yourself, brave out the custom installation. At the DOS prompt, type **SETUP /I** rather than the usual **SETUP.** If you can answer the questions Windows poses about the brand names of your computer goodies, you may overcome the problem.

✔ Windows is probably confused by something contained in two of the computer's files: AUTOEXEC.BAT and CONFIG.SYS. Unfortunately, these two files contain different codes on nearly everybody's computer, so there's no single right way to set them up. This is a job for a computer guru. Try calling the store that sold you the computer; the store may install Windows for you if you bring the computer back in.

The Mouse Doesn't Work Right

Sometimes the mouse doesn't work at all; other times the mouse pointer hops across the screen like a flea. Here are a few things to look for:

✔ If there's no mouse arrow on the screen when you start Windows, make sure that the mouse's tail is plugged snugly into the computer's rump. Then exit and restart Windows.

✔ If there's *still* no mouse arrow, perhaps the mouse is using COM3 or COM4. Windows accepts only COM1 or COM2 for mouse ports. Head back to the computer store and scream until they put the mouse on the correct port.

✔ If the mouse arrow is on the screen but won't move, Windows may be mistaking your brand of mouse for a different brand. You can change to a different mouse the same way you change to a different video mode, as described in Chapter 10. Or you can reinstall Windows by using the custom installation and choose your brand of mouse from the list on the screen.

✔ If the mouse pointer jumps around, there may be a conflict on its interrupt. You have to pull out the mouse manual and see how to change its *interrupt setting* to fix this one.

✔ A mouse pointer can jump around on the screen if it's dirty. First, turn the mouse upside down and clean off any visible dirt stuck to the bottom. Then turn the little lever until the mouse ball pops out. Wipe off any crud and blow any dust out of the hole. Pull any stray hairs off the little rollers and stick the ball back inside the mouse. If you wear wool sweaters, you may have to clean the ball every week or so.

✔ If the mouse was working fine and now the buttons seem to be reversed, you've probably hit the reverse-buttons switch in the Control Panel. See Chapter 10 to correct this inadvertent reverse.

✔ Windows comes with its own built-in mouse driver. That driver doesn't work for DOS programs, though. If you want to use a mouse for DOS programs, you need to put a mouse driver in your AUTOEXEC.BAT or CONFIG.SYS file. That way, your computer loads the DOS mouse driver each time you turn the computer on.

I'm Stuck in Menu Land

If your keystrokes don't appear in your work but instead make a bunch of menus shoot out from the top of the window, you're stuck in Menu Land. Somehow you've pressed and released Alt, an innocent-looking key that's easy to hit accidentally.

When you press and release Alt, Windows turns its attention away from your work and toward the menus along the top of the window.

To get back to work, press and release Alt one more time. Alternatively, press Esc. One or the other is your ticket out of Menu Land.

I'm Supposed to Install a New "Driver"

When you buy a new toy for the computer, it should come with a piece of software called a *driver*. A driver is a sort of translator that lets Windows know how to boss around the new toy. If you buy a new keyboard, sound card, compact disc player, printer, mouse, monitor, or almost any other computer toy, you need to install its driver in Windows. To add a new *printer* driver, gallop off to Chapter 10.

Adding a driver for a mouse, keyboard, or monitor

To add a driver for a mouse, keyboard, or monitor (Windows calls a monitor a *display*), follow these steps:

1. **Double-click on the Setup icon in the Program Manager's Main window.**

   The Setup window appears.

2. **Click on Options in the menu bar.**

   The Options menu appears.

3. **Select Change System Settings from the Options menu.**

4. **Click on the box next to the kind of toy you want to add.**

   A list of brands pops up. If you're lucky, Windows lists your brand of toy by name.

5. **Click on the brand name, and you're off to the races.**

   If your brand is not listed, click on the Other (requires disk from OEM) option and jump to the "But mine's not listed!" section.

Adding a driver for other toys

To add a driver for anything other than a printer, mouse, keyboard, or monitor, follow these steps (to add a new printer driver, turn to Chapter 10):

1. **Double-click on the Control Panel icon in the Program Manager's Main window.**

2. **When the Control Panel opens, double-click on the Drivers icon.**

3. **Click on the Add button.**

   A list of brand names pops up.

4. **If you see the brand name of your toy, click on it.**

   Everything is rosy. If the particular brand of your toy isn't listed, click on the Unlisted or Updated Driver option and start reading the "But mine's not listed!" section, which follows.

But mine's not listed!

If your new computer toy isn't listed in the Windows menu, there's still hope. When you click on Other or Unlisted or Updated Driver from the Control Panel, you see a box similar to the one shown in Figure 17-1. Now grab the disk that came with the new sound card, compact disc player, or whatever other toy you bought. If the disk is the right size for drive A, stick it in there and press Enter. If the disk fits in drive B, stick it in that drive, type **B:**, and press Enter.

Yet another box comes up, this time listing the drivers on that floppy disk (see Figure 17-2). Sometimes a disk contains only one driver; other times the dialog box lists several. Click on the name of the driver you want, click on OK, and follow the instructions that appear for your particular toy.

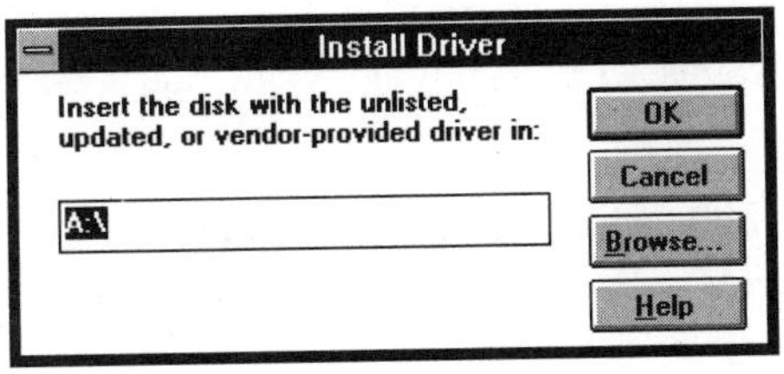

Figure 17-1:
Before
Windows
can use
a new
computer
toy, you
must install
that toy's
driver.

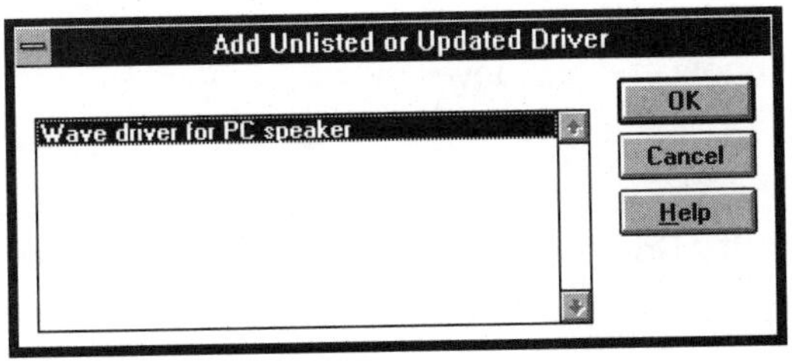

```
┌─────────────────────────────────────────────┐
│ ─        Install Driver                       │
├─────────────────────────────────────────────┤
│ Insert the disk with the unlisted,    ┌──────┐│
│ updated, or vendor-provided driver in: │  OK  ││
│                                        └──────┘│
│ ┌───────────────────────────────┐     ┌──────┐│
│ │ A:\                           │     │Cancel││
│ └───────────────────────────────┘     └──────┘│
│                                        ┌──────┐│
│                                        │Browse...││
│                                        └──────┘│
│                                        ┌──────┐│
│                                        │ Help ││
│                                        └──────┘│
└─────────────────────────────────────────────┘
```

Figure 17-2:
Sometimes
a disk
contains
only one
driver.

```
┌─────────────────────────────────────────────┐
│ ─    Add Unlisted or Updated Driver           │
├─────────────────────────────────────────────┤
│                                      ┌──────┐ │
│ Wave driver for PC speaker          │  OK  │ │
│                                      └──────┘ │
│                                      ┌──────┐ │
│                                      │Cancel│ │
│                                      └──────┘ │
│                                      ┌──────┐ │
│                                      │ Help │ │
│                                      └──────┘ │
│                                               │
└─────────────────────────────────────────────┘
```

✔ Companies constantly update their drivers, fixing problems or making them better. If the computer device is misbehaving, a newer driver may calm it down. Call the manufacturer and ask for the latest version.

✔ For floppy-disk-insertion etiquette, see Chapter 2.

✔ Not all computer toys work with Windows. Check with the store before you buy so that you aren't stuck with something that won't work.

Oh, No! I Forgot the Password to the Screen Saver

The Windows screen saver lets you use a password to secure your stuff against prying eyes. When Windows blanks the screen, you must type that password, or the screen won't unblank. Although occasionally helpful, this security measure can cause embarrassment when you forget the password after returning from lunch.

Check to make sure that no one's looking and push the computer's reset button. (You lose any work you didn't save before the screen saver kicked in.) Restart Windows and head for the Control Panel. Double-click on the Desktop icon and click on the Setup button in the Screen Saver box. Finally, click in the box next to the words Password Protected. Whew! That action disables the password-protection scheme for the screen saver.

The next time a computer guru walks by, tell him or her to remove the Password= line from the CONTROL.INI file. Then you can head back to the Control Panel and type a new password — hopefully one that's easier to remember.

Screen savers and the Control Panel are discussed in more detail in Chapter 10.

My Window Won't Sit Still

Some windows won't stay put where you leave them. For example, you line up the Program Manager flush with the edges of the screen. But, if you merely click on the title bar, the window gets up, moves over a fraction of an inch, and settles back down.

To stop this vagrancy, head for the Control Panel, double-click on the Desktop icon, and look at the Sizing Grid box near the bottom of the window. Make sure that the Granularity box is set to 0.

Windows still arbitrarily moves the windows around, but this is as good as it gets. Check out Chapter 7 for more information.

I Clicked on the Wrong Button (but Haven't Lifted My Finger Yet)

Clicking the mouse takes two steps: a push and a release. If you click on the wrong button on the screen but haven't lifted your finger yet, slowly slide the mouse pointer off the button on the screen. *Then* take your finger off the mouse.

The screen button pops back up, and Windows pretends nothing happened. Thankfully.

My Computer Has Frozen Up Solid

Every once in a while, Windows just drops the ball and wanders off somewhere. You're left looking at a computer that just looks back. Panicked clicks don't do anything. Pressing every key on the keyboard doesn't do anything — or worse yet, the computer starts to beep at every key press.

When nothing on the screen moves except the mouse pointer, the computer has frozen up solid. Try the following approaches, in the following order, to correct the problem:

Approach 1: Press Esc twice.

That action usually doesn't work, but give it a shot anyway.

Approach 2: Press Ctrl, Alt, and Delete all at the same time.

If you're lucky, Windows flashes an error message saying that you've discovered an "unresponsive application." Press Enter and Windows shuts down the program that caused the mess. You lose any unsaved work in it, of course, but you should be used to that. (If you somehow stumbled onto the Ctrl+Alt+Delete combination by accident, press Esc at the unresponsive-application message to return to Windows.)

Approach 3: If the preceding approaches don't work, push the computer's reset button.

The screen is cleared, and the computer acts like you turned it off and on again. When the dust settles, type **WIN** to start Windows again.

Approach 4: If not even the reset button works, turn the computer off, wait 30 seconds, and then turn it back on again.

Don't ever flip the computer off and on again quickly. Doing so can damage its internal organs.

My DOS Program Looks Weird in a Window

DOS programs are *supposed* to look weird when running in a window. Windows forces the computer to contort into different graphics modes. Most DOS programs look different in these modes.

However, you do have a few alternatives:

- ✔ Hold Alt and press Enter. Windows steps to the background, letting the DOS program have the whole screen. *Then* the DOS program looks normal. Hold Alt and press Esc to return to Windows, with the DOS program as an icon. Alternatively, exit the DOS program normally to return automatically to Windows.

- ✔ Play with the DOS program's fonts as described in Chapter 16.

- ✔ Buy the Windows version of the DOS program.

- ✔ Buy a more expensive graphics card that allows for even more graphics modes. Chances are, one of the modes will suit the DOS program a little better.

- ✔ Finally, you have to accept the fact that some DOS programs — usually the ones that display graphics — refuse to run in a window under Windows. They simply send you a rude error message or, in even ruder cases, no message at all. These types of programs need the whole screen to themselves.

My Disk Drive Makes Random Grinding Sounds

Disk drives can make some pretty awful grinding sounds when you use them to copy information. But under Windows, they sometimes grind even when you're *not* using them.

Windows constantly reads and writes information to the computer's hard drive, even when you're just sitting there, staring at the screen. If everything else is functioning normally, these intermittent sounds are nothing to worry about.

Floppy drives can also be noisy — especially when the File Manager has been looking at a floppy disk. File Manager sporadically peeks at the drives it shows in its windows. Each time it looks at the floppy disk, it makes random grinding sounds.

To shut it up, look for the window or icon in File Manager that shows that floppy drive. When you find the window, close it by double-clicking on the square in that window's top left corner. If the floppy drive is represented by an icon, click on it once and select Close from the menu that pops out of its head. When the drive icon or window disappears, the random growls disappear along with it.

If that floppy drive is your *only* open window, however, the window doesn't disappear. Double-click on the drive C icon along the top of the floppy-drive window; a window for drive C appears. *Now* you can close the floppy-drive window and stop the grumblings.

My Printer Isn't Working Right

If the printer's not working right, start with the simplest solution first: Make sure that it's plugged into the wall and turned on. Surprisingly, this step fixes about half the problems with printers. Next, make sure that the printer cable is snugly nestled in the ports on both the printer and the computer. Then check to make sure that it has enough paper.

Never plug in your printer cable while the computer is turned on. This seemingly innocuous action can mess up your computer's sensitive internal organs.

Then try printing from different programs, like Write and Notepad, to see whether the problem's with the printer, Windows, or a particular Windows program. Try printing the document by using different fonts. All these chores help pinpoint the culprit.

You may have to call the printer's manufacturer and ask for a new Windows *driver*. When the disk comes in the mail, follow the instructions in the "I'm Supposed to Install a New 'Driver'" section in this chapter.

If these tips don't work, it's probably time to seek out the advice of a computer guru. The guru will probably start by using Write to read the PRINTERS.WRI file in your Windows directory. This file contains tips on making different brands of printers work with Windows.

Yikes! Make Everything Go Back the Way It Started

Everybody plays around with the Program Manager when getting started. If you accidentally delete a few of Program Manager's windows or icons, or just make everything look *weird,* Windows lets you return things to normal. For complete instructions, head for the "Restoring Your Original Program Manager" section of Chapter 11.

Program Manager Lost Some of My Icons!

Sometimes icons simply disappear from Program Manager without a trace. Wouldn't it be nice if Program Manager would search through your hard drive, find all your Windows programs, and automatically add an icon for each of them?

It can. Chapter 11 shows you how to put a program's icon into Program Manager — follow the steps in the "Making Windows do all the grunt work" section.

Who's Dr. Watson?

If you're stuck with a particularly horrendous problem, you may unleash Dr. Watson, the chap who looks like this:

Dr. Watson

Like a private detective, Dr. Watson sits in the car and reads a newspaper, waiting for something terrible to happen. When Windows screams out an error message, Dr. Watson grabs it, jots down what program did what to whom, and then asks you to fill out your version of the incident. You then type what you were doing when the error occurred.

To put Dr. Watson on the job, click on File in the Program Manager and then select Run. Type the following word in the box and press Enter:

```
DRWATSON
```

That is, type **DRWATSON** with no space between the two words and then press Enter. Dr. Watson appears as an icon at the bottom of the screen. His notes appear in a file called DRWATSON.LOG in the WINDOWS directory. You probably can't make heads or tails of this file, but show it to your computer guru or Microsoft's technical support staff. Chances are, they can translate Dr. Watson's notes into a cure for the computer's ills.

As a last resort, Microsoft's technical support staff can be reached at 206-637-7098.

If you've had enough of Dr. Watson, click on him once and then choose Close from the menu that pops up from his head. To stop him from popping up again, click on his icon in Program Manager's StartUp window and then press your Del key.

"IT'S NOT THAT IT DOESN'T WORK AS A COMPUTER, IT JUST WORKS BETTER AS A PAPERWEIGHT."

Chapter 18

Error Messages (What You Did Does Not Compute)

*M*ost people don't have any trouble understanding error messages. A car's pleasant beeping tone means you've left your keys in the ignition. A terrible scratching sound from the stereo means the cat's jumped on the turntable.

Things are different with Windows, however. The error messages in Windows could have been written by a Senate subcommittee, if only they weren't so brief. When Windows tosses an error message your way, it's usually just a single sentence. Windows rarely describes what you did to cause the error. And even worse, Windows hardly ever says how to make the error go away.

Here are some of the most common error messages Windows throws in your face. This chapter explains what Windows is trying to say, why it's saying it, and just what the heck it expects you to do about it.

Not enough memory

Meaning: Windows is running out of the room it needs to operate.

Probable cause: You have too many windows simultaneously open on the screen. Or you're trying to paste a bodaciously large file (like a video) into another program.

Solutions: A short-term solution is to close some of the windows. DOS windows take up a lot of memory, so start by shutting them down. Also, make sure that you're not using any large color pictures of peacocks for wallpaper. It takes a lot less memory to tile small pictures across the screen (see Chapter 10 for information about tiling windows). If Windows still acts sluggish, close it down and start it up again.

For a long-term solution, make sure that you have plenty of empty space on the hard drive so Windows has room to read and write information. Delete any files or programs you don't use anymore.

Finally, consider buying some more memory. Windows works much better with 4MB of memory than with 2MB of memory. And 8MB of memory is better still.

Whenever you cut or copy a large amount of information to the Clipboard, it stays there, taking up memory — even after you've pasted it into another application. To clear out the Clipboard after a large paste operation, copy a single word to the Clipboard. Doing so replaces the earlier, memory-hogging chunk, freeing some memory for other programs.

Application Execution Error: Unexpected DOS error #11

Meaning: One of the Windows files has gone bad.

Probable cause: Who knows? Thankfully, this is a rare occurrence.

Solution: Reinstall Windows over itself from its original disks. Only one of the program files probably went bad, but it's too hard to figure out which one. Reinstalling Windows replaces *all* the files, including the bad one. Reinstalling Windows shouldn't affect other programs or data, but make sure that you have backup copies, anyway.

Cannot Read/Write from drive C:

Meaning: Windows can't read or write information to the hard drive.

Probable cause: Several possibilities come to mind: The hard drive is going bad, it's not compatible with Windows, or a "Virtual Memory" switch is toggled in the wrong direction.

Solution: If you're using a 386, 486, or Pentium computer, head for the Control Panel's 386 Enhanced section, look under Virtual Memory, click on the Change button, and make sure that no X appears in the Use 32-Bit Disk Access box. Some hard drives don't like this option.

Some disk-compression products can make this message surface occasionally as well. If the message recurs, consider taking the computer back to the store to have the hard drive tested or replaced if necessary. If your hard drive is going bad, buy a new one. You wanted a bigger one anyway, right?

Also, if Windows says that it can't read from your CD-ROM drive, try putting a disc in first. Then wait a few seconds before trying again. A computer can take 5 or 10 seconds to realize that a CD really *is* in there.

Not ready error reading drive A:

Meaning: Windows can't find a floppy disk in drive A.

Probable cause: There's no floppy disk in there.

Solution: Slide a disk in, push down the little lever if it's a 5 ¼-inch drive, and wish all errors were this easy to fix.

A Message Flashes, the Screen Clears, and Windows Doesn't Load

Meaning: Windows can't find a file it needs to load.

Probable cause: You've probably been fiddling with some Windows settings (video modes, mouse drivers, and so on). Or you've just moved or deleted the wrong file on the hard drive.

Once, I accidentally moved my mouse driver to a different directory. When Windows started up, it flashed the fancy Windows ad and then couldn't find my mouse driver. It flashed the name of the missing driver but then cleared the screen too quickly for me to read it. Then it left me at the DOS prompt.

Solution: This is usually a job for a computer guru because Windows depends on so many different files when it first loads. If you're in a troubleshooting mode, you may type **WIN /B** at the DOS prompt. Windows creates a text file called BOOTLOG.TXT in the Windows directory. That text file lists every file Windows tried to access as it loaded. Chances are, you can find the culprit — the altered or missing file — listed at the tail end of the BOOTLOG.TXT file.

Another option is to try using the DOS version of the Windows Setup program, but that's a job best left to a computer guru. (While in DOS, the guru needs to type **SETUP** in the Windows directory and try different settings.)

Insufficient Disk Space

Meaning: Windows has run out of room on a floppy disk or on the hard drive to store something.

Probable cause: Windows tried printing something to a disk file but ran out of space. Or your floppy disk or hard drive is simply too full.

Solution: Clear more room on that disk before printing to it. If you're not printing or copying files to a floppy disk when you see this message, save your work, exit Windows, and delete any junk files on the hard disk. BAK (backup) files and TMP (temporary) files qualify as junk files that can be deleted. Also delete any programs you don't use anymore. (For example, if you use Word for Windows as your word processor now, you probably don't need to keep the DOS version of Word 4.0 on the disk.) Also, if Windows appears sluggish after tossing this message at you, save your work, close Windows, and start it up again.

No association exists for the data file

Meaning: Windows can't find the program that created a particular file.

Probable cause: In the File Manager, you've clicked on a data file that Windows doesn't recognize.

Solution: Load the *program* that created the data file and *then* load the data file into that program. If that particular program always brands its files with a particular three-letter *extension,* try associating those files with that program, as hashed out in Chapter 12. Then you can simply double-click on the file's name to load it into the program that created it.

Not a valid filename

Meaning: DOS refuses to accept your choice of filename.

Probable cause: You've tried to rename a file by using one or more of the forbidden characters.

Solution: Turn to the section about renaming a file in Chapter 12 and make sure that you're not naming a file something you shouldn't.

There is no disk in drive A. Insert a disk, and then try again.

Meaning: Windows can't find a floppy disk in the floppy drive.

Probable cause: There isn't a floppy disk in the drive, or you've inserted one upside down or sideways.

Solution: Put a disk in the drive or head back to Chapter 2 to see how to put a disk in a drive. (A disk can fit in the drive eight possible ways — more if you bend it. Only one way works.)

Share Violation: File Already in Use

Meaning: One program is trying to use a file that another program is already using.

Probable cause: You may be trying to open a Write file that's already being displayed in another Write window. Or you may be trying to move a file in the File Manager when that file's already open on the desktop.

Solution: Look around the desktop to see what program's using the file. Close that program, and you then can use that file in the other program. If you're on a network, perhaps somebody else is using the file on his or her system.

This application has violated system integrity

Meaning: A program has done something incredibly naughty, and Windows refuses to work anymore because of it.

Probable cause: Two programs are fighting for the same piece of memory, a piece of hardware isn't getting along well with Windows, or something weird just happened out of the blue.

Solution: This is a rough one. Save your work, close Windows down, and start it back up. If this error happens with a particular program, find a newer version of that program. If it's a consistent error, find a computer guru and scream for help.

Chapter 19

Help on the Windows Help System

*J*ust about everybody's written a bizarre computer command like Alt+F4 on a sticky note and slapped it on the side of their monitor.

Windows comes with its *own* set of sticky notes built right in. You can pop them up on the screen and leave them there for easy access. In a way, they're virtually real sticky notes because they can never escape from inside the computer. Actually, it's probably better that way: You'll never find a "How to Add a Program Group" sticky note on the bottom of your shoe one evening.

This chapter covers the Windows built-in help system. When you raise your hand, Windows walks over and offers you some help.

Consulting the Windows Built-In Computer Guru

Almost every Windows program has the word Help in its top menu. Click on Help, and the Windows built-in computer guru rushes to your aid. For example, click on Help in Paintbrush, and you see the menu shown in Figure 19-1.

Figure 19-1:
Click on the
word <u>H</u>elp
when you
mean
"Help!"

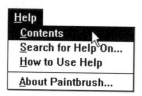

To pick the computer guru's brain, click on <u>C</u>ontents, and Windows pops up the box shown in Figure 19-2. This box is the table of contents for all the help information Windows can offer on the Paintbrush program.

Windows can offer help with any underlined topic. As the mouse pointer nears a topic, it turns into a little hand. When the hand points at the phrase that has you stumped, click the mouse button. For example, click on Flip Cutouts in the Paintbrush Help box, and Windows displays help for the topic of flipping cutouts, as shown in Figure 19-3.

Using the Windows help system is a lot faster than paging through the 600-page Windows manual. And, unlike other computer nerds, it doesn't have any Oreo gunk stuck between its teeth.

Figure 19-2:
Click on
your
problem,
and
Windows
brings up
your
answer.

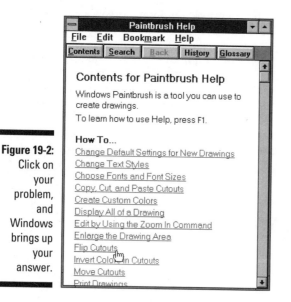

The quickest way to find help in any Windows program is to press F1, the first function key. Windows automatically jumps to the table of contents page for the help information it has for the current program.

✔ Windows packs a *lot* of information into its help boxes; some of the words usually scroll off the bottom of the window. To see them, click on the scroll bar (described in Chapter 6) or press PgDn.

✔ Sometimes you'll click on the wrong topic, and Windows will bring up something really dumb. Click on the <u>B</u>ack button at the top of the window, and Windows scoots back to the contents page. From there, click on a different topic to move in a different direction.

✔ Underlined phrases and words appear throughout the Windows help system — not just on the contents page. Whenever you click on something that's underlined, Windows jumps to a spot with information about that subject. Click on the <u>B</u>ack button to return to the last place you jumped from.

✔ If you're impressed with a particularly helpful page, send it to the printer: Click on <u>F</u>ile and choose <u>P</u>rint Topic from the menu. Windows shoots that page to the printer so that you can keep it handy until you lose it.

✔ Actually, to keep from losing it, read about sticking an electronic bookmark on that page, as described later in this chapter.

✔ If you find a particularly helpful reference in the help system, shrink the window to an icon. Click on the downward-pointing arrow in its upper right corner and keep it at the bottom of the screen. Then you can just double-click on the icon to see that page again.

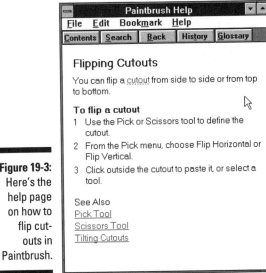

Figure 19-3:
Here's the help page on how to flip cut-outs in Paintbrush.

✔ To grab a help message and stick it in your own work, click on Edit and choose Copy from the menu. Windows then lets you highlight the helpful words you want to copy to the Clipboard. I dunno why anybody'd *want* to do this, but you *can* do it just the same.

What Does That Funny Computer Word Mean?

Windows is full of funny computer words like *pel* that don't appear in any dictionaries. To make Windows look up words for you, press F1 from the Program Manager. Then click on the Glossary button, shown in the top right corner of Figure 19-3. The Windows Glossary window pops up (see Figure 19-4).

Press PgUp and PgDn or click on the scroll bar to move up and down the list until you see the word for which you want a definition (for example, *pel*). When you find the word you want, click on it to see its definition.

✔ You don't always have to call up the Glossary to find a word's definition. Any word in the help system that has a broken underline also has a definition. Click on the word with the broken underline, and its definition pops up in a box.

✔ Click on the down arrow (the minimize icon) in the Glossary box's top right corner to make the Glossary squat as an icon. That action keeps it handy so that a simple double-click lets you look up wild Windows words like *static object.*

Figure 19-4:
The Glossary knows the definitions of weird words like *pel.*

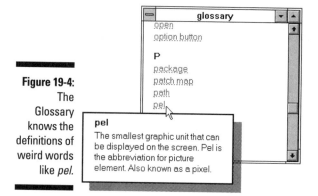

Sticking Electronic Sticky Notes on Help Pages

Windows lets you add your *own* notes to its helpful system of sticky notes. If you've made a stunning revelation and want to remember it later, follow these steps to add a paper clip to the current help topic and add your own notes to that help topic:

1. **Click on the word Edit at the top of the page.**

   The Edit menu appears.

2. **Click on the Annotate option.**

   The Annotate box appears.

3. **Start typing your own notes into the big box.**

   You can type as much as you want. Use the cursor-control keys to move around and the Delete or Backspace key to edit any mistakes.

4. **Click on the Save button when you're done entering your note.**

   Windows paper-clips your words to the current help page; a tiny picture of a paper clip appears to remind you of your additions.

Whenever you see that help page again, click on the paper clip next to the name of the topic, and your words reappear, as shown in Figure 19-5.

If you ever want to delete your paper-clipped note, click on the paper clip and click on the Delete button. Your note disappears.

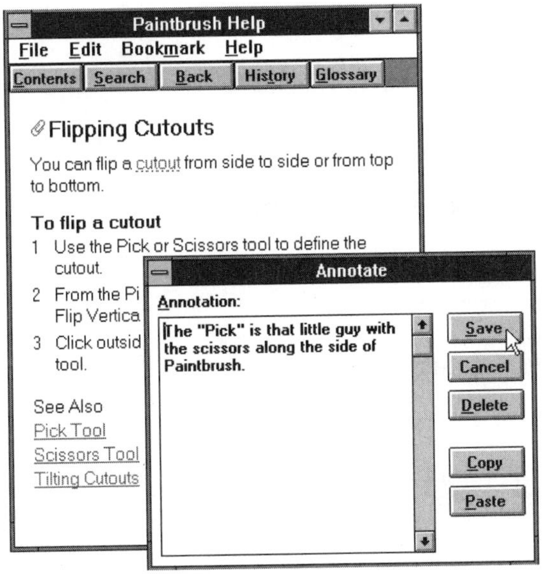

Figure 19-5:
Click on the paper clip to see the reminders you added earlier.

Finding Help for Your Problem

If you don't see your problem listed in the particular table of contents page you've accessed, there's another way to find help (although it takes a *lot* more effort). Click on the Search button at the top of any help window; the box shown in Figure 19-6 leaps to the screen. Type a few words describing your problem. As you type them, Windows shows any matches in the box below it.

If Windows matches what you type with an appropriate topic, click on the Show Topics button. Windows shows you any helpful pages of text that explain the word you've typed in. Double-click on the topic that sounds the closest, and Windows brings information about that topic to the screen.

A quicker way to find help is to click on the scroll bar to see what subjects Windows is willing to explain. If you see a subject that even remotely resembles what you're confused about, double-click on it. The topics that explain that subject appear in the bottom box. If you see a topic that looks interesting, double-click on it, and Windows brings up that page of help information.

From there, you can jump around by clicking on underlined words and phrases. Sooner or later, you'll stumble onto the right page of information. When you do, give it a *bookmark,* as described in the following section.

- ✔ The Search method of finding help usually isn't very efficient. It's easier to click on underlined words in the table of contents window and click on the Back button if that topic is not the right one.

- ✔ Windows searches alphabetically. If you're looking for help on margins, for example, don't type **adding margins** or **changing margins.** Type **margins** so that Windows jumps to the words beginning with *M.*

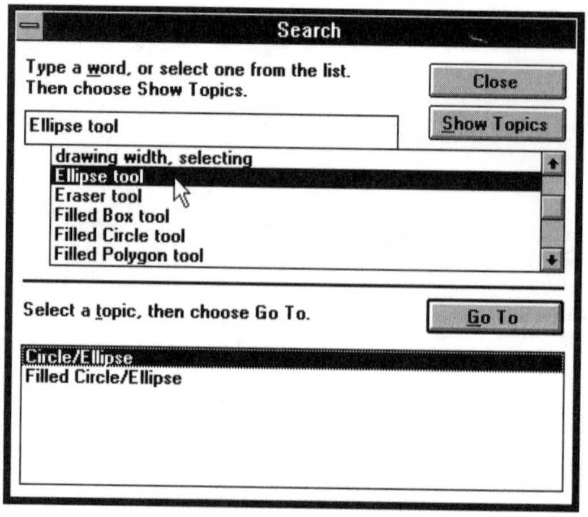

Figure 19-6:
Windows searches for help on key words.

Trying to Find the Same Page Again

The Windows help system is pretty thorough, and finding help for a particular trouble is fairly easy. But how do you return to that page a few minutes, or even a few days, later?

A couple of ways are available. If you stumbled across the right page of information just a few minutes ago and want to return to that page now, click on the History button at the top of any help window. Windows lists all the pages and topics you've seen. Double-click on the one you want to bring back, and that page appears.

The History button only keeps track of the current help session; when you close the help window, the history list disappears.

There's a better, more permanent way to relocate that perfect help page. When you've found that perfect page, click on Bookmark in the menu bar and select Define from the menu. Click on the OK button.

Now, when accessing the help system days or even years later, you can click on the Bookmark menu item. A menu tumbles down, listing the pages you've bookmarked. Click on the name of the page you're after, and Windows hops to that screen. Quick and easy.

Introduction

· ·

*T*his section isn't like your average, everyday...*For Dummies* book. It doesn't have a program to reference: the new Windows 95 software won't be on the shelf until later this year.

More than 50 million Windows users are curious about this upcoming piece of point and clickery, however, so this booklet plunges through the rumors and hype surrounding Windows 95: What is Windows 95? Is it better than Windows 3.1? What parts are different? What new programs does it come with? What sort of computer does it need? Is it worth bothering with, or is it a bother in itself?

This section is a three-part preview of Windows 95, based on a pre-release version that Microsoft slipped to me under the table; your version of Windows 95 will probably differ a little. Nevertheless, Part 1 answers the basic questions about Windows 95 — its heritage, horsepower, and computer requirements. Part 2 takes a detailed look at the biggest changes in the way Windows 95 runs programs. Part 3 examines the new programs and accessories Microsoft has packed into Windows 95.

This section is more a travel brochure than a road map. You'll find it useful for seeing the changes made in Windows 95, finding out the equipment that the software requires, and deciding whether you'd like to give the new incarnation a shot. However, you won't find the section packed with tips on actually *using* Windows 95. For that, look for the full-fledged *Windows 95 For Dummies* book, which will arrive on the scene at the same time as Windows 95.

Remember, this section was written before Microsoft even finished writing Windows 95. Chances are that a few things will change in the coming months. So if you're still reading this section in 1996, don't be surprised if some of the stuff you see in here is a wee bit different from what you see on-screen in Windows 95.

Part 1
A Brave New Windows:
Windows 95

· ·

In This Part

▶ What is Windows 95?

▶ How is Windows 95 different from Windows 3.1?

▶ Where is Windows 95?

▶ Can my computer use Windows 95?

▶ Will my old programs still work?

· ·

A new version of Windows lurks on the horizon. Referred to in hushed tones as "Chicago" during its development stages, this new version is now dubbed Windows 95. Microsoft is spending 40 million dollars to convince people to buy it.

Will Windows 95 be snapped up like a '67 Mustang? Or is it an over-hyped Edsel with a lot of chrome? This part probes the big question: Should I bother fiddling with this Windows 95 thing or what?

What Is Windows 95?

Windows 95, shown in Figure 1-1, is the latest in a long string of Windows versions. Windows 95 is destined to replace Windows 3.11, just as Windows 3.11 replaced Version 3.1, which replaced Version 3.0, which, well, you get the idea.

Microsoft tries to do three things whenever it creates a new version of Windows:

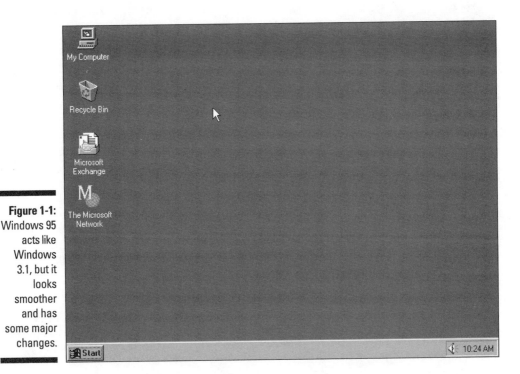

Figure 1-1:
Windows 95
acts like
Windows
3.1, but it
looks
smoother
and has
some major
changes.

First, it tries to fix the parts of Windows that currently don't work right (like the pre-1995 versions of Windows 3.1 Calculator, which come up with zero when you subtract 14.31 from 14.32).

Second, Microsoft tries to polish the parts of Windows that are a little bit awkward (like the confusing File Manager, and the program icons along the bottom of the screen that always get covered up when you're trying to find them).

Finally, Microsoft wants to make people replace their old versions of Windows so that it can make even *more* money.

✔ If you're a former Windows 3.1 user, Windows 95 may seem confusing at first — kind of like when you buy a new TV and have to get used to all those new switches on the remote control. You'll probably stumble upon some switches by accident. Others will take a little more time and effort to figure out.

✔ You don't have to run out and buy Windows 95, no matter how much Microsoft stomps its feet and claps its hands. Your current version of Windows 3.1 won't "wear out" and suddenly stop working when the newer version hits the shelves.

✔ Windows 95 still runs your old Windows 3.1 programs, as well as your old DOS programs. The opposite isn't true, however: Windows 3.1 won't be able to run any newer programs specifically written for Windows 95.

✔ Windows 95 used to be code-named *Chicago*. However, the two names refer to the same product — the version that everybody used to call Windows 4.0.

How Is Windows 95 Different from Windows 3.1?

Windows 95 does a bunch of new things that Windows 3.1 can't handle. Windows 95 replaces DOS, for example, so you don't have to deal with that C:\ stuff anymore (unless you want to — Microsoft built in a copy of the DOS prompt for the insatiably masochistic).

With Windows 95, Microsoft has expanded its "desktop" metaphor. You're no longer restricted to keeping your files as icons in Program Manager or File Manager; instead, you can spread your work all over your desktop, as shown in Figure 1-2. (And don't worry — you can still use your favorite wallpaper.)

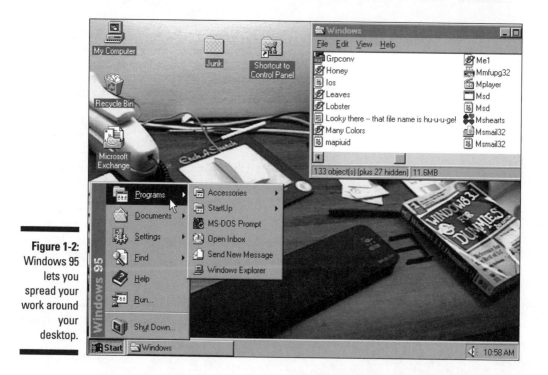

Figure 1-2: Windows 95 lets you spread your work around your desktop.

For example, you know how Program Manager makes you wade through bunches of windows to find the icon that starts your favorite program? Windows 95 dumps the Program Manager concept. Instead, you can simply toss an icon onto your desktop — that is, the back of your screen that's covered with wallpaper. Double-click that program's icon, and the program starts.

You don't need Program Manager to load programs, either. Instead, click the little Start button at the bottom of the screen. A menu leaps up, bringing a list of folders and programs to the screen.

By replacing File Manager and Program Manager with a new Desktop Computing metaphor, Windows 95 brings some substantial changes to Windows 3.1. Some people say the changes make Windows 95 easier to use; others wish Microsoft had left well enough alone.

✔ Windows 95 also lets you use long filenames, like Comparison of Early American Spatula Products instead of COMPSPAT.TXT. (Plenty more new, spiffy Windows 95 features are covered later in this section.)

✔ Other improvements aren't so subtle. For example, File Manager has been replaced by two similar programs, one called Explorer and the other cryptically called My Computer. (Luckily, Windows 95 still includes Program Manager and File Manager to placate the Windows 3.1 diehards. Unfortunately, those oldster programs don't support the long filenames that Windows 95 lets you use.)

✔ Windows 95 is a bona fide *operating system*. Previous versions of Windows are only *operating environments* — fancy DOS programs that let you run fancy programs. Windows 95 no longer needs DOS around; if you don't have a copy of DOS, you don't need to buy one. (And you're *still* able to run your old DOS programs.)

✔ Gotten used to using your left mouse button? Well, better make sure your *right* mouse button works, too. Windows 95 uses the right mouse button almost as much as the left.

So, Where Is Windows 95?

Microsoft is still working feverishly on Windows 95. Since it's not finished, nobody has the real product yet. And nobody will be able to buy Windows 95 until late 1995, either.

What some people do have are *test* copies. Technically known as *beta versions,* these are early versions of Windows 95 that Microsoft is still working on. Software developers traditionally hire *beta testers* to play with their newly written software; the beta testers then tell the developers which parts of the software don't work right.

Instead of hiring beta testers, billionaire Bill Gates is letting people pay *him* to beta-test Windows 95. Interested parties can pay around $30 for a "preview" version of Windows 95. This preview version isn't complete — it's roughly number eight in a long string of Windows 95 beta versions. And by the time you purchase this book, all the copies of the preview version may have been sold. I recommend that if you want to check out Windows 95 before it's officially released, bug your corporation's computer guru; the preview is designed to let corporations get a head start on marching toward Windows 95. (Better make sure somebody has a credit card number handy.)

- ✔ Microsoft is only releasing about 400,000 preview versions, and those copies will be snapped up pretty quickly. (After all, Microsoft sells about two million copies of the *real* Windows every month.)

- ✔ Once Microsoft hears about all the problems with the preview version — and fixes them — it will release the *real* version of Windows 95. When? The official word is August, 1995, but Microsoft isn't making any promises. The programmers say they'll release Windows 95 when it's "ready."

- ✔ If you've already picked up a copy of the Windows 95 preview version, you may want to check out my other book, *Windows 95 For Dummies.* It's just like *Windows For Dummies,* but all the Windows 3.1 stuff has been replaced with Windows 95 stuff. (Of course, this version of *Windows 95 For Dummies* is based on the *preview* version of Windows 95 — the *real* version of the book and the software won't be out until later this year.)

Can My Computer Run Windows 95?

Here's some good news: If your computer is already running Windows — and doing a good job of it — then your computer can probably run Windows 95 without too many problems. However, Table 1-1 compares the computer requirements listed on the Windows 95 box with the computer parts you *really* need to have Windows 95 work well.

Table 1-1	What Windows 95 Requires
Windows 95 Side-of-the-Box Requirements	*Windows 95 Equipment You'll Really Need*
386DX or faster	486 or Pentium
4MB of memory	8MB of memory; performance really picks up around 12MB
VGA card and monitor	Super-VGA card and monitor
One high-density floppy drive	One high-density floppy drive
10MB–15MB more hard disk space than you use for Windows 3.1 or Windows for Workgroups	At least 300MB
Mouse	Mouse with a left button *and* a right mouse button that still works

✔ You don't need a modem. But without one, you won't be able to call Microsoft's new on-line service, The Microsoft Network (dubbed MSN), and do all that Internet stuff everybody's talking about. Windows 95 comes with the software you need to dial MSN, making the service just a mouse-click away. (More dirt on MSN appears a little later in this section.)

✔ You don't need a CD-ROM drive for Windows 95, either. But installing Windows 95 from a single compact disc is a lot faster and easier than feeding your computer more than 20 floppy disks, one by one. Besides, all the multimedia programs come on compact disc these days. Windows 95 is much better at playing videos than Windows 3.1, and at least one of your friends will probably bring over a Beavis and Butthead multimedia screen-saver CD that's packed full of videos.

✔ By itself, Windows 95 runs in 4MB of memory fairly easily. But many Windows-based programs want 4MB of RAM just for themselves, meaning that your computer actually needs a total of at least 8MB of RAM. Remember: the more programs you like to run simultaneously, the more RAM you need in your computer.

✔ Windows 95 works with most of your computer's existing parts, like its video card, sound card, CD-ROM drive, and other goodies. If the parts work well with Windows 3.1, they'll also work with Windows 95.

✔ Windows 95 even works with those "clone" CPU chips from companies like AMD and Cyrix.

Passing on the driver's sidebar

Many computer parts require special Windows *drivers* — pieces of software that let Windows talk to the parts and make them work. For years, the manufacturer of the computer part also wrote the Windows driver. But if the driver didn't work, you were out of luck. For example, many video cards wouldn't work right until the manufacturers perfected their Windows drivers — a goal reached usually three to nine months after the card's release.

To avoid problems, Microsoft is including Windows 95 drivers for the most popular computer parts on the market. It's got drivers for cards from ATI, Cirrus, Compaq, Oak Technology, Media Vision, Creative Labs, Roland, Vidiola, Intel, and more.

Even though most Windows 3.1 drivers will still work with Windows 95, most manufacturers will have optimized their drivers for the new operating

system. After all, they've had plenty of time — Microsoft's been working on Windows 95 for more than two years.

Plus, Windows 95 recognizes the new Plug-and-Play technology. Plug-and-Play computers and parts are easier to install and configure. Before Plug-and-Play, people had to rely on chance when installing new parts in their computer, hoping that the components didn't fight among themselves for the computer's attention.

Windows 95 automatically identifies Plug-and-Play-compatible parts and assigns the computer's resources to them. By keeping track of who's using what part of the computer and when, Windows 95 can automatically set up newly installed parts.

Most PCMCIA cards are Plug-and-Play-compatible; so are most PCI cards, found on many Pentium computers.

Buying a computer to run Windows 95? Then make sure that the computer has either Local Bus or PCI video. Both technologies let Windows 95 sling graphics onto the screen faster. Also, make sure that the new computer is Plug-and-Play compatible. Plug-and-Play is a new technology that lets Windows automatically recognize and configure new parts when you plug them into your computer.

Will My Old Programs Still Work?

Yep, Windows 95 can still run your old Windows *and* DOS programs. In fact, if you have more than 4MB of RAM, it'll probably run your programs faster than Windows 3.1 can run them.

Your DOS games will run better under Windows, too. And they'd better: Remember, Windows 95 doesn't require DOS anymore, meaning that *all* your programs will be running under Windows — even those notoriously cranky DOS games. Some DOS programs will run in an on-screen window; the hoggy ones can take up the whole screen if they need to.

✔ You can boot back to your old version of DOS for a while, if you have to. Hold down F8 while Windows 95 is first starting up, and a menu lets you run the version of DOS that your computer was using before Windows 95 took over. (The Office Computer Guru can turn this feature off, though.)

✔ Windows 95 comes with a few of your old Windows favorites: Program Manager, File Manager, Character Map, and a few others. But some of your other favorite Windows 3.1 programs, including Paintbrush, are gone.

✔ Unfortunately, Calendar and Cardfile are gone. They've vanished, with no replacements. (Microsoft's programmers started to write replacements but gave up.)

✔ New programs will eventually begin appearing on the shelves to take advantage of the new features in Windows 95. In the meantime, however, your old Windows 3.1 favorites will still work, but don't expect them to be updated: Microsoft says it will only release Windows 95 versions of its programs; the old versions will simply fall by the wayside.

✔ Windows 3.1 programs won't be able to use Windows 95's long filenames. If you name a file SPECTACULAR. TXT while in a Windows 95 program, the file will be shortened to SPECTA~1.TXT when called up in a Windows 3.1 program.

So, Should I Upgrade?

You're the only one who can answer *this* question. If you're happy with your current version of Windows, then don't bother upgrading. There's no hurry. Wait a little while until everybody else lets all the bugs out.

Judging by the lengthy heritage Windows has enjoyed, however, and the momentum behind it, I would say that Windows 95 will eventually replace Windows 3.1. The only question is how long it will take to push the old version off the shelves.

Part 2

Looking at the Big Changes

· ·

In This Part

▶ The Start button (which replaces Program Manager)

▶ The Taskbar (which replaces the Task List)

▶ The Explorer (which replaces File Manager)

▶ The Shortcuts

▶ The Recycling Bin

▶ The Previews

▶ The Help program

· ·

*W*indows 95 looks like a friend's living room after the furniture has been rearranged: Something's new and different looking. If your friend is lucky, you'll notice the change and say how great it looks. If not, you'll walk into a couch. And first-time visitors won't notice any changes at all.

The same holds true for Windows 95. If you've been using Windows 3.1 for years, you'll be bumping into Windows 95's couches for a while until you've located everything new. Some of the programs are gone; others have been changed beyond recognition. A few of them are still hanging around to make you feel at home, however.

This part looks at the biggest changes Windows 95 makes to Windows 3.1's familiar collection of programs. Some of the changes are refreshingly fresh; others will take a little extra navigation.

Why Bother with Windows 95?

Here's the big question: Why bother buying Windows 95, going through the hassle of installing it, and learning all its new programs? Although there isn't an easy answer, Windows 95 has several strong points.

First, Windows 95 may be a little easier for beginners to figure out. Finding files and starting programs involve a lot less pointing and clicking. For example, Windows keeps track of the past 15 files or programs you've used and stores their names in a special spot. Want to load the file again? Just choose its name from list, as seen in Figure 2-1: No wading through menus or opening programs. White-gloved Windows 95 opens the car door and lets you start moving immediately.

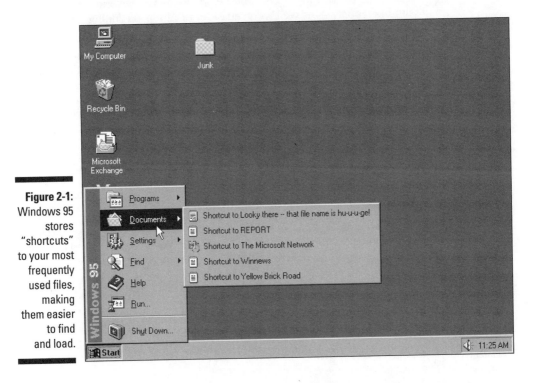

Figure 2-1:
Windows 95 stores "shortcuts" to your most frequently used files, making them easier to find and load.

You see lots more little buttons with pictures on them — *icons* — used in Windows 95 programs. Don't know what the little triangles in Media Player are supposed to do? Then rest your mouse pointer over them, as shown in Figure 2-2. After a few seconds, a window pops up on-screen, explaining the triangles' reason for living. (Some icons don't offer this explanatory feature, however.)

Windows finally allows for longer filenames with Windows 95, as shown in Figure 2-3. After 15 years of frustration, IBM-PC users can call their files something more descriptive than RPT_15.TXT. In fact, you can use 255 characters to describe your computer creations.

Ready to upgrade your computer? Windows 95 can give you a hand with its upgraded Plug-and-Play wizards. Windows 95 Plug-and-Play technology keeps better track of the parts inside your computer and can alert you when internal brawls start. Better yet, it stops brawls from even starting by making sure computer parts aren't assigned the same parts of your computer when they're first installed.

✔ Windows 95 can still run your Windows 3.1 programs and many old Windows 3.0 programs. Because those old programs weren't designed for Windows 95, however, they can't take advantage of its special new features. You won't be able to *multitask* — run several programs simultaneously — as well when an older program is running. And the old Windows programs are still stuck with eight-character filenames.

✔ Windows 95 automates many computing chores. To install a program, for example, just push the floppy disk (or compact disc) into the drive and double-click the Add/Remove Programs icon in the control panel. Windows searches your computer's disk drives for the installation program and runs it automatically. Windows 95 can automatically search for any new hardware you've installed, too, recognizing quite a few of the most popular upgrades.

✔ Tired of twiddling your thumbs while Windows formats a floppy? Windows 95 can handle floppy chores in the background so you can continue playing your card game. (The new card game — FreeCell — is an incredibly delicious time-waster, by the way.)

✔ Dare I say the word *Macintosh*? Windows looks more like the age-old Mac every year. That means Windows 95 will make Macintosh users feel more at home than ever. OS/2 users will find a little resemblance as well.

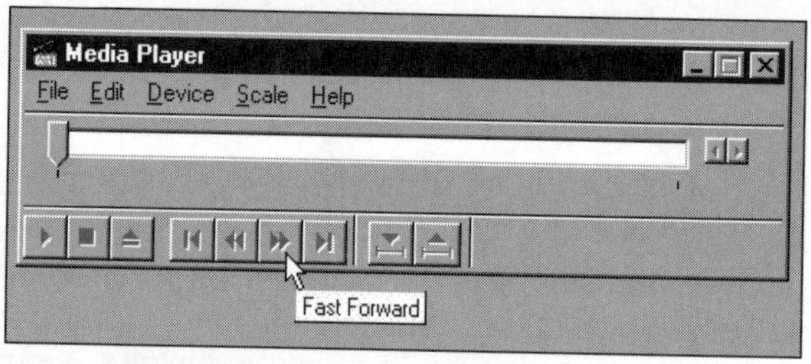

Figure 2-2: Rest your mouse pointer on a confusing icon or button to find out its purpose.

Figure 2-3: Windows 95 allows files to have more than eight characters. Finally!

The Start Button (Program Manager's Replacement)

Perhaps the biggest change in Windows 95 comes with the Start button. Yep — one little button replaces the huge Program Manager. It works like this: Click on the Start button, shown in the bottom-left corner of Figure 2-4.

Once it's clicked, the Start button shoots a menu from the top of its head, revealing several folders, as shown in Figure 2-5.

Figure 2-4:
Program
Manager's
replacement.

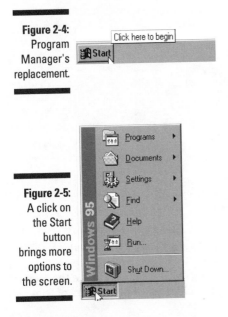

Figure 2-5:
A click on
the Start
button
brings more
options to
the screen.

See the little arrows next to some of the folders on the menu? Hold the mouse over the word next to the arrow, and a new menu bursts from its side, as shown in Figure 2-6.

Want to open an Accessory? Hold the mouse pointer over the word Accessories, and a handy menu of your Windows accessories appears, as shown in Figure 2-7.

Figure 2-6:
Holding the
mouse
pointer over
the word
Programs
brings an
organized
list of
programs to
the screen.

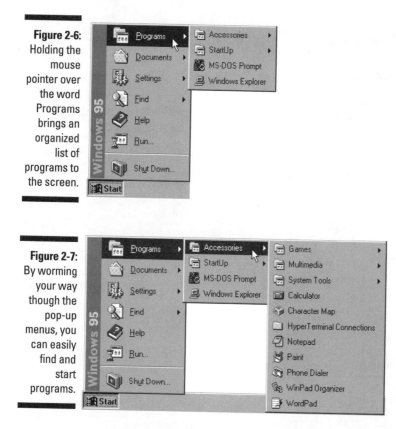

Figure 2-7:
By worming
your way
though the
pop-up
menus, you
can easily
find and
start
programs.

Click on the name of the program you'd like to start, and it leaps to the screen. Unlike Program Manager, where piles of windows often cover up the program you're after, the Start button keeps everything organized. Plus, since the menus pop up automatically, you don't need to keep clicking through layers of windows.

Here are some of the changes and replacements you Windows 3.1 users should be aware of:

- Newly installed programs are automatically added to the Start button, just as they're added in Program Manager.

- Each of those folders on the Start button's menu used to be a program group window in Program Manager.

- Just as you can add, delete, and change the names of Program Manager's program groups, you can customize the Start button menus to suit the way you work. Or you can ignore them and let Windows 95 add programs to the Start list automatically.

✔ To find and start programs with the Windows 3.1 Program Manager, you have to double-click on everything, over and over. The Start button, by contrast, has boiled the action down to two clicks. After you click on the Start button, rest your mouse button over the other menus to have them pop up automatically. When you see the name of the program you're after, click it to bring it to life.

✔ Don't like the Start button concept? Then ignore it. Windows 95 still includes Program Manager for Windows 3.1 die-hards.

✔ Just like Program Manager, the Start button comes with a StartUp folder. Any program listed in that folder automatically starts running when you first load Windows 95.

The Taskbar (Which Replaces the Task List)

Ever misplaced an icon at the bottom of your screen, lost beneath a sea of open windows? Microsoft listened carefully to complaints and revamped the icon concept. Now, minimized windows are absorbed into the Taskbar, shown along the bottom of the screen in Figure 2-8.

The Taskbar always fills an edge of your screen; windows never cover it up (unless you deliberately turn on its hide feature). When the Taskbar is on top, so are your program's pushbuttons.

The Taskbar along the bottom of Figure 2-8 lists the programs currently running in the background: the FreeCell card game, the CD Player, a drawing in the Paint program, and the Calculator. See how the Calculator program's title looks a little different on the Taskbar? That's because the Calculator is currently running on the desktop, and all the others are running in the background, waiting to be used.

But there's more: See the little speaker in the bottom-right corner of the Taskbar in Figure 2-8? That's the volume control for sound cards, thankfully. When a rowdy program STARTS SOUNDING LIKE THIS, just click on the speaker. A sliding lever pops up, shown in Figure 2-9, making it easy to turn down the sound: No more searching for the sound card's special volume control program.

See the Taskbar's clock, right next to the speaker? Rest your mouse pointer over the time, and Windows 95 pops up with the date, as shown in Figure 2-10. Or double-click on the clock, and a menu appears for changing the date or time.

With the Taskbar, it's a lot easier to juggle programs without losing any.

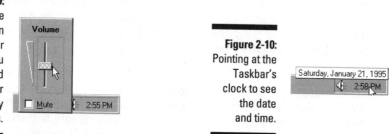

Figure 2-8:
Minimized
windows
are no
longer icons;
they're little
sections on
the Taskbar
along the
bottom of
the screen.

Figure 2-9:
The little
speaker on
the Taskbar
lets you
silence loud
programs or
amplify
quiet ones.

Figure 2-10:
Pointing at the
Taskbar's
clock to see
the date
and time.

✔ The Taskbar replaces the Task List found in Windows 3.1. In fact, just as pressing Ctrl+Esc brings up the Task List in Windows 3.1, pressing Ctrl+Esc in Windows 95 summons the Windows 95 Taskbar and Start button if they happen to be hiding.

✔ What happens if you're running a whole *bunch* of programs? Each program's name still appears on the Taskbar. However, Windows 95 shrinks the amount of Taskbar real estate allotted to each program's name. Eventually, those tiny Taskbar chunks become too small to read comfortably.

✔ The Taskbar doesn't have to sit along the bottom of your screen. You can drag it to the top, for example, or leave it sitting along an edge as a column. Or you can make the Taskbar *invisible* so that it only appears when you move your pointer to the edge of the screen. Or you can make the Taskbar thicker, allowing more room for listing open programs.

The Explorer

File Manager brings the most confusion to Windows 3.1. After all, Windows is supposed to be an escape from bothersome DOS concepts like "paths" and "system files." Under Windows, computing dilemmas are supposed to be mild things, like choosing between two new Bart Simpson icons.

But the merry atmosphere of Windows ends whenever File Manager arrives on-screen. Instead of assigning sounds to Barney icons, File Manager forces people to choose between somber "Tree and Directory" views and wade through "Expand Branch," "Collapse Branch," and "Expand One Level" terminology.

Windows 95 fixes some of the rough spots with two programs: Explorer, shown in Figure 2-11, and the cryptically named My Computer program, shown in Figure 2-12.

Both programs let you organize your files; you can copy, delete, rename, move, print, and view them, check their size, and perform other basic bits of computer housekeeping. The two programs work in decidedly different ways, however. It's as if two gangs of Microsoft programmers couldn't decide which program was better, so they tossed in both.

Of the two programs, Explorer works the most like File Manager. The Explorer window is divided in half, with folders on one side and a folder's contents on the other. To see what's in a particular folder, just click on it — the files inside that folder are then listed on the other side of the window.

The My Computer program takes a slightly different tack. Instead of keeping everything self-contained inside one window, it spills new windows across the screen. It starts with a single window full of folders, as seen in Figure 2-12. Double-click on the folder you'd like to peek into, and My Computer opens a second window, listing the selected folder's contents. See an interesting folder in the new window? Double-click on it, and a third window pops open, listing *that* folder's contents.

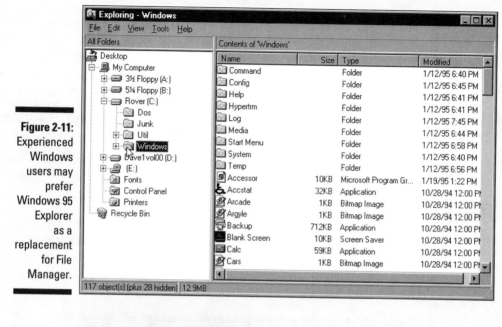

Figure 2-11: Experienced Windows users may prefer Windows 95 Explorer as a replacement for File Manager.

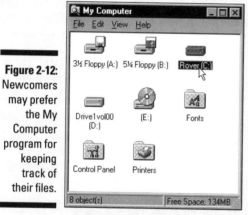

Figure 2-12: Newcomers may prefer the My Computer program for keeping track of their files.

Play with both of them to see which approach you prefer. Chances are, you'll be like Microsoft's indecisive programmers: You'll like both of them for different reasons.

- ✓ The My Computer program makes it easy to copy and move files: Just drag a file from one window to another.

- ✓ The Explorer usually involves less pointing and clicking. Plus, there's less cleanup after you've found your file: You don't have to close all those extraneous folders that My Computer leaves lying around the desktop.

✔ Both programs differ from File Manager in that they show more than files: They also let you access your Control Panel and control your printer's output.

✔ The Windows 95 Explorer doesn't come in an Eddie Bauer model with leather seats.

Other Windows 95 Features Worth an Ogle

This section can't cover all the new stuff that's going into Windows 95; you need *Windows 95 For Dummies* for that. But here are a few other Windows 95 features you'll probably find yourself using — *if* you decide to upgrade, that is.

Shortcut buttons

Windows 3.1 lets you open programs and files through little pushbuttons — icons — stored in Program Manager's windows. Windows 95 dumps Program Manager but holds on to the icon concept. Now the icons are called Shortcuts, and they're movable pushbuttons, ready to be installed in easy-to-reach locations.

The easiest place to reach is probably the desktop itself. For example, if you find yourself using FreeCell constantly, you can stick a Shortcut for it onto the Windows 95 desktop.

Then, when you play a game of FreeCell, you can simply head for the Shortcut button on your desktop (see Figure 2-13). You don't need to search for the button in a bunch of panels and folders.

✔ You can create shortcuts for data files as well as programs. For example, you can put sounds, movies, or fax cover templates on the desktop, ready for quick access.

✔ A shortcut can be easily identified by the little arrow in its bottom corner, as seen in Figure 2-14. The *real* program is on the left; its shortcut is on the right.

✔ Another way to add a shortcut is to click on the desktop with the right mouse button. When the menu appears, click on New and choose Shortcut. A Browse box then lets you sort through your files, in a way that's similar to how My Computer and Explorer work. Click on the file you'd like to have appear, and a shortcut appears on the desktop.

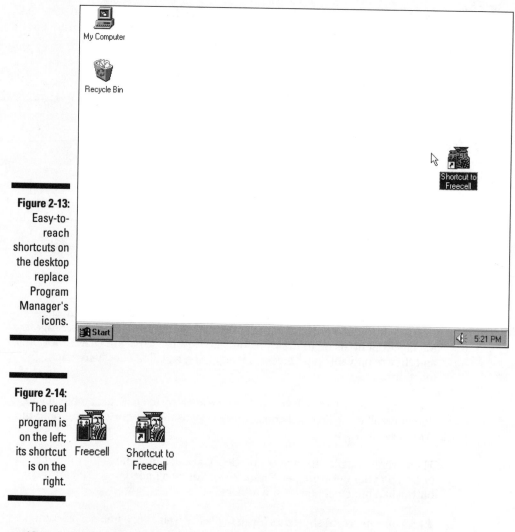

Figure 2-13:
Easy-to-reach shortcuts on the desktop replace Program Manager's icons.

Figure 2-14:
The real program is on the left; its shortcut is on the right.

Freecell Shortcut to Freecell

✔ Shortcuts — just like the Program Manager icons they replace — can be safely deleted. They're merely an extra pushbutton for starting a program; they don't affect the program itself.

✔ Shortcuts are spread throughout Windows 95 folders. For example, the Control Panel window contains shortcuts for accessing font files and different printer setups.

Finding recently used programs and files

When you open an envelope on your desk and it disappears a few minutes later, you know it's still on your desktop — somewhere. But computers make you search a lot farther than a desktop to find recently opened files.

But that's changing. Attentive Windows 95 keeps track of your most commonly used files and stores their names in a list through the Start button, as shown in Figure 2-1.

Looking for a letter or report you wrote just a few hours ago? Then don't bother hunting for it; just click on the Start button and rest the pointer over Documents. A new menu shoots from the Start button's side, listing the files you last accessed. Click on the name of the file you're after; Windows 95 grabs the program that created the file and brings them both to the screen.

Recycle Bin

So you deleted a file, slapped your forehead, and cursed yourself for deleting something so important. Happens to everybody. Microsoft's Undelete utility sometimes helps retrieve a deleted file, but the new Recycle Bin goes one step further: It holds on to your deleted files. If you decide down the road that you didn't *really* want to delete a file, the undamaged file is waiting for you in the Recycle Bin.

Nothing special happens when you delete a file. It vanishes. But double-click on the Recycle Bin icon at the end of the day (or before lunch hour, depending on the size of your hard drive), and you see the names of your deleted files waiting for you. Choose Empty Recycle Bin from the File menu, and your deleted files are destroyed for good.

(The name "Recycling Bin" not only sounds politically correct, but Apple had already taken the words "Trash Can" for the Macintosh computer, which has been doing the same thing for a decade.)

File Previews

Computers are not only time savers, but they're time wasters, too. For example, how can you tell what's inside a file? Only by loading it into the program that created it and peeking — an oft-repeated, laborious process.

Windows 95 comes with a way to peek inside files *without* loading the program. From within Explorer, click on the program's icon with your right mouse button. Choose Quick View from the menu that pops up and stand back as the file's contents appear on your screen. Figure 2-15 shows a Lotus 1-2-3 file, as an example.

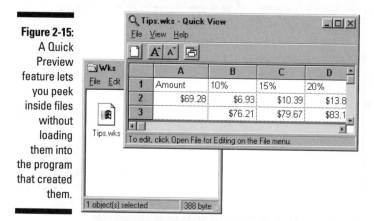

Figure 2-15:
A Quick
Preview
feature lets
you peek
inside files
without
loading
them into
the program
that created
them.

More helpful Help program

Windows 95 comes with a lot more features than any other version of Windows
or DOS. Thank goodness it comes with a lot more of a Help program, too. For
example, have you ever asked for help in a Help program, only to be told you
have to click your way through a bunch of folders to buttons in a different area?

The Windows 95 Help program not only tells you where you need to go, but it
takes you there as well. Don't know how to set your computer's clock? Press
the Help key — F1 — and Windows 95 tells you which program to use for
changing the clock's time and date. In fact, the Help program not only tells you
what program to use, it comes with a special button, seen in Figure 2-16. Just
click on that button, and the Help program automatically fetches the clock-
setting program for you. It's about time!

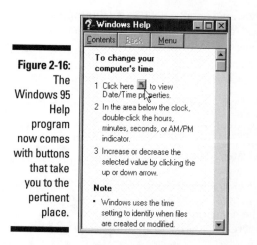

Figure 2-16:
The
Windows 95
Help
program
now comes
with buttons
that take
you to the
pertinent
place.

Part 3

The New Goodies in Windows 95

. . . .

In This Part

▶ Replacements for Windows 3.1 programs

▶ The Microsoft Network on-line service

▶ HyperTerminal

▶ WordPad

▶ Phone Dialer

▶ FreeCell

▶ CD Player

▶ Backup

. . . .

*W*indows 95 comes with bunches of new goodies, but fewer of the old goodies. This part gives the rundown on what Microsoft has stuffed into and pulled out of the Windows box.

Remnants Remaining in Windows 95

Like an evolving creature, Windows has changed fairly drastically from Windows 3.1 to Windows 95. To see if your favorite programs have been improved, removed, or destroyed, check out Table 3-1; it lists Windows 3.1 programs and their Windows 95 replacements.

Table 3-1	Windows 3.1 Programs and Their Windows 95 Replacements
The Windows 3.1 Program	*Its Windows 95 Equivalent*
Program Manager	Start button (Program Manager is still included, if you prefer to stick with it)
File Manager	Explorer and My Computer programs (File Manager is still included, if you like it better, and Windows 95 lets you change the My Computer program's name to something more personable, too)
Write	Replaced by WordPad, which adds features
Paintbrush	Replaced by Paint, a drawing program with similar features
Cardfile, Calendar	Gone with no replacements (a Personal Information Manager called WinPad didn't make it into the final cut)
Character Map, Calculator, Notepad, Media Player, Sound Recorder, MS-DOS prompt, Object Packager, Solitaire	Still the same in Windows 95
Terminal	Replaced with HyperTerminal, a telecommunications program with many more features
Control Panel	Replaced by Control Panel window, a similar collection of icons
PIF Editor	Replaced by Properties sheet: Click on a DOS program's icon with the right button and choose Properties from the menu to tweak the program's settings
Clock	Replaced by a permanent clock on the Taskbar
Clipbook Viewer	Still included, but supplemented with Scraps, a new concept for moving snippets of information around

✔ If you install Windows 95 over Windows 3.1, you'll be able to hang on to most of your favorite Windows 3.1 programs.

✔ Hang onto your Windows 3.1 disks. That way, you can copy some of your old Windows 3.1 programs back onto your computer if you don't like the Windows 95 replacements.

✔ Microsoft hadn't finished writing Windows 95 at the time I finished this section; the programmers may have changed their minds and changed a few programs around by the time this section — and Windows 95 — makes it into your hands.

The Microsoft Network On-Line Service

Most people have heard about *on-line services*, where you can hook your computer up to the phone lines and, under the pretense of making direct deposit payments through your checking account, swap pictures of your cat wearing a beret with new-found friends on the Cat User Group.

Microsoft, smelling money, started its own on-line service to compete with CompuServe, America Online, Prodigy, GEnie, the Internet, and the plethora of other on-line services that hatch each day.

Windows 95 comes with software that's itching to access what's known as The Microsoft Network. Seen in Figure 3-1, The Microsoft Network looks more like a Windows program than an on-line service. It uses the same folders and format used by Windows 95 as it spreads itself across your desktop.

✔ Don't bother searching through the Windows 95 box for mail-in forms to subscribe to The Microsoft Network. Instead, the sign-up form is right on the Start button's menu. Point and click, and Windows 95 starts dialing. (That's why all the other on-line services are a little bit worried about the competition.)

✔ Just as you can place pictures, sounds, and charts in a Windows word processor file, you can place pictures, sounds, and charts in messages swapped over The Microsoft Network. For example, you can easily paste a picture of yourself (or your cat) into a message to a friend.

✔ The Microsoft Network offers the standard on-line fare: electronic mail, bulletin boards, "chat rooms," file libraries, and Internet newsgroups. Because Microsoft is running the show, you can find lots of technical support for Microsoft products on-line, as well.

✔ The Microsoft Network will be accessible in more than 35 countries. Vacation planners can send messages to members in London before traveling there and ask for the names of the best pubs.

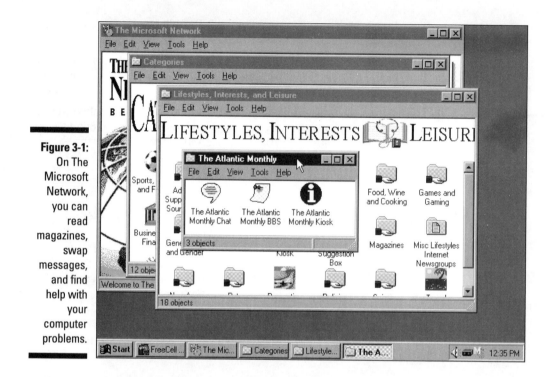

Figure 3-1:
On The
Microsoft
Network,
you can
read
magazines,
swap
messages,
and find
help with
your
computer
problems.

HyperTerminal

The old Windows modem program, Terminal, can handle the basics of logging on to a BBS and grabbing files, but it's not fancy enough for today's more sophisticated Internet surfers. Terminal doesn't come with Windows 95, but its replacement, HyperTerminal, makes modeming a lot easier.

Shown in Figure 3-2, HyperTerminal lets you assign a different icon to each on-line service or BBS that you call.

HyperTerminal can automatically figure out what settings to use for most places that you call. And because Windows 95 figures out what brand of modem you're using as part of the installation process, HyperTerminal automatically knows your modem's language, too.

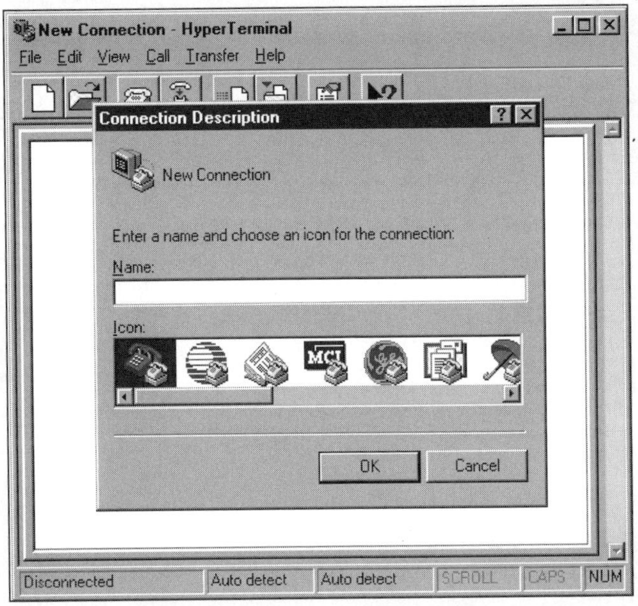

Figure 3-2:
HyperTerminal
comes with
ready-made
icons for
popular
on-line
services.

[HyperTerminal dialog screenshot: New Connection - HyperTerminal window with a "Connection Description" dialog box titled "New Connection," prompting "Enter a name and choose an icon for the connection:" with Name field, Icon selection row, and OK/Cancel buttons. Status bar shows Disconnected, Auto detect, Auto detect, SCROLL, CAPS, NUM.]

- ✔ HyperTerminal does a lot more stuff automatically than Terminal, making it a little easier to use. But HyperTerminal has a lot more features to figure out than Terminal, which brings its friendliness level back down by a few notches.

- ✔ The old Windows Terminal program can only download files using two settings: XMODEM and Kermit. Windows 95's HyperTerminal program supports the much speedier ZMODEM and YMODEM formats in addition to XMODEM and Kermit.

- ✔ World travelers with Windows 95 on their laptops will appreciate HyperTerminal's support for the dialing codes used by a wide variety of countries, from Afghanistan to Zimbabwe.

- ✔ Modem hounds can choose among ANSI, Minitel, TTY, Viewdata, VT100, and VT52 terminal emulation.

WordPad

The new word processor in Windows 95, WordPad isn't much different from Write, the old word processor. WordPad adds a few new features, however, as shown in Figure 3-3: You can automatically insert the time and date, add bullets to highlight important points, and use different colors for different words.

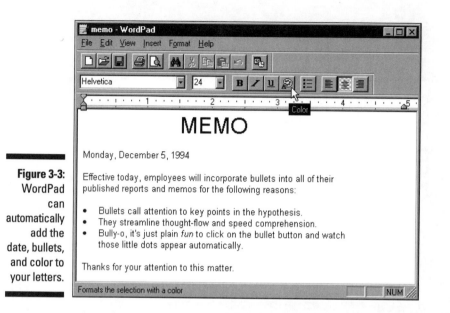

Figure 3-3:
WordPad
can
automatically
add the
date, bullets,
and color to
your letters.

> ✔ Still using Word for Windows 2? Then you're outta luck: WordPad can read and write in the Word for Windows 6 format, but it can't read Word for Windows 2 files. (It can still read your old Write files, though.)

> ✔ Still no spell checker. No columns or tables, either.

See the word Color floating beneath the mouse pointer, near the word MEMO, along the top of Figure 3-3? That word popped up when the mouse pointer hovered over WordPad's little palette icon. Microsoft realized that people are tired of guessing what icons are supposed to mean, so little pop-up explanations appear when the mouse pointer rests over certain icons. An even more detailed icon explanation appears along the window's bottom, also shown in Figure 3-3.

Phone Dialer

The Windows 95 Phone Dialer spiffs up your desktop telephone, even if it's a really cheap one. First, it lets you assign your most frequently dialed phone numbers to pushbuttons, as shown in Figure 3-4.

Then, if you just click on the button, Phone Dialer dials the call. In addition, Phone Dialer keeps track of the last calls you made using the program. Can't remember whether you made that important call yesterday morning? Choose Show Log from the Tools menu, and you can see a list of the phone numbers you've dialed, when you dialed them, and how long the conversations lasted.

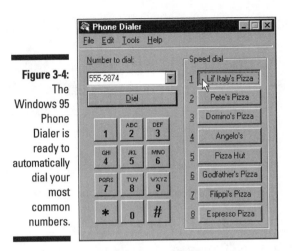

✔ Phone Dialer can be handy for making those complicated long-distance calls that require too many digits to remember.

✔ Phone Dialer offers a few more options for dialing than found in the old Windows 3.1 Cardfile. The Phone Dialer can dial using a calling card number, turn call waiting on and off, and dial extra numbers to reach outside lines.

✔ Using Phone Dialer on your laptop in the hotel room? Phone Dialer automatically sets up your call for dozens of countries, from Albania to Zambia. (And Afghanistan and Zimbabwe, too.) Lots of international stuff in Windows 95.

FreeCell

The Windows 3.1 favorite time-waster, Solitaire, has been passed up by a new contestant: FreeCell. Although FreeCell looks a lot like Solitaire, it plays a lot different. As shown in Figure 3-5, FreeCell works in more opportunities for easy double-clicking: Instead of making you drag the cards around, FreeCell simply jumps them into place.

The object is pretty simple: Sort the cards in order by suit and number from Ace to King on the four upper-right squares. While moving the cards up there, you can move other cards temporarily to the four "free cells" on the upper-left side.

✔ FreeCell comes with 32,000 different games. So far, none of them has been proven unbeatable.

✔ If you're looking for a challenge, try the games numbered 285; 27,006; and 31,465. In fact, you may find one or two other difficult ones as well.

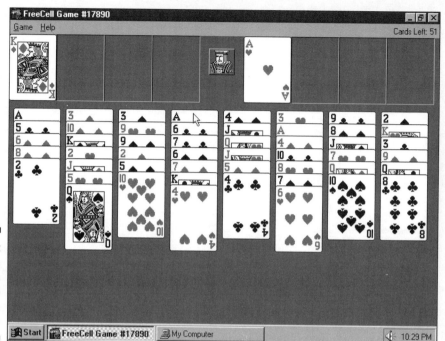

Figure 3-5:
Aces along
the top edge
of FreeCell
make for a
rough game.

> ✔ Moved the wrong card? Quick, press F10. That's the Undo button, but it undoes only if you press it before clicking on another card.

> ✔ There's a way to cheat, but Microsoft might fix it if someone from the company sees it here. If this secret still works when Windows 95 makes it to the shelf, you'll find it in *Windows 95 For Dummies.*

CD Player

Adding a CD-ROM drive to a computer doesn't always add multimedia as much as it adds Bachman Turner Overdrive to the lunch hour. Most multimedia computer owners pop a musical CD into the computer's disk drive now and then.

Windows 3.1's Media Player can play music CDs, but Windows 95 comes with a full-fledged CD Player, shown in Figure 3-6.

The CD Player lets you add song titles to the menu as well as create your own play lists. Or, if you're feeling random, choose the Random Order setting to make Windows 95 act like a jukebox. Now, if it could just come with a pool table. . . .

✔ An easy-to-find menu item brings up the volume control — no frantic searching to save your ears.

✔ Don't remember what some of those buttons do? Just rest your mouse pointer over one of them, and Windows 95 sends a message to the screen to help you out. In Figure 3-6, for example, the CD Player says that the two triangles you're pondering let you jump to the previous track on the CD.

✔ Looking for a certain song but can't remember which one it is? Then choose the Intro Play option. It automatically plays the first few seconds of every song on the CD until you recognize the one you're after.

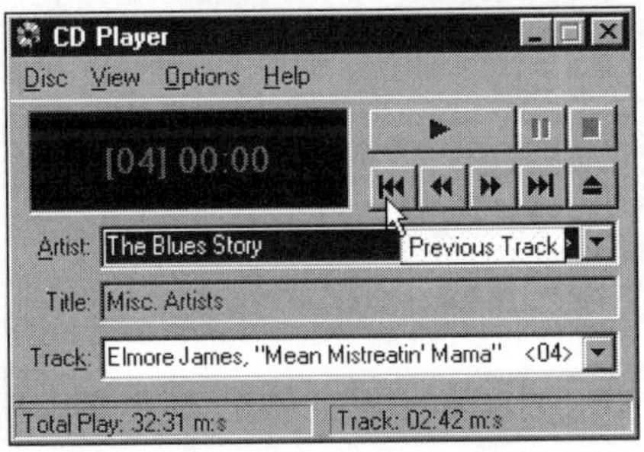

Figure 3-6:
The
Windows 95
CD Player
lets you
keep track
of your
songs.

Backup

Everybody knows that you're supposed to make backup copies of your computer's information. The problem is finding the time to do it.

The Windows 95 Backup program, shown in Figure 3-7, isn't anything really special, except in one key area: It can handle long filenames. The old-school, DOS-based backup programs can only handle eight-character filenames, so they can't make reliable Windows 95 backups.

To keep Windows 95 users from treading dangerously, Microsoft tossed a Backup program in with Windows 95 until all the other companies update their backup programs.

Once you tell the Windows 95 Backup program which programs to save, it copies them to floppy disks or a tape backup unit. (You can see the flourish in Figure 3-8.)

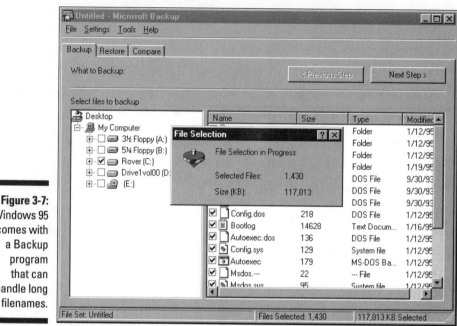

Figure 3-7:
Windows 95
comes with
a Backup
program
that can
handle long
filenames.

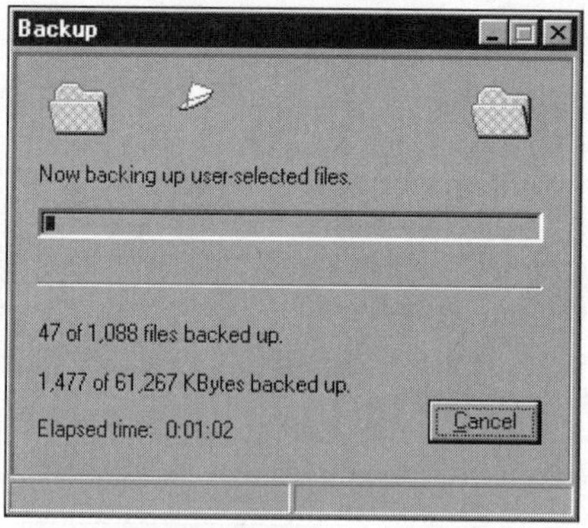

Figure 3-8:
The Backup
program
shows a
cartoon of
papers
flying
through the
air during
the Backup.

✔ Windows 95 has a lot more attention to detail than Windows 3.1. See the little top spinning in Figure 3-7 and the little paper flying through the air in Figure 3-8? Those "animated icons" roam the place.

✔ If you haven't bought a tape backup unit yet, now may be a good time to put one on your shopping list. They've come way down in price, and copying huge hard drives onto hundreds of floppies is a bore, even if Windows 95 *does* let you play FreeCell while you're doing it.

Part VI
Windows for Workgroups

In this part...

*I*n the beginning, Windows newcomers didn't have to bother fiddling with networks. After all, people only used networks in offices where bunches of computers were strung together with spiraling cables. Networked offices automatically came with a harried Network Guru to solve everybody's computing problems (eventually).

So when Microsoft came out with its networked version of Windows — Windows for Workgroups — nobody had to learn it. (Well, the harried Network Gurus had to, but they're used to punishment.)

But now, things have changed. First, some manufacturers install Windows for Workgroups on all their computers, even the ones heading for people's homes. Second, many harried Network Gurus are too tangled in cable to come running when network users raise their hands with a question.

This part of the book is for people who find themselves stuck with Windows for Workgroups, either because some salesperson put it on their new home computer or because their office computer guru is getting a wee bit harder to find.

Chapter 20

Windows on a Network

• •

In This Chapter

▶ What is a network?

▶ What is Windows for Workgroups?

▶ How does Windows differ from Windows for Workgroups?

▶ Just tell me how to "log on" and "log off" a network!

▶ Making Windows for Workgroups run faster

• •

*I*f you're lucky, someone in your office knows how this whole networking thing works. Any time you run across a problem, give this technical wizard a call and let him or her worry about the headaches in getting your computer to work on the network.

But if the techno-wizards have stopped responding when you raise your hand (after all, they're expected to fix the coffee machine, too), this chapter will pitch in. You won't find any techno-babble here — just plain-English explanations to help you understand networks better so that you can get your work done.

If you're using Windows for Workgroups but your computer *isn't* wired to another computer somewhere — it's not on a *network* — you don't need to read this entire chapter. Just check out the last section, which tells you how to play the new card game that comes with Windows for Workgroups.

What Is a Network?

In the old days when computers cost millions of dollars, only large corporations and the government could afford them. To save money, people shared a computer: the expensive computer sat safely in one room, and the people using it sat in another room, tapping on keyboards connected by a long cord. That way, even their clumsiest mistakes couldn't damage the precious computer in the other room.

Years later, personal computers became so cheap and plentiful that companies could afford to put one on every employee's desk. Pretty soon, each employee not only wanted a computer, but also a printer, modem, hard disk, and scanner.

Rather than bankrupt themselves by buying all that extra computer equipment, companies came up with another solution. Why not buy *one* printer, hard disk, or modem and let all the personal computers share it? By using this strategy, companies can buy less equipment, save money, and still keep everyone happy (almost).

Connecting personal computers with a cable enables users to share the same printer or modem. When two or more computers are linked with cables, allowing them to work together, they're called a *network*.

- Networks let bunches of computers share the same pieces of expensive *equipment*, just like office workers usually share the same copy machine.

- Networks let people share *files* between their computers so that nobody has an excuse to get up.

- Networks let people pass *messages* between computers, making it quicker to pass around gossip, er, memos.

What Is Windows for Workgroups?

Windows for Workgroups is plain ol' Microsoft Windows, but with a few extra goodies designed for networks. For example, if your computer is connected to a network, Windows for Workgroups lets you edit files stored on somebody else's hard disk, send messages to your coworkers about your updates, and even print that newly edited file on somebody else's printer.

The term *workgroup* simply means a collection of people performing similar tasks. For example, the people in a sales department may be considered a workgroup, the people in the marketing department may form another workgroup, and the people in the accounting department may be a third workgroup. Technically speaking, the slaves who built the Egyptian pyramids were in one workgroup and the slaves who built the Great Wall of China were in another workgroup.

- Organizing computer users in a network or workgroup lets people share information more easily. Need information stored on Fred's computer? Just yank it off as if it were stored on your own computer. Want to get other people's ideas without scheduling a meeting that nobody really wants to attend? Pass notes electronically and let your coworkers review your idea at their convenience.

- Windows for Workgroups offers the same graphical user interface that people have already used in Microsoft Windows. By tacking on the conveniences of pull-down menus, windows, and icons, Windows for Workgroups makes networks simple, easy, and (supposedly) fun to use.

How Does Windows Differ from Windows for Workgroups?

At first glance, Windows and Windows for Workgroups look exactly alike. In fact, you can use Windows for Workgroups on a single computer — even if it's not hooked up to any type of network.

The most noticeable difference between the two programs shows up in File Manager; a few other changes pop up in Print Manager and the Clipboard. Windows for Workgroups comes with a few extra network programs, and it's slightly faster at grabbing files off the hard drive.

The Windows for Workgroups File Manager looks just like the regular File Manager except for a special toolbar along its top. The toolbar lets you connect to another computer's hard disk and share its files (see Figures 20-1 and 20-2).

Figure 20-1:
The File
Manager in
Windows.

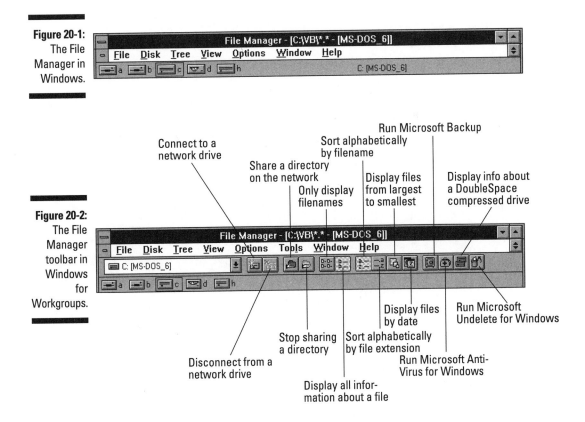

Figure 20-2:
The File
Manager
toolbar in
Windows
for
Workgroups.

The Print Manager in Windows for Workgroups also includes a special toolbar that lets you use printers connected to other computers on the network (see Figures 20-3 and 20-4).

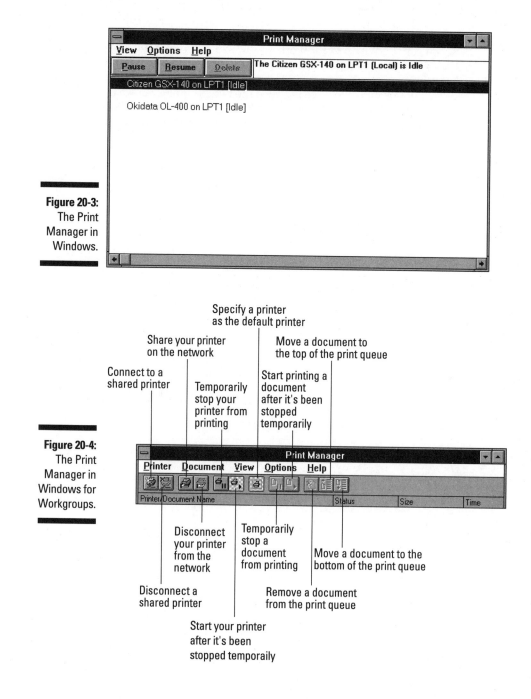

Figure 20-3:
The Print Manager in Windows.

Figure 20-4:
The Print Manager in Windows for Workgroups.

The Clipboard Viewer in *regular* Windows, shown in Figure 20-5, lets you cut, copy, and paste items between programs. Windows for Workgroups renames this program the *ClipBook Viewer,* shown in Figure 20-6, and lets you cut, copy, and paste items between programs on different computers. This means that you can write a document on your computer, cut out a paragraph, and then paste it in somebody else's document stored on another computer.

Or somebody could snatch a copy of that paragraph from your Clipboard and paste the paragraph into their own document, on their computer across the room.

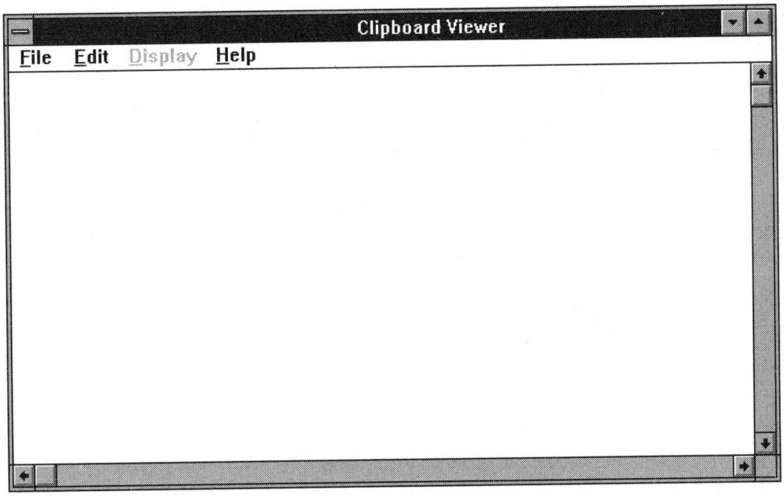

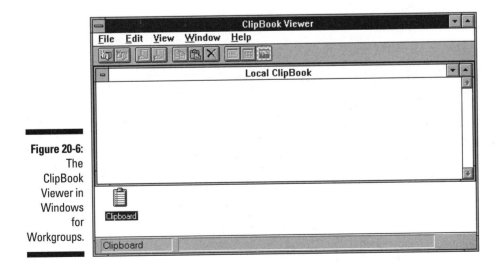

Figure 20-5:
The
Clipboard
Viewer in
Windows.

Figure 20-6:
The
ClipBook
Viewer in
Windows
for
Workgroups.

Windows for Workgroups also comes with a bunch of programs designed for network stuff, as shown in Figure 20-7 and described in the following list:

Figure 20-7:
Windows for Workgroup's special networking programs.

✔ A mail program allows you to exchange messages and files with other people on the network (instead of walking to their desks carrying a floppy disk).

✔ A chat program lets you type messages back and forth to other people on the network (you can look like you're working when you're really gossiping about the other people in your office).

✔ An appointment scheduling program helps you organize your time and lets others see when you're busy.

✔ A fax program enables you to send and receive faxes through a fax modem connected to the network.

Essentially, Windows for Workgroups is nothing more than a slightly faster version of Windows with added network capability. For that reason, many people use Windows for Workgroups whether or not their computers are connected to a network.

In fact, Microsoft claims that Windows for Workgroups can run up to 70 percent faster than ordinary Windows. Then again, back in the late '80s, Microsoft claimed that OS/2 would be the operating system of the future.

Just Tell Me How to "Log On" and "Log Off" a Network!

A network connects your computer to other computers. From your computer, you can examine all the files stored on other computers connected to the network. But just because the physical wires are plugged in correctly doesn't automatically mean that you can start using the network. Before you can use a network, you must *log on,* which is a fancy term for telling the computer, "Hey, I want to use the network now!"

To log on to the network (assuming that the network works properly), do the following:

1. **Type WIN at the DOS prompt and press Enter.**

   You always start Windows that same way, and it should look like this:

   ```
   C:\> WIN
   ```

   If you're lucky, Windows for Workgroups will simply hop onto the screen, and you'll be ready to go. But if you're working for a corporation or large company, you'll probably have to type in a password, described in the next step.

2. **Make sure that your name is correct in the Logon Name box, type your password into the Password box, and click the OK button, seen in Figure 20-8.**

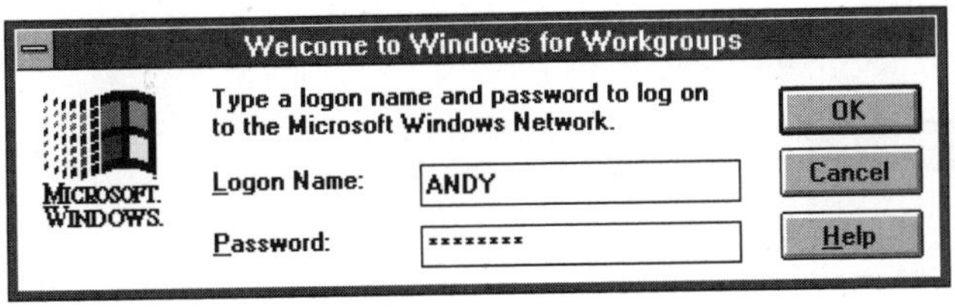

Figure 20-8:
A form for logging onto a Windows for Workgroups network.

The logon box is smart enough to always list your particular name in the Logon Name box, saving you some time. In fact, you'll never have to change that box — unless you're trying to log in on somebody else's computer.

Be careful when typing in your password: The computer types in asterisks as you type in letters. That prevents prying eyes from peeping at your password, but it also prevents you from seeing if you've typed in a mistake.

✓ Passwords can only be 14 characters long. Windows for Workgroups starts beeping after the fifteenth character.

✓ If you're logging in for the first time, Windows for Workgroups may ask if you'd like to create a *password list.* Feel free to create one. By filling out a few password forms similar to the Logon Name box — choosing passwords for any shared printers or other resources — you can tell Windows for Workgroups to automatically enter in those additional passwords in the future. Whenever you type in your initial logon password, the computer pulls all your other passwords from the master list, saving you from computerized bureaucracy.

✔ Windows for Workgroups locks up your password list when you log off the network or log off Windows for Workgroups. That keeps people from sneaking in later and using your password list.

 ✔ When thinking up a password, don't use your own name — that's too easy for enemy invaders to guess. For the best protection, change your password often.

To log off from the network, follow these steps:

1. **Open the Network group window (shown in Figure 20-7) from Program Manager.**

2. **Double-click on the Log On/Off icon.**

3. **A dialog box appears, asking whether you're sure you want to log off. Click Yes.**

Windows for Workgroups displays a Log On/Off dialog box, letting you know whether you have successfully disconnected from the network, as shown in Figure 20-9.

Figure 20-9:
The Log On/
Off dialog
box.

When you log off from a network, other people on the network can still access your computer's directories, printer, fax, and so on, but you can't access anyone else's computer.

To log back on to the network after logging off, follow the same steps. Oddly enough, you get absolutely no message from Windows for Workgroups letting you know whether you successfully logged on or not. Just assume that everything is working okay and get back to work.

Sharing hard disk directories

With a network, two or more people can share a directory stored on another computer. This capability lets everyone store files in one central location (and also creates the risk that everyone's work will be lost because it's stored in a single central location).

When you start Windows for Workgroups, coworkers on the network can't use any of your directories, no matter how much more money they make than you. To share your directory with other people on the network, you have to tell Windows for Workgroups which directory you want to share. It gets a little technical, but hey, you're on a network.

A shared directory can be one of three types:

- ✔ Read-Only
- ✔ Full
- ✔ Depends on Password

With a *Read-Only* directory, other people can run programs stored in the directory and read files, but they cannot modify any files or store new files there. This type of directory is great when you want to share information but you're worried that your coworkers might screw up the files.

With a *Full* directory, anyone can modify, change, rename, move, delete, destroy, mutilate, and otherwise wreak havoc on your directory. In other words, use the Full option only if you trust your coworkers. It gives them maximum control over your directories.

With a *Depends on Password* directory, you can password-protect your directory. If people know the right password, they can get full access to your directory. Otherwise, they get only read-only access.

Making a shared directory

Before you can share your file directories with others, you need to tell the network, "See this directory? I want to share it with everyone else on the network."

To share a directory on your computer with others, follow these steps:

1. **Open the File Manager.**

2. **Highlight the directory that you want to share.**

   Just click on the directory's name with the mouse. For the purposes of example, let's say that you're sharing your VIRUS directory with your coworkers.

3. **From the Disk menu, choose the Share As command, as shown in Figure 20-10.**

   The Share Directory dialog box appears, as shown in Figure 20-11.

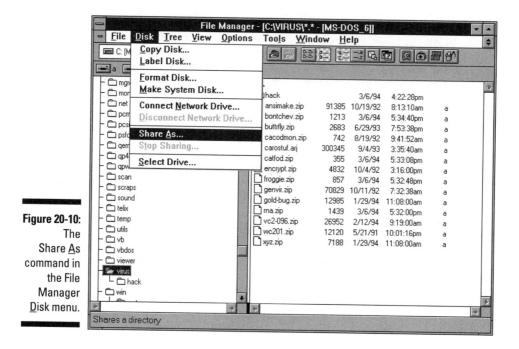

Figure 20-10:
The
Share <u>A</u>s
command in
the File
Manager
<u>D</u>isk menu.

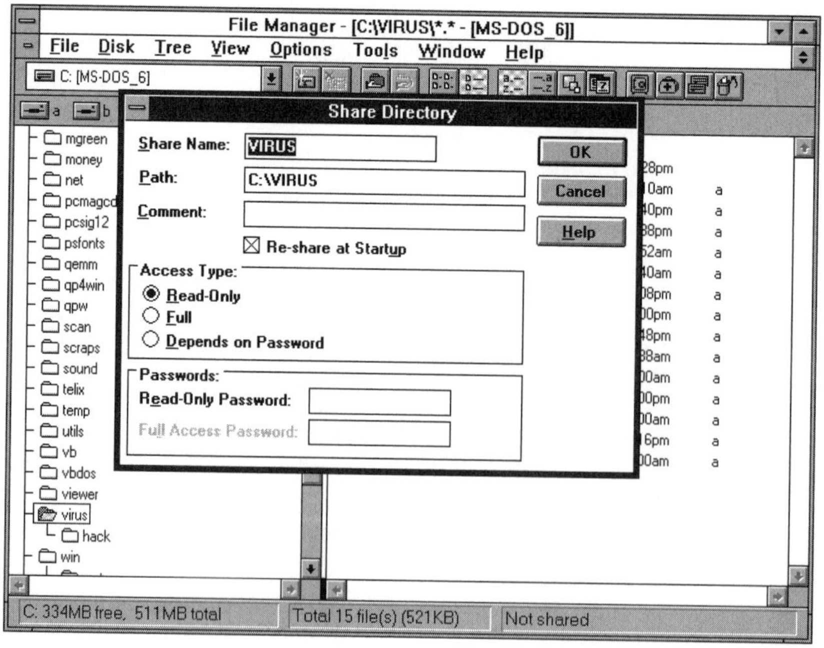

Figure 20-11:
The Share
Directory
dialog box.

4. Type a name for your shared directory.

If you don't type a name, Windows for Workgroups uses the current name of the directory.

5. Choose an Access Type.

As described in the preceding section, choose Read-Only, Full, or Depends on Password. If you choose Depends on Password, enter a password that any new users will have to enter before being allowed access.

6. Choose OK.

Anyone else in the network can now use your shared directory. The newly shared directories will appear with a little hand beneath their folder icon in File Manager.

Using a shared directory

After someone creates a shared directory, everyone else on the network can converge on it like a flock of ravenous vultures. (Of course, if the shared directory has a password, the vultures need to enter a password before they can start tasting the directory's files.)

To use a shared directory stored on another computer, follow these steps:

1. Open the File Manager.

2. From the Disk menu, choose the Connect Network Drive command.

The Connect Network Drive dialog box appears, as shown in Figure 20-12.

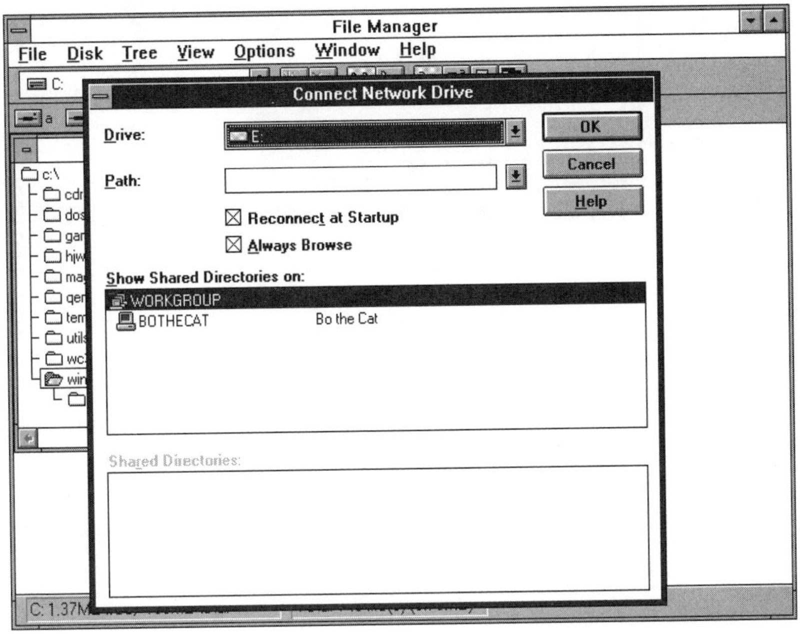

Figure 20-12:
The Connect
Network
Drive dialog
box.

3. **In the Show Shared Directories on: list box, highlight the computer containing the shared directories that you want to use.**

The Connect Network Drive dialog box then shows all the shared directories available on the computer you chose (see Figure 20-13).

4. **Highlight the shared directory you want to use and then press Enter.**

File Manager will display the shared directory on-screen. Depending on how the other computer is set up, you may need to type in a password first, however.

When you're ready to disconnect from the shared directory, follow these steps:

1. **Open the File Manager.**

2. **From the Disk menu, choose the Disconnect Network Drive command.**

3. **Double-click on the drive you no longer need.**

Disconnecting a shared directory from the network

After you've shared a directory with others, you may want to revert back to stoic individualism and remove the directory from the network so that other people can't access it any more.

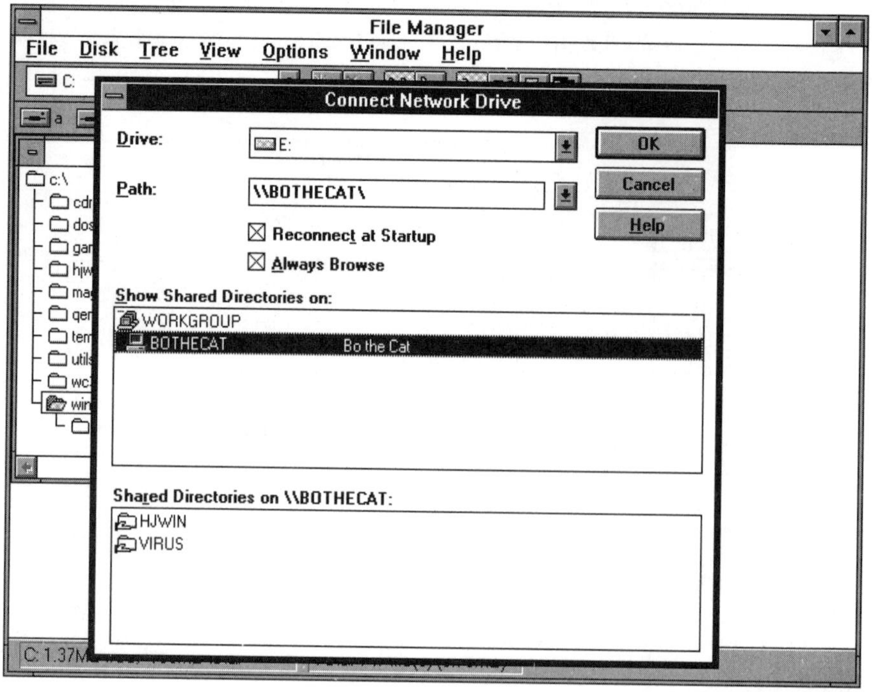

Figure 20-13:
The Connect
Network
Drive dialog
box showing
shared
directories.

To remove a shared directory from the network, follow these steps:

1. **Open the File Manager.**

2. **From the Disk menu, choose Stop Sharing, as shown in Figure 20-14.**

   The Stop Sharing Directory dialog box appears (see Figure 20-15).

3. **Highlight the directory you want to stop sharing and press Enter.**

If other people are using the directory that you want to disconnect from the network, you see the dialog box shown in Figure 20-16. Better check to see what they're up to before kicking them off your computer.

Sharing printers

Not everyone can afford the latest, high-speed, full-color laser or inkjet printer. As a cheaper alternative, the boss usually gets all the good equipment and everyone else has to fight over the old printers. But if the boss connects the good printer to a network, everyone can send documents to it.

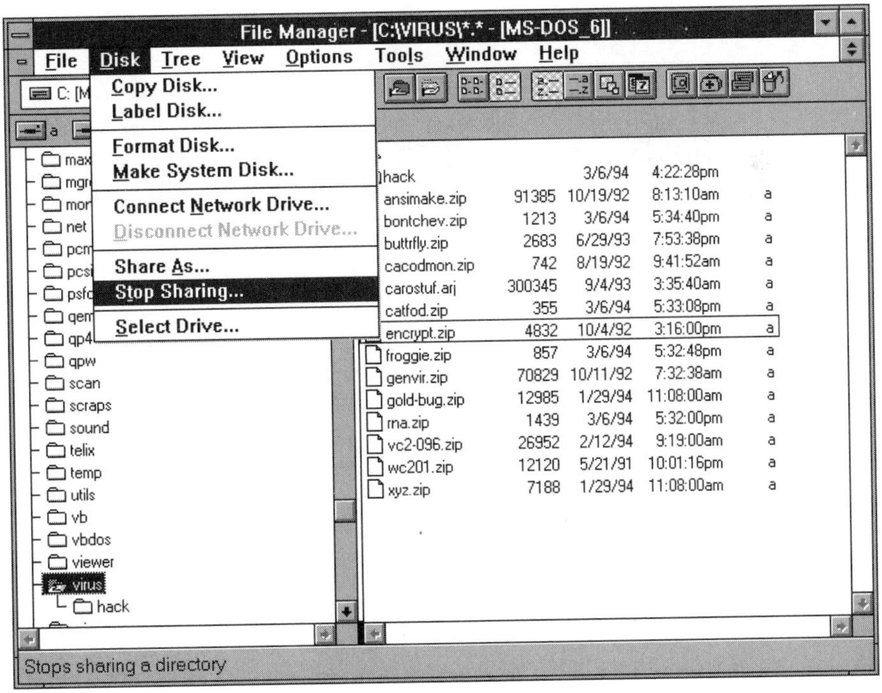

Figure 20-14: The Stop Sharing command in the Disk menu.

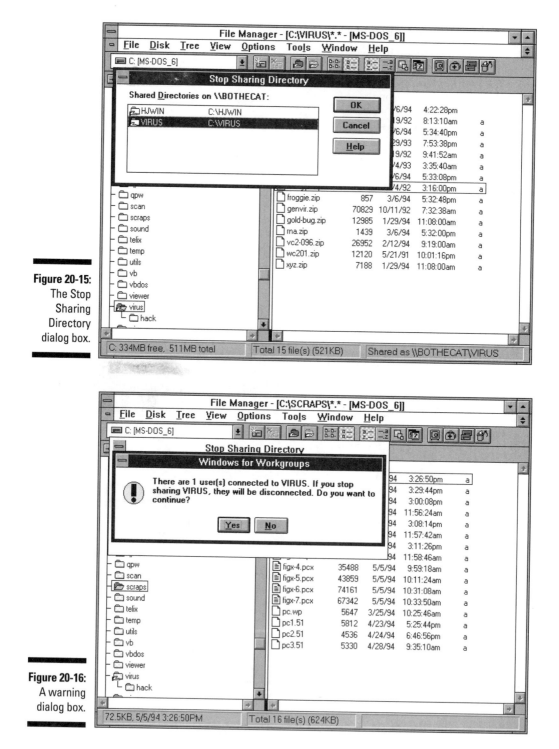

Figure 20-15:
The Stop
Sharing
Directory
dialog box.

Figure 20-16:
A warning
dialog box.

Making a shared printer

If you happen to have a good printer connected to your computer, it's tempting to hog it all for yourself. However, if your boss says that you either have to share your printer or get fired, compromise and make your printer available to everyone else on the network.

To make a shared printer, follow these steps:

1. Open the Print Manager.

2. Highlight the printer you want to share with others.

Just click on the name of the printer that you want to share.

3. From the Printer menu, choose Share Printer As, as shown in Figure 20-17.

The Share Printer dialog box appears, as shown in Figure 20-18.

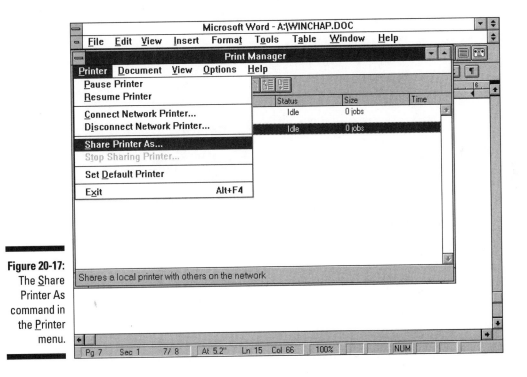

Figure 20-17:
The Share Printer As command in the Printer menu.

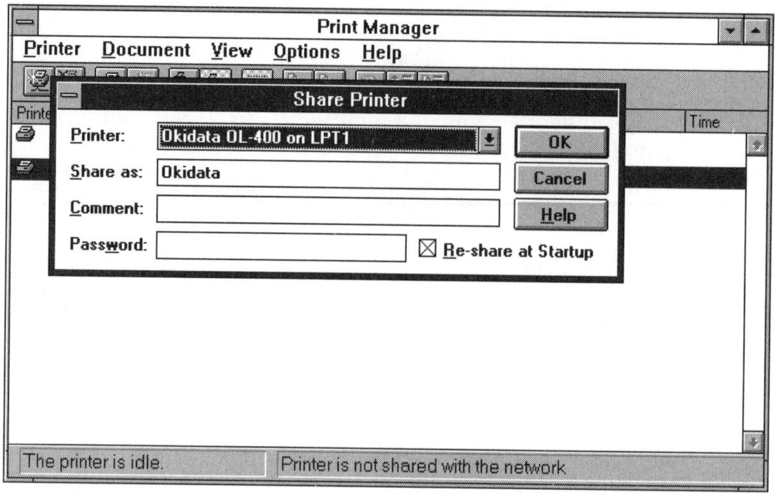

Figure 20-18:
The Share
Printer
dialog box.

4. Choose OK.

The Print Manager makes your chosen printer a shared printer (see Figure 20-19).

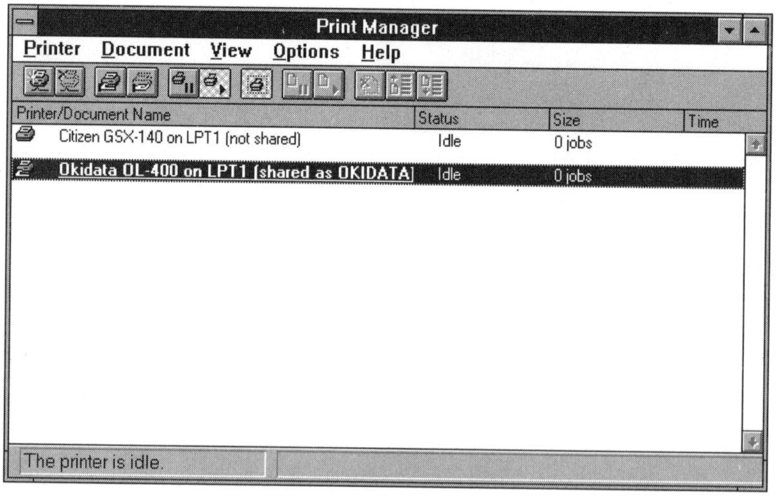

Figure 20-19:
The Print
Manager
with a
shared
printer
highlighted.

Using a shared printer

After someone makes a printer a shared printer, everyone else can connect to and start sending documents to that printer.

To use a shared printer, follow these steps:

1. **Open the Print Manager.**

2. **From the Printer menu, choose the Connect Network Printer command (see Figure 20-20).**

   The Connect Network Printer dialog box, displayed in Figure 20-21, appears.

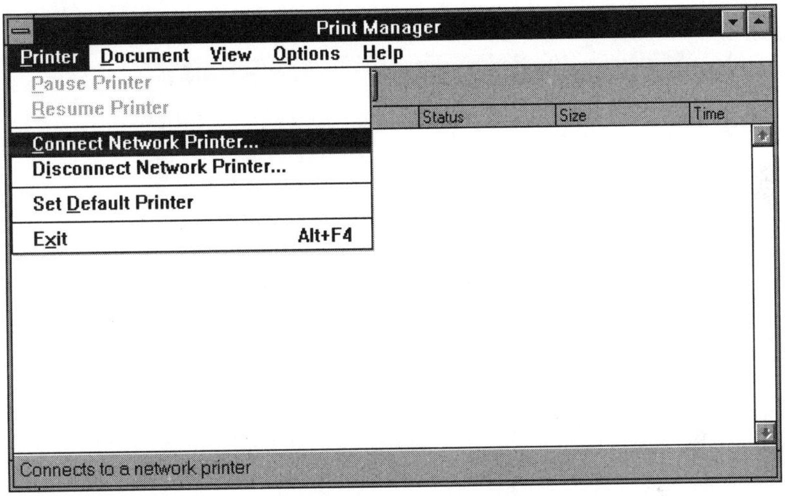

Figure 20-20:
The Connect Network Printer command in the Printer menu.

Figure 20-21:
The Connect Network Printer dialog box.

3. **In the Show Shared Printers on: list box, highlight the computer attached to the printer you want to use.**

   The Shared Printers list box shows all the available printers you can use (see Figure 20-22).

4. **In the Shared Printers list box, highlight the printer you want to use and press Enter.**

   The Print Manager appears, showing the name of the network printer on-screen, as in Figure 20-23.

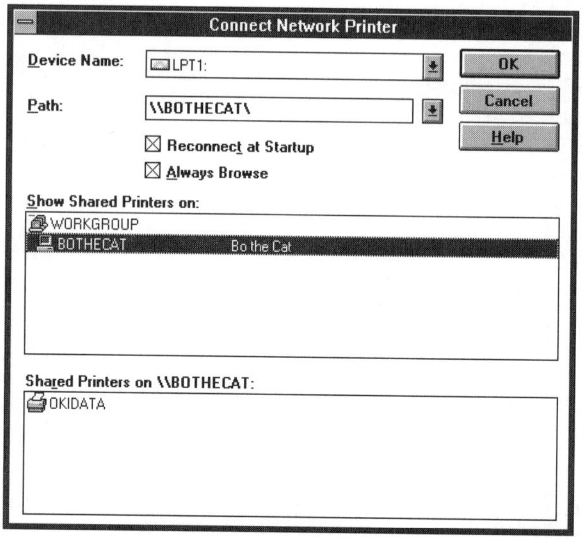

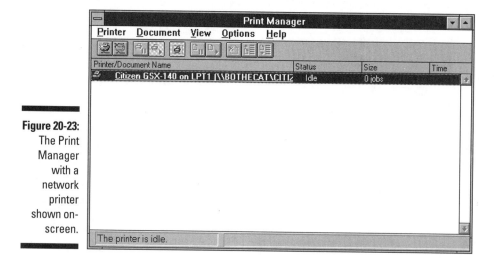

Figure 20-22:
The Shared Printers list box in the Connect Network Printer dialog box.

Figure 20-23:
The Print Manager with a network printer shown on-screen.

When you print something, it goes through the network and prints on the shared printer.

Disconnecting a shared printer from the network

If you're feeling selfish and want to stop sharing your printer with everyone else on the network, you can disconnect your printer at any time.

To disconnect a shared printer from the network, follow these steps:

1. **Open the Print Manager.**

2. **From the Printer menu, choose the Stop Sharing Printer command (see Figure 20-24).**

   The Stop Sharing Printer dialog box shown in Figure 20-25 appears.

3. **Highlight the printer you want to stop sharing on the network and press Enter.**

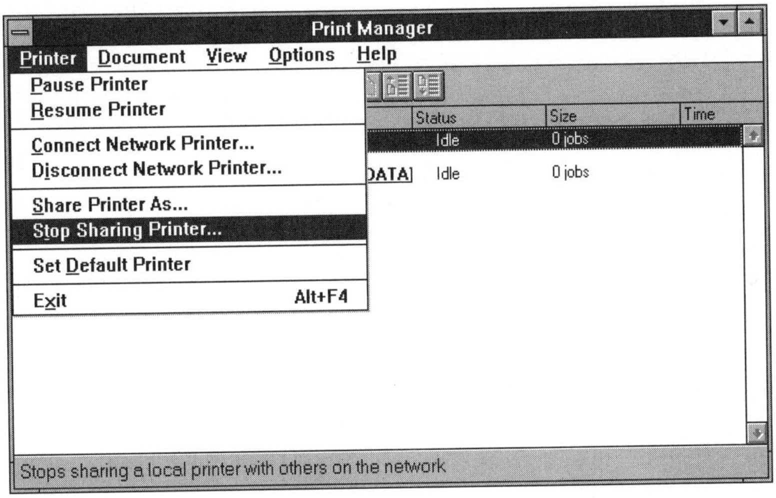

Figure 20-24: The Stop Sharing Printer command in the Printer menu.

```
┌─────────────────────────── Print Manager ──────────────── ▼ ▲ ─┐
│ Printer  Document  View  Options  Help                          │
│ Pause Printer                    │▓│▒│                          │
│ Resume Printer                   ─────────────────────────────  │
│                                  │ Status    │Size     │Time   │
│ Connect Network Printer...           Idle      0 jobs          ▲│
│ Disconnect Network Printer...   )ATA]  Idle    0 jobs           │
│                                                                 │
│ Share Printer As...                                             │
│ █Stop Sharing Printer...█                                       │
│                                                                 │
│ Set Default Printer                                             │
│                                                                 │
│ Exit                  Alt+F4                                    │
│                                                                 │
│                                                                ▼│
│ Stops sharing a local printer with others on the network        │
└─────────────────────────────────────────────────────────────────┘
```

Chatting with someone else

If you don't want to get caught chatting with your coworkers by the water cooler or break room, the wonders of modern technology can come to your rescue. You're not only allowed to chat on a network, but you're also *supposed* to.

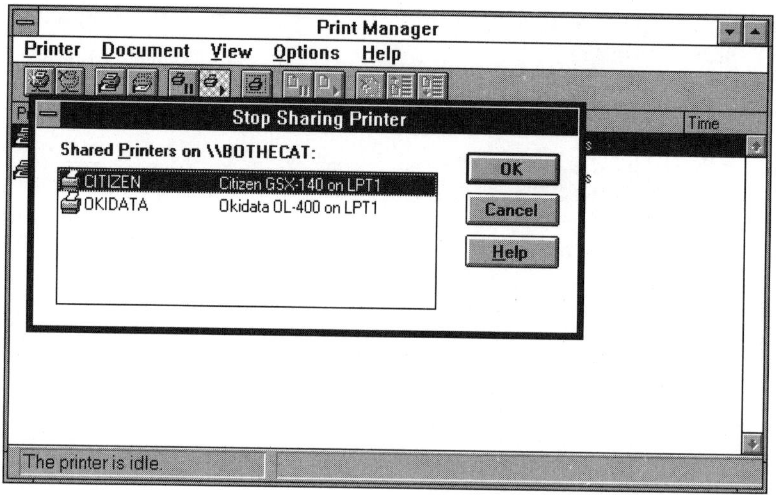

Figure 20-25:
The Stop
Sharing
Printer
dialog box.

With Windows for Workgroups, you can chat with anyone else on the network. As you type, your message appears on the other person's screen. When that person types a message back, his or her words appear on your screen. Because it looks like you're diligently typing at your computer, your boss won't know that you're really just gossiping over the network.

Contacting someone to chat

Before you can chat with someone over the network, you must first connect to that person's computer.

To connect someone else on a network to chat, follow these steps:

1. **Choose the Chat icon from Program Manager's Network group.**

   The empty Chat window shown in Figure 20-26 appears.

2. **From the Conversation menu, choose the Dial command, as shown in Figure 20-27.**

   The Select Computer dialog box appears (see Figure 20-28).

3. **Highlight the computer you want to chat with and press Enter.**

   The computer user you're dialing periodically hears an annoying beep, which lets that user know that you're trying to call. When the person you're calling finally answers your call, your Chat window splits in half.

4. Type your message.

Everything you type appears not only on *your* screen, but also on the other person's screen.

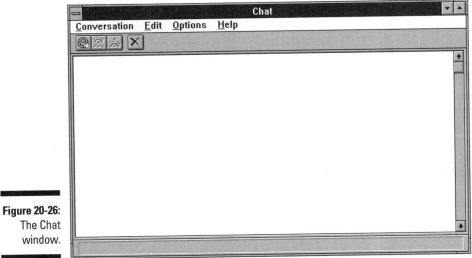

Figure 20-26:
The Chat window.

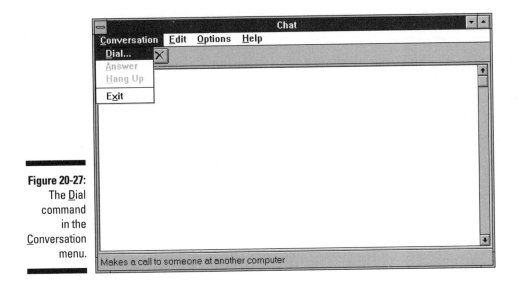

Figure 20-27:
The Dial command in the Conversation menu.

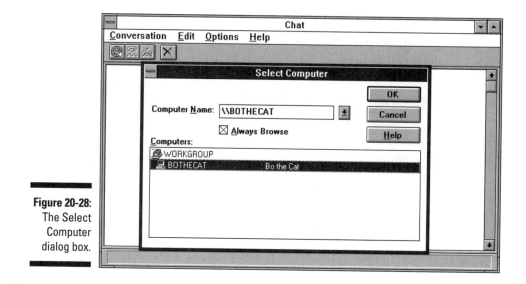

Figure 20-28:
The Select
Computer
dialog box.

Answering a call to chat

If you're using your computer and suddenly hear an annoying beep, somebody's trying to call you to chat.

To chat with the person calling you, follow these steps:

1. Choose the Chat icon.

The Chat window appears.

2. From the Conversation menu, choose the Answer command, as shown in Figure 20-29.

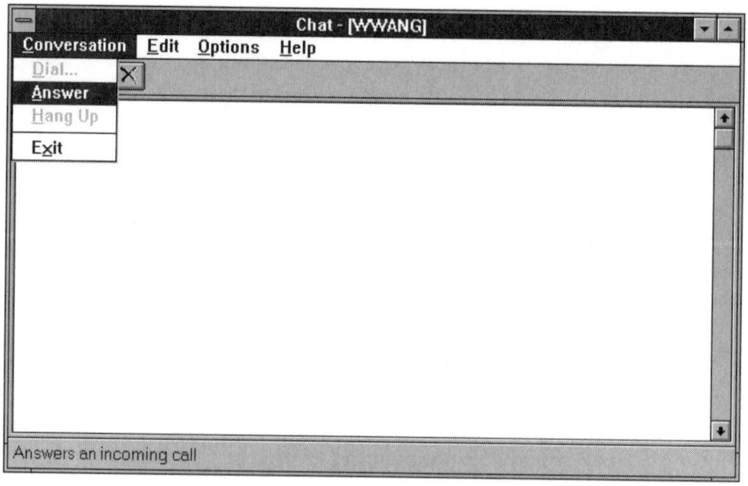

Figure 20-29:
The Answer
command
in the
Conversation
menu.

The annoying beeping goes away and the Chat window splits in two, as demonstrated in Figure 20-30.

3. Type a message.

Whatever *you* type appears in the top half of the Chat window. Whatever the other person types appears in the bottom half of the Chat window (see Figure 20-31).

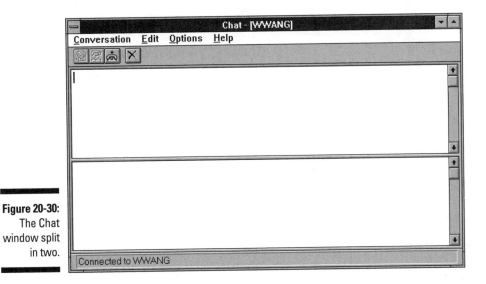

Figure 20-30:
The Chat window split in two.

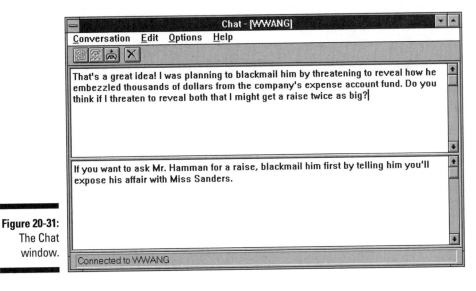

Figure 20-31:
The Chat window.

Disconnecting a chat

Eventually, your boss will get suspicious about two people on the network giggling uncontrollably, and you'll have to stop chatting.

To quickly disconnect a chat, follow these steps:

1. **From the Conversation menu, choose the Hang Up command, as shown in Figure 20-32.**

   The bottom half of the Chat window displays a telephone icon to let you know that you have hung up (see Figure 20-33).

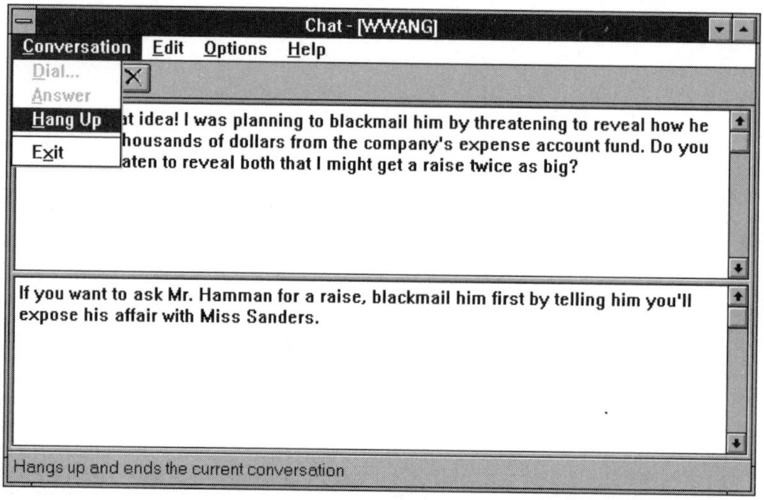

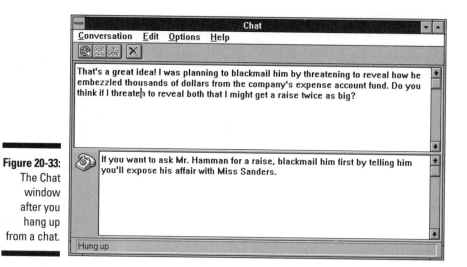

Figure 20-32: The Hang Up command in the Conversation menu.

Figure 20-33: The Chat window after you hang up from a chat.

TECHNICAL STUFF

Making Windows for Workgroups run faster

Plain old Windows uses 16 bits to transfer data to the hard disk. Windows for Workgroups uses 32 bits to transfer data to the hard disk. Although common-sense mathematics may make you think that Windows for Workgroups should be twice as fast, it's not. According to Microsoft, it can be up to 70 percent faster (but the company isn't as loud about saying exactly *what* it can do 70 percent faster).

If you're connected to a network, the person in charge of the network should have completed the following steps for you. But if you're using Windows for Workgroups on a computer not connected to a network or if you're the person in charge of the network, make sure that Windows for Workgroups is using 32 bits to transfer data by following these steps:

1. **Load the Control Panel and choose the 386 Enhanced icon.**

   The Enhanced dialog box appears.

2. **Choose the Virtual Memory button.**

3. **Choose the Change button.**

4. **Choose the Use 32-Bit Disk Access option.**

5. **Change your Swapfile setting to Permanent.**

6. **Choose the 32-Bit File Access option.**

7. **Choose OK.**

   The Virtual Memory dialog box appears.

8. **Choose Yes.**

   Another Virtual Memory dialog box appears.

9. **Choose Restart Windows.**

   Windows reboots and then returns to the screen. This time, however, it should be a little bit faster when reading or writing information to the hard disk.

A Hearty Game of Hearts

Getting tired of Solitaire and the cute little sun that sticks out its tongue? Sick of Minesweeper, now that you know how to cheat? Keep your chin up: Windows for Workgroups comes with a terrific game of Hearts, as shown in Figure 20-34.

Double-click on the Hearts icon in the Games program group of the Program Manager, and the game appears. The game works just like *real* Hearts. One person tosses a card onto the table, everybody else tosses down a card of the same suit, and the person with the highest card grabs the pile. The tricky part? You want the *lowest* score — any card with a heart is one point, and the queen of spades is worth 13 points.

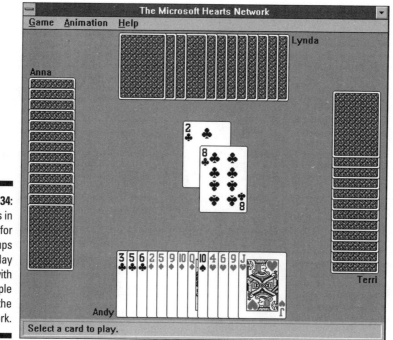

Figure 20-34:
Hearts in
Windows for
Workgroups
lets you play
cards with
other people
on the
network.

✔ There's a catch. If one player grabs all the hearts and the queen of spades, that player doesn't get any points, and all the other players are penalized 26 points.

✔ Nobody around at the office? The computer fills in for the other three players, and you can still play. In fact, you can play Hearts even if your computer isn't hooked up to a network.

✔ Cheat alert: The computer automatically sorts your cards by suit at the screen's bottom. However, it doesn't sort the cards that represent the other player's hands — the cards around the edges. Therefore, you can't get an idea of what cards the other players have by watching the position of their cards.

Part VII
The Part of Tens

The 5th Wave   By Rich Tennant

"NO, YOU'RE IN THE CASTLE COMPUTER ROOM. THAT'S THE 'WIZARD OF NERD'. YOU WANT 'OZ'—TWO DOORS DOWN ON YOUR RIGHT."

In this part...

*E*verybody likes to read Top Tens in magazines —
especially in the grocery store checkout aisle when
you're stuck behind someone who's just pulled a rubber band
off a thick stack of double coupons and the checker can't find
the right validation stamp.

Unlike the reading material at the grocery store, the chapters
in this part of the book don't list ten new aerobic bounces or
ten ways to stop your kids from making explosives with
kitchen cleansers. Instead, you find lists of ways to make
Windows be more efficient — or at least not as hostile. You
find a few tips, tricks, and explanations of eccentric acronyms
like *DLL.*

Some lists have more than ten items; others have fewer. But
who's counting, besides the guy wading through all those
double coupons?

Chapter 21

Ten Aggravating Things about Windows (and How to Fix Them)

. . . .

In This Chapter

▶ Bypassing the menus

▶ Keeping track of multiple windows

▶ Fixing the Print Screen key

▶ Saving your favorite Program Manager layout

▶ Understanding why DOS programs run too slowly

▶ Lining up two windows on the screen

▶ Updating a floppy disk's contents in the File Manager

▶ Hearing sounds *without* buying a sound card

▶ Making Windows start automatically

. . . .

"**W**indows would be great if only . . . (insert your pet peeve here)." If you find yourself thinking (or saying) this frequently, this chapter is for you. This chapter not only lists the most aggravating things about Windows, but it also explains how to fix them.

Those Zillions of Mouse Menus Take Forever

Windows has a zillion menus you can work through with the mouse, but you don't have to use them. If you want, you can use the keyboard to quickly select everything that you can click on in a menu.

Look closely at the words on the menu bar, along the top of each window. Some-where in every word, you can spot a single underlined letter. Press and release the Alt key and then press one of the underlined letters you see in a word. Try pressing the F in File, for example. Presto! The File menu leaps into place. Look for underlined letters on the newly displayed File menu. For example, now press S for Save. Presto again! Windows saves the current file, without a single mouse click.

To save a file in nearly any Windows program, press and release Alt, then press F, and then press S. It's that simple (after you memorize the combination, that is).

You find these underlined letters everywhere in Windows. In fact, you've been seeing underlined letters in this book as well. They're the keys you can use to avoid rooting through all the menus with a mouse.

- ✔ A list of the most commonly used key combinations is included in the Cheat Sheet at the front of this book.

- ✔ For some keys, you hold Alt while pressing a function key. For example, to close any Windows program, hold down Alt and press F4 (Alt+F4).

- ✔ If you accidentally press Alt and are stuck in Menu Land, press Alt again. Alternatively, press Esc and bark loudly until it lets you out.

It's Too Hard to Keep Track of All Those Windows

You don't *have* to keep track of all those windows. Windows does it for you with the Task List. Hold Ctrl and press Esc or simply double-click anywhere on the wallpaper, and the Task List rises to the forefront.

The Task List lists every currently open window by name. Double-click on the window you want, and that window hops to the top of the pile.

Even better, shrink all the windows into icons except for the window you're cur-rently working on. Then call up the Task List and click on the Tile button to line everything up neatly on the screen.

In Chapter 8, you find more soldiers to enlist in the battle against misplaced windows.

My Print Screen Key Doesn't Work

Windows takes over the Print Screen key (labeled *PrtSc, PrtScr,* or something even more supernatural on some keyboards). Instead of sending the stuff on the screen to the printer, the Print Screen key sends it to the Windows Clipboard, where it can be pasted into other windows.

- ✔ Some keyboards make you hold Shift while pressing Print Screen.

- ✔ If you hold Alt while pressing Print Screen, Windows sends the current *window* to the Clipboard — not the entire screen.

- ✔ If you *really* want a printout of the screen, hold Shift and press Print Screen to send a picture of the screen to the Clipboard. Paste the contents of the Clipboard into Paintbrush and print from there. (That's explained in Chapter 13.)

It Doesn't Remember My Favorite Program Manager Layout

Even after you've spent hours arranging the windows in the Program Manager, Windows isn't smart enough to think you want to save that particular layout. You must specifically tell Windows to save your changes. Follow these steps to instruct Windows to save your final arrangement of windows for the next session:

1. **From the Program Manager, click on <u>O</u>ptions.**

   The <u>O</u>ptions menu appears.

2. **Select <u>S</u>ave Settings on Exit.**

   The next time you start up Windows, Program Manager will look the same way it did when you last exited Windows: if you left it looking messy, then it will look messy, or, if you left it looking neat, it will look neat.

If you prefer that your Program Manager always look the same, however, regardless of how much you've changed it around during your current session, try this trick instead:

1. **Arrange Program Manager the way you want it to *always* look.**

2. **While holding down Shift, double-click on the box in Program Manager's upper left-hand corner.**

   Yep, that's the box that usually closes a program down. But when you hold Shift, you're telling Program Manager to simply save its current settings. (This trick only works with Program Manager and File Manager, however.)

3. **Deselect the <u>S</u>ave Settings on Exit option from Program Manager's <u>O</u>ptions menu.**

   Make sure that the little check mark does *not* appear next to the <u>S</u>ave Settings on Exit option. Now your Program Manager will always look the same when you start Windows. (If you make a change you want to keep, however, be sure to repeat the first two steps in this section, or Program Manager won't remember your changes.)

I Can't Find the Right Icon in Program Manager

Windows-based programs are notoriously self-centered. Whenever you install a new program in Windows, that program invariably creates a new program group window in Program Manager. After a few months of use, Program Manager becomes too cluttered with program groups for you to find anything.

Plus, that plethora of program group windows robs Windows of resource muscle it could be using elsewhere. The solution? Start cleaning up Program Manager by organizing your program group windows.

- ✔ For example, make *one* program called CDs and fill that window with all the icons for your CD programs. Then delete all the program group windows where those programs originally came from.

- ✔ If you have a lot of games, make a single program group called Games and drag all the icons for game programs into it. Then delete the games' program group windows.

- ✔ Chapter 11 has more information about reorganizing program group windows.

 To move an icon from one program group to another, drag it there: Point at it with the mouse and, while holding down the mouse button, point at the program group where you want to move the icon. When you let go of the mouse button, Program Manager moves the icon to the new program group.

My DOS Programs Run Too Slowly under Windows

DOS programs almost always run more slowly under Windows than if they had the whole computer to themselves. And they run the slowest when they're in a window.

Running DOS programs in a full screen speeds them up a little, as does beefing up the computer: adding more memory, upgrading to a faster 386, 486, or Pentium computer, and buying a bigger hard drive.

What's the best solution? Well, Windows is like a camper shell that is put on a pickup truck. Although the truck is more comfortable, it is slower and can't go underneath low bridges. To get back the speed and maneuverability, you simply have to remove the shell (or buy a more powerful engine).

That means don't run DOS programs under Windows. Simply exit Windows before running the program or buy the Windows version of that program.

It's Too Hard to Line Up Two Windows on the Screen

With all its cut-and-paste stuff, Windows makes it easy for you to grab information from one program and slap it into another. With its drag-and-drop stuff, you can grab names of files in the File Manager and drag them into the Program Manager to install them as icons.

The hard part of Windows is lining up two windows on the screen, side by side. That's where you need to call in the Task List. First, put the two windows anywhere on the screen. Then turn all the other windows into icons by clicking on the downward-pointing arrows in the top right corners of the windows.

Now call up the Task List by double-clicking on the wallpaper. Alternatively, hold Ctrl and press Esc. Click on the Task List's Tile button; the two windows line up on the screen perfectly.

The Task List always lines up windows *vertically*. If you want them lined up horizontally, hold the Shift key while clicking on Tile. Pretty sneaky, huh?

The File Manager Shows the Wrong Stuff on My Floppy Disk

The File Manager sometimes gets confused and doesn't always show what's on the disk drive. To prod it into taking a second look, press the F5 key.

I Need an Expensive Sound Card to Hear Any Cool Sounds

When creating the latest version of Windows, Microsoft experimented with some software that could play sounds on computers that didn't have a sound card. The software could play sounds through the computer's built-in speaker — the one that beeps all the time.

Unfortunately, the software didn't work on every computer they tried it on. Some computers have itty-bitty speakers that don't make much noise; other speakers are buried too deep in the case to be audible.

Because it didn't work on everybody's computer, Microsoft left it out of the final package. However, if you want to try Microsoft's internal speaker driver, you can download it from Microsoft's bulletin board system. Reach the Microsoft bulletin board system at 206-637-9009. You need a modem and Terminal, which is Windows' communications program (and probably a computer guru to watch and make sure that you're doing it right).

When you've downloaded the driver, install it as described in Chapter 17. The sounds aren't as loud or as clear as they can be with a sound card, but they are a lot cheaper.

If you're not up for the downloading experience, ask just about any computer nerd for a copy. It's a pretty widespread file.

Also, for Alice Martina Smith in Indianapolis, the driver only works with Windows programs — not DOS programs. It won't work with your old Battle Chess program, even if you run it in a slow DOS window.

I Want to Make Windows Load Automatically Each Morning

Some people use Windows constantly for all their computing needs. Others just load it up when they're ready for a game of Solitaire.

If you're tired of typing **WIN** every time you turn on the computer, you can tell the computer to run Windows automatically. The key is changing a file called AUTOEXEC.BAT in the computer.

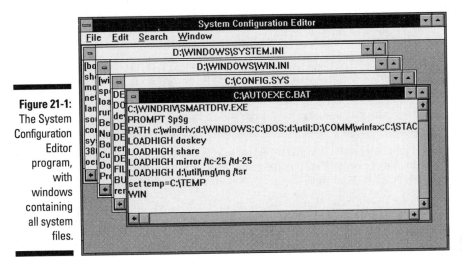

Figure 21-1:
The System
Configuration
Editor
program,
with
windows
containing
all system
files.

A computer's AUTOEXEC.BAT file contains many cryptic computer code words that you should not change. Don't ever change anything in that file unless you have a specific reason.

To change the AUTOEXEC.BAT file so that it contains the instructions to start Windows whenever you turn on the computer, follow these steps:

1. **Click on File at the top of the Program Manager.**

   The File menu appears.

2. **Select Run from the menu.**

   A command line box pops up.

3. **Type the following into the box, just like this:**

   ```
   SYSEDIT
   ```

   A program appears, making the screen look something like the one shown in Figure 21-1. Your screen will look slightly different.

   The SYSEDIT program works just like Notepad, but it holds four special system files in separate windows. The AUTOEXEC.BAT file for your computer sits on the top of the pile.

4. **Just as you would in Notepad, add the word** WIN **to the bottom of the AUTOEXEC.BAT file.**

   Make sure that you type **WIN** by itself on the bottom line. You don't even have to press Enter after typing **WIN**.

5. **Close the SYSEDIT program by double-clicking on its Control-menu box.**

   The Control-menu box is that little square in the top left corner of the window.

6. **If you're *sure* that you've done everything right, click on Yes when SYSEDIT asks whether it should save your changes.**

   If you think something may have gotten bungled a little, no matter how small, click on Cancel to try again or click on No to give up.

   ✔ If you *don't* want Windows to load whenever you turn on the computer, do the opposite: Remove the word *WIN* from the bottom of the AUTOEXEC.BAT file.

   ✔ Before you fiddle around with the AUTOEXEC.BAT file, it's wise to make a copy of it to a floppy disk and put it away for safekeeping. If you change something for the worse, and the computer won't work, copy that file from the floppy back to the C:\ directory. The File Manager, discussed in Chapter 12, is up for that task.

Nerdy stuff to ignore

The SYSEDIT program brings four files to the screen: AUTOEXEC.BAT, CONFIG.SYS, WIN.INI, and SYSTEM.INI. Each file contains settings pertaining to your particular computer setup.

AUTOEXEC.BAT: This file contains lists of commands you can normally type at the DOS prompt. By putting them in this file, the computer types them itself when it first runs. It's usually a mixture of DOS commands and program names.

CONFIG.SYS: References to most of the computer's hardware hang out in here. Most of the computer gizmos require *drivers,* special software that describes how the gizmos are to be addressed. The CONFIG.SYS file lets the computer know the proper etiquette for addressing the gizmos.

WIN.INI: Windows and its staff of programs keep their settings in here. When you change the colors in Windows, or tell one of its programs which printer to use, those commands usually are remembered here.

SYSTEM.INI: This file is the most complicated because it contains information Windows uses when dealing with the computer's hardware. It tells Windows what fonts work best on the monitor, for example, or how to take advantage of the computer's 386-class chip.

Computer nerds diddle with these files for hours, moving the settings around, plugging in different numbers, or even rearranging the order of the lines. However, fiddling with any of the settings in these files is like moving around the cables in a car's engine: There's a good chance it won't start unless you know exactly what you are doing. That's why you should leave these files for the computer nerds to play with.

Chapter 22

Ten DOS Commands You Shouldn't Run under Windows

. . . .

In This Chapter

Dangerous first-degree offenders:

▶ CHKDSK /F

▶ FDISK

▶ RECOVER

▶ SELECT

▶ FORMAT C:

Recently paroled commands:

▶ APPEND

▶ ASSIGN

▶ JOIN

▶ SUBST

▶ SHARE

▶ FASTOPEN

Plus 8 dangerous DOS 6 commands:

▶ DBLSPACE

▶ DEFRAG

▶ EMM386

▶ MEMMAKER

▶ MSCDEX

▶ NLSFUNC

▶ SMARTDRV

▶ VSAFE

. . . .

Don't bother reading this chapter if you use Windows exclusively. But, if you ever double-click on the MS-DOS icon in the Program Manager to make a DOS prompt appear, give this chapter a brief look.

Some parts of DOS don't get along well with Windows. Some DOS commands are downright deadly; others are only hazardous under certain conditions.

So, if you *shell to DOS* under Windows, don't type any of these commands. Here's the list of offenders, and the reasons why they're bad for the health of Windows.

Dangerous First-Degree Offenders

These commands are the worst. They don't sound any worse than the others, but they're sneakier. Avoid them at all costs.

CHKDSK /F

What it does: Normally, this command roots through the hard drive for any files that look weird and fixes them.

Why you shouldn't use it: When Windows runs, it makes a lot of files look weird. If CHKDSK /F tries to fix them, it messes them up instead. (You can use the CHKDSK command without the /F option, however.)

FDISK

What it does: This command sets up new hard drives when they're used for the first time.

Why you shouldn't use it: Your hard drive is already set up. Typing this command just messes it up.

RECOVER

What it does: Supposedly, RECOVER helps salvage information from a damaged disk.

Why you shouldn't use it: In the process of frantically grabbing information, RECOVER renames all the files to unrecognizable code words and moves everything around. *Never* use this command, even when you're *not* using Windows.

SELECT

What it does: This command installed early versions of DOS.

Why you shouldn't use it: Windows simply doesn't like or need this command. Because DOS is already installed on your computer, SELECT just louses things up.

FORMAT C:

What it does: This command wipes the hard drive clean.

Why you shouldn't use it: You lose everything on the hard drive: Windows, your data, and anything else you've stored there. You can use the FORMAT command to format your floppy disks, however, by typing **FORMAT A:** or **FORMAT B:**. Just never use the *C* with this command (or *D* or *E* or *F*, if your hard drive has those letters).

Recently Paroled Commands

The following commands aren't quite as bad as the first set. But don't use them anyway — especially just to see what happens.

APPEND, ASSIGN, JOIN, and SUBST

What they do: DOS wizards play with these commands to make their directories act like disk drives and vice versa.

Why you shouldn't use them: They're fine for DOS wizards, but they confuse everybody else, including Windows. They play too many games with your disk drives.

SHARE

What it does: When added to the AUTOEXEC.BAT file as a single line, SHARE prevents two programs from fighting over the same piece of data.

Why you shouldn't use it: SHARE is fine when it's in the AUTOEXEC.BAT file. In fact, you may ask a DOS guru to put it there for you. Share is *not* fine when you type it at the DOS prompt under Windows, however, because it doesn't work correctly. It must be loaded *before* you let Windows out of the bag.

FASTOPEN

What it does: This command supposedly lets the computer open files a little bit faster.

Why you shouldn't use it: It confuses Windows about exactly what files are open.

DOS 6 Commands to Avoid While Running Windows

Using DOS 6 or DOS 6.2? Then add these commands to the forbidden list. Don't click on these program's names while working in File Manager, and don't type their names at the DOS prompt while Windows is waiting in the background.

DBLSPACE

What it does: Known as DoubleSpace, it compresses all the files on your hard drive and gives you room to stuff even more files onto it.

Why you shouldn't use it: Don't run DBLSPACE until you've installed Windows on your hard drive. Although it won't complain at first, Windows doesn't like being installed on a compressed hard drive: Complaints about `Corrupt swap files` will surface soon enough.

DEFRAG

What it does: Organizes the files on your hard drive so they're easier and faster for your computer to locate.

Why you shouldn't use it: When Windows is running, it's holding onto big chunks of your hard drive; when DEFRAG starts grabbing those chunks, too, Windows gets annoyed.

EMM386

What it does: Cooks up and dishes out different types of memory to different types of programs.

Why you shouldn't use it: EMM386 is a complicated little beast; running it from within Windows will confuse your computer.

MEMMAKER

What it does: Organizes your 386- or 486-computer's memory so all your programs can get the right slice.

Why you shouldn't use it: Windows has already grabbed a bunch of memory, so MemMaker isn't supposed to run until you've exited Windows.

MSCDEX

What it does: Tells your computer to look for a certain disk drive.

Why you shouldn't use it: Windows counts all the disk drives when it comes to the screen; it doesn't like new ones jumping in.

NLSFUNC

What it does: Helps set up a keyboard for foreign language characters.

Why you shouldn't use it: This command might accidentally switch languages while Windows lurks in the background; when Windows comes back to the screen, it might insist you type in French.

SMARTDRV

What it does: SmartDrive lets Windows grab information from your hard drive a little bit faster.

Why you shouldn't use it: Your computer automatically loads SmartDrive before you start Windows.

VSAFE

What it does: VSAFE is the DOS version of Anti-Virus, the program that sniffs out evil, data-damaging programs.

Why you shouldn't use it: Windows runs best with the Windows version of Anti-Virus, not the DOS version.

You'll find more information about DOS 6 in *MORE Windows For Dummies*.

Chapter 23

Ten Programs That Make Windows Easier (or More Fun)

· ·

In This Chapter

▶ Installing a Windows program

▶ Using Symantec's Norton Desktop for Windows

▶ Using MicroHelp's UnInstaller

▶ Using Berkeley System's After Dark 2.0

▶ Using Delrina's WinFax Pro

▶ Using Wired for Sound Pro

· ·

*I*t took more than five years, but Windows is trendy! It seems that more companies are releasing Windows programs than DOS programs. Some are simply Windows versions of popular DOS programs. Others are designed exclusively for Windows.

The surprising thing is that you already know how to use most of them without taking them out of the box! Like with any other Windows program, you can save their contents by clicking on File and Save. And you can print a file by clicking on File and Print.

Now, if you can just figure out how to print a burp sound. . .

Installing a Windows Program

Installing a program means taking the disks out of the box, putting them in the floppy drive, and copying them to the hard drive. The final step is kicking everything in different places until it finally works. Luckily, Windows does most of the kicking for you.

Start by examining the software box closely and then tearing the shrink wrap off with your teeth. Next, paw through all the goodies in the box until you find a floppy disk marked number 1. Then follow the steps below.

1. **Insert the floppy disk into drive A.**

   Not sure about floppy disks, drives, or As? Chapter 2 covers the ins and outs.

2. **Load File Manager.**

   If File Manager's not already on-screen, double-click on its icon in Program Manager.

3. **Double-click on the drive A icon.**

   It's in the upper left corner of File Manager or its window. A double-click on the drive A icon shows the files currently living on the floppy drive. (File Manager's covered in Chapter 12, by the way.)

4. **Double-click on a file called README.TXT or README.WRI.**

   If you don't see a file named README.TXT or README.WRI in File Manager, move ahead to Step 5. But if you do spot one of those files, double-click on its name and read its contents in Notepad or Write. It may have important instructions about your particular brand of computer. Or it may be full of indecipherable gibberish. Nod earnestly and move to Step 5.

5. **Double-click on a file called SETUP.EXE or INSTALL.EXE.**

   A double-click on either of those files makes the program start installing itself. Whew. If there isn't a file called SETUP.EXE or INSTALL.EXE, you have to install the file yourself. First, create a subdirectory on your hard drive. Then copy all the floppy disk's files to that directory. (Both steps are covered in Chapter 12.) Finally, put an icon for that program in Program Manager, a chore covered in Chapter 11. (The process can be tedious — so tedious that it's described in a lot more detail in *MORE Windows For Dummies*.)

Answering question after question (the grill session)

The next step in the installation process involves the software bugging you with questions. Most pieces of software ask you to type your name and your company's name, for example. Do so and press Enter. Then the software probably asks where you'd like the program to be installed in your computer.

Advanced computer users are very picky about just where the new program should live on the hard drive. Everybody else just presses Enter and lets the program install itself wherever it wants.

Some programs ask whether it's OK to "modify the CONFIG.SYS and AUTOEXEC.BAT files." Go ahead and click on Yes. Again, computer geeks (including me) yell shrilly if a program tries to play with those two files. Everybody else shrugs his or her shoulders and says, "Go for it."

In between all this interrogation, the computer usually asks you to keep feeding it floppy disks. Keep sticking the appropriate disk in the appropriate drive until the program says it's installed. Finally, some programs say that they need to close Windows down and rev it back up. Again, let it have its way. Make sure that you save any open files before letting the program shut Windows down, however.

Trying to make it work

If everything went as planned, the software appears as a new icon in the Program Manager. In fact, the program probably created an entire program group window for itself, even if it contains just one little icon.

Now comes the big test: Double-click on the icon to see whether the program greets you with a friendly message. If its friendly message contains the words *error, could not find,* or *Oh no!,* something went wrong. It's time to invite a computer guru over for an Oreo lunch or root through the software box until you find the technical support phone number.

- ✔ The more complicated your computer setup, the better the chances are that something will go wrong. Incoming software can walk into walls if the hard drive has a drive C *and* a drive D, for example. Or, if you run a disk-compression program like Stacker or any sort of memory manager, the software can get lost and end up on the wrong plane.

- ✔ Many programs create an entire program group window for a single icon. If the Program Manager's getting too crowded, drag that icon to a different program group — perhaps one named Applications. Then delete the empty program group, a hatchet job that's explained in Chapter 11.

- ✔ If you find a piece of paper in the software box that says *Read Me First,* at least glance at the first few paragraphs. You may find a clue as to why the software is tracking cellular phone conversations rather than balancing your checkbook.

Using Symantec's Norton Desktop for Windows

In a way, Windows has a split personality. When you want to play with a program, you head for the Program Manager and start clicking on the little pictures. But, if you want to play with any of that program's files, you must head for a second program, the File Manager.

To turn Windows' two heads into one, several companies sell yet another program. Norton Desktop for Windows (see Figure 23-1), for example, strives to replace both the Program Manager and the File Manager.

Norton Desktop for Windows works sort of like the Program Manager. You can keep little icons along the bottom of the screen, and you can keep program groups right along the side of the screen.

But it grabs disk-drive icons from the File Manager and sticks them along the other side of the screen. Double-click on the disk-drive icon, and you can see the files on the hard drive or a floppy drive.

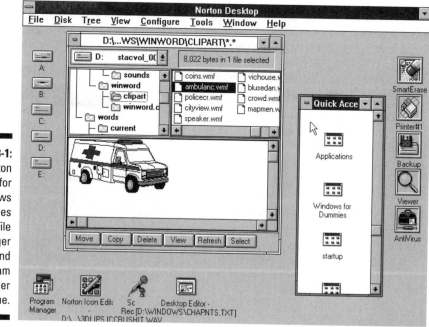

Figure 23-1: Norton Desktop for Windows combines the File Manager and Program Manager into one.

With Norton Desktop for Windows, you can literally *see* the files. Norton Desktop for Windows comes with *file viewers.* Click on a file, and Norton Desktop for Windows shows you what's inside it. Forgotten what UVULA.BMP looks like? You don't have to call it into Paintbrush. Just click on its name and click on the View button. The contents of UVULA.BMP appear in a window.

Norton Desktop for Windows comes with a wide variety of computer-nerd utilities as well. It can dredge the entire hard drive for all files containing the word *lunch,* for example, so finding lost files is easier. It can repair damaged disks, back up the hard drive, look for viruses, and keep you busy for hours trying to figure out what everything else does. In fact, its manual is thicker than the 600 pager that comes with Windows!

✔ Norton Desktop for Windows contains a wide variety of tools for a wide variety of tasks. It's designed for people who like to fiddle with their computers. In fact, even if you don't use it much, the computer nerd who tries to fix your computer will probably rev it up.

✔ Make sure that you have at least 9MB of free space on the hard drive if you want to install all the Norton Desktop for Windows programs. Alternatively, you can save space by picking and choosing the parts of the program you want to install.

✔ Although it's called the Norton Desktop for Windows, it's sold by a company named Symantec.

Using MicroHelp's UnInstaller

After a program is installed in Windows, it's stuck — just like gum dropped onto the carpet. Deleting the program's icon from Program Manager just removes its On button — the program's files stay spread throughout your hard drive.

In addition, Windows often takes notes about a program's special requirements — and the program doesn't erase those notes when it's deleted. Simply put, getting rid of a Windows program can turn into a major event.

So MicroHelp came up with UnInstaller for Windows, shown in Figure 23-2.

MicroHelp UnInstaller for Windows can pry unwanted Windows programs off your hard drive, no matter how strongly they are attached. UnInstaller can also wipe unnecessary or duplicate files from your hard drive, freeing space for more important things.

If your hard drive's getting cluttered and you're thinking about getting rid of some unused Windows programs, think about putting UnInstaller to work.

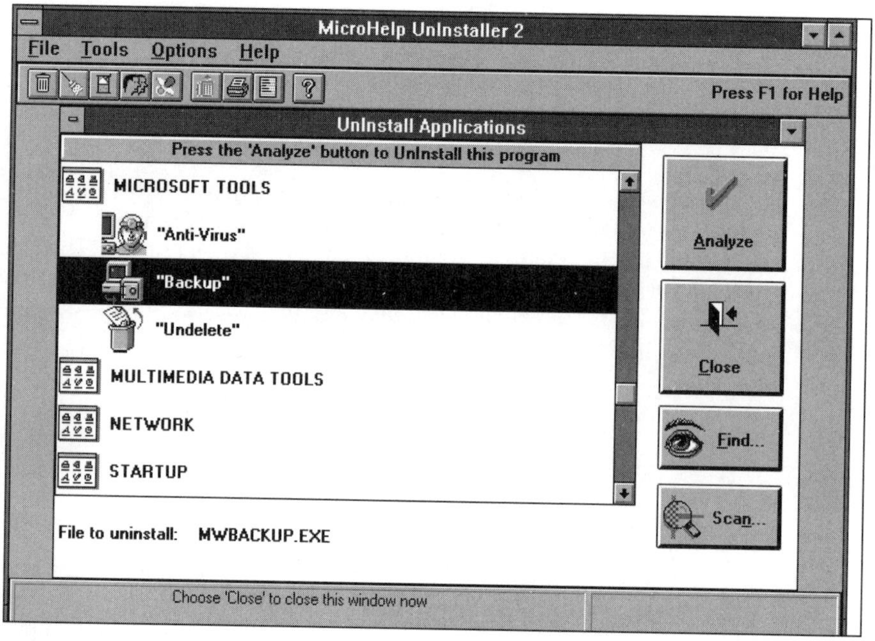

Figure 23-2:
MicroHelp
UnInstaller
for
Windows
can remove
unwanted
Windows
programs
and wipe
unnecessary
files from
your hard
drive.

```
┌──────────────────────────────────────────────────────┐
│                MicroHelp UnInstaller 2           ▼ ▲  │
│ File  Tools  Options  Help                            │
│ ┌──┬──┬──┬──┬──┬──┬──┬──┬──┐                           │
│ │🗑│  │  │  │  │  │🖨│  │? │        Press F1 for Help  │
│ └──┴──┴──┴──┴──┴──┴──┴──┴──┘                           │
│ ┌─────────── UnInstall Applications ──────────────▼─┐ │
│ │   Press the 'Analyze' button to UnInstall this    │ │
│ │                    program                        │ │
│ │  ▦ MICROSOFT TOOLS                    ↑  ┌───────┐ │ │
│ │      🖥 "Anti-Virus"                     │   ✓   │ │ │
│ │      🖥 "Backup"                         │Analyze│ │ │
│ │      🗑 "Undelete"                       └───────┘ │ │
│ │  ▦ MULTIMEDIA DATA TOOLS                 ┌───────┐ │ │
│ │  ▦ NETWORK                               │  🚪←  │ │ │
│ │  ▦ STARTUP                            ↓  │ Close │ │ │
│ │                                          └───────┘ │ │
│ │  File to uninstall:  MWBACKUP.EXE        ┌───────┐ │ │
│ │                                          │  👁   │ │ │
│ │                                          │ Find..│ │ │
│ │                                          └───────┘ │ │
│ │                                          ┌───────┐ │ │
│ │  Choose 'Close' to close this window now │  🔍   │ │ │
│ │                                          │ Scan..│ │ │
│ └──────────────────────────────────────────└───────┘─┘ │
└──────────────────────────────────────────────────────┘
```

Using Berkeley Systems' After Dark 3.0

Thousands of years ago, computers constantly displayed text in neat little rows on the screen. Eventually, those neat little rows *burned* themselves onto the monitor: You could see a faint outline of the rows, even when the monitor was turned off.

So somebody invented a *screen saver,* a program that blanks the screen if nobody touches the keyboard for a while. A touch of the spacebar brings the screen back to life. The blanking effect helps prevent a constantly displayed insurance form from burning itself onto the screen.

With today's color monitors and the wide variety of images they're displaying, *burn-in* is pretty much stuck in computer history books. Yet screen savers have not only survived, but they've evolved into an art form, as shown in Figure 23-3.

Like convertible Cadillacs from the '60s, screen savers aren't really necessary, but they can be a lot of fun. The premier screen saver, Berkeley Systems' After Dark, comes with more than 30 different *modules,* replacing a simple blanked-out screen with flying toasters, tropical fish, bouncing marbles, and dozens of other frivolities.

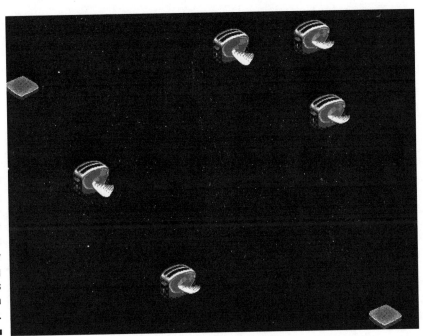

Figure 23-3:
The After
Dark for
Windows
legendary
Flying
Toasters
screen
saver.

✔ Windows comes with several built-in screen savers, so After Dark is more of a fun purchase than a tax-deductible business expense.

✔ If you want to write it off anyway, however, say it's for security: You don't want anybody looking at your work while you're out to lunch.

✔ Oh, and it takes up about 5MB of hard disk space.

Using Delrina's WinFax Pro

Fax machines are a necessary nuisance in life, but Delrina's WinFax Pro makes faxes a lot easier to deal with: There's no wait at the fax machine, and there's no slimy fax paper to make you want to constantly wipe off your hands.

WinFax Pro pretends it's a printer. When you're ready to send a fax, head for the File menu and click on Print Setup. You'll find WinFax listed as an available printer.

Click on the name WinFax and then print just as you would with any other printer. A box pops up; enter the fax machine's phone number. If you've sent a fax to this machine before, pluck the number from the pop-up list.

That's it! What you see on the screen will soon appear on a fax machine somewhere else in the world. If somebody sends *you* a fax, a box appears on the screen, telling you that a file's on the way. Keep on working until the fax is inside the computer and then let WinFax show it to you on the screen. You can print it, if it's something good. Otherwise, delete it as you would any other file.

WinFax is easy to install, easy to use, and easy to send faxes to the deli with your lunch orders.

✔ Before you can use WinFax, you need a *fax card,* a gizmo that slips inside the computer. Some modems can send faxes, too. For example, Cardinal's 9600 FaxModem can send faxes with WinFax, as well as call up other computers through Terminal, Windows' built-in modem program.

✔ Faxes sent with WinFax look better than if you print them and send them on a plain old fax machine. Because you send the fax directly from the computer, you don't send any dirt or squished gnats from the fax machine's rollers.

Using Wired for Sound Pro

Sound card owners have doubtlessly fiddled with the Windows Control Panel, assigning different sounds to different events. For example, you can set up Windows to scream when it's first loaded or howl when it leaves the screen.

The Control Panel stops the fun after you assign sounds to seven events; Wired for Sound Pro picks up the slack. It comes with more than 200 sounds to assign to different actions. There's no barf sound, but you can find plenty of other, even more disgusting noises.

✔ Wired for Sound Pro works with any sound card that works with Windows: Sound Blaster, Pro AudioSpectrum, or any other card that has Windows drivers.

✔ It also has a sound editor, letting you piece together your own sound effects on those slow days. A talking alarm clock reminds you of appointments, and a system monitor tells you personally when Windows is running out of memory.

✔ Disk space? Count on devoting about 5MB of hard disk space for all that fun. Or buy the CD-ROM version and save space by copying only the sounds that you want to hear.

Microsoft Bob

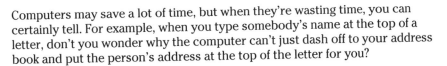

Microsoft Bob

Computers may save a lot of time, but when they're wasting time, you can certainly tell. For example, when you type somebody's name at the top of a letter, don't you wonder why the computer can't just dash off to your address book and put the person's address at the top of the letter for you?

Microsoft is trying to make computers a little more polite with a concept called "Bob." Bob is a computer program that puts a front door on your computer screen. What do you do next? Because there's no manual, let the little cartoon character in the corner be your guide, as seen in Figure 23-4.

Figure 23-4:
Bob comes
with several
different
guides,
each with
its own
personality.

Bob lets you head to the living room and write letters, pay bills, and keep track of car or house maintenance, and helps you perform all the other wonderful tasks that computers were supposed to make so much easier for us. Want to pay the bills? Then click on the checkbook sitting on the table. Write a letter? Click on the pencil and paper. With Bob, you don't have to remember a program's name, because there aren't any names.

All the programs try their best to look out for each other: You add a friend's birthday and address to the Address Book, and it automatically marks the birthday on the Calendar that hangs over the mantel. Before the big day, the Calendar reminds you of the birthday, giving you time to reach for the Letter Writer. The Letter Writer's smart enough to retrieve the friend's address from the Address Book and include it in the letter. Whew.

By putting computing tasks in a real-life setting, Bob tries to make foreign concepts like computing seem more familiar. Want to change your computer's time and date? Don't bother searching for a program. Just click on the clock hanging from the living room wall. The clock opens up so you can change the time, just like in real life.

- Bob is a whole new way to use computers, that's for sure. Some people will enjoy the cartoons and friendly guides. With its simple and friendly Bob concept, Microsoft envisions people keeping computerized household records that are so detailed that the baby-sitter will be able to replace the correct fuse in the fuse box.

- Other people will say that computers simply *aren't* fun, no matter how heavy the shenanigans — they'll prefer the quick and dirty programs that let them spend as little time around their computers as possible.

- Bob tries hard to please. Its electronic mail box swaps talk with the Internet, CompuServe, Prodigy, and America Online. It pays bills electronically. It lets you inventory your house or track your car maintenance, and it explains how to remove butter stains from the carpet.

- Tired of computing? Then head for Bob's living room and spend time rearranging the furniture, choosing between architectural styles and moving the plants around the rooms. No hurry to pay the bills, anyway.

- Bob's certainly no saint. He requires a fast, 33Mhz 486 computer, about 40MB of hard disk space, and at least 8MB of RAM. And he's a little slow at times — you have to wait for the little cartoon characters to waddle around from room to room.

- Don't expect the programs to be powerhouses, either. They don't save files in formats easily recognizable by other programs. And don't bother using the Letter Writer for big reports, because there's no search feature.

- Remember, Bob's just a child. After he grows past his awkward years, he might be just what millions of computer users have been asking for: a simple way to do simple things.

Chapter 24

Ten Expensive Things You Can Do to Make Windows Better

. . . .

In This Chapter

▶ Buy more memory

▶ Shell out the bucks for a bigger hard drive

▶ Order a 386, 486, or Pentium computer

▶ Put a graphics accelerator card on the credit card

▶ Purchase a shell program

▶ Beg for or borrow a bigger monitor

. . . .

Give a Ford Fairlane to the right teenage boy, and he'll get right to work: boring out the cylinders, putting in a high-lift cam, and adding a double-roller timing chain. And replacing the exhaust system with headers, if his cash holds out.

Computer nerds feel the same way about getting under the hood of their computers. They add a few new parts, flip a few switches, and tweak a few things here and there to make Windows scream.

Even if you're not a computer nerd, you can still soup up Windows a bit. Take the computer back to the store and have the *store's* computer nerd get under the hood.

This chapter talks about what parts to ask for, so you don't end up with high-lift cams rather than more memory.

Buy More Memory

If you bought a 386, 486, or Pentium computer, the salesperson probably tried to talk you into buying more memory, or RAM, for the computer. Windows probably talks just as loudly about this issue as the salesperson.

See, Windows can read and write information to RAM very quickly. The phrase *lightning quick* comes to mind. But, when Windows runs out of RAM, it starts using the hard drive for storage. Compared with RAM, hard drives are slow, mechanical dinosaurs. If you're short on memory, you hear the hard drive grinding away as you switch between programs and Windows frantically tries to make room for everything.

Windows runs very slowly on a computer with only 2MB of RAM. Twice that amount of RAM speeds things up more than twice as much. With 8MB of RAM, Windows can juggle programs even more quickly (and without dropping them as often).

If you're tired of waiting for Windows, toss the computer in the back seat, take it back to the computer store, and have the store people put some more RAM inside.

- ✔ After Jeff in the back room puts the memory chips inside the computer, he'll flip some switches on the computer's *motherboard* so that it knows that the new chips are there. People who plug the chips in themselves often don't flip the right switch and then wonder why their new chips don't work. (Some newer computers don't have a switch; they know automatically when they have more memory to play with.)

- ✔ Different computers can hold different amounts of RAM. Some can't handle more than 8MB of RAM; others can be stuffed with 32MB or more. Before buying more memory, check with your dealer to make sure that your computer has room for it.

Shell Out the Bucks for a Bigger Hard Drive

Right on the box, Microsoft recommends that the computer have at least 10MB of free hard drive space in order to run Windows. That's if you want to run *Windows* and no other programs.

If you buy Microsoft Word for Windows, however, that program wants more than 20MB of hard drive space for all its bells and whistles. Add a few other hoggy Windows programs, and you run out of room quickly.

Norton Desktop for Windows wants about 10MB of hard disk space. Plus, you should leave part of the hard drive empty so that Windows has room to move around.

The moral is to look for the biggest hard drive you can afford. Then borrow some money and buy one that's slightly bigger.

Order a 386, 486, or Pentium Computer

Windows works on a 286 computer, but just barely. It's really designed for a 386, 486, or Pentium computer and the special features of those particular microprocessors.

As a bare minimum, a 386SX computer can handle Windows' special 386 Enhanced mode, letting you run more programs at the same time as well as run DOS programs in their own windows. But the 386SX crawls along pretty slowly.

A 386DX computer can run in the same Enhanced mode, but a little faster. A 486SX is even faster, followed by the 486DX. The Pentium is the current speed demon. Balance your need for speed with your checking account balance.

You can find this 386/486/Pentium stuff thrashed out in Chapter 2.

Put a Graphics Accelerator Card on the Credit Card

When tossing boxes and bars around, Windows puts a big strain on the computer's *graphics card,* the gizmo that tells the monitor what information to put on the screen.

Windows also puts a strain on the computer's *microprocessor,* the gizmo that tells the graphics card what to tell the monitor.

A graphics accelerator card eases the burden on both parties. Simply put, a graphics accelerator is a hot-rodded graphics card. It replaces the VGA or Super VGA card and contains a special chip that handles the dirty work of filling the monitor with pretty pictures.

The result? Dialog boxes that zip onto the screen almost instantly. You no longer have to wait for Windows to repaint the screen when you move windows around. Everything just looks a little snappier.

- ✔ You probably don't need to upgrade the monitor when buying an accelerator card. A Super VGA accelerator card works just as well with a Super VGA monitor as the regular Super VGA card does.

- ✔ Upgrading the computer from a 386 to a 486 or Pentium also speeds up the graphics, even if you don't buy an accelerator card.

- ✔ A computer with special *VESA local bus video* can speed graphics up the fastest. Unlike accelerated video cards, however, you can't drop *local bus video* cards into just *any* computer. Only computers built with a special *local bus video slot* can use those cards.

- ✔ And if you're using a Pentium computer with a PCI slot, look for a PCI video card. That's currently the fastest breed of video card for a Pentium.

Purchase a Shell Program

Windows may be silk compared to a DOS canvas, but it still has some rough edges. To smooth things over, some people use a *shell program.* For example, Norton Desktop for Windows, described in Chapter 23, can completely replace Program Manager and File Manager. Other shells, like TabWorks, replace Program Manager's group windows with tabs, like those found in a notebook.

Some people swear by these shell programs. Others say that they're just one more program to learn.

Beg for or Borrow a Bigger Monitor

Part of the problem with the Windows stack-of-windows approach to computing is the size of the screen. The Windows desktop is the size of the monitor: about one square foot. That's why everything constantly covers up everything else.

To get a bigger desktop, buy a bigger monitor. The new 17-inch monitors offer almost twice the elbow room as the standard 12 inchers. You have more room to put windows side by side on the screen, as well as more room to spread icons along the bottom. The new 20 inchers give you an executive-sized desktop but at a mahogany price.

✔ Before buying, make sure that the new monitor and video card can work together as a team. Not all cards work with all monitors.

✔ If you have a stack of phone books holding up one side of your desk, buy a new desk when you buy the new monitor. Those big monitors can weigh 50 pounds or more.

Chapter 25
Ten Atrocious Acronyms

In This Chapter

▶ Ten (plus eight) acronyms in alphabetic order

▶ Helpful pronunciation tips so you won't just mumble them quietly

▶ What they mean to computer nerds

Computer geeks have a certain fascination for long, complicated strings of words. They've reduced these syllables into short grunts called *acronyms*.

This chapter lists, in alphabetic order, what the nerds are saying, what their grunts stand for, and what those grunts are supposed to mean.

ASCII

What it stands for: American Standard Code for Information Interchange

Pronunciation: ASK-ee

What they're talking about: A standard for saving information — usually words and numbers — so that most other programs can read it.

BIOS

What it stands for: Basic Input/Output System

Pronunciation: BUY-ohss

What they're talking about: Information stored inside a computer that tells programs how the computer is designed. For example, if a program wants information to go to the printer, the program politely tells the BIOS, which subsequently sends the information to the printer. Windows sometimes by-passes the BIOS and sends information directly to the computer's parts. This procedure is faster but can sometimes confuse the rest of the computer.

DDE

What it stands for: Dynamic Data Exchange

Pronunciation: Dee-dee-ee

What they're talking about: A way Windows programs can share information automatically in the background. Today, OLE is much more fashionable.

DLL

What it stands for: Dynamic Link Library

Pronunciation: Dee-ell-ell

What they're talking about: A file containing information for a program. You can find bunches of files ending with DLL on the hard drive. Don't think that they're trash and delete them, or you'll have some wide-eyed programs wandering around the system, searching for their DLLs.

DRV

What it stands for: Driver

Pronunciation: DRY-ver

What they're talking about: Drivers contain brand-specific information about a computer's parts: printers, mice, monitors, and other goodies. You see files ending in DRV scattered throughout the hard drive. Don't delete them, or Windows won't be capable of talking to your computer's parts.

EMS

What it stands for: Expanded Memory Specification

Pronunciation: Ee-em-ess

What they're talking about: A special part of the computer's memory used by some DOS programs. When filling out a DOS program's PIF, you may need to check this option.

IBM

What it stands for: International Business Machines

Pronunciation: Aye-bee-em

What they're talking about: A huge computer company that designed the first widely accepted PC and then tried to catch up as all the other companies started copying and bettering its design. Windows requires an IBM-compatible computer.

INI

What it stands for: Initialization

Pronunciation: IN-ee (as opposed to an OUT-ee)

What they're talking about: A file containing customized instructions for a program. Many Windows programs look for their own INI file to make sure that they're working according to the user's whims. For example, WIN.INI contains information about the way you like Windows: its colors, the settings you've made in the Control Panel, and other information.

Don't mess with the INI files unless you have a specific reason to do so. Changing them around can seriously affect how programs run in Windows.

IRQ

What it stands for: Interrupt Request Line

Pronunciation: Aye-are-cue

What they're talking about: The way parts of a computer can get the attention of the computer's main processor. For example, every time you move the mouse, the mouse sends a signal down its IRQ to the computer's processor, which stops what it's doing and displays the mouse's new position on the screen. Each device needs its own IRQ; if two computer toys try to share one IRQ, both work in a wacky way.

OLE

What it stands for: Object Linking and Embedding

Pronunciation: Oh-ell-ee

What they're talking about: A way to merge different kinds of data into one file. For example, you can stick an icon into a letter file; when people click on that icon, they hear your voice telling them that they're fired. You also can double-click on a numerical chart within a letter file; a chart editor pops up, letting you change the figures around.

PCX

What it stands for: Nothing

Pronunciation: Pee-see-ex

What they're talking about: Some guy thought of a way to store graphics in computer files. He picked the letters PCX out of the blue. Today, PCX is one of the most widespread graphics standards. Paintbrush can read and write graphics as PCX files; so can most other graphics programs.

PIF

What it stands for: Program Information File

Pronunciation: Piff (rhymes with *sniff*)

What they're talking about: A file containing instructions Windows needs to nurse along troublesome DOS programs. The PIF contains information about how that program expects to find memory and other things important for making DOS and Windows live together pleasantly.

RAM

What it stands for: Random-Access Memory

Pronunciation: Ram (rhymes with *cram*)

What they're talking about: The memory Windows reads and writes to when making stuff happen on the screen. When the power's turned off, RAM erases itself.

ROM

What it stands for: Read-Only Memory

Pronunciation: Rahm (rhymes with *bomb*)

What they're talking about: Memory that can't be written to — only read from. For example, a computer's BIOS is stored in ROM. Computerized microwave ovens and other fun consumer electronic goodies sometimes store their instructions on ROM chips as well.

TMP

What it stands for: Temporary

Pronunciation: Temp

What they're talking about: In most cases, these are the files Windows creates to hold miscellaneous information. Windows normally deletes these files when you close the Program Manager. If Windows exits the screen less gently, however (through a crash or power outage, for example), Windows leaves these files lying around on the hard drive. If you come across a file that starts with a tilde (~) and ends in the letters TMP, you can safely delete it from the hard drive as long as Windows isn't currently running.

TSR

What it stands for: Terminate and Stay Resident

Pronunciation: Tee-ess-are

What they're talking about: This software loads and then hangs out in the computer's memory. Some TSRs are drivers (see "DRV"); others are actual programs. DOS looks at two files, AUTOEXEC.BAT and CONFIG.SYS, to see which TSRs it should load. Sometimes TSRs fight each other for memory space, causing crashes. In fact, if you mention your computer troubles to nerds, they almost always rub their chins and say, "Hmmm, have you tried a clean boot without any TSRs?" Answer them with, "Well, no. Why don't you come over and we'll give it a try?"

UAE

What it stands for: Unrecoverable Application Error

Pronunciation: You-ay-ee (rhymes with *you, baby*)

What they're talking about: Earlier versions of Windows sometimes crashed for no apparent reason. Before it zonked itself into unconsciousness, it would say that it had experienced a UAE. The latest version of Windows doesn't have UAEs anymore. Instead, the errors are labeled with a bunch of other terms, as described in Chapter 18.

XMS

What it stands for: Extended Memory Specification

Pronunciation: Ex-em-ess

What they're talking about: The special type of memory that comes with 286, 386, 486, and Pentium computers. Normally, DOS programs can't touch it. Windows comes with a memory manager, however, which can harness that memory and even dole it out to DOS programs when they run in Windows.

Glossary

Windows comes with its own Glossary program. Described in Chapter 19, it's just a mouse-click away. Press F1 while in any program that comes with Windows — Write, for example — and click on the Glossary button shown in Figure G-1.

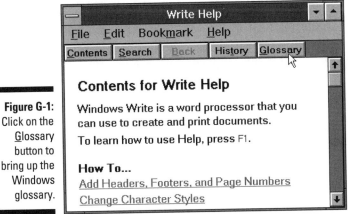

Figure G-1: Click on the Glossary button to bring up the Windows glossary.

But for those times when your computer's not even turned on, here's a list of some of the more common Windows words you'll encounter.

32-bit: Computers push their information through "pipes." The first IBM PC used eight pipes. The next version, the 286, used 16 pipes. A 386 computer can use 32 pipes, but most programs just shoot their stuff through 16 pipes. For extra speed and power in computer networks, Windows for Workgroups can use all 32 pipes at the same time when moving information to or from a hard disk.

8514/A: One of the more expensive (and esoteric) video cards released by IBM and now copied by other companies.

active window: The last window you clicked on — the one that's currently highlighted — is considered active. Any keys you press affect this window.

AUTOEXEC.BAT: A file that an MS-DOS computer reads when you first turn it on. The file contains instructions that affect any subsequently running DOS programs — and Windows, as well.

bitmap: A graphic consisting of bunches of little dots on-screen. They're saved as bitmap files, which end with the letters BMP.

border: The edges of a window; you can move the border in or out to change the window's size.

case-sensitive: A program that knows the difference between upper- and lowercase letters. For instance, a case-sensitive program considers *Pickle* and *pickle* to be two different things.

click: To push and release a button on the mouse. Windows prefers its clicks to come from the mouse's *left* button. (If you're left-handed and want to switch the mouse buttons, head for the mouse section of Chapter 10.)

Clipboard: A program that keeps track of information you've cut or copied from a program. It stores that information so you can paste it into other programs.

command prompt: The little symbol that looks like C:\ or [C:\] or A:\ or something similar. It's the place where you can type instructions — *commands* — for DOS to carry out.

CONFIG.SYS: A file that your computer reads every time it boots up. The file contains information about how the computer is set up and what it's attached to. Both DOS and Windows programs rely on information contained in the CONFIG.SYS file.

cursor: The little blinking line that shows where the next letter will appear when you start typing.

default: Choosing the default option enables you to avoid making a decision. The *default option* is the one the computer chooses for you when you give up and just press Enter.

desktop: The area on your screen where you move windows and icons around. Most people cover the desktop with *wallpaper* — a pretty picture.

directory: A separate *folder* on a hard disk for storing files. Storing related files in a directory makes them easier to find.

double-click: Pushing and releasing the left mouse button twice in rapid succession.

drag: A four-step mouse process that moves an object across your desktop. First, point at the object — an icon, a highlighted paragraph, or something similar. Second, press and hold your left mouse button. Third, point at the location to which you'd like to move that object. Fourth, release the mouse button. The object is "dragged" to its new location.

drop: Step four of the *drag* technique, described above. *Dropping* is merely letting go of the mouse button and letting your object fall onto something else, be it a new window, directory, or area on your desktop.

DRV: A file ending in DRV usually lets Windows talk to computer gizmos such as video cards, sound cards, CD-ROM drives, and other stuff. (DRV is short for *driver.)*

file: A collection of information in a format designed for computer use.

format: The process of preparing a disk to have files written on it. The disk needs to have "electronic shelves" tacked onto it so that DOS can store information on it. Formatting a disk wipes it clean of all information.

highlighted: A selected item. Different colors usually appear over a highlighted object to show that it's been singled out for further action.

icon: The little picture that represents an object — a program, file, or command — making it easier to figure out that object's function.

INI: Short for *initialization,* INI usually hangs on the end of files that contain special system settings. They're for the computer to mess with, not users.

maximize: The act of making a window fill the entire screen. You can maximize a window by double-clicking on its title bar — that long strip across its very top. Or you can click on its maximize button — that button with the upward-pointing arrow, located in the window's upper-right corner.

memory: The stuff computers use to store on-the-fly calculations while running.

minimize: The act of shrinking a window down to a tiny icon to temporarily get it out of the way. To minimize a window, click on the minimize button — that button with a downward-pointing arrow, located near the window's upper-right corner.

multitasking: Running several different programs simultaneously.

network: Connecting computers with cables so that people can share information without getting up.

operating system: Software that controls how a computer does its most basic stuff: stores files, talks to printers, and performs other gut-level operations.

path: A sentence of computerese that tells a computer the precise name and location of a file.

program: Something that lets you work on the computer: Spreadsheets, word processors, and games are *programs*.

RAM: Random-Access Memory. See *memory*.

subdirectory: A directory within a directory, used to further organize files. For example, a JUNKFOOD directory might contain subdirectories for CHIPS, PEANUTS, and PRETZELS. (A CELERY subdirectory would be empty.)

Task List: A pop-up box that lists all your currently running programs. To see it, press Ctrl+Esc or double-click on a blank area of your desktop.

virtual: A trendy word to describe computer simulations. It's commonly used to describe things that *look* real but aren't really there. For example, when Windows uses *virtual memory,* it's using part of the hard disk for memory, not the actual memory chips.

VGA: A popular standard for displaying information on monitors in certain colors and resolutions. It's now being replaced by SVGA — Super VGA — which can display even more colors and even finer resolution.

wallpaper: Graphics spread across the background of your computer screen. The Windows Control Panel lets you choose among different wallpaper files.

window: An on-screen box that contains information for you to look at or work with. Programs run in *windows* on your screen.

Index

(continued)

Title	Author	ISBN	Price
INTERNET / COMMUNICATIONS / NETWORKING			12/20/94
CompuServe For Dummies™	by Wallace Wang	1-56884-181-7	$19.95 USA/$26.95 Canada
Modems For Dummies™, 2nd Edition	by Tina Rathbone	1-56884-223-6	$19.99 USA/$26.99 Canada
Modems For Dummies™	by Tina Rathbone	1-56884-001-2	$19.95 USA/$26.95 Canada
MORE Internet For Dummies™	by John R. Levine & Margaret Levine Young	1-56884-164-7	$19.95 USA/$26.95 Canada
NetWare For Dummies™	by Ed Tittel & Deni Connor	1-56884-003-9	$19.95 USA/$26.95 Canada
Networking For Dummies™	by Doug Lowe	1-56884-079-9	$19.95 USA/$26.95 Canada
ProComm Plus 2 For Windows For Dummies™	by Wallace Wang	1-56884-219-8	$19.99 USA/$26.99 Canada
The Internet For Dummies™, 2nd Edition	by John R. Levine & Carol Baroudi	1-56884-222-8	$19.99 USA/$26.99 Canada
The Internet For Macs For Dummies™	by Charles Seiter	1-56884-184-1	$19.95 USA/$26.95 Canada
MACINTOSH			
Macs For Dummies®	by David Pogue	1-56884-173-6	$19.95 USA/$26.95 Canada
Macintosh System 7.5 For Dummies™	by Bob LeVitus	1-56884-197-3	$19.95 USA/$26.95 Canada
MORE Macs For Dummies™	by David Pogue	1-56884-087-X	$19.95 USA/$26.95 Canada
PageMaker 5 For Macs For Dummies™	by Galen Gruman	1-56884-178-7	$19.95 USA/$26.95 Canada
QuarkXPress 3.3 For Dummies™	by Galen Gruman & Barbara Assadi	1-56884-217-1	$19.99 USA/$26.99 Canada
Upgrading and Fixing Macs For Dummies™	by Kearney Rietmann & Frank Higgins	1-56884-189-2	$19.95 USA/$26.95 Canada
MULTIMEDIA			
Multimedia & CD-ROMs For Dummies™, Interactive Multimedia Value Pack	by Andy Rathbone	1-56884-225-2	$29.95 USA/$39.95 Canada
Multimedia & CD-ROMs For Dummies™	by Andy Rathbone	1-56884-089-6	$19.95 USA/$26.95 Canada
OPERATING SYSTEMS / DOS			
MORE DOS For Dummies™	by Dan Gookin	1-56884-046-2	$19.95 USA/$26.95 Canada
S.O.S. For DOS™	by Katherine Murray	1-56884-043-8	$12.95 USA/$16.95 Canada
OS/2 For Dummies™	by Andy Rathbone	1-878058-76-2	$19.95 USA/$26.95 Canada
UNIX			
UNIX For Dummies™	by John R. Levine & Margaret Levine Young	1-878058-58-4	$19.95 USA/$26.95 Canada
WINDOWS			
S.O.S. For Windows™	by Katherine Murray	1-56884-045-4	$12.95 USA/$16.95 Canada
MORE Windows 3.1 For Dummies™, 3rd Edition	by Andy Rathbone	1-56884-240-6	$19.99 USA/$26.99 Canada
PCs / HARDWARE			
Illustrated Computer Dictionary For Dummies™	by Dan Gookin, Wally Wang, & Chris Van Buren	1-56884-004-7	$12.95 USA/$16.95 Canada
Upgrading and Fixing PCs For Dummies™	by Andy Rathbone	1-56884-002-0	$19.95 USA/$26.95 Canada
PRESENTATION / AUTOCAD			
AutoCAD For Dummies™	by Bud Smith	1-56884-191-4	$19.95 USA/$26.95 Canada
PowerPoint 4 For Windows For Dummies™	by Doug Lowe	1-56884-161-2	$16.95 USA/$22.95 Canada
PROGRAMMING			
Borland C++ For Dummies™	by Michael Hyman	1-56884-162-0	$19.95 USA/$26.95 Canada
"Borland's New Language Product" For Dummies™	by Neil Rubenking	1-56884-200-7	$19.95 USA/$26.95 Canada
C For Dummies™	by Dan Gookin	1-878058-78-9	$19.95 USA/$26.95 Canada
C++ For Dummies™	by Stephen R. Davis	1-56884-163-9	$19.95 USA/$26.95 Canada
Mac Programming For Dummies™	by Dan Parks Sydow	1-56884-173-6	$19.95 USA/$26.95 Canada
QBasic Programming For Dummies™	by Douglas Hergert	1-56884-093-4	$19.95 USA/$26.95 Canada
Visual Basic "X" For Dummies™, 2nd Edition	by Wallace Wang	1-56884-230-9	$19.99 USA/$26.99 Canada
Visual Basic 3 For Dummies™	by Wallace Wang	1-56884-076-4	$19.95 USA/$26.95 Canada
SPREADSHEET			
1-2-3 For Dummies™	by Greg Harvey	1-878058-60-6	$16.95 USA/$21.95 Canada
1-2-3 For Windows 5 For Dummies™, 2nd Edition	by John Walkenbach	1-56884-216-3	$16.95 USA/$21.95 Canada
1-2-3 For Windows For Dummies™	by John Walkenbach	1-56884-052-7	$16.95 USA/$21.95 Canada
Excel 5 For Macs For Dummies™	by Greg Harvey	1-56884-186-8	$19.95 USA/$26.95 Canada
Excel For Dummies™, 2nd Edition	by Greg Harvey	1-56884-050-0	$16.95 USA/$21.95 Canada
MORE Excel 5 For Windows For Dummies™	by Greg Harvey	1-56884-207-4	$19.95 USA/$26.95 Canada
Quattro Pro 6 For Windows For Dummies™	by John Walkenbach	1-56884-174-4	$19.95 USA/$26.95 Canada
Quattro Pro For DOS For Dummies™	by John Walkenbach	1-56884-023-3	$16.95 USA/$21.95 Canada
UTILITIES / VCRs & CAMCORDERS			
Norton Utilities 8 For Dummies™	by Beth Slick	1-56884-166-3	$19.95 USA/$26.95 Canada
VCRs & Camcorders For Dummies™	by Andy Rathbone & Gordon McComb	1-56884-229-5	$14.99 USA/$20.99 Canada
WORD PROCESSING			
Ami Pro For Dummies™	by Jim Meade	1-56884-049-7	$19.95 USA/$26.95 Canada
MORE Word For Windows 6 For Dummies™	by Doug Lowe	1-56884-165-5	$19.95 USA/$26.95 Canada
MORE WordPerfect 6 For Windows For Dummies™	by Margaret Levine Young & David C. Kay	1-56884-206-6	$19.95 USA/$26.95 Canada
MORE WordPerfect 6 For DOS For Dummies™	by Wallace Wang, edited by Dan Gookin	1-56884-047-0	$19.95 USA/$26.95 Canada
S.O.S. For WordPerfect™	by Katherine Murray	1-56884-053-5	$12.95 USA/$16.95 Canada
Word 6 For Macs For Dummies™	by Dan Gookin	1-56884-190-6	$19.95 USA/$26.95 Canada
Word For Windows 6 For Dummies™	by Dan Gookin	1-56884-075-6	$16.95 USA/$21.95 Canada
Word For Windows For Dummies™	by Dan Gookin	1-878058-86-X	$16.95 USA/$21.95 Canada
WordPerfect 6 For Dummies™	by Dan Gookin	1-878058-77-0	$16.95 USA/$21.95 Canada
WordPerfect For Dummies™	by Dan Gookin	1-878058-52-5	$16.95 USA/$21.95 Canada
WordPerfect For Windows For Dummies™	by Margaret Levine Young & David C. Kay	1-56884-032-2	$16.95 USA/$21.95 Canada

Fun, Fast, & Cheap!

CorelDRAW! 5 For Dummies™ Quick Reference
by Raymond E. Werner

ISBN: 1-56884-952-4
$9.99 USA/$12.99 Canada

Windows "X" For Dummies™ Quick Reference, 3rd Edition
by Greg Harvey

ISBN: 1-56884-964-8
$9.99 USA/$12.99 Canada

Word For Windows 6 For Dummies™ Quick Reference
by George Lynch

ISBN: 1-56884-095-0
$8.95 USA/$12.95 Canada

WordPerfect For DOS For Dummies™ Quick Reference
by Greg Harvey

ISBN: 1-56884-009-8
$8.95 USA/$11.95 Canada

Title	Author	ISBN	Price
DATABASE			
Access 2 For Dummies™ Quick Reference	by Stuart A. Stuple	1-56884-167-1	$8.95 USA/$11.95 Canada
dBASE 5 For DOS For Dummies™ Quick Reference	by Barry Sosinsky	1-56884-954-0	$9.99 USA/$12.99 Canada
dBASE 5 For Windows For Dummies™ Quick Reference	by Stuart J. Stuple	1-56884-953-2	$9.99 USA/$12.99 Canada
Paradox 5 For Windows For Dummies™ Quick Reference	by Scott Palmer	1-56884-960-5	$9.99 USA/$12.99 Canada
DESKTOP PUBLISHING / ILLUSTRATION/GRAPHICS			
Harvard Graphics 3 For Windows For Dummies™ Quick Reference	by Raymond E. Werner	1-56884-962-1	$9.99 USA/$12.99 Canada
FINANCE / PERSONAL FINANCE			
Quicken 4 For Windows For Dummies™ Quick Reference	by Stephen L. Nelson	1-56884-950-8	$9.95 USA/$12.95 Canada
GROUPWARE / INTEGRATED			
Microsoft Office 4 For Windows For Dummies™ Quick Reference	by Doug Lowe	1-56884-958-3	$9.99 USA/$12.99 Canada
Microsoft Works For Windows 3 For Dummies™ Quick Reference	by Michael Partington	1-56884-959-1	$9.99 USA/$12.99 Canada
INTERNET / COMMUNICATIONS / NETWORKING			
The Internet For Dummies™ Quick Reference	by John R. Levine	1-56884-168-X	$8.95 USA/$11.95 Canada
MACINTOSH			
Macintosh System 7.5 For Dummies™ Quick Reference	by Stuart J. Stuple	1-56884-956-7	$9.99 USA/$12.99 Canada
OPERATING SYSTEMS / DOS			
DOS For Dummies® Quick Reference	by Greg Harvey	1-56884-007-1	$8.95 USA/$11.95 Canada
UNIX			
UNIX For Dummies™ Quick Reference	by Margaret Levine Young & John R. Levine	1-56884-094-2	$8.95 USA/$11.95 Canada
WINDOWS			
Windows 3.1 For Dummies™ Quick Reference, 2nd Edition	by Greg Harvey	1-56884-951-6	$8.95 USA/$11.95 Canada
PRESENTATION / AUTOCAD			
AutoCAD For Dummies™ Quick Reference	by Ellen Finkelstein	1-56884-198-1	$9.95 USA/$12.95 Canada
SPREADSHEET			
1-2-3 For Dummies™ Quick Reference	by John Walkenbach	1-56884-027-6	$8.95 USA/$11.95 Canada
1-2-3 For Windows 5 For Dummies™ Quick Reference	by John Walkenbach	1-56884-957-5	$9.95 USA/$12.95 Canada
Excel For Windows For Dummies™ Quick Reference, 2nd Edition	by John Walkenbach	1-56884-096-9	$8.95 USA/$11.95 Canada
Quattro Pro 6 For Windows For Dummies™ Quick Reference	by Stuart A. Stuple	1-56884-172-8	$9.95 USA/$12.95 Canada
WORD PROCESSING			
Word For Windows 6 For Dummies™ Quick Reference	by George Lynch	1-56884-095-0	$8.95 USA/$11.95 Canada
WordPerfect For Windows For Dummies™ Quick Reference	by Greg Harvey	1-56884-039-X	$8.95 USA/$11.95 Canada

FOR MORE INFORMATION OR TO ORDER, PLEASE CALL ▶ 800. 762. 2974

For volume discounts & special orders please call
Tony Real, Special Sales, at 415. 655. 3048

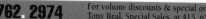